The Music
Management Bible

MUSIC MANAGERS FORUM

An organisation representing the interests of artists/management worldwide. For details, contact James Sellar at:

MMF (Head Office)
1 York Street
London W1U 6PA
Tel: (+44) (0)870 8507 800
Fax: (+44) (0)870 8507 801
Email: info@ukmmf.net
Web: www.ukmmf.net

Printed and bound in Great Britain by Antony Rowe Limited, Chippenham

Published in the UK by SMT, an imprint of Sanctuary Publishing Limited, Sanctuary House, 45-53 Sinclair Road, London W14 0NS, United Kingdom

www.sanctuarypublishing.com

ISBN: 1-84492-025-9

The Music Management Bible

Music Managers Forum

smt

Contents

MMF Training Opportunities

The training division of the Music Managers Forum, MMF Training, has been established for over six years. Our first constituency was – and still is – those involved in artist management. However, as the artist manager is arguably the only professional whose role it is to know and understand something about every aspect of the music industry, our programmes are becoming increasingly relevant to practitioners in every sector of the industry.

When we first began delivering our music-industry learning programmes in 1995, our objectives were straightforward and simple. They remain unchanged:

1   To develop further knowledge and understanding of our industry amongst industry professionals.

2   To develop recognised business skills and professional standards

3   To open up debate and explore key industry issues

4   To create legally binding agreements which are fair and reasonable to all parties.

We now offer a range of programmes including:

Network Learning Sessions – Comprehensive and practical information on all key aspects of the recording, publishing, live and merchandising industries from industry professionals in a networking environment.

Bespoke Programmes – Music-business masterclasses tailor-made to your needs.

International Projects – A chance for existing and aspiring industry professionals from across the world to learn about industry practice in each other's countries.

Facilitated by Stuart Worthington (Head of Education and Training for the MMF), our service is provided in conjunction with knowledgeable and experienced guest speakers representing all sectors of the music industry.

Our programmes are designed to complement the ever-increasing number of academic and vocational training courses that provide opportunities to learn about the music industry. Our intention is to provide an alternative method of learning – designed by professionals for professionals – using a format that is as much about networking as it is about learning, and that can accommodate the business activities and lifestyles of busy entrepreneurs and professionals. As the MMF develops its membership and associations across the world, our learning programmes have become an integral part of the process of developing and agreeing professional standards in our global industry.

As new technology changes the whole structure of our industry, we are beginning to interact with broadcasters, telecommunication companies and Internet service providers in ways that we never imagined. Our learning programmes are as much about political change and networking as they are about learning. We hope to continue to help each other to develop opportunities for our artists and our industry.

HOW TO BOOK

If you would like to reserve a place at any of our events, please complete one of our booking forms and return it to us at the MMF Training Office, at the address on page 2, along with the necessary deposit. For information on all other services send a request to: admin@mmf-training.com

MMF Training Office
Ground Floor
Fourways House
57 Hilton Street
Manchester
M1 2EJ
Tel: (+44) (0)161 228 3993
Fax: (+44) (0)161 228 3773
Email: admin@mmf-training.com

The Contributors

ANDREW THOMPSON has been a commercial lawyer since qualifying as a solicitor in 1977, and since 1978 has specialised in music. In 1983 he co-founded Lee & Thompson Solicitors. In 1993 he helped form the MMF and is still its company secretary. He lectures frequently on music-industry topics, and is the major contributor to this book.

ANDY ALLEN, through his company, Backstreet International Merchandise, has been involved with merchandising for the past ten years, working with bands such as Blur, Pulp, Skunk Anansie and Supergrass, and has also managed bands such as Swervedriver and Reef.

STEVE BRICKLE was founding MD of Giant Merchandising, whose clients included Paul McCartney, Michael Jackson and Prince. He now runs a web management company.

BERNARD DOHERTY has managed publicity campaigns for David Bowie, Rod Stewart, Paul McCartney, The Rolling Stones and The Brit Awards. He co-ordinated the publicity for Live Aid, and has run PR campaigns for Stevie Wonder and Janet Jackson. He is chief executive officer of PR company LD.

ANDREW FORBES is a partner in Forbes Anderson, a firm of solicitors which specialises exclusively in media and entertainment dispute resolution. He is an expert in music industry disputes, including those involving management contracts, recording, publishing and copyright.

MARTIN GOEBBELS is a director of Robertson Taylor Insurance Brokers, having joined them in 1978, and has played a pivotal role in their development as the leading brokers to the entertainment industry, with clients ranging from bands of all stature, promoters, agents, venues and record and publishing companies. Martin has also spoken on panels at many of the major music conferences, including MMF workshops.

JEF HANLON has been lead guitarist, roadie, tour manager and agent, and has promoted tours with Gary Glitter, Bob Hope, The Village People and BB King. In 1998, he produced *Bugs Bunny* on Broadway. For two years, he was president of the Agents' Association of Great Britain. He is a past chairman of the MMF and founder member of the Concert Promoters' Association.

RUSTY HANNAN is an artists manager who has also distinguished himself as an outstanding production and tour manager.

HARRY HODGKIN is a practising barrister, arbitrator and mediator with ADR Chambers. He specialises in commercial law, new media and information technology.

MARTIN HOPEWELL, of Primary Talent and founder of the International Live Music Conference, was recently inducted onto the MMF British Music Roll of Honour for outstanding services to the music industry.

DENNIS MUIRHEAD is an artist and record producer manager, consultant lawyer and mediator with ADR Chambers. He was the founding chairman of the UK MMF and serves on the Council. He is a moderator and panellist at music-industry events.

TERRY O'BRIEN is chairperson of the National Acoustic Music Association, founder of the Playpen Acoustic Club in London's Earls Court and owner of the Playpen record label.

NIGEL PARKER has qualified as a barrister, solicitor, trade-mark attorney and mediator, specialising in copyright and entertainment law. He currently practises as a legal, business and public-affairs adviser representing major artists and music-industry organisations.

RUPERT SPRAWSON is a solicitor with the London firm of Davenport Lyons.

DAVID STOPPS began his career as promoter of the Friars Club in Aylesbury, which played a part in the development of Genesis, David Bowie, U2, The Jam and The Clash. He has also managed a number of artists, including Marillion, Howard Jones and Miriam Stockley. He is a member of the MMF Council and the British Copyright Council.

Introductions

By Chris Morrison

Oh, hell. At the beginning of May I promised James Sellar, General Secretary of the MMF, that I would write a preface for this book and deliver it by the end of May. Now I'm two weeks late and the MMF enforcement police are booting down the door. I was full of good intentions, but then life intervened!

So what am I going to write about? Make it up as I go on or go on as I make it up? As I've been managing musicians for 35 years, maybe I'll tell you what it was like then and compare it to how it is today. Not maybe, that *is* what I'll do. Sooo...

THEN – My first office was in the front half of a disused fish-and-chip shop in Kilburn, London

NOW – My office is under the elevated section of the A40 flyover in west London.

THEN – One of the first groups I managed was Danta, an Afro-rock band that featured a 45-year-old bearded white Yorkshire man who dressed in a leopard skin, played congas and ate and breathed fire. That is, until a ball of fire he breathed out blew back and singed off his facial hair. From then on, he just played congas.

NOW – Among the artists I manage is a group of cartoon characters by the name of Gorillaz. One group member is a 12-year-old Japanese guitarist who doesn't speak English. The drummer is a large African-American who is possessed by the spirit of a dead rapper which appears out of his head. There is a very cool but vacant lead singer and a zombie-obsessed bass player.

THEN – The first group I managed which got a record contract were paid a royalty of 1% of the retail price of a record in the UK and ¹/₂% in the rest of the world. They recorded in mono in a huge studio in London.

NOW – Blur recorded their latest album, *Think Tank*, in a studio in London, a house in Morocco and a barn in Devon. It was recorded using Pro Tools and all the latest technology. They get more than 1% royalty in the UK and more than ¹/₂% in the rest of the world.

THEN – Thin Lizzy's 1970 recording contract with Decca Records was three and a half pages long.

NOW – The Gorillaz recording contract with EMI was over 100 pages long.

THEN – Publishers' 'standard' contract with writers was for 50%/50% split of receipts in the UK, life of copyright and small (if any) advances. The publishers claimed that they could not exist on less.

NOW – Publishing deals are offered at 80%/20% per cent splits 'at source' (in favour of the artist), five to ten years' licence of copyright and substantial advances. Publishers are richer than ever!

THEN – Recording contracts paid the performer a royalty based on the retail price of the record, recording costs were recoupable tour shortfall was non-recoupable, there were no videos and TV advertising was unheard of. The record companies made a gross profit per vinyl record of about £1.50, the artist about £1, including producer royalty.

NOW – Recording royalties are based on dealer price, recording costs are recoupable, as is tour shortfall and video costs, and TV advertising are almost standard. (The artist normally contributes 50% of the cost of the campaign from royalties). With the advent of CDs, the record companys' gross profit per unit sold has now reached about £4–£5 and the artist makes about £1.50 per unit from which to pay his costs. What's wrong with this picture?

THEN – Vinyl was the only game in town. First were 78rpm 12" singles, then along came 7" 45rpm singles and 33^1/$_3$rpm long-play records – but it was all vinyl, and all mono!

IN BETWEEN – There have been – and still are, is in some instances – eight-track cartridges (now collectable), cassettes, 12" singles, LPs, stereo and, for a short, while quadraphonic vinyl.

NOW – There is CD, MiniDisc, DVD, downloads, DVD audio, MP3, mobile phones – the list of music carriers is expanding all the time.

Now Glastonbury has been and gone, June is over and I've written about one-third of what I should have. I get calls from James Sellar and the MMF every hour, on the hour. My delay has caused the book to be delayed. My conscience troubles me.

James tells me that the book is serious and weighty, and I get the feeling that my being a little flippant is slightly disapproved of, or just disapproved of.

So what is it like to be a manager for 35 years? I can't tell you in a couple of pages; it's a book in itself, and I haven't written it yet. I'm not sure I ever will, if it's this hard to write a couple of pages!

A manager probably has a closer relationship with his or her artists than any other person in the music business. You have to care, yet you have to be detached. It is your artist's career you're helping and guiding, so you advise, they decide.

The best music comes from the heart, from inside. It tells of every aspect of human joy and pain. The people who write it and perform it feel those emotions more intensely than others, so don't expect them to be easy to work with. They will, on occasions, be difficult, make bad decisions, blame you, be angry and probably be very badly behaved. Without them, your job and those of everyone else in the rest of the industry do not exist. You are privileged. Try to remember that when you're rowing with the record company *and* your artist, when nobody likes you because you're trying to make a round peg fit in a square hole.

Unless you have exceptional and extraordinary success, don't expect to get rich. If your deal is based on 20%, you will earn between 20p and 40p per record sold, for which your artist receives a royalty and hopefully writes. (That's the 40p end!) To remind you, the record company makes from £4 to £5 gross profit per record sold.

If you're managing artists today, you are doing so at a time of great change, of more uncertainty and greater excitement than ever before. And the changes are more rapid and volatile than ever before.

At the start of the 20th century, music was distributed by sheet music. It required the consumer to be able to play an instrument. Then came Bakelite rolls, vinyl discs and all the rest of the carriers. The distributors and record companies had a monopoly on distribution. Now there is the internet and they have lost that monopoly. Worldwide physical record sales have declined by 30% over the last two years. Everyone's income is threatened and everyone has an opinion (including me) as to how it will resolve.

Remember, 100% of the world population listens to music. When records were the main form of dissemination, only 8% paid for it. My company manages some of the best writers and performers of music. All I have to do is keep an open mind, investigate the alternatives and figure out how my artists receive payment for their work from the population of the world. It's not music that's in trouble – there is no alternative, everyone will still listen; it's just the business model that is changing.

So, for all of you who are already managing artists or aspiring to manage artists, remember the first rule of management: THERE ARE NO RULES!

Chris Morrison
July 2003

20 Good Reasons For Joining The MMF

1   Giving managers the status they deserve

2   Discounts for music business conferences

3   Discounted education courses for new managers

4   Higher level education courses

5   EU networking and funding opportunities

6   Worldwide networking and info gathering on developing markets

7   Strengthening artist management agreements

8   Simplifying and strengthening other music business agreements

9   Pursuing payment from hidden income streams

10   New technology – protecting artist's and manager's rights

11   Lobbying government and industry

12   Information helpline service on management issues

13   Surgeries and MMF 2000

14   Member discounts and special offers

15 Regular information updates

16 Links with other industry bodies

17 Trade discount of the manager's handbook

18 Annual roll-of-honour dinner

19 Setting standards

20 MMF member conferences

---

1 • GIVING MANAGERS THE STATUS THEY DESERVE

In the early days of the '60s and '70s, when managers first played a significant role in the music business, they suffered a bad press, which in some cases was entirely justified. The press perceived managers as Mafioso-style rogues, charlatans who were exploiting musicians. Then, throughout the '80s and '90s, the manager's role became more and more sophisticated and professional, to the point at which now there are many degree courses in Artist Management. The MMF is dedicated to giving modern managers the status they deserve alongside accountants, lawyers and record-company executives for the crucial role they hold within the music industry.

2 • DISCOUNTS FOR MUSIC BUSINESS CONFERENCES

The MMF is continually securing significant discounts to music-industry conferences such as Midem, SXSW, PopKomm and In The City. Associate members attending any two of these conferences can save in excess of the annual MMF membership subscription.

3 • DISCOUNTED EDUCATION COURSES FOR NEW MANAGERS

The MMF runs regular courses around the UK aimed at educating people in key areas in the music industry. The modules for these courses usually run over two evenings and cover such topics as recording agreements, publishing agreements, artist management agreements, touring, new technology, collection societies, accounting, etc. These courses are currently available at a price of £25 per module for MMF members, compared with £50 for non-members.

4 • HIGHER-LEVEL EDUCATION COURSES

The MMF is currently embarking on staging a series of high-powered one-day seminars for the higher-level executives in the music industry, such as lawyers, accountants, top managers, publishers and record-company executives. These courses will be priced competitively with other such commercial seminars but will be far more dynamic than anything else available in the UK. Substantial discounts will be available for MMF members.

5 • EU NETWORKING AND FUNDING OPPORTUNITIES

The MMF is very active in Europe, where they are setting up a European MMF network. The aim is to have MMF chapters in every European country. It may also be possible to access European funding for such uses as tour support and cultural exchanges, etc. The MMF also holds the position of observer at the EMO (European Music Office).

6 • WORLDWIDE NETWORKING AND INFORMATION GATHERING IN DEVELOPING MARKETS

There are active MMF organisations around the world, including the USA, Canada and Australia. The MMF is also very keen to set up sister organisations in the Far East and in the emerging developing countries. European artists have been very successful in territories such as the Far East and the Pacific Rim, and the MMF will continue to interface with the music business in those territories.

7 • STRENGTHENING ARTIST MANAGEMENT AGREEMENTS

A great deal of work has been done in this key area. The MMF Subcommittee on Copyright and Contracts has developed a comprehensive paper entitled *MMF Guidelines To Artist Management Agreements*, which uses an example of an artist management agreement free of law-speak, together with notes of explanation on each clause. This document is a cornerstone of the MMF and emphasises how vulnerable the manager's position is in such agreements. Fundamentally, it seeks to strengthen and protect the manager's position and rights in a fair and reasonable way. The MMF has also developed a standard letter of engagement which covers a short initial trial period prior to a long management agreement form being negotiated. Both of these documents are available to MMF members.

8 • SIMPLIFYING AND REFORMING OTHER MUSIC-BUSINESS AGREEMENTS

The MMF is constantly monitoring other music-business agreements, such as recording and publishing contracts for new clauses which may not be in artists', and therefore the managers', interests. The MMF is also concerned with the reforming of various industry norms, such as the assignment of copyright and packaging deductions in recording contracts, as well as a host of other old-fashioned and blatantly unfair conditions.

9 • PURSUING PAYMENT FROM HIDDEN INCOME STREAMS

This is an area being monitored constantly by the MMF, and one which gave rise to an enormous amount of work following the 1996 UK Copyright legislation amending the 1998 Copyright Act. This legislation became law as the result of a EU Directive concerning public-performance income from recordings. As a direct result of this new legislation, a new collection society was formed under the name of AURA (the Association of United Recording Artists), which not only monitors and collects UK income but for the first time is able to access public-performance income from many foreign countries. AURA campaigns specifically for the rights of contracted featured artists and seeks to ensure that artists are paid in keeping with their status and the contributions they make to recordings.

10 • NEW TECHNOLOGY - PROTECTING ARTISTS' AND MANAGERS' RIGHTS

The MMF continues to monitor new developments in technology, particularly regarding the internet, new sound carriers, etc. The MMF supports BMR and is also an active member of the British Copyright Council, an organisation which interfaces with the Department of Trade and Industry in connection with legislation concerning new technology and other copyright issues.

11 • LOBBYING GOVERNMENT AND INDUSTRY

In addition to the MMF's active participation in support of British Music Rights and the British Copyright Council, as well as giving active support from time to time to the BPI and IFPI in their campaign against piracy, the MMF is also very active in direct government lobbying on many issues, including the current controversial communications and licensing bills and the so-called 'New Deal' for budding musicians on welfare benefit. The MMF also works with the DFEE and the soon to be formed Sector Skills Council (SSC) for the music industry. We help campaign for improved education opportunities in the field of artist management. We feel that this is crucial if the UK is to maintain its position in the global music industry.

12 • INFORMATION AND HELPLINE SERVICE ON MANAGEMENT ISSUES

The MMF offers a general information service to its members via its London office on all issues concerning artist management. If the permanent staff cannot answer a question, the enquirer will be referred to a senior MMF member with specialist knowledge and experience in the area of concern. The MMF also has access to specialist music-business lawyers and accountants who can often help with specific problems and information.

13 • 'SURGERIES'

This is a key area of the MMF's work. The MMF runs these discussion sessions aimed at enlightening and informing members of the latest developments on a wide variety of music related issues. These take place usually monthly at a venue in central London. Apart from being very lively, informative and fun, they provide a great opportunity to network and catch up on the latest gossip.

14 • DISCOUNTS AND SPECIAL OFFERS

Various key music-industry companies support and sponsor the MMF. Some of these companies are able to offer special deals and discounts to MMF members in areas such as studio hire, equipment rental and insurance.

15 • REGULAR INFORMATION UPDATES (ELECTRONIC AND PRINTED)

The MMF website is widely accessed across the entire industry, both in the UK and overseas. It is regarded as an invaluable source of information, not only with regard to MMF matters but also general industry issues.

The MMF is a dynamic, pro-active organisation, and is usually to be found on the cutting edge of all controversial music-industry issues. The reason for this is that managers are the only group within the industry that have to deal with every aspect of the industry on a daily basis. They are therefore uniquely positioned to comment and act on issues of importance. The MMF newsletter reflects this, and the MMF is constantly striving to improve and expand its presentation.

16 • LINKS WITH OTHER INDUSTRY BODIES
To help its members, the MMF works closely with other trade associations and industry bodies and, where available, provides them with access to their information and resources.

17 • PUBLICATION OF THE MANAGERS' HANDBOOK
The MMF (in conjunction with Sanctuary Publishing) has published this book, *The Music Management Bible*, the definitive industry reference book on artist management and related issues.

18 • MMF BRITISH MUSIC ROLL-OF-HONOUR DINNER
This prestigious annual ceremony is becoming regarded more and more as one of the landmark social highlights of the British music industry year. Each year, the event takes place in London and inducts key industry figures onto the MMF Roll Of Honour. Past inductees include Rob Dickins, John Kennedy, Gail Colson, John Peel, Geoff Travis and Jeanette Lee, Muff Winwood, Peter Reichart, Bob Grace, Richard Park, Ed Bicknell, Martin Hopewell, John Hutchinson, Rupert Perry and the legendary manager's manager Peter Grant.

19 • SETTING STANDARDS
The MMF represents and promotes high ethical standards in music management to which MMF members are expected to adhere. Many MMF members include the MMF logo on their letterheads to symbolise good management practice.

20 • SPRING/AUTUMN CONFERENCES
We hold up to two conferences during each year, each of which provides a full day's programme of industry-led panels and networking opportunities for our members. Subjects are always wide-ranging and pick up on any current hot topics. As a result, these conferences are always sold out. They are subsidised by the MMF and have proved to be extremely useful, value-for-money exercises.

1 Management Contracts

By Andrew Thompson

The music business is just that: a business. For all the artistic aspirations of a particular musician, if he wishes to succeed as a professional recording artist then his art must be pursued within a competitive business environment. Occasionally, an artist will manage his own business affairs (or, in the case of a band, one or two members may assume responsibility for this task). This sometimes works quite well if the person is businesslike and if the act is focused in its area of activity, although the artist will usually need to rely heavily upon professional help from solicitors and accountants. However, most artists aren't particularly businesslike. Moreover, the logistics of organising a successful recording career are normally so complex that the artist would never have time to deal with the business side of things on his own. Also, an important part of the management function involves 'selling' the artist, and it's difficult for an artist to sell himself. For most artists, therefore, perhaps the single most important decision of their careers is their choice of manager.

This chapter will cover the nature of management and look at how to find the right manager. The legal framework of the arrangement will also be reviewed, along with the component parts of a typical management contract.

PART 1: THE MANAGER

1.0 finding a manager

1.1 WHEN?

Generally, the sooner the appointment is made, the better. The manager prefers to have a clean slate with which to work. For example, it wouldn't usually be a good idea for an artist to negotiate a record deal and then ask a manager to take over. That said, this situation doesn't often arise – the artist would typically look for a manager as the first stage towards securing a record deal. In any event, many A&R executives prefer to deal with managers rather than artists (when it comes to negotiating deals, at least), and often the artist will benefit from the additional validity brought to his project by the involvement of a respected manager. Nevertheless, artists shouldn't rush into management arrangements. There are many different types of manager, and it's better for the artist to wait until he finds the right manager rather than for him to be panicked into hiring the wrong one. Moreover, the artist/manager relationship is a personal one, and so, as with all personal relationships, the parties involved should initially proceed with some caution.

1.2 HOW?

Sometimes the manager will find the artist. It's corny, but it does often happen that, after a gig, somebody (not always smoking a cigar) will come backstage and insist that he is the man to make the artist rich and famous. Generally, however, the artist will need to adopt a more pro-active approach. He should first set about compiling a shortlist of potential candidates, and he should also talk to all of his contacts in the industry. One possible approach is to identify other admired artists and find out about their management arrangements (although it's not necessarily sensible for an artist to be with a manager who already looks after a similar, and therefore competing, artist). An artist looking for a manager could check the MMF web site for advice at www.ukmmf.net

1.3 PRESENTATIONS

It's rarely worthwhile sending out circulars in bulk in the hope of attracting a manager. The artist will need to approach the targeted manager personally, or find somebody who is prepared to do so on his behalf. The artist should put together a presentation package of some kind, like a tape of a few of his best songs, even if they're in rudimentary demo form. One or two photographs and a short biography, together with any press cuttings, would also be useful. Successful managers are generally very busy people, and it usually proves counter-productive for artists to be too pushy. Most managers will have the courtesy to respond to approaches, but they need to be given a little time.

1.4 WHAT TO LOOK FOR IN A MANAGER

When they have a shortlist of managers demonstrating a positive interest in them, artists should consider the following points:

- How experienced is the manager?

- How successful has he been? And has that success been in a similar field?

- How long has he worked in the music industry? And in what different capacities?

- Does the manager have a good reputation? What are his reputed strengths?

- Is he primarily a business manager or a creative manager?

- How long has he managed any other artists with whom he's been involved in the past? (The artist should try and talk to those other artists.)

- Does the manager have the type of personality that the artist is looking for? For instance, is he the aggressive type, or perhaps more diplomatic?

- Where is the manager based? What back-up is available? What kind of office facilities does he have?

- How much time will the manager be able to spend on the artist's affairs?

- How convinced does he seem of the artist's talent?

- How extensive are his contacts in the industry?

- Does he have experience of the industry outside the UK? For example, does he have contacts in America?

- Does he have good negotiating skills?

- Will he or his staff be able to deal with the details efficiently – for example, returning phone calls, dealing with correspondence, maintaining proper financial records, etc?

- If the artist already has a recording or a publishing deal, does the manager have any history of dealing with the companies concerned? If so, what do the key personnel at those companies think of him?

1.5 THE DECISION

An artist should adopt a thorough and professional approach to the selection process, but ultimately he must rely on his own judgement in determining whether or not the management relationship would be an effective and successful one.

1.6 BUSINESS MANAGERS

There is a trend in the UK towards following the US practice of dividing responsibility between a general manager and a business manager. The general manager will have responsibility both in assisting the artist in determining the overall strategy for the artist's career and for the day-to-day implementation of that strategy and will have some input in relation to creative and artistic matters, while the business manager will have responsibility for financial matters. For this reason, business managers tend often to be accountants. They will often work closely with artists' lawyers. There is often some sense in dividing responsibilities between a general manager and a business manager, but this will depend upon the circumstances of the particular case and the particular talents of the manager concerned. If there is to be a division of responsibilities in this way, it is crucial for the artist that there is good communication between all three parties and that there is a good working relationship between the general manager and the business manager, since otherwise there is an obvious danger that mistakes will occur and bickering will ensue.

1.7 HOME-GROWN MANAGERS

The manager is often found close to home. He may be a close relative or, perhaps, a school friend. In such cases, the manager is unlikely to have much experience, but there may be compensating benefits. If the parties are happy to work together, there is little reason why the customary industry terms should not apply, and there is just as much reason to formalise the arrangements. The position is more complicated in the case of a group of artists who decide that one member of the group should double as the manager. This often leads to arguments either over money or as a result of the imbalance of power between the manager member or members and the non-manager members. Logically, if one band member assumes all of the usual management functions, there is no reason why he shouldn't be paid management commission at the same rate and in the same manner as any other manager, but this inevitably leads to a significant economic imbalance between the parties which tends to give rise to resentments.

Of course, in the case of a successful band, there's unlikely to be time for any one person to be both artist and manager. In other cases, where the management role is perhaps limited to basic correspondence and bookkeeping and one band member is better equipped to deal with this than the others, the group may agree to pay a modest fee.

Many groups below a certain level of activity and/or success divide up management responsibilities between themselves. No payment is made for their services, even though inevitably the contributions will be unequal.

2.1 THE DANGER OF DELAY

What should the artist do once he's found a suitable manager prepared to take him on? Most artists – certainly those at a preliminary stage in their careers – are reluctant to enter into discussions with a new manager about the formal terms which should apply; they're particularly shy about making a long-term commitment. Likewise, many managers are reluctant during the early stages to ask an artist to sign a contract for fear of giving the wrong signals – this kind of approach benefits nobody. The manager is unlikely to perform to the best of his ability unless he feels confident and secure in his relationship with the artist. If the artist consistently avoids any discussion over the formal terms which are to apply, the uncertainty is likely to lead to problems: either there will be a dispute as to the basis on which the manager has been working, or ill will may develop as a result of one side feeling let down by the other. Of course, the artist – and the manager, for that matter – should exercise some caution before committing to a long-term arrangement. Nevertheless, this doesn't justify burying one's head in the sand; as soon as the artist and manager begin working together, efforts should immediately be made to formalise the arrangements.

2.2 PROCEDURE

The management contract is usually prepared by the manager or his solicitor and presented to the artist. It's important from the artist's point of view that he receives expert independent advice from his own solicitor. Moreover, it's also important from the manager's point of view that the artist is independently advised (see the section on 'The Legal Framework' below). Many managers are reluctant to incur legal fees in relation to a management contract, because during the preliminary stages there is often no income being generated by the project. Artists tend to be still less inclined to incur legal fees, usually for the simple reason that they have no money. Unlike a recording or publishing agreement, no money is payable to the artist upon signing a management agreement. Despite these constraints, however, it's important that both parties to a management contract are properly advised. There needn't be protracted (and therefore expensive) negotiations between lawyers. Before the lawyers are instructed, the parties should try and agree between themselves the basic principles which are to apply (although each party should accept that whatever is agreed will be subject to legal advice). This and the following chapter are intended to assist in that process.

1.0 the nature of the contract

1.1 THE DIFFICULTY OF ENFORCEMENT

Management contracts are essentially straightforward by nature. They're contracts for the supply of personal services. A management contract will describe the services to be provided by the manager and will specify how he is to be paid for those services. The main significance of this is that a management contract can't be specifically enforced. The obvious analogy of this is an employment contract. An employer may enter into a fixed-term employment contract with an employee for, say, three years. If the employee leaves without good cause after one year, he would be in breach of the employment contract, and the employer would be able to sue the employee for breach of contract. Generally, however, the only recourse available to the employer in any such legal proceeding would be for an award in damages. The employee would be compelled to pay the employer a sum of money equal to any financial loss which the employer would be able to prove – to the satisfaction of the court – that he has actually suffered as a result of the breach of contract. However, the employer generally wouldn't be able to obtain an order for specific performance from the court (ie the employee wouldn't be forced to work for the employer for the remaining two years). An artist and his manager are in a similar position; the manager will be entitled to damages if the artist walks away from the management contract before its term has expired, but he will generally be unable to compel the artist to continue to allow the manager to represent him.

1.2 ALTERNATIVE ARRANGEMENTS

Partly for the reason mentioned above, some managers try to protect their positions by entering into alternative contractual arrangements with their artists. It used to be quite common for a de facto manager not to enter into a management agreement but instead to require the artist to enter into recording and publishing agreements, the effect of which was that the 'manager' was exclusively entitled to the artist's songwriting and recording services and owned the copyright and all other rights in the artist's songs and recordings. The 'manager' would then seek recording and publishing deals for the artist, but it would be the 'manager' – in his guise as a production company or a publisher – who would enter into the agreements with the third parties concerned. Often, the 'manager' would also require the signing of a management contract. In this way, he could prevent the involvement of any other manager and would secure a financial interest (by means of management commission) in any of the artist's earnings from activities other than recording and songwriting. In the worst cases, the 'manager' would retain all of the recording and publishing income, would pay a royalty of some kind to the artist, and would then claim a percentage commission on that royalty income, under the terms of the management contract. Arrangements of this kind are nowadays generally frowned upon, so that, when an artist is presented with a contract by a manager, that contract will normally be a management contract rather than a recording or publishing contract. However, this isn't to say that production contracts (ie recording contracts entered into with small record-production companies) don't have a place in the music business. Arrangements of this type may be justifiable in their own right. (See Chapter 3 for more information concerning this area.)

1.3 UNDUE INFLUENCE

The courts may set aside an agreement if it has been entered into under circumstances where undue influence has been brought to bear by one party of the contract against another. In the context of a management contract, this doesn't mean that the artist has to show that he was taken to the pub and made to get drunk before signing the agreement, or that a gun was held to his head; there is what is known as a presumption of undue influence if the relationship is one of trust and confidence. Trust and confidence lie at the very heart of any relationship between a manager and an artist, and therefore the presumption of undue influence immediately arises. If the court is to be persuaded to recognise a management contract, the presumption of undue influence has to be rebutted. There is an automatic suspicion that the manager – who is usually older, more experienced and more businesslike than the artist – has in some way exerted pressure on the artist to accept the terms of the contract in question. The only effective means by which to rebut this is for the manager to show that the artist was independently advised, preferably with the help of a lawyer who has specialist knowledge of the music industry. This would normally be sufficient for the manager to demonstrate that there had been a genuine negotiation in relation to the terms of the contract, and that its contents were properly understood by the artist, or at least that the artist was given an opportunity to fully understand its implications.

PART 3: THE CONTRACT

1.0 duration

1.1 CONTRACTS TERMINABLE UPON NOTICE

Some management contracts don't run for a fixed term, and instead continue indefinitely unless and until either party serves a given period of notice. This period of notice would normally be three or perhaps six months, although in some cases there are more sophisticated provisions for the serving of notice so that, for example, the agreement may only be brought to an end once a particular album cycle has reached its conclusion.

1.2 FIXED-TERM CONTRACTS

Most management contracts provide for a minimum fixed period, usually between three and five years, and there is an unwritten rule that management contracts shouldn't continue for longer than five years. The general feeling is that, if a manager were to insist upon a longer period, the artist may be able to challenge the validity of the agreement, on the basis that it represents an unreasonable restraint of trade. However, there's no black-and-white rule to the effect that a five-year contract is enforceable but that anything longer isn't.

There's a current trend for management contracts to run for a given number of album cycles rather that for a specified period of years, ie for perhaps three cycles (with a cycle being defined for this purpose as the period of time which involves writing, rehearsing and recording an album, and then until the end of any promotional or touring activity in relation to that album).

1.3 TYPICAL DURATION

However, most management agreements run for three, four or even five years. This would include any option period so that, for example, the agreement may run for three years but at the end of the initial period the manager has an option to extend for another year or two. Sometimes the option to extend will be available to the manager only if certain targets have been achieved during the initial period – perhaps a minimum level of earnings, or a given chart position.

1.4 TRIAL PERIOD

There may often be a trial period of some kind. A typical trial period would be for six months, and this would usually work in one of two ways. The parties may sign a simple agreement on the basis that if, at the end of the trial period, both parties wished to proceed, then both parties would negotiate the terms of a more formal, longer-term agreement. (There is an example of such a letter of engagement in Chapter 2, 'MMF Guidelines For Artist Management Agreements'.) Alternatively, a formal agreement would be negotiated from the outset. However, whilst this agreement would run for five years, for example, there would be a provision to the effect that either party could terminate at any time during the period of, say, 30 days following the expiration of the initial six months. Managers are naturally reluctant to agree to a trial period of this kind, because this may result in them performing a great deal of preliminary work for no purpose. Therefore, the approach adopted by many managers is to include a provision to the effect that the artist is able to terminate the management agreement after a given period – perhaps twelve or 18 months – in certain defined circumstances (eg if at that point the artist has failed to enter into a recording contract).

1.5 EXCLUSIVITY

The duration of the deal represents the period during which the manager is exclusively entitled to represent the artist. This exclusivity rarely works the other way around – the artist wouldn't expect to be exclusively entitled to the manager's services (although some management contracts specify that the manager may not manage more than a given number of other artists). Typically, with a new recording career, a great deal needs to be done during the early stages for relatively small reward. A manager signing a contract with a new band will often face a lengthy period of hard work before the project is in good enough shape to be presented to record companies. The whole process of negotiating a record deal is usually a long and arduous one. After the record deal has been signed, further work will need to be done in preparing, rehearsing and recording the material. Also, the record company may wish to release a single before committing to the release of an album.

For all of these reasons, it might easily be a year or two after signing the management contract before the first album is released. This may be followed by an extensive period of touring to promote the album. Assuming that the album is successful enough for the record company to exercise its option for the next album, there may then be another delay before suitable material is prepared and recorded. Because of this, a three-year management contract will often fail to cover more than one album, and a four-year management contract will often cover no more than two albums. The artist's first album will have to be unusually successful for this to be sufficient to recoup the record company's initial expenditure and give rise to commissionable recording income, and it usually takes some time for even a successful artist to build a reasonable sales base. It's therefore not difficult to envisage circumstances whereby a manager may work very hard over a period of three or four years to establish an artist only to find that the artist then decides that he wishes to appoint another manager, or to look after his own affairs, leaving the ex-manager with a commission entitlement in relation to perhaps only two albums, just before the watershed is achieved with the third album (see the section on 'The Watershed' in Chapter 3). It's for this reason that managers seek the protection of long-term, exclusive management contracts. The difference between a five-year contract and a four-year contract may be critical.

2.0 the scope of the agreement

2.1 TERRITORY

A typical management contract will grant the manager the exclusive right to represent the artist in all areas of the entertainment industry, throughout the world. Sometimes the agreement may be territorially restricted in some way, most typically when a separate manager is engaged for the American market. For example, if there are two managers, one for each of two territories – perhaps North America and the rest of the world – each manager will usually only earn commission upon earnings arising in his territory. However, UK-based managers usually object to the exclusion of America, or indeed of any other territory. The income from the territory to be excluded may well make the difference between financial success and failure.

There are also practical difficulties concerned with having two separate managers, in that they may pull in different directions, and each will have a vested interest in persuading the artist to concentrate his attention in the one territory at the expense of the other. One practical way of dealing with this is for a UK manager to insist upon worldwide rights but to agree to appoint a separate US manager. However, the appointment will be made by the UK manager so that, effectively, the US manager reports to the UK manager. The UK manager will still expect some financial reward from the activities in the US, so if he's entitled to 20% commission on worldwide earnings, for example, he may agree to pay perhaps 10% (ie one half) of the commissionable earnings originating in the US to the US sub-manager, so that he still receives the remaining 10%.

2.2 NON-MUSIC ACTIVITIES

As well as territorial restrictions, the scope of the manager's appointment may be limited in other ways. Ordinarily, the manager will wish to represent the artist in relation to all of his activities in the entertainment industry. The artist may wish to restrict his manager's influence to activities in the music industry. With a new artist, however, this would probably be unfair to the manager, because in all likelihood any opportunity for the artist to profit from other activities will arise only as a result of the artist's success in the music industry. For example, the artist may be offered a part in a film, or he may decide to write a book. If an artist already has a career in another area of the entertainment industry – if he's an actor with a theatrical agent representing him in this area, for example – then the management contract would need to recognise this. A manager will sometimes agree that, if at some future stage the artist becomes involved in acting or literary endeavours, the manager will then agree to appoint a theatrical/film or literary agent of the artist's choice. To centralise the arrangement, the manager might insist that the appointment of agents of this kind must be made by him, so that any agent will be a sub-agent of the manager rather than employed directly by the artist. As with an overseas manager, the manager may agree that all or part of the sub-agent's commission is to be subtracted from the manager's commission.

2.3 AREAS OF RESPONSIBILITY

It's impossible to be too precise about the respective duties and obligations of the parties under a management contract, apart from certain obvious matters, such as the manager's obligation to account to the artist for any money in the specified manner. Each artist has his own view of what a manager should do and how he should go about it, and likewise each manager will have a different approach to his work and will attach different priorities to the various aspects of his remit. Some artists expect the manager to be at the artist's beck and call day and night to sort out every problem, whether professional or purely personal, and some managers accept that baby-sitting an artist is part of the job. Others, however, generally don't take kindly to being pestered outside normal business hours (while accepting that, in the music business, 'normal' doesn't mean 9am to 5pm). It's not really the manager's job to pay the artist's domestic bills and generally deal with any personal crises. Nevertheless, a successful (and therefore busy and often egotistical) artist will often expect this kind of service from his management company. The best answer for the manager is to provide the artist with a personal assistant, employed by the management company but available to do the artist's bidding on the basis that the cost of employing the person involved is recoverable from the artist's earnings. The personal assistant's job specification will often be complex. Some of the his responsibilities will be managerial, and others will be of the nannying variety, and so a sensible compromise, often, is that only part of the assistant's salary is recoverable.

We're a long way from achieving any recognised set of standards, in terms of exactly how a manager's role is defined, and we probably never will, because so much depends upon the particular requirements of the artist and the very personal nature of the arrangements worked out between the artist and his manager. While a formal management contract will make some attempt to specify the respective obligations of the parties, in practice the contract is likely to be of little help in this area. In the MMF's suggested form of contract in the next chapter, an attempt is made to illustrate in some detail the respective obligations of the parties.

3.0 the manager's remuneration

3.1 COMMISSION

On rare occasions, and usually only if he is well established, the artist may engage a manager on the basis that he will be paid an agreed fee or salary. However, in the vast majority of cases, the manager will be paid by way of commission. This recognises that the music business is a volatile one, and that success is by no means guaranteed. The manager runs the risk of working very hard but failing to achieve success with the artist, in which event he earns little, or nothing. Conversely, if success is achieved, the manager may be rewarded handsomely. The obvious benefit from the artist's point of view is that the manager won't have to be paid unless there's some money with which to pay him. Of course, the artist usually has only one career, and thus one chance of success, while if the manager represents other artists he'll have more than one chance of achieving success.

3.2 COMMISSION RATES

Commission rates have crept up over the years, and there are sound reasons for this. Historically, the manager was nicknamed 'Mr 10%', although by the 1970s the usual rate of commission was 15%. Nowadays, managers invariably charge 20%, and sometimes a manager will charge

25%, although this is rarely thought to be justifiable. An inflated rate of this kind might arguably be reasonable in the case of a powerful and successful manager putting together a 'manufactured' band, or if the manager is prepared to work exclusively for the artist involved. The principal reason for this increase in rates is that, when a lesser rate of perhaps 10% or 15% might have applied, the remaining terms of the typical management contract would have been more demanding, from the artist's perspective. For example, the manager might have expected to receive his commission on the gross income arising from any contracts entered into during the currency of the management contract. The management contract might have run for five years, but if the artist were to enter into a long-term recording agreement towards the end of the five years, for example, the manager would nevertheless expect his commission on all earnings under that agreement, even though a large part of those earnings may have been attributable to recordings made after the expiration of the management contract. Today, a manager wouldn't usually expect to receive commission on recordings made or songs written after the expiration of the management contract, even though he may have negotiated the terms of the recording and publishing deals governing those subsequent recordings and songs. Moreover, most managers now accept that commission will be calculated on the gross income only after deduction of certain expenses. Not only that, but the manager will often have to accept that, following the end of the management contract, there will at some point be a reduction, or even a cut-off, in his commission entitlement. For these reasons, the rate of commission has increased to its usual rate of 20%.

The rate of commission may be affected by what is agreed as to the extent of the manager's involvement. A manager may wish to limit his involvement to the business side of things – he may not wish to be available day and night to deal with creative issues and personal crises. If he's prepared to accept that he's offering something less than a full management service, the manager may be prepared to accept a less substantial rate of commission. A business manager, for example, will usually charge 5%. This will sometimes mean that the artist pays 25% in total, but more often the general manager will accept 15%. On this basis, the artist may be better off because, while he'll still be paying 20% (15% to the general manager and 5% to the business manager), there may be a saving in accountancy fees. In many cases, however, the business management services will be provided by the business management consultancy arm of an accountancy practice, and while that consultancy will charge 5%, an associated accountancy practice may still charge separately for bookkeeping and other accountancy services. The MMF's position is that the absence of any bookkeeping function on the part of the manager does not justify a reduction in management commission.

3.3 VARIABLE RATES

Sometimes, different rates of commission apply for different types of income. For example, an artist may argue that, since a manager has had little or no involvement in the songwriting process – as opposed to recording and touring activities – commission should be paid in relation to publishing income at a lesser rate. This is a spurious argument that is rarely accepted by managers. After all, it's partly the manager's work which helps create the circumstances in which the value of the artist's publishing rights may be enhanced.

3.4 COMMISSIONABLE INCOME

Generally speaking, the manager will be entitled to commission calculated at the agreed percentage rate, but only from the artist's earnings arising from those activities which fall within the scope of the agreement during the term of the management contract. A manager would rarely expect to receive commission upon income attributable to work done by the artist (ie recordings made and songs written) after the expiry of the contract. However, the manager would usually expect to receive commission on income received during the term of the management contract from work undertaken by the artist prior to commencement of the management arrangements. This prevents, for example, a manager taking on a new band and being excluded from commission from the earnings attributable to the band's first album simply because the songs were perhaps written and the recordings made prior to the manager's involvement. If the artist is already established and there is a stream of income from past commercial activities, the artist may wish to exclude all or part of that income for commission purposes. The manager may object to this on the basis that it will be the work completed during the currency of the management contract which reactivates any back catalogue and gives rise to any current earnings from that back catalogue. The artist would usually concede this point, although he may be reluctant to do so if he is already paying commission on that income to an ex-manager.

3.5 CALCULATION OF COMMISSION

The old principle that the manager's commission is calculated by reference to the artist's gross earnings has been eroded in a number of respects.

Recording Income

The manager will usually be paid his commission on the amount of recording income actually received by the artist – ie all advances and any royalties which are actually paid. To the extent that royalties accrue but aren't paid to the artist because they are used for recoupment purposes, those royalties are not commissionable. If the record company pays an advance which is inclusive of recording costs, those costs are non-commissionable. Most recording contracts now provide for cost-inclusive advances, and this gives rise to some difficulty. If a record company pays £200,000 inclusive of recording costs, how does the manager calculate his commission when the recording costs are not yet known? The record company might pay, say, £50,000 initially and then the remaining £150,000 following completion of recording after first deducting any recording costs (which the record company usually pays on behalf of the artist). The manager would take his commission on the initial £50,000 and would usually accept that he would commission the balance only once the album had been recorded and the actual recording costs had been ascertained. If the £200,000 is paid 'up front', the manager should either defer the calculation and payment of his commission or reach agreement with the artist for an 'on account' payment. Sometimes, if he fears profligacy in the recording studio, the manager may insist upon a cap for the costs of the recording (for the purposes only of calculating his commission).

Publishing Income

The manager will expect to be paid his commission calculated by reference to the gross income paid to the artist. There are fewer complications involved with publishing income, as there are so few expenses. Some artists try to exclude from commission any performance income received by the writer direct from the PRS. The PRS accounts direct to the writer for the writer's 6/12 share of any performance income, and accounts separately to the

ery small when expressed as a percentage of the gross. Touring activities
may generate little or no profit during the early stages of an artist's career,
but the artist is likely to continue with his efforts, perhaps with the record
company underwriting any loss by way of 'tour support' as a means of
promoting record sales. If a tour grosses £1,000,000, for example, and the
expenses total £800,000, leaving £200,000 profit, the artist is likely to be
unimpressed with the suggestion that the entirety of that £200,000 (ie 20%
of the gross) should be paid over to his manager.

Some managers accept that commission should be calculated upon net
touring income, ie only on any profits that remain after the deduction of all
expenses. A prudent manager will at the very least impose some element of
control over those expenses so that, if the artist is profligate and insists on
taking suites at five-star hotels and travelling everywhere by chauffeured
limousine with a large entourage, for example, this doesn't impact unfairly
on his management commission.

The MMF believes that it is inappropriate for managers to charge
commission only upon net earnings. They take the view that the manager is

heavily involved in the artist's touring activities, often having to gear up the management operation in order to cope with the level of work involved, and that the manager therefore needs to know that he's assured of some income from his investment of time and labour. An obvious and standard compromise is that commission is calculated on the gross income after the deduction of certain specified (but not all) expenses. Another approach is for the commission to be calculated on the net profits after the deduction of all expenses, but also for a fee of some kind to be paid to the manager to defray or help defray any additional overhead expenses, with that fee then treated as an expense to be taken into account when determining the profits.

Managers sometimes make comparisons between the amount of work which has to be undertaken by the manager in relation to a particular tour and the amount of work required on the part of the booking agent. The manager may argue that it's unfair for the artist to accept that the booking agent should be paid his fee – which is usually 10% or 15% and calculated upon the gross income (the booking agent will always insist that this method of calculation applies for the payment of his commission) – while the manager is expected to rely on a share of the net profits. However, this argument doesn't take account of the fact that the booking agent doesn't earn from other sources – for example, from the additional record sales which a promotional tour is designed to achieve. Nevertheless, a manager would usually be far more heavily involved in any tour than the booking agent.

Sometimes, the manager will not only mastermind the touring arrangements but will also provide day-to-day tour-management services. If the manager or a member of his staff acts as tour manager, thus avoiding the expense of engaging a specialist, then the manager may justifiably argue that he should be paid separately for those services. Alternatively, he may argue that the degree of involvement on his part supports his assertion that he should be paid a sum in direct relation to the gross income. Similarly, if the manager has sufficient experience to do so, it's possible for him to dispense with the booking agent altogether and book the dates himself. Again, this might justify a greater financial involvement on his part.

4.0 post-term commission

4.1 POST-TERM ACTIVITIES

A manager generally isn't entitled to any commission relating to income attributable to activities undertaken after the expiration of the contract. However, some managers don't entirely accept this principle, and argue to the effect that they should earn commission (if, perhaps, at a reduced rate) on, say, the next album to be recorded after the end of the deal – although perhaps only if the manager negotiated the record deal under which that album is to be recorded.

4.2 FUTURE COMMISSION

A manager will often accept that he has no entitlement to commission relating to any activities that were undertaken after the end of the contract, but he will in return demand that he will expect to receive his full commission on all income arising from those activities undertaken during the term of the management contract, irrespective of when that income is actually received. For example, if a management contract runs for five years, and during that period three albums are recorded, the manager would then expect his full commission on the relevant earnings from those three albums whenever those earnings arose, even to the extent that the albums in question were still generating income in 20, 40 or 60 years' time.

4.3 POST-TERM REDUCTIONS

The artist will often argue that there should be a reduction in commission at some point, that perhaps commission should continue to be payable at the full rate – perhaps 20% – for five years after the end of the management contract, but that this should then be reduced to 10% in relation to income received over the next five years, and that the entitlement should then cease altogether. The artist will advance two arguments in support of an arrangement of this kind: firstly, he will point to the fact that, assuming that he continues with his career, he'll need to find a new manager, who will no doubt insist on receiving commission during the currency of the new management contract on earnings received from the exploitation of the artist's back catalogue, even if at a reduced rate; and secondly, he'll argue that any future income from the exploitation of the artist's past work will be generated in large part by his continuing efforts to maintain his profile and the direct promotion of his earlier material, through concert performances and the like. The issue is controversial, and many managers don't accept that their financial interest in a particular body of work should reduce with the passage of time. In many cases the point may be largely academic because, if full commission continues to be paid for, say, five years after the end of the management contract, this may catch the vast majority of the total income which is generated from the body of work in question. Again, however, the question of whether or not cut-off provisions should apply rather depends upon the circumstances of each case. A manager who provides a complete service and manages the artist to the exclusion of all other interests is more likely to object to provisions of this kind.

A post term commission entitlement is often referred to as a *pension* and, in keeping with this concept, there is some merit in the argument that the longer a manager is involved in the artist's career, the greater the protection he should receive. One simplistic way of dealing with the issue is to make the period during which the post-term commission entitlement applies co-terminus with the duration of the management agreement so that, if the manager is in place for three years, for a further three years he should continue to benefit from the income which is generated from the work which was done during the initial three years. Likewise, if the manager is involved for ten years, he should continue to enjoy the income generated from what was done during that ten-year period for a further ten years. The MMF's recommendation is that commission should continue to be paid at full rate for two years after the end of the term and thereafter should be payable at half rate in perpetuity.

5.0 expenses

5.1 OUT-OF-POCKET EXPENSES

A manager will invariably require reimbursement of his expenses, although this should extend only to expenses incurred by the manager specifically on behalf of the artist – the manager's overhead costs shouldn't be recoverable from the artist.

5.2 APPROVALS

Some artists require the right to approve any expenses to be incurred above a particular limit. This is a prudent precaution during the early stages of the business relationship but tends to become unnecessary and cumbersome once the working relationship has been properly established.

REIMBURSEMENT

There's often some controversy over how expenses are to be reimbursed. Most managers accept – partly out of practical necessity – that expenses are recoverable only from commissionable income. Others take the view that, since the expenses have been incurred specifically on the artist's behalf, those expenses should in effect be treated as loans, and should be repayable on demand. This gives rise to the unedifying prospect of a project failing and the management relationship coming to an end, with the manager then presenting the impecunious artist with a demand for the repayment of outstanding expenses. No management contract will impose an obligation on a manager to incur any particular expenses, and most managers will readily accept that, if they agree to incur a particular expense, they do so at their own risk, in the sense that this will only be reimbursable if there is sufficient commissionable income.

One possible compromise is that, if the commissionable income is insufficient, any outstanding expenses would be repayable out of the artist's future entertainment-related income, even if that income isn't commissionable because the management agreement has come to an end. If the manager insists on this, the artist might at least try to ensure that reimbursement is made only out of an agreed share of future income, in order to avoid the risk of there being a period during which he loses all of his earnings to his ex-manager.

accounting

USUAL METHOD

Traditionally, the manager has always controlled the artist's income. He is responsible for ensuring that earnings from the artist's activities are paid in full and on time, and he regularly prepares management accounts – perhaps on a semi-annual or quarterly basis – showing all income received and all expenses incurred. Each set of accounts is accompanied by a cheque in favour of the artist for the amount due. This system often still applies, although semi-annual accounting is now frowned upon. Most managers agree to account to their artists either quarterly or perhaps even monthly.

ALTERNATIVE METHOD

There is a growing trend among artists to take control of their own money. Some artists feel that, if a manager is entitled to 20%, it's nonsense for him to receive 100% and then account to the artist for 80%. Rather, it's more sensible for the artist to receive 100% and to account to the manager for his 20%. Some managers are delighted at this; looking after the money is obviously important, but many managers see this as a time-consuming and dreary function, and if the artist is prepared to do it and still pay the manager his 20% then he may not complain. Other managers view artists as not particularly businesslike and sometimes unreliable, and think that they need to take control of the money themselves in order to ensure that they both get paid. Also, the significance of expenses shouldn't be underestimated; it's likely that, during the early stages of an artist's career, the aggregate of the manager's commission and expenses will represent the lion's share of any available income.

PITFALLS

Many managers will gladly relinquish this task of accounting, but only on the proviso that the artist employs a reputable firm of chartered accountants to receive all income on the artist's behalf and to pay the manager's commission and expenses on the presentation of invoices. Some artists think that, in this way, their money will be safer, although this isn't necessarily true; unfortunately, in recent years, there have been a number of well-publicised cases of music-business accountants acting improperly with their clients' money. Perhaps in the music business, as in any other, not all managers are trustworthy. Of course, the vast majority of them are, and the plain fact is that, unless the artist has a proper degree of trust in his manager, he shouldn't enter into a management relationship with him in the first place. The problem is that it's not always efficient to have payments cleared through an accountant's office; an accountant will naturally charge for his services, and these charges will usually have to be borne by the artist rather than by the manager. All in all, there's perhaps a lot to be said for the traditional accounting arrangements, coupled maybe with some contractual safeguards for the artist. For example, the artist might insist that his money is paid into a separate client account held by the manager rather than mixed in with his own money, and he might also demand suitable rights of audit.

termination

TERMINATION FOR BREACH

With a fixed, long-term contract, either party will usually have a contractual right of termination in certain carefully-defined circumstances – ie if the other party is declared bankrupt, convicted of an offence involving dishonesty, or is incapacitated for an extended period due to illness or accident and is unable to fulfil his obligations. More controversially, the artist may require the right to terminate the contract in the event that the manager is in breach of the material terms of the agreement. This is a dangerous position from the manager's point of view, because it enables the artist to walk away from the contract, arguing – for whatever (perhaps spurious) reason – that the manager hasn't been performing his obligations properly. This merely has the effect of muddying the contractual waters, which benefits the artist in the sense that the manager may be dissuaded in those circumstances from suing him for breach of contract.

KEY-MAN CLAUSES

If the management contract is with a management company, rather than with an individual, the artist will usually insist that the individual with whom he will be dealing must be named in the contract, on the basis that, if he ceases to be available, the artist is entitled to terminate.

2 MMF Guidelines For Artist Management Agreements

By David Stopps, For The MMF Copyright And Contracts Sub-Committee

This chapter includes the MMF's own guidelines for artist management agreements. This document, which has already been used in several legal cases, such as the Shaun Ryder case, was compiled by the MMF Copyright and Contracts Sub-Committee under the chairmanship of the author.

Following the example long form written contract contained herein a section on verbal agreements and an example of a temporary 'letter of engagement' is given which is useful in the initial relationship between an artist and a manager. This is followed by a brief discussion of some alternative arrangements which a manager and an artist could consider. Some notes are also included concerning the judgement in the Shaun Ryder case which may be helpful. Although English law uses the doctrine of precedent in such cases for guidance, it does not necessarily follow that another court would come to the same conclusion in a case where the facts were materially different.

It is best to think of artist management agreements as a kind of marriage. It is essential that both sides get on with each other. The artist management agreement should be the only time in the artist's career in which the artist and the manager sit on opposite sides of the table. Thereafter, both the artist and the manager should work together as a team with success being the common goal. When an agreement is reached, both sides should feel reasonably comfortable with it. If one side feels very happy and the other unhappy it will not have achieved the balance needed for a good working agreement. The artist/manager relationship has to be based on trust and regular discussion on all the issues. It is important that the artist is told as much as possible, both good news and bad news at an appropriate time (eg it is generally not a good idea to deliver bad news just as the artist goes on stage!)

The agreement itself should clearly lay out the ground rules, but there will always be unusual situations which will need discussion and should be resolved within the spirit of common sense and compromise by all concerned. If there are any special arrangements made, they should always be made in writing and signed by both parties.

It is absolutely essential that the artist receives independent legal advice from a specialist music business lawyer. If not, the enforceability of the contract will be weakened considerably.

When a band is starting out there is usually very little money available and the prospect of incurring huge legal fees is daunting. Lawyers are aware of this and are usually happy to either charge a very low fee or postpone payment until a recording or publishing advance is secured in the hope that future work will be forthcoming. Sometimes the manager will pay the artist's legal fees with the manager being reimbursed when income starts to flow through. In either case the artist and the manager should get a quote from their respective lawyers before work commences. The MMF can provide a list of specialist music business lawyers who specialise in the music business which could be passed on to the artist. If the artist is a member of the Musicians' Union they can also provide legal advice for a comparatively low fee.

In the '60s and '70s, artist management agreements were often unfairly weighted in favour of the manager. During the '80s, however, artists' lawyers successfully gained more ground for the artist to the point where many current agreements are now often unfairly weighted against the manager. (For example, some artist lawyers try to insist that managers do not commission PRS income which the MMF recommend is firmly resisted.) This has the effect of reducing the incentive for managers and encourages poor quality management. Also, if the agreement does not reward the manager adequately, the manager may have to take on extra artists simply to survive, which will mean that less time can be devoted to the artist which is not in the artist's interest.

From the manager's point of view it is important that the conditions in the agreement fall broadly in line with industry norms and are not unreasonable. If the contract as a whole is too harsh a court may take the view that the contract puts the artist in a position of being in restraint of trade.

Both the manager and the artist should clearly understand that time is valuable.

The manager's expert advice, whilst not charged by the hour as in the case of lawyers, and accountants, clearly has a substantial value. If the manager is investing large amounts of time and/or money the manager needs to be compensated for this risk in a way which is reflected in the commission structures.

At the end of the day the most contentious issues in these agreements are likely to be the post-term commission arrangements and the touring income commission arrangements. It is important for both the manager and the artist that a fair workable agreement is achieved in these areas.

It is very important for a manager to try and provide a thorough and high quality management for the artist. It is therefore a much better idea for managers to focus on one or two artists than to take on too many and spread themselves too thin, unless their businesses are structured with enough full-time staff to adequately administer a larger number of artists. The MMF is dedicated to providing education for managers and raising professional standards.

The best way of explaining the way in which these agreements work is to give an example of an artist management agreement such as can be seen below.

THE CONTRACT

Both the artist and the manager should use a specialist music-business lawyer. Failure of the artist to receive independent advice from such a lawyer may jeopardise the enforceability of the contract. It is also essential that the manager and the artist use different lawyers. Every situation is different and will have its own unique set of circumstances. The following example is therefore intended to be a guide to understanding such contracts, hopefully providing help in arriving at a fair agreement for both parties. This is an example of an artist/management contract based on the precepts of the preceding chapter, with notes of explanation and advice.

1.   *The Artist hereby appoints the Manager who agrees to carry out the Manager's Duties in relation to the Artist's career throughout the Territory during the Term.*

2.   *The Artist shall pay commission to the Manager at the Commission Rate during the Commission Term on all Commissionable Income earned by the Artist from the Artist's Career.*

3.   *The Manager shall pay the Manager's Expenses as defined in the Schedule.*

4.   *The Artist shall pay the Artist's Expenses as defined in the Schedule.*

5.   *The Artist and the Manager shall each have the right to audit the other not more than once in any (_____) month period. Such audit shall require 30 days written notice and must take place within normal office hours. If no objection is raised to an accounting statement rendered by either party within (_____) years of its date, such statement will be deemed correct and binding.*

With audit rights, it is common to agree that if the party being audited is shown to have underpaid by more than 10% then in addition to reimbursing the shortfall (plus interest) they are also obliged to pay the cost of the audit. The right to audit is usually limited to no more than once in any 6- or 12-month period. The number of years to raise an objection is typically two or three years.

Then either:

6.   *The Manager shall, during the Term, collect all income on behalf of the Artist and shall pay it into a bank account exclusively dedicated to the Artist. The Manager shall only use funds deposited in such account for purposes directly connected to the Artist's career.*

or:

6.   *The Artist shall be responsible for all accounting concerning the Artist's Career including all book keeping, tax returns, invoicing, receipts and payments etc. From time to time the Manager will invoice the Artist for Commission which shall be paid within (___) days of receipt.*

If adopting the second approach ignore sections 8, 9.4 and 9.5 from the Schedule. It is important that the manager keeps a separate bank account for each artist. The number of days in which the invoice should be paid could be anything from 10–30 days.

7. *After the expiry of the Term the Artist shall every (_____) months produce statements to the Manager showing all income and Commission due and shall on receipt of an invoice from the Manager pay the Commission due within (_____) days of receipt of the invoice.*

It is normal for the Artist to be obliged to produce statements every three months. The number of days in which the invoice should be paid could be anything from 10–30 days.

8. *The Artist and the Manager shall each have the right to terminate the Term by written notice if the other:*

    8.1.1 *is declared bankrupt or enters into a composition or agreement with creditors, or*

    8.1.2 *is convicted of an offence involving dishonesty, or*

    8.1.3 *is in material breach of this agreement and shall not have remedied that breach within 30 days of written notice of being required to do so, or*

    8.1.4 *is incapacitated due to illness or accident for a period exceeding (_____) days.*

The normal period of incapacity is three to four months but it could be anything from six weeks to 12 months. A contract might also provide for a temporary replacement manager in such circumstances. Anyone can have an accident or become ill and it seems unreasonable that managers having suffered one misfortune then have to suffer another by losing their artists. The MMF therefore recommends a period of at least four months.

    8.2 *If either party terminates the term this shall not affect either party's rights or obligations that are intended to continue in force beyond the Term.*

9.   No variation of this agreement shall be binding unless made in writing and signed by both parties.

10.   Any notice or consent to be given under this agreement shall be effective if sent by registered or recorded delivery post to the other party at the address given in the Schedule. Service shall be deemed to take place on the day following posting.

11.   Nothing herein shall constitute a partnership between the Artist and the Manager.

12.   The Artist and the Manager herein acknowledge that they are advised to seek independent specialist music business legal advice from a qualified music-business lawyer before signing this agreement.

13.   The Manager has the right and authority to negotiate with third parties on the Artist's behalf.

14.   This agreement shall be governed by (_____) law and both parties agree to submit to the exclusive jurisdiction of the High Court of Justices in (_____).

For UK managers we recommend that 'English' and 'England' are inserted respectively. The law in Wales and Northern Ireland is identical to those of England as far as these agreements are concerned, whilst the law in Scotland is very different. If most of an artist's work takes place in Scotland the contract could be governed by Scottish law but a manager in this position would nevertheless still be advised to have a contract governed by English law because there is a great deal more precedent in English law and the majority of UK specialist music business lawyers are based in London.

A manager dealing with an artist who is based abroad and who insists on dealing in the law of a foreign country must be very careful to research the laws concerning contracts. For example, in California contracts for personal services are restricted to seven years.

15.   Terms used in this agreement shall have the meanings described in the Schedule, heretowhich is hereby incorporated into this agreement.

the schedule

1. The Artist: (_____)

The Artist could be an individual, a partnership or a limited company. The Artist's real name should appear here together with their stage name (if any) and their current address. If the Artist is a band each member of the band's real name together with their stage name (if any) and their current address and the current name of the band should be shown. If the Artist is a band there will need to be provision here for changes in the band's personnel with an obligation for new joining members to be party to this agreement. Also a band will need to have a separate 'band agreement' which will deal with such issues as how income is to be split between each band member and the provisions in the eventuality of a band member leaving.

If the artist is contracted as a limited company it will be necessary to have an inducement letter wherein the artist is held personally responsible for the provisions of the agreement.

2. The Manager: (_____)

The manager could be an individual, a partnership or a limited company. If contracted as the latter the artist may wish to have a 'key man' clause inserted in the agreement obliging the manager's personal services to be available, the failure of which would be a breach.

If either party contracts as a limited company, that company is not entitled to legal aid in the event of a dispute. A company is also likely to be asked by the court for a security deposit before the case starts.

3. Territory: (_____)

If managers are not managing the Artist for the world make sure that they are clear about who the other managers are in other territories and of their roles in the international picture. If they are principal managers then they should have the right to appoint third-party managers in foreign territories.

In this case it is important for them to make sure that the commission arrangements are clear and that the artists are not paying double commission.

4.   *Term: (_____) years/months commencing on (_____). Thereafter the Term continues until either party gives (_____) months' notice of termination.*

The term could be anything from six months to five years. Some managers prefer to go for a comparatively short term, perhaps one year, and to have a three-month notice of termination from either side after that period so that, for example, the term continues indefinitely after one year until one party gives notice to the other that the term will end in three months. The advantage of this is that the manager has a stronger negotiating position in regard to the other terms of the contract. Artists are also reassured that, if things don't work out, they are not tied to the manager for a long period of time.

On the other hand some managers feel that they will need to invest a great deal of hard work into an artist in the early stages, probably with very little commission and that they therefore need a longer term in order to feel secure about making that investment of time and effort.

Another common arrangement is to have a term of perhaps two or three years with options for a further one or two years. The options can only be taken up by the manager if the manager has achieved certain income levels for the artist.

Yet another approach is to define the term in albums rather than in years. In the '70s an artist would typically release one album per year. These days, however, an artist may be lucky to get two albums released in the first four years. It may therefore be a much better approach to define the term as two or three albums in the same way that it is defined in recording and publishing contracts. If this approach is adopted it is essential that a long-stop term is also included as a contract cannot be open-ended (eg two years commencing from a certain date or until six months after the release of the third album, whichever is the longer, provided that in no circumstances will the basic term exceed five years.)

In some cases the manager may reach an arrangement with the artist wherein, if the manager is unsuccessful in procuring a recording agreement or publishing agreement within perhaps 12–18 months then the term has an earlier termination date.

Generally speaking, the MMF recommends that a fixed term does not exceed five years. In the Shaun Ryder case the court held that a seven year term (comprising an initial term of three years and two two-year options not related to earnings) was unreasonable. The court observed that it is usual in the music industry for an earnings target to be included to legitimise a further period which is the subject of an option, and that it was unreasonable for an option period not to be tied to an earnings target. (See Chapter 4, 'Enforceability Of Agreements'.)

5. *Commission Rate: (_____)%*
    Not withstanding anything to the contrary in this agreement, the commission payable to the manager by the Artist in respect of touring and live performance income shall be (____)% of the gross fees in respect of touring and live performance or (____)% of the net profit from touring and live performance whichever is the greater.

The generally accepted commission rate for managers in the music industry is 20%. In practice, however, this can range from 10% to 25%. Take the example of a manager investing a lot of money into a new band and giving them a tremendous amount of time and belief. In such a situation it might be quite reasonable for the manager to take 25%. It may also be appropriate for a manager to take 25% if he or she agrees to manage the artist exclusively. In such a situation it is common to agree that the commission rate lowers to 20% if the manager manages more than one or two other artists.

For a very well-established artist looking for a new manager, the new manager will know that there is very little or no risk involved and that therefore there is quite a lot of money in the picture. In such a case the manager might be willing to agree a commission of 10%–15% or even operate on a flat-fee basis.

In the other extreme there has been a new phenomenon in recent years wherein a high level manager has created a band by holding auditions or by taking a band on via a TV talent competition in which they are involved. By virtue of the manager virtually guaranteeing massive TV exposure, or in the case of the manager creating the band and investing very large sums of money, commissions as high as 50% are rumoured to have been agreed. Whether a court would find this level of commission acceptable in such circumstances remains to be tested but in such a case it may be better to enter into some kind of joint venture with the band or artist as will be briefly discussed later in this chapter.

TOURING INCOME

In practice there are many different arrangements in place for touring income varying from a straight 20% of the gross to 20% of the net profits only. A large proportion of tours lose money or break even (often with record company tour support). If the manager only has a 20% of the net profits agreement this means he or she cannot take any commission on the tour. Furthermore, the manager has had to pay for all of the management staff and office costs etc connected with the tour. In such a case the manager has done a tremendous amount of work (usually much more than the booking agent) and ends up with a considerable financial loss. Also if there is tour support from a record company, this represents a further loss to the manager as it is usually fully recoupable from royalties which would otherwise have been commissionable. The MMF therefore feels that 20% of the net profits only is unreasonable from the manager's perspective unless the tour is making a substantial profit, and its recommendation is that management should take at least 10–15% of the gross touring income (less VAT/other taxes) or 20–30% of the net profits, whichever is the greater.

Another approach is for the manager to take a fixed fee for managing the tour or for an arrangement to be worked out on a tour-by-tour basis by reference to the budgeted costs and income. Yet another basis is that the manager gets at least the same as the highest paid person on the tour. The level of an appropriate touring commission rate can be influenced by several other factors: is the manager also the tour manager or the booking agent or both?; is the artist a solo performer or a band?; and who is in control of touring costs? For example, if the manager also provides and pays for the services of a tour manager it would be quite reasonable to fix an all-in touring commission rate of 17.5% of the gross.

Some managers favour adding an additional clause so that the touring commission rate can be reviewed in the light of how the artist's career develops. Such a clause might read:

> From time to time and at the request of either party the fairness of this clause can be reviewed.

This clause is not recommended by the MMF as it could lead to difficulties and disputes. However, some managers favour its inclusion and have made it work successfully. If the arrangement is changed in such a review it is important to remember to get the change agreed in writing and signed by both parties. If an agreement is reached for a percentage of the gross and the artist is unable to pay the manager due to cash flow difficulties then the amount should be rolled up with interest and paid when the artist is in a position to do so. This process also applies to commission generally.

Merchandising and sponsorship income associated with a tour or a retail merchandising agreement should, in the MMF's view, be treated separately and should be commissioned at the normal commission rate rather than be included in the calculation of touring losses and profits.

When negotiating tour support with a record company it is important to insist that management commission is an acceptable tour cost. It is also important to clarify that merchandising income is not included as tour income in the tour accounts. For some illogical reason some record companies accept booking agency commission as a *bona fide* expense but refuse to accept management commission. Apart from being illogical this is also demeaning to managers and unfair to artists and in the MMF's view this should not be accepted. It is important to raise these issues with the record company as early as possible and preferably when the recording agreement is originally negotiated. That is the only point at which the manager may have the upper hand over the record company. It may also be possible to negotiate with the record company that the record company will pay the manager a weekly fixed fee when on tour, and international airfares in the early stages of the artist's career when touring will need tour support.

We suggest a 'tour' be defined as a series of more than six dates in any monthly period. If several 'one-off' dates occur in a month then these can be grouped and the commission calculated on a monthly basis.

In the 21st century, as record sales decrease due to such factors such as illegal CD burning, an artist's income is in many cases shifting from recording and publishing income towards touring income. For artists who have ceased to have hit albums and hit singles touring income represents their main income stream so it is very important to consider the above carefully and arrive at fair and workable percentages for both parties.

It is interesting to note that in the Shaun Ryder case the court decided that a touring commission rate of 20% of the gross was reasonable!

6. Commission Term: (_____)

An accepted principle of artist management agreements is that the manager should continue to receive commission after the term has expired for their achievements during the term. In the UK this is known as 'post term commission'. In the USA it is known as the 'sunset clause'.

Many managers believe strongly that commission should be payable in perpetuity on income resulting from work carried out during the term and this is a view supported by the MMF. If an album is successful it is generally so because of the combined efforts of the artist, the manager and the record company. Many recording contracts are for life of copyright which for sound recordings in the UK is currently 50 years from first release. Therefore the artist and the record company will receive income in perpetuity (or for life of copyright) so why shouldn't the manager? The manager is usually a key component in the success of an album, and that expertise and hard work deserves to be rewarded. Similarly life of copyright in songwriting (musical works and lyrics) currently has a term of 70 years after the death of the last person who participated in the song-writing for a particular song which in practice could be 130 years if the song was written when the artist was 20 and the artist died at the age of 80. Post-term commission in perpetuity is something that is likely to be challenged by artist lawyers but it is the MMF's view that a manager should be firm in insisting this continuity of commission as it is both fair and reasonable.

It may be the case that a compromise is reached by which the manager's commission is payable at full rate for a period after the term, which is then followed by one or two periods in which the commission reduces, the last of these being in perpetuity. For example, full rate for the first two or three years following the end of the term of the management agreement, and half rate in perpetuity (or until copyright expires by law) thereafter.

If the commission does reduce, a second manager may be able to negotiate with the artist for the difference between the commission being paid to the first manager and the commission rate. If the previous works were commissionable at the full rate in perpetuity by the old manager, it may be a good idea to approach the old manager (with the approval of the artist) to negotiate a commission split on previous works. After all, if a new manager invests a tremendous amount of work on current and future works, and the work is successful, this could well stimulate back catalogue sales, which would benefit the old manager. It may therefore be in the old manager's interest to encourage the new manager to try very hard in this respect by agreeing to a split commission which would provide a further incentive.

In any case, except in unusual circumstances, the aggregate of the commissions of the old manager and the new manager would not exceed the commission rate. It is also important to define which works will be commissionable on a post-term basis. It could be any of the following:

(a) anything created during the term (writing or recording);
(b) anything recorded during the term (either demos or masters);
(c) anything released during the term.

It is interesting to note that in the Shaun Ryder case the court was critical of a clause which gave the manager the right to commission on an album both recorded and released after the end of the term of the management agreement. It was also not persuaded that commissioning post term in perpetuity *at the full rate* of commission was reasonable.

7.   *Artist's Career. All activities in the (_____) industry, including without limitation the creation of Works as defined in 11 below.*

Either 'music' or 'entertainment' should be inserted here. 'Entertainment' has broader scope and would include such things as literary and dramatic works if appropriate.

8.   *Artist's Account: Bank Address: (_____).*
      Bank Account Number: (_____).
      Signatories: (_____) (_____).
      Interest if either party owe money to the other: (_____)% over the (_____) base rate.

It is completely reasonable for the manager to charge interest if commission or expenses cannot be paid. If a payment of income or corporation tax payment is late the Inland Revenue will automatically charge interest and the situation should be exactly the same for management commission and expenses.

9.   *Manager's Duties:*

9.1   *To use the Manager's reasonable endeavours to advance and promote the Artist's Career.*

9.2   *To advise and consult with the Artist regarding the collection of income and the incurring of expenditure, and to use the Manager's reasonable endeavours to ensure that the Artist gets paid.*

It's important that the manager and the artist regularly consult and discuss the development of the artist's career, both in terms of assessing its past and present success and its future direction.

9.3   *To consult regularly with the Artist and to keep the Artist informed of all substantial activity undertaken by the Manager, and to discuss the Artist's career development generally and to offer constructive criticism periodically.*

9.4   *To maintain records of all transactions affecting the Artist's Career and to send the Artist a statement within (_____) days of the end of each calendar quarter disclosing all Income, the source of Income, expenses, commission and other debts and liabilities arising during the preceding three months.*

The period between the end of the quarter and the statement can be anything from 30–120 days. It can often take a considerable time to document and account the financial activity of a particular quarter, especially if the artist is on a world tour. The MMF therefore suggests that managers try to negotiate as long a period as reasonably possible. If the accounts are late, for some reason, an artist may rightly claim breach of contract. Supplying the accounts 120 days after the quarter end is not unreasonable, and for those cases where a tour straddles two accounting periods it may be necessary to have a one-off agreement signed to the effect that the accounting will be deferred to the end of the period following the end of the tour. In a case such as this it is important to have a clear written agreement signed to this effect before the start of the tour.

> 9.5 *To obtain the artist's approval for any expenditure over £(_____) for a single cheque or £(_____) over a period of one calendar month.*

This is sometimes seen in artist management agreements, and provides the artist with some protection against the manager misusing his or her money. In practice it is vital that there is trust between the artist and the manager. This limitation can also be a practical problem if, for example, the manager is in England and the artist is in Australia and funds are needed quickly.

> 9.6 *To advise the Artist on appointing booking agents, accountants, lawyers, sponsors, merchandisers and other agents with due consideration to the Artist's moral views.*

It is important that both the artist and the manager feel comfortable and are able to work with third-party professionals. It is also important that the manager is aware of the artist's political and moral views and does not commit the artist to anything inappropriate.

10. *Artist's Duties:*

> 10.1 *To carry out to the best of their ability and in punctual and sober fashion all reasonable agreements, engagements, performances and promotional activities obtained or approved by the Manager.*

> 10.2 *To attend promptly all appointments and to keep the Manager reasonably informed of the Artist's whereabouts and availability at all times.*

10.3 To reveal to the Manager all income, including – but not limited to – PRS, PPL, GVL, MU, AURA, PAMRA, touring overages, and radio and television appearance monies paid directly to the Artist.

10.4 To refer promptly all approaches and offers from third parties concerning the Artist's Career to the Manager.

10.5 Not to engage any other person to act as the Artist's manager or representative in connection with any aspect of the Artist's Career.

10.6 To consult regularly with the Manager concerning the development of the Artist's Career and to accept that it is part of the Manager's job to offer constructive criticism from time to time.

10.7 To keep the Manager fully informed and to consult regularly concerning all anticipated expenditure to be incurred by the Artist, and to obtain the Manager's approval with regard to recording costs, video costs, equipment costs and touring costs.

11. Works:

11.1 Sound recordings (including demos).

11.2 Visual recordings (including film and video).

11.3 Literary, dramatic and musical works.

11.4 Merchandising, sponsorship of any name, logo, artwork or trade mark owned by or associated with the Artist.

11.5 Performances and appearances by the Artist in concert or on radio, television or film.

11.6 Recordings of other artists produced, engineered, programmed or arranged by the Artist.

In each case (11.1–11.6) created or substantially created during the Term.

12.   *Income (shall mean both 12.1 and 12.2):*

   12.1   *Commissionable Income*

   All gross fees and sums of money payable and accruing to the Artist in respect of exploitation of the Works or otherwise arising from activities in the Artist's Career excluding Non-Commissionable Income.

   12.2   *Non-Commissionable Income:*

   12.2.1   *Sums paid by or on behalf of the Artist as budgeted, recoupable recording costs or budgeted recoupable video costs.*

   12.2.2   *Royalties, advances or fees paid or credited by or on behalf of the Artist to any third-party producers, mixers, programmers or engineers, to an agreed budget.*

   12.2.3   *Monies paid or credited to the Artist as tour support, to an agreed budget.*

   12.2.4   *In the event that the Artist enters into a separate production and/or publishing agreement with the Manager then income from such agreements shall be non-commissionable income.*

The word 'budgeted' has been included in the above to allow the commissionable income to be calculated in a fair and reasonable way. The responsibility for budgeting should rest jointly between the artist and the manager, but if, for example, the recording costs for an album go wildly over budget, it may be necessary for the artist and the manager to come to an agreement as to how much commission should be taken.

   The modern tendency is for recording contract advances (sometimes called 'recording funds') to be inclusive of recording costs and if this is the case, the manager and the artist are faced with the problem of deciding how much of the recording advance should be set aside for recording (which is non-commissionable income) and how much should be regarded as commissionable income. It is a good idea to come to a separate written agreement with the artist every time a new album recording advance is received so that an agreed level of the advance is deemed to be commissionable income. For instance, it could be the case that the entire advance is spent on recording costs, in which case the manager would earn absolutely nothing.

It may also be possible to insert a re-assessment clause wherein both parties agree on an adjusted level of commissionable income when the recording of the album has been finished. Also if the artist buys recording equipment with the advance this should be regarded as commissionable income as the artist is acquiring an asset.

13. *Manager's Expenses: General office and business costs, including:*

> *Office rent;*
> *Local property tax on office;*
> *Management staff salaries and wages;*
> *Management staff Social Security payments;*
> *Manager's office equipment, including:*
> > *Computers;*
> > *Fax machines*
> > *Photocopiers;*
> > *Pagers*
> > *Mobile phones;*
> > *Office telephone system;*
> > *Audio and audio-visual equipment*
> *Manager's car and associated costs;*
> *Manager's legal fees;*
> *Local telephone, fax and e-mail costs;*
> *Miscellaneous office expenses.*

14. *Artist's Expenses: Any expenses reasonably incurred in connection with the Artist's Career whether incurred by the Manager or the Artist other*

than the Manager's Expenses including but not limited to the following:
Commission payable to a booking agent or other agents;
Costs/wages payable to a Tour Manager;
Mailshots on behalf of Artist;
Advertising on behalf of Artist;
Artwork on behalf of Artist;
Management long-distance phone and fax charges, if specifically on behalf of Artist;
Hotel room charges;
Air fares, rail fares and sea fares;
Courier charges on behalf of Artist;
Manager's reasonable subsistence (food, etc) when on tour or away from the office on business on Artist's behalf;
(____) pence per mile for Manager's car journeys in the UK (to be reviewed annually);
Car hire, taxis and other travel costs when business is carried out on behalf of the Artist by the Manager or the Manager's personal assistant;
Expenses incurred by the Manager prior to the commencement of this agreement to the sum of £(_____).

The above to be pro rated if work for other artists is also being carried out.

This is an example of a typical arrangement for expenses, although the specifics will vary. Telephone systems are now available wherein a code can be used to accurately charge each call to the appropriate artist. If the manager does not have this technology another arrangement is to agree a standard monthly fee to the artist for long distance, mobile and international telephone calls. Also, the mileage rate charged for the manager's car journeys, will vary according to the engine capacity of the manager's car. The AA, the RAC or the Inland Revenue will be able to supply the current rates.

END OF SCHEDULE

VERBAL AGREEMENTS

Some very high-level managers operate using verbal or 'handshake' agreements and seem to have made them work. It may be that they are so confident in their own abilities that they feel secure enough that the artist will not be tempted to go elsewhere.

In the UK verbal agreements for services such as an artist management agreement are enforceable by law whereas in the USA such agreements have to be in writing.

The problem of course with a verbal agreement is that whilst they may work very well when things are going well, they can prove problematic if there is a dispute. In such a dispute it can often end up as one person's word against the other's especially if there were no witnesses when the verbal agreement was made. It is therefore advisable, if possible, to have reliable witnesses to such an agreement and to try and cover as many of the issues such as term, commission rates, what is commissionable, post-term commission arrangements, touring commission rates, reimbursable expenses etc as clearly and as precisely as possible.

Another advantage of a verbal agreement is that it is more likely to be acceptable to the artist, at least in the initial stages. Many agreements have failed due to a manager being too demanding in the initial stages by perhaps insisting that a full long-form management agreement is signed before they will do any work. An artist's lawyer might well advise the artist against this hasty and perhaps heavy-handed approach which could instil doubts in the artist's mind about the suitability and possibly the integrity of the manager.

As mentioned earlier, the negotiation of the artist management agreement is the only time in the artist's career where the artist and the manager are on opposite sides of the table and this negotiation needs to be handled sensitively and diplomatically so that both the artist and the manager retain their enthusiasm for moving forward together. It can be traumatic for the artist to have just met a suitable manager only to be thrown into heavy negotiations with that manager right at the beginning.

In general, even if at the very beginning the agreement is a verbal agreement it is always better to get the agreement in writing as soon as practicable so that both sides know as clearly as possible where they stand, but as stated above, in a way that does not damage the spirit of the relationship.

legal limitations and implied terms

for verbal contracts

A court may impose certain legal limitations on the relationship between an artist and a manager if there is no written agreement. Some of the implied terms a court might impose are:

1   The Manager will not allow a conflict of interest to arise between themselves and the artist.

2   The Manager will represent the Artist with fiduciary care (ie the manager will diligently and honestly represent the Artist with due care and attention and will not misuse confidential information regarding the Artist or misrepresent the Artist in such away as to cause the Artist damage).

3   The Manager will keep accurate books of account in regard to artist's income and expenditure, together with all bank statements, invoices and receipts, etc.

short-term trial period letter of engagement

There is a third way! Whilst at the very beginning the relationship between the artist and the manager will almost certainly be verbal, a very short one page letter of engagement can be agreed for an initial trial period. This should be signed as soon as practicable after the initial meetings have taken place. Such a letter of engagement sets out the very basic arrangements under which the manager will manage the artist in the short term until both sides feel comfortable to move ahead with negotiations of a long form agreement as above. It is arguable whether or not the artist needs legal advice for such a short, simple and temporary agreement. If the artist wishes to take legal advice they can of course do so but what tends to happen is that the artist lawyer will expand and change this letter agreement with extended riders etc in which case it might be better to go straight into negotiations of a long form agreement in the first place. Although this simple letter agreement has as far as we know never been tested in court, at least it sets out something in writing to show the basic way the parties intend to operate. The MMF would advise that such a temporary agreement has a term of no more than six months.

On the next page there is an example of such a letter of engagement from the manager to the artist on the manager's headed paper:

ALTERNATIVE AGREEMENTS

An artist management agreement as shown above is an agreement for services. The problem with such agreements is that they leave the manager vulnerable to being dismissed by the artist. The manager is acting as an agent to the artist and does not hold any property rights in the artist's works. If the relationship breaks down the only recourse that the manager has is either to come to a settlement with the artist or to sue for damages in the courts. No court will ever force an artist to continue working with a manager if they don't wish to. Rather they will award the aggrieved party damages based on the current situation.

Many managers are unhappy with the lack of security provided in such agreements and are pursuing alternative arrangements wherein they own all or part of the artist's copyrights.

Such agreements could be:

1   A partnership agreement with the artist wherein the copyrights are jointly owned;

To: (Artist(s) Name(s) and Address(es))
Date

Dear _____

Further to our meetings and discussions to date, please take this letter as confirmation that ....(Manager) will act as your exclusive manager throughout the world for a trial period of (.........) months from the above date, after which either you or ....(Manager) must give 30 days' notice to the other to effect termination.

During this trial period you agree to pay us commission of (......)% on any income received by you in the entertainment industry, except for any income specifically intended as recording costs, video production costs or as tour support. You further agree to re-imburse reasonable expenses incurred by ....(Manager) on your behalf as per the attached expenses schedule. In regard to live performances, the commission payable to us will be reduced to (......)% of the gross income received.

At the end of the trial period, you or ....(Manager) may elect to terminate the management relationship or move forward with negotiations for a long-form artist management agreement. In either case, payment to ....(Manager) of commission and expenses must be paid to ....(Manager) within 60 days of receipt of the invoice which we will submit.

If you sign this letter, you are entering into a legally binding agreement.

If the above is a correct reflection of the agreement we have reached, please confirm this by your signature(s) below.

Yours sincerely

...........................(Manager)

Confirmation of agreement by (name and address of Artist(s))

Signature...

Date...

The expenses as per the example in clauses 14 and 15 of the schedule above should be attached to this temporary letter of engagement.

2   A limited company wherein the manager and the artist are directors and the copyrights are owned by the limited company;

3   A production company agreement either owned by the manager or jointly owned with the artist;

4   A publishing agreement wherein the manager owns the publishing entity or it is co-owned with the artist.

In all the above cases, the manager (although that title may need to be dropped) would have an intellectual property ownership interest in the artist's work which puts him or her in a far stronger and more secure position. It is essential, however, that if the manager becomes a production company and/or the publisher that no management commission is taken in either case. This would be considered to be a conflict of interest.

In the case of a split-copyright ownership arrangement the accounting procedures may become more complicated than for a conventional management commission arrangement. Specialist legal and accounting/taxation advice should be sought prior to entering into such deals.

production company agreements

Of the above, the production company route is becoming more common. In this business model the manager may cease to be the manager in title but may nevertheless provide management services but without commission. The manager becomes the production company. The difficulty here is that the manager has to find the money to make an album, which can be a very high risk investment. Production agreements are typically 50/50 to 70/30 in the artists favour. The production company makes the album and then licenses it to record companies around the world. The recording costs for the album are first deducted from any incoming advances together with any other allowable expenses and the net is then split between the production company and the artist according to the split agreed.

The advantage to the artist of a production company agreement is that the copyright in the recording will often be owned by the production company for a far shorter period than would be the case with a major record company who will often demand that they own the copyright for life of copyright (a practice that the MMF are campaigning to end!), which is currently 50 years from first release. The term in a production company agreement might be for only ten years whereafter the artist would get ownership of the copyright in the recordings back (provided the album is recouped), which is extremely attractive for the artist. In this way the production company can only license the recordings for ten years to a major record company as those are the only rights it has, which works to the advantage of the artist. Also although the artist will have to split their royalties with the production company a record company will generally pay a higher royalty rate to a production company than to an artist signing directly as they don't have to pay recording costs. They also know exactly what they are getting as, at least the first album is usually finished when it is licensed which saves the record company risk and A&R costs. The other significant advantage to the artist if they sign to a production company is that the production company can protect the artist from unreasonable demands from the record company and provide another tier of support to the artist in every area. In some cases this could mean the difference between success and failure.

Although the production company or publisher may also provide management services in the initial stages, albeit without charging the artist any commission, the artist would be free to engage a manager on a traditional agreement for services at any time if they so wish.

Alternatively a management agreement could exist in addition to production and/or publishing agreements provided it states clearly in the management agreement that commission will not be taken on income from such additional agreements (see 12.2.4 above)

In regard to where the artist enters into a publishing agreement with the manager it may be possible to provide for the term of the publishing agreement to be for the duration of the management agreement plus, for example, ten years. If the publishing splits were, for example, 75/25 at source in the UK and 80/20 on receipts outside the UK and no commission was payable this could give the artist a net financial gain in percentage terms over traditional management arrangements and would give the manager greater security – ie, if a writer were to enter into a traditional

75% at source deal with a major publisher then a manager would expect to commission at 20% leaving the writer with in effect 60% of at-source earnings. If the manager sets up their own publishing company then the net pay-through to the artist would need to be higher than 60% at-source for the artist to be better off. The complication here is the issue of advances from third parties which should be paid through to the artist if received by the manager's publishing company. Another advantage to the artist of this arrangement is that royalties are likely to be paid through more quickly than would be the case with a major publisher.

The extreme of this is that the manager has a management agreement, a production agreement and a publishing agreement with the artist all running concurrently. This situation has, as far as we know, never been tested in court but provided the artist has received independent advice from a specialist music business lawyer and the manager does not take management commission on the publishing and production company income, the terms of all three agreements are reasonable and the manager acts in an honest and professional manner, the MMF is advised that such a situation would be lawful. If such a situation were to be challenged it would be on the basis that the manager had a conflict of interest. We will have to wait for a court judgement to be made in such a case before certainty can be established. As such, the MMF strongly recommends that any manager intending to use this business model should first take independent legal advice.

This document was created by the MMF Copyright and Contracts Sub-Committee. The members of this committee, who gave a great deal of unpaid time, were as follows: David R Stopps (Chairman), Nigel Parker, Peter Jenner, Phil Nelson, David Enthoven, Tim Clark and Jazz Summers. Special thanks also to Robert Horsfall and Tim Gardner for consultancy.

Any enquiries about this document should be addressed to:

MMF (Head Office)
1 York Street
London
W1U 6PA
Tel: (+44) (0)870 8507 800
Fax: (+44) (0)870 8507 801

Email: info@ukmmf.net
Web: www.ukmmf.net

or to

David R Stopps
Friars Management Limited
33 Alexander Road
Aylesbury
Buckinghamshire
HP20 2NR
Tel: (+44) (0)1296 434731
Fax: (+44) (0)1296 422530
Email: DavidStopps@FMLMusic.com

3 Recording Contracts

By Andrew Thompson

The recording contract is the principal means by which a recording artist earns his living. Without a record deal, his ability to exploit his talent is limited. The recording contract is also the principal means by which a record company acquires its stock-in-trade. Record companies may also buy 'catalogues' of recordings made by other record companies under their own recording contracts. Without recording contracts there would be very few recordings. Without recordings there would be limited opportunities for songwriters and music publishers to exploit their songs. The recording agreement affects every aspect of the recording artist's career and its importance cannot be over-emphasised.

In Part 1 of this chapter, we will look briefly at how a recording artist might find a record deal, and at the different types of deal which might be available. In Part 2 we will then look more closely at the component parts of a typical recording contract, before examining the financial aspects of recording contracts in Part 3. Finally, in Part 4, we will deal with some of the more general considerations which apply once a recording artist has secured a record deal.

PART 1: THE DEAL

1.0 finding the deal

1.1 THE TEAM

Few would-be recording artists are lucky enough to find worthwhile recording contracts. There is no easy way to get a deal. We would all like to think that talent is the main factor. But talent alone is not enough. Good luck plays a large part (although, to some extent, a recording artist can help make his own luck). Nor is there any right or wrong way to go about finding a deal. Artists can rarely secure a deal on their own, if only because it is difficult for artists to sell themselves. The first aim is therefore to ensure that the right team of people is in place to support the artist.

1.2 THE MANAGER

In most cases, an artist appoints a manager before obtaining his first record deal. Sometimes a manager, or someone else with contacts and experience, may agree to help secure a deal whilst not wishing to remain involved beyond that. In return he may ask for a finder's fee.

This approach can be problematic. The strength of the overall team is important for the record company. In deciding whether or not to offer a deal, the company wants to feel comfortable with the organisation of the recording project. In particular, the company must have confidence in the artist's manager. So the record company may resist dealing with someone who is merely 'shopping' for a deal with no intention of following through with continuing help and support. Sometimes a company will sign an artist without a manager. In most cases, though, the company would then try to ensure that a manager is put in place.

1.3 AGENTS

If the artist is gigging regularly, his booking agent may help to get a deal. However, the major booking agencies are reluctant to sign artists until they have a good live following. Often, this only happens once a record deal is in place.

1.4 LAWYERS

A music business lawyer can sometimes help with getting a deal. Most lawyers are only of real help once a record company has shown some interest. There is a limit to what the lawyer is able to do in securing that interest in the first place. A specialist lawyer (like anybody else working in the industry) might manage to put a demo tape on the right desks at selected record companies. He might even ensure that the tape is given proper consideration. However, distributing demo tapes is rarely enough, on its own, to get a deal.

1.5 THE PITCH

Every recording project is different. Even if it is not different, it must be presented as if it is. So a 'story' must be developed around the particular project before this is 'pitched' to record companies. The individual talent of the artist will always be the central feature of the story. There will be many other factors involved, including the songs and perhaps the intended producer, and perhaps the past history of those involved in the project. The story takes time to develop and a record deal never turns up overnight.

1.6 PUBLISHERS

Assuming the artist writes some or all of his own material, there is the question of whether to sign a record deal or a publishing deal first. Some years ago, the conventional wisdom was that a record deal should be secured before a publishing deal. The theory was that the record deal would give extra value to the publishing rights. It is now more common for an artist to enter into a music publishing deal before a record deal. (See Chapter 4, Part I para 2.0). Once a publisher is involved, this means that there is then one more member of the team who can give real help in securing the record deal. The existence of the publishing deal may also give the record company added confidence.

1.7 WHICH COMPANY?

Sometimes it never rains but it pours. When, finally, one record company shows interest, others may suddenly follow. There is nothing more likely to awaken a record company's interest in the artist than interest from another company. If the artist is lucky enough to have a choice between companies, how should he choose? Firstly, he should look at the company's current roster of artists. Consider whether those artists and their success (or otherwise) suggests that the company will properly understand and work effectively with the artist in question. On the other hand, an artist may want to avoid a company which already has a similar artist competing in precisely the same field. This need not necessarily be a problem. However, artists must compete with others on their label for limited marketing and promotion budgets.

1.8 INDIVIDUAL EXECUTIVES

Don't set too much store by a company's past successes. All major companies have labels of which they are rightly proud. An artist should concentrate on the label's recent track record rather than its historic success. Look carefully at the current MD, head of A&R (and any other significant A&R staff) and head of marketing . Talk to them about their careers, what they have done and what they still hope to achieve.

Remember, however, that record company executives are not generally known for their loyalty. Artists may have to sign for six albums but key executives change jobs frequently. Financial considerations will affect any choice. If competing deals are roughly comparable in financial terms, the deciding factor should normally be the level of enthusiasm shown. You cannot always be sure that a company is as enthusiastic as it seems. The amount of money offered is a good indication of enthusiasm, but it is only one indication.

Despite the risk of key executives leaving to join another label, the most important factor is the artist's relationship with the person bringing in the deal. How experienced is that person? How much power does he have within the organisation? How much do you trust him to do all of the things he has promised?

2.0 indie or major?

2.1 THE CONVENTIONAL DEAL

Although all record companies and publishers have standard forms of contract, no two deals are ever quite the same. In this section we'll look more closely at the component parts of a typical record deal. For this purpose we assume that the deal is with a major. Under this type of deal, an artist signs exclusively to the company on a long-term basis. The company owns all of the recordings made during the full length or *term* of the agreement. The artist earns royalties on record sales. Those royalty earnings are used by the company to pay off, or *recoup*, any advances paid to the artist, including any recording costs and certain other expenses.

Within that framework there is a great deal of flexibility. Every negotiation and every contract will have a distinct flavour of its own. Nevertheless, the basic ground rules remain the same.

2.2 INDEPENDENTS

One way to break free of these limitations is to sign to an independent label. A key question for an artist is often whether he should sign with an indie or with a major. At the beginning of 2003, the majors are BMG, EMI, Sony, Universal and Warner and their various affiliates and labels. For many years there was a middle category of substantial record companies which did not own their own manufacturing plants and distribution networks, eg Island, Virgin, Chrysalis, A&M and Geffen. All of these companies have now been bought by the majors. This middle tier has therefore all but disappeared. Most recently, Mute gave up its independence when it was acquired by EMI.

2.3 FLEXIBILITY

The major apparent advantage of signing to an indie is that the artist may retain greater creative or artistic control. The deals offered by indies tend to be more flexible, and the financial terms are sometimes more acceptable to artists.

2.4 CREATIVE CONTROL

Majors usually insist on either total or limited control over certain elements of the creative process – for example, the choice of songs, producer and studio. The major will wish to control these elements if it does not approve of the artist's plans.

Indies are reputed to be more sympathetic to the artist's wishes. They will generally allow the artist to go in whatever artistic direction he wants. One reason for this more sympathetic approach is that an indie invests significantly less in an artist than a major, in terms of 'up front' money put at risk. Also, indies are usually run by people with a particular understanding of the artists they sign and their music. On the whole, they can relate better to their artists on a musical and artistic level.

This is not to say that A&R managers at the majors never have this level of understanding. However, an A&R manager at a major will tend to look after several artistically different acts. The investment in his artists (which will usually be more substantial than that made by an indie) will increase the pressure to secure immediate chart success rather than allowing the artist to develop more naturally and gradually.

Also, the key A&R man at an indie is often the owner of the company. He is more free to make decisions than his counterpart at the major. He does not have to justify the company's expenditure to a managing director, chairman or finance director (none of whom may like a particular artist's work) when sales are not going that well.

Nevertheless, there is a tendency to exaggerate a major's ability to control the artistic process. A record company cannot physically force an artist to record a particular song or work with a particular producer.

Some A&R managers at the majors have immense experience and understanding. A good A&R manager will operate as a catalyst for all of the ideas and other artistic ingredients involved. Indies tend to have smaller artist rosters than the majors. The majors tend to have different priorities from time to time with the result that some artists may be neglected. Different records by different artists may be competing for a gap in the major's release schedule. Indies tend not to have these problems – or if they do they are not quite so marked.

2.5 SHORT OR LONG TERM

All majors expect a new artist to sign an agreement committing the artist to record probably five or six albums. An A&R manager might sign an artist to a six-album deal only to join another company a year or so later. Indies generally will not demand such a long-term commitment. The deal may be limited to as little as one album. Even if the indie wants options for additional albums, this may matter less to the artist because of the creative factors. Indies often allow an artist to develop at his own pace, and so avoid the pressures of becoming a 'mainstream' act too quickly, with the artistic compromises this may involve. An artist might start off with an indie and move to a major later. If he is successful and receives some critical acclaim with the indie, he might then extract a better deal from the major over creative issues.

2.6 TERRITORY

All the majors expect to sign artists for the whole world. This applies even if their overseas associates (often part of the same multinational empire) have shown no particular interest in the artist. Indies, however, often limit their recording agreements to just a few countries (eg UK only, or Europe, or the World excluding North America). This allows the artist to make separate agreements with other record companies in the countries not covered by the initial deal. Artists can then choose companies which are genuinely enthusiastic about them, or which might for other reasons be 'stronger' in that territory.

If the artist secures separate deals overseas, he will benefit by having more than one royalty stream. Even if the indie insists on a worldwide deal, the indie will have more flexibility in sub-licensing outside the UK to companies genuinely interested in the artist. Indies will sometimes agree to share with the artist any advances they receive from their overseas associates.

2.7 ROYALTY RATES

A typical royalty rate on album sales for an artist signing to a major would be, say, 20% for UK sales; 18% in major countries such as Germany, France, the USA and Japan; and 16% for the rest of the world. (What all this means is examined more carefully in Part 3.) The higher rate for the 'home' territory – in this example, 20% – is sometimes referred to as the *headline* rate of royalty. Lower rates apply outside the home territory because the company itself merely receives a royalty from its licensee and will wish to maintain a reasonable margin between the royalty received and the royalty passed to the artist. However, an artist signing to a different company in each territory will expect to obtain a headline rate because, by signing direct to the overseas companies, he is cutting out the middle man.

2.8 SHARE OF PROFIT

An artist signed to an indie will often be paid a share of profit or *net receipts* instead of a percentage of the price of each record sold. The profit share is usually 50% of the indie's net receipts. This might increase (or *escalate*, in record-company jargon) for later albums and perhaps for overseas income.

The relationship between an artist and an indie is more like a partnership.

The artist takes less money up front (sometimes none) on the basis that, if the artist succeeds, he and the record company share more or less equally in the fruits of his success. Again, this is examined more carefully in Part 3.

2.9 FINANCIAL INSECURITY

However, there are considerable problems with the indie route. An indie is more likely than a major to have cashflow problems or perhaps go bust. It may not have the sophisticated structures, financial disciplines and professional management of the majors. This becomes a matter of particular concern when an artist 'breaks' (whether domestically or internationally) because at that stage substantial investment is needed to maintain the artist's momentum and to capitalise fully on all opportunities.

2.10 INTERNATIONAL

If there are separate deals for different territories, the artist or his management will become heavily involved in liaising with and co-ordinating the different distributors. Each company needs masters, information and promotional material. Each will expect the artist to tour in its territory and may not be very tolerant of the artist's other commitments. With a single deal with a major, many of these problems are avoided. It is for the major's International Department to look after all these conflicts.

2.11 ADVANCES

Indies do not usually pay substantial advances to their artists. Conversely, majors often do so, which gives a degree of financial security. Similarly, indies are less inclined to allow the artist to spend as much on recording costs so the indie artist is less likely to use the top studios and producers. Once an artist breaks, majors are more likely to have the resources to exploit the opportunities fully. They can fund more expensive videos and more substantial marketing campaigns, including TV advertising. Majors can usually co-ordinate international campaigns more effectively.

2.12 STRENGTH IN DEPTH

Majors employ talented, creative people in specialised departments, such as A&R, Marketing, Press, Promotions and International. Many staff at majors have worked in the record industry for a long time. The personnel at the smaller indie labels may not have such wide or detailed experience of all aspects of the development of artists, and of maintaining success once it has been achieved. If an artist has creative flair, or an experienced and creative manager, then he will have less need to call upon a major's resources. However, few artists have these abilities and resources; they need record companies to provide guidance, advice, support, commitment and money.

2.13 THE FINAL CHOICE

Some of the more interesting artists in recent years have come from indies. Other artists, signed to majors, may well have made less impact had they been on indie labels. Some bands which either have (or pretend to have) the indie mentality get suffocated when they move to a major. In choosing between the indies and majors, there are perhaps five crucial factors:

2.13.1 **Current A&R Relationship** – How good is the artist's relationship with his A&R manager when he signs the deal?;

2.13.2 **Future A&R relationship** – How likely is the A&R relationship to survive? Will it break down – for example, because the A&R manager is put under intolerable pressure from the 'men in grey suits'? Or will it end simply by the A&R manager leaving to pursue his career elsewhere?;

2.13.3 **The Artist's Ability** – Might his particular talents be stifled by the major approach? The cliché of the difficult second novel applies equally to musicians. Some artists clearly have enduring appeal while others come and go. Those that fail might blame the stifling atmosphere at a major; those that endure might well have succeeded wherever they were;

2.13.4 **The Artist's Management** – How competent and experienced is the artist's management team? How quickly can they adapt to the artist's changing fortunes?;

2.13.5 **The Artist's Style** – a pop or mainstream rock artist may be better suited to a major, given its marketing machinery; an alternative rock or dance artist is arguably better off with an indie, at least during the early stages.

3.0 the proposal

3.1 FALSE HOPES

Typically, artists suffer a series of false starts. Record companies frequently offer encouragement, leading to misplaced optimism on the part of the artist. Too often, record companies appear keen when they have no real enthusiasm. In the worst cases, a company may ask for more demos, or suggest other changes, without any genuine expectation of signing a deal, so the artist can be led down a cruel cul-de-sac.

3.2 WHO MAKES THE FIRST MOVE?

Nevertheless, with luck, sooner or later a record company will decide to proceed. At that point, the record company will ask what deal the artist is looking for. Often, the artist's reaction is to panic, because he does not know what he is looking for. Logically, a company which has expressed interest in signing an artist should put forward its proposals for a deal. This rarely happens in practice. The company wants the artist to put forward a proposal. The initial proposal is one of the most vital stages of the negotiating process. All of the team members should be involved in formulating it. However, the initial proposal should not be over-complicated; it should deal with the suggested length of the deal, the territory, the product commitment and the basic financial terms for the initial recordings. It is probably better not to complicate the initial proposal with the financial arrangements for subsequent recordings. The proposal should also raise features of the deal which are thought to be important but non-standard.

3.3 HIGH OR LOW?

The artist should take care that the proposal is pitched sensibly in terms of what the record company is likely to agree to do and pay. The artist must avoid asking for too little but there is a danger in asking for too much. The artist therefore needs a team member (perhaps his manager, but probably his lawyer) with experience of comparable deals.

4.0 the legal framework

4.1 PRACTICALITIES

Much of what happens in the music business cannot be understood without an outline knowledge of certain legal issues. The most important of these, in the context of recording contracts, is the doctrine of *restraint of trade*. Put simply, the law provides that an agreement which unreasonably restricts a person's ability to carry on his trade cannot be enforced against him. This assumes immediate importance only when there is a dispute between the parties to an agreement. When that happens, an artist may try to escape from his obligations under the agreement by arguing that it is, and always has been, unreasonably in restraint of trade. No record company would make a substantial investment in an artist if it felt there is a real risk that the artist might at some stage avoid his obligations in this way. The issue of restraint of trade therefore has a significant impact on the obligations imposed by record companies on artists.

Many commercial agreements involve a restraint of trade to a greater or lesser degree. The courts will only enforce a particular agreement if persuaded that the restraints which it imposes are reasonable. A recording agreement is a restraint of trade because of the element of exclusivity. The agreement gives the record company the exclusive right to the artist's services as a recording artist. The artist may not carry on his trade for any other person or company. Any recordings made by the artist during the agreement automatically belong exclusively to the record company.

The extent of the restraint differs from agreement to agreement and from company to company. In the case of an agreement with a major, a typical deal will be worldwide, for perhaps five or six albums. During the term of the agreement (and it may take ten years or more to record and deliver five or six albums), the artist is prevented from recording for anyone else. There will also be other restrictions – for example, for a period of time (perhaps five years) after the end of the deal, the artist will be prevented from recording for anybody else any of the songs which were recorded during the term of the recording agreement. This is known as a *re-recording restriction*.

If an artist claims in any legal proceedings against a record company that his agreement is in unreasonable restraint of trade, the court will take into account all the terms of the agreement. Restraint-of-trade cases involve an exhaustive consideration of evidence, as to what is, or is not, reasonable. Such cases may run for many weeks. It follows that they are expensive, which helps to explain their rarity. It is difficult to extract hard-and-fast rules from decided cases, because they depend so much on their particular facts.

Except in extreme cases, lawyers find it difficult to give definitive advice as to whether or not a particular agreement might constitute an unreasonable restraint of trade and so be set aside. In 1990 the court set aside Holly Johnson's recording agreement with ZTT on the grounds that it constituted an unreasonable restraint of trade. Similarly (although the facts in each case were very different), in 1993 the court set aside The Stone Roses' recording agreement with Silvertone for similar reasons. However, more recently, George Michael failed in his bid to set aside his agreement with Sony Music. The decision in George Michael's case has caused some confusion because it is difficult to square this with the decisions in the Holly Johnson and Stone Roses cases.

4.2 LEGAL ADVICE

One factor which prejudiced George Michael's position is that he had renegotiated his contract several times since first entering into a recording contract (as a member of Wham!) with Sony. On each occasion, Michael had been properly advised by experienced music-industry lawyers. In any restraint-of-trade case, the court will take into account not only all of the terms of the agreement but also the circumstances in which the agreement was entered into. It is for this reason that the adequacy of any legal advice is of crucial significance.

It is obviously sensible for any artist to obtain proper legal advice for his own benefit, but, moreover, it is equally vital from the record company's perspective that the artist is seen to have been properly advised. A prudent record company will insist that there is clear evidence that the artist has been independently advised. For example, if the manager's lawyer deals with the matter on behalf of the artist, the record company may wish to be satisfied that, whilst the lawyer concerned also acts for the manager, nevertheless – as far as his dealings in relation to the recording contract are concerned – the lawyer has taken his instructions from the artist direct, or has at least explained the nature and content of the contract direct to the artist.

If the record company is particularly prudent, it will strive to ensure that there is a genuine negotiation. This need not mean that the record company has to make concessions that it is unwilling to give, but it does mean that the record company should avoid the approach of refusing to negotiate and of merely adopting the 'take it or leave it' approach. One particularly irritating habit on the part of record companies is that of refusing even to attempt to justify a particular provision but simply to insist upon its inclusion in the contract on the basis that it is 'company policy'. The prudent record company will at least try to justify and explain why it insists upon a particular provision.

One practical ramification of all of this is that, since it is quite as important for the record company as it is for the artist that the artist should be properly advised, most record companies will agree to pay or at least make a contribution towards the artist's legal fees (although usually on the basis that this is to be treated as a further advance against royalties).

4.3 LESSONS

Record companies have learnt many lessons from the restraint-of-trade cases affecting the music industry. They try to make sure that their recording agreements are as safe as possible from attack. One of the major criticisms raised against recording contracts has been their excessive duration. Whereas the majors used to ask for a total of seven or eight albums (sometimes as many as nine or ten), after the decisions in the Holly Johnson and Stone Roses cases this crept down to five or six albums. If a record company insists on a maximum of, say, six albums, this is probably because it has been advised that to ask for more carries an unacceptable risk. If the company were confident of justifying seven or eight albums, it would no doubt insist upon them.

5.0 production agreements

5.1 WHAT IS A PRODUCTION DEAL?

A production agreement is the name usually given to a recording contract between an artist and a company which is neither a major record company nor an independent record company but which is in the business of making recordings which it then licenses or assigns to a record company.

5.2 WHY SIGN ONE?

An artist might prefer to sign a record contract with a record company rather than a production company for the obvious reason that the production company is a 'middle man', with the inevitable consequence that the artist's earnings are reduced.

In Chapter 1, we considered the practice of *de facto* managers seeking to improve upon the strength of their position by requiring the artist to sign a production agreement in addition to a management agreement. In fact, in recent years there has been a proliferation of production agreements. The reason for this is that the growing financial crisis with which the major record companies have been grappling for some years has led to substantial cost-saving measures, including numerous redundancies. There has been a reduction in both the quality and quantity of A&R staff, so there has been a trend for the record companies to look more and more to outside teams of producers and writers. At the same time, recording technology is cheaper and better, encouraging a proliferation of privately owned small-scale recording studio facilities. As a result, the number of direct signings to record companies is reducing. The number of production deals is increasing dramatically.

5.3 PITFALLS

The difficulty with a production deal is that, typically, the intention on the part of both the artist and the production company is that they should ultimately secure the involvement of a properly funded record company. For this reason, the production company will usually insist upon acquiring all of those rights which it will need in the event that it is able to secure an appropriate record deal. Hence, the production company will typically seek options for up to five or six albums so that the artist is required to enter into what is potentially a very long-term commitment with a production company which cannot guarantee the involvement of a record company. The production company has no ability by itself to release any records and probably cannot or will not pay any advances to the artist beyond payment of recording costs, which often is limited to the use of the production company's own limited studio facilities.

The production contract will usually provide for any net profits to be divided between the production company and the artist (in much the same way as profits are commonly shared between an independent record company and the artist). Typically, there might be a 50:50 split of profits in relation to any first album but so that the artist receives a greater share in relation to subsequent albums.

The production company 'produces' the recordings so that often there will be no third-party producer royalties. Accordingly, an artist signing direct to a major record company for a royalty of 20% of the dealer price might have a net entitlement of, say, 16% (because the 20% royalty would be inclusive of any third-party producer royalties and a producer might typically receive a 4% royalty). If the record deal were entered into through a production company and the production company receives the same 20% royalty, this might be split equally (so that the artist receives only 10% rather than 16%).

The best practical protection for the artist is to have a right of approval over any record deal with a third party and the right to terminate the production deal if a suitable record deal is not found within a reasonable period.

5.4 TELEVISION TALENT SHOWS

A further example of how the major record companies rely upon outside parties is the fashion for the creation of instant high-profile recording artists through televised talent contests such as *PopStars*, *Pop Idol* and *Fame Academy*. In these cases, the agenda is dictated by the television production companies. It will be a requirement of entry into the contest that if the contestant reaches a certain stage then he must sign a number of contracts. He will be required to take legal advice on the agreements and will be entitled to withdraw if he wishes, but for practical purposes he will have no real bargaining power. The television production company will require him to enter into a long-term recording agreement either with the television production company itself or with a specified record company (on the understanding that there will be a participation on the part of the television production company in the record company's profits) and will also be required to enter into merchandising and sponsorship agreements, probably a live concert performance agreement and possibly a songwriting agreement. In extreme cases, he will also be required to enter into a management agreement.

PART 2: THE CONTRACT

1.0 the term

1.1 LONG-TERM CONTRACTS

As explained in Part 1, most UK majors ask for up to five or, perhaps, six albums when signing new artists. US record companies, when signing in the US, still tend to ask for seven or eight albums. Elsewhere – in Germany, France and Scandinavia, for example – there is less obsession with long-term contracts.

One advantage in following the indie route is that contracts are usually less demanding, particularly in terms of duration. An indie may be prepared to conclude a deal for just one record or with a very limited number of options. Generally, the artist needs the contract to last long enough to ensure that the record company is reasonably committed, but not so long that the record company can stifle the artist's career, whether artistically or financially.

1.2 DEVELOPMENT DEALS

In many cases, the record company will not be prepared to commit immediately to recording an album. Instead, it may ask for one or two singles, with the right to call for sufficient additional material to comprise an album. This type of agreement is often called a *development deal*, and these are generally unsatisfactory for artists. Whilst the company will not be obliged to continue beyond the singles stage, it may nevertheless insist upon options for up to, say, five or six albums. Accordingly, the artist is entering into potentially a very long-term commitment, despite having only a very limited commitment from the company in return.

The other problem with development deals is that the artist may suffer from inordinate delays. In order to explain why these delays may occur, we first need to describe how the term of a typical recording agreement is structured.

1.3 EXTENSION PERIODS

In a six-album deal, for example, the artist will usually be contracted to the company for an initial contract period of one year. This is followed by five further successive option periods of one year each. The record company alone may decide in each case whether to exercise its option and so enter into each subsequent contract period. On the face of it, therefore, if all the options are exercised, the contract continues for six years. This might sometimes be referred to as a *six-year deal* but would usually (and more accurately) be referred to as a *six-album deal*. The reason why this description is more accurate is because of the 'extension' provisions. Each contract period will run for 12 months or, if longer, until a set period following delivery or, more usually, until the release of the album recorded during that contract period.

In the first contract period, recording of the album usually does not begin until the agreement has been signed. The recording process is often lengthy. Then, once the completed album has been delivered to the record company, there will be a further delay before it is released. One reason for this hold-up is that majors often have crowded release schedules. Moreover, marketing and promotion campaigns have become more sophisticated. Accordingly, lead-in times – ie the periods between delivery and release – have become longer.

It may be sensible to avoid the release of an album during August (when everybody is away on holiday) or during November and December (when there is a deluge of releases competing for the Christmas market).

Generally, there may be a delay of perhaps three to six months after delivery before the album is released. The contract may provide for a further period of extension following release of as much as a further six months. This gives the record company time to evaluate the success of the album before deciding whether or not to exercise the option for the next period. The problem may be worse in later option periods because recording will not begin until after the option has been exercised. Only then will money be made available for recording. The artist may still have outstanding touring commitments to fulfil in relation to the promotion of the previous album before he begins writing and recording the next album.

For all of these reasons, a typical 'album cycle' might be two years in length. In the case of a six-album deal, this might therefore take, say, 12 years to fulfil.

1.4 DELAYS

A development deal may be structured on the basis that, during the first contract period, only one single is to be delivered. The record company may have an option to enter into a further contract period during which perhaps the artist must deliver a second single. Only then might the record company be obliged to decide whether or not to commit to a third period during which the first album would be recorded. The artist might record two singles only to find that the record company does not wish to continue. In the meantime, as a result of the extension provisions, there might have been a delay of perhaps a year or two. This is why, for the artist, development deals are generally to be avoided if possible.

A preferable alternative is to persuade the record company to finance some high-quality demonstration recordings without the benefit of a formal contract. If both sides are pleased with the result then a record deal (with a proper commitment on both sides) may be negotiated. The record company is exposed to some degree because the artist may try to use the demos to 'wind up' the deal by seeking interest from other companies. However, a pragmatic company may be prepared to adopt this approach with the confidence of knowing that it is far ahead of its competitors in terms of building a relationship with the artist.

1.5 HOW MANY OPTIONS?

The artist should restrict the company to as few options as possible. There may be a temptation to attach more significance to other aspects of the recording agreement – perhaps the advances and royalties.

In fact, the difference between a five-album and a six-album deal may be very significant. In the majority of recording contracts, the option for the second album is not exercised. Even when it is exercised, the option for the third album may not be exercised. As a general rule, if a third album is delivered, this demonstrates that the artist has achieved some real success. The artist should by then be a recognised talent with a secure sales base.

In some cases, a first album will be so successful that the artist will more or less immediately achieve significant wealth and status. However, although an artist about to record his fourth album may be perceived as successful, and though he may have benefited from a number of substantial advances, nevertheless (for reasons explained in Part 3), his royalty income might not yet have begun to flow.

The artist may wish to flex his muscles at around this stage and attempt to re negotiate his deal, and the issue of re-negotiation of recording contracts is dealt with in more detail in Part 4. At the point at which a record company requires an artist to deliver a fourth album, the artist will find it more difficult to secure significant improvements if the record company can call for a maximum of six or more albums. The task of renegotiation would be far easier if the deal were for only five albums.

In summary, if a record deal is not going to survive beyond the first few albums then it does not matter whether the maximum number of albums allowed for is five, ten or any other number. However, if a contract survives beyond three albums (at which point the stakes are higher all round) then every extra album for the company wins the company perhaps two more years before it may have to give the artist improved terms.

2.0 product commitment

2.1 ARTISTIC STANDARDS

As we have seen, the artist may have to deliver up to five or six albums. The recording agreement will be more precise about exactly what has to be delivered. Generally, the albums must be studio recordings rather than live. Also, the company will want to set a minimum standard. At worst (for the artist), the company will be entitled to reject any recordings which the company (in its absolute discretion) decides are commercially unsatisfactory, whatever that means. Ideally, for the artist, the record company's right to reject master recordings should apply only if they are technically unsatisfactory for records to be made from them. A suitable compromise is usually found.

2.2 ADDITIONAL MATERIAL

In addition, the company may acquire the right to insist upon a minimum number of additional tracks for use as B-sides. An album used to be defined as a minimum of ten tracks with a minimum playing time of, say, 30 minutes. With the advent of CDs, an artist now has to deliver a minimum of, say, 12 tracks (plus additional B-sides if required) with a minimum playing time of perhaps 40 or 45 minutes. All of this is of particular significance for the artist if the advances to be paid are expressed to be inclusive of any recording costs (see Part 4).

2.3 TWO ALBUMS FIRM

Sometimes a record company will agree (using accepted industry slang) to *two albums firm*. This means that the company does not have an option for a second album but commits to it from the outset. A company will only reluctantly agree to this, and usually only in the face of fierce competition to sign an artist.

On the face of it, two albums firm represents a victory for the artist; it shows real commitment from the record company. It shows that the company is taking a long-term view and is prepared to proceed with the second album, even if the first does not immediately bring the anticipated level of success. However, in some respects a two-album-firm commitment can be a double-edged sword. If the company loses interest after the first album, the artist is nevertheless exclusively contracted for a significant further period. The record company may become obstructive in recording the second album or, perhaps worse, may allow it to be recorded but then put no effort into its promotion. Arguably, the artist might have been better off had the company committed to one album and failed to pick up its option for the second. This would leave the artist free to pursue his career elsewhere. This is less true at the present time, when record deals are more than usually difficult to come by.

That said, the usual outcome where the record company loses interest is a negotiated settlement of some kind. The artist is released from the contract and is paid a reduced sum of money in return for agreeing that the company no longer has to pay the advance and recording costs for the second album. The company might also be paid an 'override' (ie a royalty of perhaps two or three on subsequent sales of that album) by the artist's new record company. Alternately, on occasions, as part of any settlement, the artist may be given copyright in the masters for the first album.

2.4 'GREATEST HITS' AND LIVE ALBUMS

Sometimes (but rarely) a 'greatest hits' album may qualify as a product-commitment album. For example, the company may agree to restrict the deal to five studio albums rather than six, on the basis that, in addition to the five studio albums, the company will be entitled after a given period to compile and release a 'greatest hits' album. This would represent a victory of sorts for the artist because in reality this means that he has to deliver only five albums rather than six. Ordinarily, not only will the record company own all of the material but it will have unrestricted rights of exploitation. A company rarely accepts any restriction on its ability to release a greatest hits album.

Similarly (but again, rarely) a company may accept that one of the albums to be delivered will be a live album. Ordinarily, if a live album is recorded, the company automatically acquires exclusive rights to it, without any reduction of the minimum product commitment, and without any obligation on the part of the company to pay any advance for it, or even to release it.

2.5 EXCLUSIONS
Recording agreements are invariably exclusive. If the artist records additional material beyond the contracted minimum product commitment, the record company will own all of the additional material.

Most recording agreements contain limitations upon this exclusivity. For example, the artist may normally undertake session work (within defined limits) and may record TV and radio broadcasts, provided the TV and radio companies undertake not to exploit those recordings, except by means of broadcast. Established bands may negotiate a deal which relates solely to recordings made by the band itself, leaving the individual members to pursue solo projects outside the scope of the deal. Record companies are very nervous of this arrangement; if they have to agree to important limitations of this kind, they will always insist that any solo or other work must not interfere with the band's promotional activities. Release dates must be carefully monitored.

Record contracts do not normally extend to the artist's separate activities as a record producer or engineer, but, given the increasing confusion between performance and production in some areas of contemporary music, provisions are in some cases included which limit the extent to which an artist may work as a record producer for third parties.

3.0 territory

3.1 WORLDWIDE DEALS
Where a major signs a new artist, the company's right to manufacture and sell records will invariably extend worldwide. In special circumstances, particular territories may be excluded – for example, a non-UK artist launching

his worldwide career from the UK may already have recording arrangements in place in his home territory. An artist moving to a major from an indie may have granted rights in future recordings to overseas licensees. Here, the territories in question are simply not available to the major.

3.2 RESTRICTED-TERRITORY DEALS

Majors do not like to give up any territory. This is not only because they will lose profits from sales in the excluded territory, but also because the company will be at risk, throughout its territory, from imports of records coming from the excluded territory.

In practice, the excluded territory will often be the USA and Canada. This territory accounts for more than one third of worldwide record sales. For that reason alone, most artists aspire to success there and record companies do not want to give up their rights there.

An artist may wish to exclude North America because he thinks that his company's US affiliate is either inept or is likely to dismiss the artist's talents, and that the UK company has little or no influence over its US affiliate. If so, the artist may prefer to achieve success elsewhere before concluding a deal direct with a US-based company which likes his work.

Split-territory deals like this will give rise to separate income streams. If the artist recoups in one territory, he will enjoy royalty income from that territory. If the deal was for the world, the accrued royalties from the recouped territory would be used to recoup generally. This area is dealt with in Part 3.

3.3 INTERACTION

Split-territory deals are complex. Release dates have to be co-ordinated to reduce the problem of imports. Usually, all distributors want to use the same artwork. There would be little point in each company making its own videos. So, if the world is divided into two (or more) separate territories, then, in addition to negotiating the two recording agreements, a separate agreement is needed between the artist and both the record companies regulating dealings between them. Another disadvantage is the high level of legal fees involved in setting up these arrangements.

A less attractive alternative for the artist is for him merely to have a right of approval over the identity of the record company's US licensee. Most majors would only give such an approval right as between the various US labels owned by that major. An artist has to be in an exceptional negotiating position to secure a split-territory deal, however, and usually has to be in a strong position even to secure a right of approval over the US licensee.

4.0 creative issues

4.1 APPROVAL RIGHTS

The issues of most concern to the artist are usually the selection of songs, choice of producer and studios, approval of mixing and re-mixing, control over artwork and photographs, and control over videos, including the approval of any storyboard and of the director and producer involved. An artist might look for other approval rights over financial matters rather than creative issues – for example, since all recording costs and at least a proportion of promotional video costs will be recouped from his royalties, it follows that the artist should ideally have a right of approval over recording and video budgets, and any other recoupable expenditure.

4.2 CONTROL

There are four basic alternatives to the above scenario:

4.2.1   The record company has complete control (ie what it says goes);

4.2.2   The record company has control, subject to an obligation to consult with the artist;

4.2.3   Both parties must mutually agree upon the matters in question (perhaps on the basis that, in the event of a stalemate, the company and the artist have an alternate casting vote);

4.2.4   The artist has complete control.

Most agreements contain a mixture of these four alternatives. A new artist is unlikely to achieve complete control and would normally be happy with a mix of consultation rights and, in certain key areas, mutual approval.

5.0 the record company's obligations

5.1 ONE SIDED?

Recording contracts issued by majors now stretch to 60 or 70 pages. About a third of the agreement is taken up with financial provisions, most of which – as we will see in Part 3 – deal with the various means by which the artist's basic royalty is reduced.

The bulk of the contract is for the company's benefit. It imposes obligations on, and extracts warranties (legally binding promises) from, the artist. Beyond the obligation to pay an advance and possibly, at some future time, some royalties, it is difficult to find anything in the document that imposes any obligation on the company.

5.2 RELEASE COMMITMENTS

One exception is that most recording agreements now include a release commitment of some kind. This would appear to favour the artist, but appearances can be deceptive.

Record companies rarely agree to a positive commitment to release a particular record in a particular territory within a given period. A company would probably give such a commitment only for a record which has already been made and for which there is an obvious market. In such a case, there is little benefit to the artist in securing a binding release commitment, because commercial reality will ensure the record is released in any event.

The main reason for the release commitment is to satisfy the company's concern that, without this there might be a stronger argument that the agreement constitutes an unreasonable restraint of trade. Courts do not look favourably upon an exclusive recording contract which does not contain an obligation to make the artist's work available to the public.

Most release commitments are not 'positive' commitments; they are best described as 'negative' release commitments. Typically, release obligations relate only to the UK, apply only to minimum commitment albums (not singles) and provide that the album must be released within, say, six months of delivery. If the company fails to release within that period, the artist may serve a *cure notice*. This gives the company a further period – perhaps 60 days – from its receipt of the cure notice in which to release the album.

If the company has still failed to release the album by the end of the cure period, the artist's only remedy is usually to serve a further notice on the company terminating the contract. In other words, the artist will no longer be obliged to record for the company. Since the company has persistently refused to release the album, this usually would not cause the company any difficulty. Moreover, all rights in the unreleased album would still rest with the company.

5.3 REVERSION
In order to make release obligations more effective, the artist should try to shorten the periods involved and to ensure that, if the right of termination arises, copyright in the unreleased album automatically reverts to the artist. This is difficult to achieve, but the company may agree to it, on repayment of all or part of the recording costs and/or in return for a small royalty (normally referred to as an *override*) on any subsequent sales of the album through a third party.

5.4 OVERSEAS RELEASES
In practical terms, disputes are more likely to arise over the company's failure to release a particular record overseas, especially North America. Even a successful artist may have difficulty in securing a release in the US. The US is such a large market that the costs involved in breaking a new artist are much greater than elsewhere. Each artist has to compete both with American artists and with other foreign artists for the limited promotion and marketing resources of his US affiliate. The US affiliate may not wish to prioritise the artist. The UK company, which must grant rights to its US affiliate, may have no real influence, if any, over the extent to which the US affiliate exploits those rights.

5.5 TERRITORIAL REVERSIONS
With the above in mind, the artist should try to secure a positive commitment of some kind for the release of his records, not only in the US and Canada but all other major territories. Ideally, if the company fails to release in any overseas territory, all rights for that territory should revert to the artist – ie not only for the unreleased album but for all future recordings.

This is very difficult to obtain and is in any event problematic because usually the company has secured worldwide rights on the basis that it makes and pays for all of the recordings. There is a natural reluctance to give up copies of the masters to the artist or to some other record company in another territory. This would give rise to difficulties over the appropriate contribution (if any) towards recording costs, how videos are to be dealt with, how to deal with imports and other practical matters. Often, the best that may be achieved is a provision that the artist can compel his record company to license another company in any territory in which its regular licensee is unwilling to release the album.

However, even this is not always possible, because the internal licensing arrangements between the affiliates of a major may not easily permit the grant of a licence to anyone outside the major's own group. Moreover, if this arrangement is accepted, the company is likely to insist upon some reduction in royalties (certainly if the royalty paid by the licensee is less than the artist's royalty for sales in that territory plus a reasonable profit margin for the company).

5.6 IS A RELEASE COMMITMENT WORTH HAVING?

The trend has been for release commitments to become more convoluted and of less practical relevance. Forcing a company to release a record is of questionable value. Releasing a record is one thing, but marketing and promoting it in a positive manner is quite another. Many release provisions benefit the record company rather than the artist, by limiting its exposure in the event of non-release.

5.7 MARKETING AND PROMOTION

It is difficult to persuade any record company to give a precise commitment on marketing and promotion. Sometimes, a company will agree to use 'all reasonable endeavours to exploit', but this is fairly meaningless. What the artist needs (but rarely gets) is a commitment that the company will spend a minimum sum on direct marketing and promotional expenses. Sometimes a company will agree to appoint independent promoters to support a record and may commit to spending a minimum sum on this. Beyond this, a company might commit to a minimum number of promotional videos (perhaps one or two for each album) in accordance with an agreed budget. Sometimes a company will accept a contractual commitment to provide a certain amount of 'tour support' – ie to make good the shortfall of expenditure over income from an approved promotional tour.

However, even if tour support is paid, the company will insist on numerous rights of approval. Tour support is normally treated as a further advance, 100% recoupable from the artist's royalties.

6.0 ownership

6.1 COPYRIGHT
Almost without exception, the company owns copyright in the artist's recordings for the full period of copyright, which lasts for 50 years from first release. This feature of recording agreements reflects the perhaps outdated view that an artist's work is effectively available for outright purchase. This approach was traditionally taken in music publishing. Twenty years ago it was still common for writers to grant copyright in all songs to the publisher for the full life of copyright, which in the case of any song is now for the life of the composer plus a further 70 years. This is now unusual.

6.2 YOU PAY, WE OWN
The record company's position with regard to copyright is difficult to justify when coupled with the practice of recouping all recording costs from the artist's royalty. Provided that sufficient records are sold, the company is repaid its recording costs by the artist by deduction from his royalties. The practice of insisting upon outright ownership of copyright is seen by some as an abuse of record company power.

6.3 COPYRIGHT REVERSION
A very successful artist may eventually succeed in obtaining reversion to him of copyright in his recordings. This would rarely be granted by way of concession. It would normally only reluctantly be conceded in a renegotiation. In effect, the artist will pay a price for the reversion of copyright, usually in the form of an agreement to record more material for the company.

6.4 RESTRICTIONS

The artist may succeed in imposing restrictions on how the record company's rights may be exercised. The company is more likely to grant concessions to the artist over artistic matters than marketing. Artistic controls are dealt with in Section 4.0, 'Creative Issues', while marketing controls are covered in Paragraph 6.6.

6.5 ARTWORK

The artist will often require the right of approval over any artwork. Usually, the record company will pay all artwork origination costs on a non-recoupable basis. In the absence of any agreement to the contrary, the company (as between the company and the artist) will own the artwork. The artist may nevertheless have a right of approval. In other cases, the artist will insist on the right to originate artwork, in which case he may own the artwork.

Sometimes the company will pay the origination costs up to an agreed budget but will nevertheless accept that the artist owns any available rights. The artist will then grant the company a licence to use it for the promotion and sale of his recordings. This leaves the artist free to exploit the artwork for other purposes (eg on T-shirts and other merchandise) without having to seek approval from the record company. Record companies may sometimes refuse to allow an artist to make use of its artwork for merchandising unless the artist pays all or part of the origination costs. In some cases (though rarely, nowadays), record companies insist on a share of any merchandising profits from the use of their designs.

If an outside designer is commissioned or freelance photographer used, a clear assignment of copyright should be obtained. If this is not done, copyright in the artwork will remain with the creator while the artist and record company will have an implied licence to use the artwork for its intended purpose on the record's packaging. Further consents may be required before the artwork may be used for merchandising or other purposes.

6.6 MARKETING RESTRICTIONS

The record company may agree to seek the artist's prior written consent to certain acts – for example, for the deletion of his records from the company's catalogue less than, say, two or three years after release; for release of his records on a different label; for recoupling certain tracks with other recordings on compilation albums and the like; for using his recordings as premiums whereby his records are given away as an incentive to purchase another product (see Part 3); for the grant of any synchronisation licence to use a recording in a TV ad or film; or, perhaps more importantly, before selling his albums at less than full price before, say, one or two years after initial release.

Whilst some restrictions are useful, the artist should be cautious of imposing unnecessary restrictions. In theory, the record company will know best how to market his recordings.

However, problems often arise after an artist leaves his record company. His new company's carefully planned marketing campaign might be damaged by the previous record company's re-release of earlier material. Accordingly, the artist may seek to impose restrictions on the release or the frequency of release of 'greatest hits' albums. However, these problems may be exaggerated; an artist's previous record company's activities are unlikely to damage the new company's efforts seriously. Indeed, sometimes an increased activity in respect of the artist's earlier recordings will produce additional income for the artist at a time when he is likely to be unrecouped with his new company.

7.0 group provisions

7.1 LEAVING MEMBERS

Any group recording agreement will include *leaving-member provisions*. These tend to be controversial because they are very restrictive and are increasingly complex. Their basic effect is that an artist who signs a deal as a member of a group may find that, even after he has left the group, he is still tied to the record company.

Despite their restrictive nature, record companies are confident that leaving-member clauses are reasonable. No sensible company, they argue, would invest substantial sums of money in a group without protection should the group split up. No recording agreement compels a group of artists to remain together, as this would be too restrictive; instead, if the group disbands, or a member leaves, the company insists upon the right to continue with the leaving members. The company retains complete flexibility. It may continue with the remaining members and drop the leaving member, it may drop the remaining members and continue only with the leaving member, it may continue with all members, or it may drop all members.

If the group disbands, all members are treated as leaving members. The company may continue with all or any of them.

If a band split is acrimonious and the company wants to continue with all members, this may give rise to a conflict of interest on the part of the record company, as a number of warring factions will be competing for priority in recording budgets, release schedules and promotion and marketing budgets. In practice, the record company will normally agree to release one side from the contract, usually in return for a payment of some kind. This is often financed by a new record company and may be coupled with an override royalty on sales of that artist's subsequent recordings.

7.2 CROSS RECOUPMENT

The artist should try to ensure that, if the company exercises a leaving-member option, any royalties payable to the leaving member may be used to recoup only the leaving member's share of any unrecouped balance on the group's royalty account at the time of his departure. The leaving member will probably have to concede that his share of royalties from group recordings on which he performs may be used towards recoupment of any advance (or other recoupable sums) paid under his new leaving-member contract.

7.3 LEAVING MEMBERS' COMMITMENT

Ordinarily, a leaving-member contract will be on the same terms as the existing group contract for the balance of the commitment then outstanding. If the member leaves after four albums have been recorded under a six-album deal, the leaving-member contract should cover only two albums. The company may argue that, as it now has to invest in a new project, it needs the protection of a higher minimum number of albums, but the artist should resist this. The company may also try to insist that a lower royalty rate should apply for any leaving member. Again, whilst this used to be common practice, it is now usually successfully resisted.

7.4 SOLO WORK

A band member may not need to leave if he can work as a solo artist separately from his commitments as a member of the group. A recording agreement will rarely include separate provisions dealing with a solo commitment unless a particular group member has a specific project in mind when the deal is being negotiated. A group member may have to leave the group if he is determined to pursue a particular project, which involves the risk of being dropped by the record company and then failing to secure a deal elsewhere.

8.0 controlled compositions

8.1 BACK TO BASICS

Most recording agreements contain what are known as *controlled compositions clauses*. This is the part of the recording agreement which interlocks with the publishing arrangements of artists who write and compose their own material. The aim of controlled compositions clauses is to reduce the mechanical (ie publishing) royalties paid by the record company for the use of the artist's own compositions.

Before explaining controlled compositions clauses in more detail, we must look at the differences between recording and publishing. Every recording contains at least two copyright works: the copyright in the recording itself (which is normally owned by the record company) and separate copyrights in the music and the lyrics of the song featured on the recording (which are owned in the first place by the writers of the music and words of the song). If the writer has entered into a publishing contract, then usually, under the terms of that agreement, he assigns copyright in the words and music to the music publisher.

8.2 MECHANICAL LICENCES

Each time the record company manufactures a CD or other record, it copies, or reproduces, the music and lyrics of the song. Unless that reproduction is authorised, this will amount to an infringement of copyright in the song. The record company must therefore obtain permission from the owner of the copyright in the song for it to be featured on the record. This permission is known as a *mechanical licence*, because it allows the record company to reproduce the song by mechanical means.

There is a set rate for the mechanical licence which has been negotiated between organisations representing publishers and record companies. In most European countries, the rate paid by the record company to the owner of copyright in the song (usually the music publisher) is 9.306% of the dealer price of the record, although in the UK the lower rate of 8.5% applies.

8.3 AVAILABILITY OF LICENCE

Recording agreements include a warranty (a legally binding promise) from the artist that the publisher will grant the record company a mechanical licence on standard terms for every song used on recordings made under the agreement. The artist should take care that this warranty does not extend to songs written by other people (particularly if the record company has chosen the material).

8.4 THE USA AND CANADA

The position is more complicated for records manufactured in the USA and Canada. Outside these territories, it does not matter how many songs are used on an album because the total mechanical royalty liability will be the same: the appropriate percentage of the dealer price of the record. On a 20-track album, each song will receive a payment equal to one-half of what would be paid for a track on a ten-track album – the record company's liability remains the same.

In North America the mechanical royalty is not calculated as a percentage of the price of the record; instead, record companies pay a fixed fee per song. The US Copyright Tribunal increases the per song rate from time to time, partly to take account of inflation. The rate as at 1 January 2002 was eight cents per song.

This gives rise to two problems for record companies. Firstly, it means that an album with an unusually large number of songs will attract too high a mechanical royalty payment. The second problem for the record companies is that they perceive the US per song rate to be too high. US record companies have decided that they should have to pay only 75% of the 'statutory' per-song rate. Accordingly, US record companies use controlled compositions clauses to oblige artists to grant mechanical licences of their own works at 75% of the statutory rate.

These clauses also usually limit each company's liability to a maximum of ten times the reduced per-song rate for any album, no matter how many songs are used on that album. Although this problem affects only North

America, record companies outside North America insist on controlled compositions clauses so that they can comply with their obligations to their North American licensees.

8.5 THE PUBLISHER

The artist's publisher (if he has one) must approve the controlled compositions clauses before the record deal is signed. Otherwise, if the publisher later refuses to accept them, the artist will be in breach of the recording agreement. This will normally give the record company the right to claw back any excess mechanical royalties from payments otherwise due to the artist.

Understandably, publishers are very sensitive about controlled compositions clauses because those clauses are intended specifically to reduce their income. Of course, major publishers are affiliated to major record companies and perhaps as a result their criticisms are tempered. A ritual dance has developed whereby the artist (or his lawyer) sends the controlled compositions clauses to his publisher and asks for confirmation that the publisher will comply with them. The publisher often expresses outrage at the idea of a reduced mechanical royalty rate and seeks numerous amendments to the clauses. Depending on the flexibility or otherwise of the record company, the publisher may sometimes improve the provisions. The publisher may insist on dealing with the record company direct, but usually any dialogue between the publisher and record company will be conducted through the artist's lawyer. After all the huffing and puffing, the publisher will accept the controlled compositions clauses.

No publisher will run the risk of being responsible for the failure of negotiations over a record deal. Some record companies agree, even for new artists, to pay more than 75%. Successful artists should expect to secure 100% at some stage.

Some companies are more flexible than others. Sometimes a built-in escalation may be agreed so that, for example, the rate improves from 75% to 85% after a given number of sales in the USA, and then perhaps to 100% when a higher level is reached. Since CDs now tend to carry more than ten tracks, it is sometimes possible to agree a restriction of say 12 rather than 10 times the per-song rate for CDs, if not for cassettes.

Most controlled compositions clauses attempt to set the per-song rate at the rate in force at the time that the master CD is first delivered. The publisher will wish to apply the rate in force at the time of manufacture of the record.

PART 3: MONEY

1.0 overview

1.1 THE BASIC ROYALTY SYSTEM

Under the system operated by the majors, the company pays for everything and assumes all financial risk. However, certain expenses are recovered, or *recouped*, from the artist's royalties; the artist never has to pay money back to the company from his own pocket. Recoupment forms a very significant part of the calculation of the payments to be made to the artist. A common misconception is that recoupment has something to do with profit. However, the point at which recoupment occurs bears no relation to the point at which the company may begin to make a profit.

1.2 RECOUPABLE EXPENDITURE

So what is recouped from the artist's royalty, and how does this work? The artist will be entitled to a royalty for each record sold. The calculation of the per-unit royalty is complex (see Paragraph 3.0 of this section).

Assume the royalty for each album sold is £1. If the company sells 100,000 albums, the artist is owed £100,000 in royalties. The company will first recoup from this any advances previously paid to the artist and any other recoupable expenditure. Recording costs are always recoupable while manufacturing and distribution expenses are not recoupable – nor, ordinarily, are marketing and promotional expenses. However, a number of grey areas have developed.

1.3 WHAT IS RECOUPABLE?

1.3.1   Recording Costs – Recording costs are fully recoupable, and the recording agreement will include a wide definition of such costs which will extend to studio costs, musicians' fees, equipment hire, travel and accommodation expenses, producers' fees and so on. The definition will also extend to cutting and mastering costs. But where does the recording process end? One grey area is the extent to which mixing costs incurred after delivery of the finished master should be treated as a recoupable recording cost.

Some companies (and artists) like to release many different mixes of a particular single. Arguably, this is more in the nature of a marketing exercise, so the costs involved should be borne by the company on a non-recoupable basis. An artist very rarely achieves this; the best that might be done is to restrict the company's ability to recoup remixing costs from royalties which accrue in relation to each particular remix.

1.3.2   **Remixing Costs** – Aside from marketing exercises of that kind, record companies often spend substantial sums on mixing and remixing an album, even before any of the material is released. Again, these costs are recoupable. As a limited means of protection, an artist should try to secure a right of approval over the budget for any remixing.

1.3.3   **Promotional Video Costs** – As a rule, promotional costs incurred by a company are non-recoupable. However, the company will argue that promotional video costs are in the nature of recording costs, which are recoupable. The usual compromise is that 50% of video costs are recoupable from the artist's record royalties. The company will invariably insist that any video costs which are unrecouped (including the 50% which is not recoupable from record royalties) may be recouped from video royalties. The opportunities to profit from videos are generally limited to the release of compilation videos, video jukebox payments and broadcast. The recoupment provisions in place ensure that the artist is unlikely ever to receive any income from the exploitation of promotional video material.

1.3.4   **Independent Promotion Costs** – An artist may try to persuade the company to use independent promoters. Many companies will resist this because they have their own in-house promotion teams and will not wish to incur the expense of outside promoters. However, independent promotion is sometimes the only means of ensuring that a new release is given sufficient priority and is worked hard enough. The company is likely to insist that some or all of the costs must be recoupable.

US companies tend not to have strong in-house promotion teams. Some cynics assume that this is because it would not be seemly for a record company employee to do some of the things which promotion teams have to do in order to help break a new record. It is difficult in the US to break a new artist without liberal use of independent promoters (and US independent promoters are particularly expensive). Often, the pressure to use independent promoters tends to come from the artist or the artist's manager. The company will often turn this pressure back on the artist/manager by insisting on the right to recoup all such expenditure.

1.3.5   **Tour Support** – Likewise, there will often be pressure from the artist/manager for the company to provide tour support. Again, this is a promotional expense. The artist would not be touring at a loss (which is what gives rise to the need for tour support), except to promote record sales. At one time, tour support payments tended to be 50% recoupable, but in recent years the trend has been for 100% of any such payments to be recoupable.

1.3.6   **Television Advertising** – Most recording contracts allow the record company to decide whether or not it wishes to spend money on television advertising. However, the company claws back all or part of the costs either by reducing the royalty payable on sales promoted by the advertising campaign (see Paragraph 3.8.4 in this section) or by treating all or part (often only 50%) of advertising costs as recoupable.

1.4 PROFIT SHARES

The alternative to the basic royalty system is the profit-sharing arrangement. No major would be interested in sharing its profits, but most indies adopt this approach. Again, the indie pays for everything and assumes all of the financial risk. However, the relationship between the indie and the artist is more in the nature of a joint venture – the artist supplies his talent, the indie provides its resources, and they split any profits, usually 50/50.

This system bears no relation to the basic royalty system, so they are difficult to compare. For example, an artist might be offered 50% of the net profits from an indie, with no advance beyond actual recording costs. A major might offer a traditional royalty deal of, say, 20% of the dealer price of each record sold and an advance exclusive of recording costs of £50,000. Even if the artist knows how many records the indie is likely to sell compared with the major, it will not be possible to work out in advance which deal is more financially attractive, as it will depend on the amount of recoupable expenditure spent by the major and on the total expenses incurred by the indie. The equation would also have to take into account the cost-effectiveness of the indie's manufacturing and distribution arrangements.

In working out profits, the indie deducts all expenditure from its total receipts from the exploitation of the recordings, including recording costs, remixing costs, mechanical royalties, manufacturing costs, artwork origination costs, promotion, advertising, marketing costs, distribution fees and any other costs directly related to the recordings. Only the indie's own overhead costs are excluded.

1.5 A PRACTICAL EXAMPLE (PROFIT SHARE V ROYALTY)

Using the example in Paragraph 1.4 above, and giving ourselves the benefit of hindsight, let us investigate, in relation to a particular album, which deal is financially better for the artist. We will make the following assumptions:

1.5.1   Recording costs are £50,000. Indies are normally more sparing about recording costs, but for this example, we'll assume that the costs would have been £50,000 either way.

1.5.2   The album sells 100,000 copies. The major might argue that, given its resources and more efficient distribution arrangements, it would expect to sell more than the indie, but again, for the sake of simplicity, we will ignore this.

1.5.3   The dealer price is £7 (excluding VAT). The dealer price of a full-price cassette album might be around £6.99, and the dealer price of a full price CD might be around £8.89, but for this exercise we will assume an average of £7.

1.5.4 The royalty offered by the major after taking into account packaging allowances and other royalty mitigation provisions, and after deducting any share of the royalty payable to the producer, averages out between the different formats at, let us say, £1 per unit. (For the sake of simplicity, we will ignore the fact that singles will probably have been released from the album, which would also affect the royalty position).

1.5.5 The indie receives only £4 of the £7 dealer price after deduction of a £2 distribution fee and £1 manufacturing and printing costs.

1.5.6 The indie spends £20,000 in marketing and other allowable expenses.

1.5.7 The total mechanical royalties on 100,000 album sales amounts to, let us say, £50,000.

1.5.8 Video costs are £20,000 (ignoring the fact that the major would normally make available a bigger budget for this than the indie).

Based on these rough-and-ready assumptions, the indie would receive the £7 dealer price less the manufacturing and distribution costs of £3, making £4 per album. On 100,000 sales, total income would be £400,000. Out of this, it would have to recover £140,000 of expenditure (recording costs, copyright royalties, marketing and video costs), leaving £260,000. On a 50/50 split, the artist would receive £130,000.

How would the artist fare with the major? At £1 per unit the artist would earn £100,000 royalties on 100,000 sales. This would be set against £110,000 of total recoupable expenditure (made up of the £50,000 advance 50% of the £20,000 video costs and £50,000 recording costs). The artist's royalty account would therefore still be unrecouped by £10,000.

Accordingly, in this example, the artist would eventually receive £130,000 from the indie, but from the major he would receive only the £50,000 'up front' advance.

This example serves to illustrate the differences between the two systems, but not too much should be read into the result. The first point a major would make in relation to this example is that, for a new artist seeking mainstream success, the marketing and promotion costs will often be enormous. Under the traditional royalty system, most of those costs would be non-recoupable, and so entirely borne by the record company, whereas, even if the indie could afford to meet costs at that level, they would all be taken into account in determining the net profits.

An established artist signed to a major would certainly expect to earn more if he was paid 50% of the company's net profits from the sale of his records than if he was paid a royalty (even a particularly high rate of royalty) under the traditional system. It should also be borne in mind that 50% of the major's net profits would probably be greater than 50% of the indie's net profits from the same sales because the indie's costs are normally far higher. For example, the major has its own distribution network; the record label will have to pay modest distribution fees to its affiliated distribution company, but indies generally pay higher distribution fees to their distributors (anything between 15% and 35% of the dealer price).

A 50/50 net profits deal means, clearly, that profits are divided in the ratio 1:1. Typically, under the traditional royalty system, profits are likely to be divided in a ratio nearer 2:1 or even 3:1 in the record company's favour.

1.6 WHO TAKES WHAT?

Let's look at the cost structure from a different angle. What happens to the money paid by the customer in the record shop? A full-price CD album might sell for £14.99. The dealer has to account to HM Customs & Excise for VAT, which at the rate of 17.5% is £2.62, leaving the dealer with £12.37. The PPD (published price to dealer) of the record might be £8.45 exclusive of VAT. In the case of a dealer with multiple stores (such as Woolworths and WH Smith), the dealer will have sufficient clout to secure a substantial discount. We will assume discounts of 10% across the board for this exercise, although the discounts are often far greater. This means that, ignoring VAT, the record company receives £7.61 leaving £4.76 for the dealer.

What happens to the £7.61 received by the record company? The record company has to pay a mechanical royalty of 8.5% of the dealer price. This amounts to 64p. If the artist wrote the song, a substantial part of this will find its way back to him under his publishing deal.

The record company is then left with £6.97. Part of this is paid to the distributor as a distribution fee in return for physically putting the record in the shop. For a major, distribution will be undertaken by another company within the same group. Nevertheless, a fee (probably quite low) will have to be paid. For an indie, the distribution fee will be quite substantial. Assuming a distribution fee for the indie of 20% of the published dealer price, this amounts to £1.70, leaving the indie with £5.27. If the major has to pay only a 10% distribution fee (ie 85p), then it is left with £6.12.

The record company has to pay the manufacturer for any printing/pressing/duplicating costs. Again, the major may pay less than the indie per unit (because of economies of scale), but for this exercise we will assume total manufacturing costs of 50p per unit both for the major and for the indie. This leaves the major with £5.62 per unit. Out of this, the major will have to account to the artist for his royalty. If we assume a rate of 20% of the dealer price (inclusive of the royalty payable to the producer) after deduction of a packaging allowance of 25% (see Paragraph 3.0 in this section for a more detailed explanation of this) then the artist will receive £7 x 75% x 20% – ie £1.05. This will not begin to apply until sales are sufficient to reach recoupment, so that the major will be left with £5.62 per unit for a good many sales but then reducing to £4.57 per unit.

The indie, meanwhile, would be left with £4.77 per unit (because it has to pay higher distribution fees), which is split with the artist after any other expenses have been deducted. If there is a profit-sharing arrangement, then it is difficult to see clearly how the unit price for a particular record might be divided. In the case of the traditional royalty system, the breakdown (based upon the above example) in the case of a full price CD sold by a major (ignoring the fact that the artist royalty will be available for recoupment, and remembering that the artist royalty is usually inclusive of the producer's royalty) is as follows:

Customs & Excise	£2.62
Dealer	£4.76
Publisher	£0.64
Distributor	£0.85

Manufacturer	£0.50
Artist and Producer	£1.05
Record Company	£4.57
	£14.99

On this analysis, the record company takes a little over four times the combined amount taken by the artist and producer. However, this is an over-simplistic approach. After taking into account all of the marketing and promotional expenditure (but ignoring the record company's overhead costs), the profit ratio might typically be in the region of 2:1 or, even nearer, 3:1 in favour of the record company. This conclusion is supported by the evidence in the George Michael case. The record companies argue, of course, that they need to retain profits in this ratio in order to support their substantial overhead costs (including all of the A&R costs written off in relation to unsuccessful artists).

2.0 advances

2.1 HOW DO THEY WORK?

An advance is a pre-payment of royalties and is recoupable from those royalties. However, the advance is non-returnable. Royalties take a long time to work through the system and often longer to reach a level sufficient to achieve recoupment. The majority of recording contracts remain 'unrecouped', ie the artist never receives a royalty cheque. The safest approach for an artist (in terms of forward financial planning) is therefore always to approach a record deal on the basis that any income will be limited to the contractual advances (although beware of cynicism – see Paragraph 4.0 in this section).

2.2 COSTS INCLUSIVE?

It is usually preferable for an artist's advances to be exclusive of recording costs so that the record company pays recording costs (up to an agreed budget and on a recoupable basis) in addition to the advances stated in the contract. The advantage is that the artist can plan and budget for his general expenditure.

In a long-term record deal, part of the advance for the first album is normally paid on signature and the balance on delivery (or perhaps release) of the album. The date on which the balance of the advance is paid is therefore uncertain. Nevertheless, under a costs exclusive deal the artist can more easily make sensible financial plans than if the advance includes recording costs. Even though a recording-costs budget may be set, it is notoriously difficult to keep within it. A company will often insist on a costs-inclusive deal even though, when the deal is signed and the advance agreed, neither party has a clear idea of the likely recording costs.

On the other hand, if the artist has control over the recording process and has developed a degree of skill in producing first-rate recordings at a modest cost (perhaps he already has his own home recording studio), there may be an advantage in securing a costs-inclusive deal. The costs-inclusive advance may be greater than the aggregate of any personal advance he might have obtained, together with any actual recording costs. Against this, of course, if the artist does have his own recording facilities, the company may use this to its own advantage by depressing the level of the advances which might otherwise have been paid.

2.3 HOW MUCH?

Historically, UK record companies paid an advance to the artist and, separately, paid all of the record costs. Most deals are now costs inclusive. In the case of an album deal the advance for the first album might fall in the range of £50,000–£150,000. This will obviously be affected by the nature of the music and how it is to be recorded. There is from time to time the exceptional case which would fall way outside this suggested range.

Usually, the size of any advance is determined at least in part by the artist's actual financial requirements so that, for example, a solo artist might expect a lower advance than a group. However, if the artist's negotiating position is strong, the level of the advance may be determined less by actual need and more by a combination of market forces and the record company's perception of likely sales.

When negotiating an advance, figures preferably should not be plucked out of the air. The artist or his manager should at least attempt to justify what is asked for. A record company does not expect to support a life of luxury for a new artist but it does have to recognise that basic living costs must be covered. Likewise, the manager has to be paid since he also has a living to earn, so his commission entitlement should be factored into the equation. Beyond this, funds may be required for equipment and/or stage clothes and/or perhaps a van to carry the equipment. Lawyers and accountants also need to be paid. Perhaps the lead vocalist would benefit from singing lessons, which will also have to be paid for.

The record company will want to know the publishing situation. If the publishing deal is in place, the record company may suggest that it is unreasonable for the record company to underwrite all of the artist's anticipated expenditure and that the artist should approach his publisher for part of the funding. If no publishing deal is in place, the record company will suggest to the artist that he finds one. In the case of a group with perhaps one principal songwriter there is the problem that the songwriter will (understandably) not wish to allow his publishing income to subsidise the group's recording activities.

2.4 CROSS-RECOUPMENT

Essentially, all royalties which accrue under an agreement will be used to recoup all advances. For example, if the first album is an expensive flop but the second album takes off, the company can use royalties from the second album to recoup the costs of the first album as well as the second album (and the third and later albums). This concept of cross-recoupment is sometimes referred to as cross-collateralisation.

Sometimes (but rarely) the artist may be able to impose restrictions on the company's cross-recoupment rights. For example, if the company has control over the artist's back catalogue and a new deal is structured for future recordings, the company might agree that royalties from the back catalogue will be free flowing and will not be used to recoup advances paid for new recordings.

As we have seen, a company may occasionally agree to recoup remix costs only from the remix in question. Sometimes (probably only after a renegotiation) royalties from a particular territory or territories may be free-flowing. Alternatively, they might be available for recoupment only of advances which are paid specifically in relation to sales in that territory. For leaving members, there should be limitations on the company's cross-recoupment rights between the original agreement and any leaving member agreement (see Paragraph 7.0 in Part 2 of this chapter).

2.5 ASSOCIATED AGREEMENTS

None of the majors now insists that an artist must sign a publishing contract with its publishing affiliate as a condition of entering into a recording contract. Even if by choice the artist does sign a publishing contract with an affiliated company, there would be no cross-recoupment other than in extraordinary circumstances. For example, perhaps in the context of tax planning arrangements, the record company and the publishing company might be persuaded to pay substantial advances during a particular financial year, but only on condition that cross-recoupment will apply.

Smaller companies still sometimes insist that an artist signs recording and publishing contracts with related companies. This should usually be resisted, but if recording and publishing contracts are signed with the same company (or with affiliated companies) it should be made clear that there is to be no cross-recoupment between them.

3.0 royalties

3.1 RETAIL OR DEALER PRICE?

Some few years ago, most UK record deals provided for the calculation of record royalties on the retail price of records sold. For some while, most deals have provided for record royalties to be calculated on the dealer price. In the distant past, record royalties were calculated on the wholesale or dealer price, but as some record companies also owned record shops, there was a feeling that the price might be manipulated. The artist's best protection was to have his record royalty calculated on the price at which the record was actually sold to the ultimate customer. With the abolition (many years ago) of retail-price maintenance and, more recently, the increasing competitiveness of the retail sector, confusion has developed over the prices at which records are in fact sold by retailers. Even though a company may suggest a retail price, there tends to be fierce discounting. Accordingly, there is uncertainty over the accuracy of the retail prices used for royalty calculations.

Before the current mechanical royalty rate of 8.5% of dealer price was established by the Copyright Tribunal, the mechanical royalty rate was 6.25% of the retail price. In those days, in order to resolve the uncertainty over retail prices, the MCPS and BPI agreed a formula to establish a notional retail price by multiplying the dealer price by a fixed percentage. This procedure is no longer necessary in the case of mechanical royalties which are now calculated on the dealer price (see Chapter 6, Part 2, Paragraph 1.2 for an explanation of mechanical royalties). Many contracts are still in operation under which record royalties (as opposed to mechanical royalties) are calculated on the retail price. This is now calculated on an 'uplifted' dealer price in a manner similar to that previously adopted by the MCPS and BPI in relation to the calculation of mechanical royalties. The notional retail price is calculated by multiplying the dealer price by something between (usually) 125% and 132%. In some agreements, the same result is achieved by calculating royalties on dealer price but uplifting the royalty rate by a similar margin.

3.2 PACKAGING DEDUCTIONS

Until recently, all majors insisted on perpetuating the ludicrous system whereby royalties are reduced by the application of packaging deductions or allowances. Though described as 'packaging allowances', they bear no relation to actual packaging costs. Many years ago, when packaging allowances were first introduced (at more modest rates), the companies tried to justify them by arguing that the royalty should attach to the music or the record but not its package. Few companies attempt to justify packaging allowances any more and most will candidly admit that the allowances are merely artificial reductions. For many years arguments over packaging allowances often generated ill will between the parties. Since the companies have given up attempting to justify the allowances, artists and their advisers have been more ready to accept them. The general approach now is to accept packaging allowances with a metaphorical shrug of the shoulder and to concentrate on securing an appropriate rate of royalty, having allowed for the fact that the royalty rate will be reduced by the packaging allowances.

For example, an artist may be entitled to a royalty of say 18% of the dealer price. The record company will insist upon a packaging allowance of usually up to 20% for vinyl discs and cassettes, 25% for CDs and 30% or even 35% for videos. Accordingly, in the case of a CD, the 18% royalty is not 18% at all; it is 18% of 75% (ie the dealer price less the 25% packaging allowance). In other words, the royalty rate being offered is 13.5%. The company will not offer 13.5%. Instead the company will insist upon offering 18% of 75%. Very few people are fooled by this.

In 2002, BMG had the courage to simplify its royalty calculation provisions by, in particular, abolishing packaging deductions. It offers reduced rates of royalty but is able to demonstrate that its current offers are at least as favourable as the offers it previously made at the higher rates under its old royalty system. Progress at last!

3.3 RETURNS AND NET SALES

Royalties are not calculated on the number of records manufactured, although mechanical royalties usually are; instead they are payable on *net sales*, ie records sold (rather than given away) and not returned. In some territories (notably North America), records are sold on a sale-or-return basis, which means that the dealer can send all or any of them back to the distributor if he is unable to sell them. In the UK, records are sometimes sold on a sale-or-return basis, but only in exceptional circumstances (eg where there is an expensive TV advertising campaign and the only way the distributor can persuade dealers to buy enough stocks to meet expected demand is to reassure them that they can return unsold records). However, in the UK there is what is known as a *returns privilege*, under which dealers may return up to 5% of records distributed to them. A dealer might take 5 records each from 20 artists on the same label, totalling 100 records. Under the returns privilege, he may send back a total of five records. If he chooses to return five records by one artist, that artist suffers 100% returns. The dealer may in any event return faulty records.

Until recently, many companies accounted to the artist only upon 90% of net sales. Using the example of the 18% royalty, the effective rate for a CD is in fact 18% x 75% (to allow for the 25% packaging allowance) x 90% – ie 12.15%. This practice is said to date back to the days of the old 78rpm shellac records. In those days, royalties were calculated on 90% of records manufactured, on the rough-and-ready assumption that 10% of all records broke. This has no relevance today. 'Net sales' will in any event be defined in order to exclude faulty products or returns. However, most notably, Virgin Records still generally account on 90% of net sales, and so do some US record companies.

3.4 ROYALTY BASE PRICE

In order to calculate what an 18% royalty of dealer price is worth, we need to establish what is usually referred to as the royalty base price. Although we talk of '18% of dealer', in fact the royalty is not calculated on the actual dealer price, but on an artificial price, which is arrived at by deducting the packaging allowance from the dealer price. In addition, the artist should be aware of the possible impact on the royalty base price of discounts. Ideally, the artist's royalty should be calculated by reference to the PPD (published price to dealers) less only the packaging allowance.

In some cases, however, the royalty is calculated not on the PPD but upon the actual dealer price after discounts. All distributors have what they refer to as *file discounts*, ie different discounts depending upon the category of dealer involved. Woolworths will command bigger discounts than the independent corner record shop. However, these discounts usually do not affect the royalty base price.

3.5 FREE GOODS

A further complication arises by virtue of what is known as the *free goods policy*. There is confusion over what is meant by 'free goods'. Sometimes this means records given away free for genuine promotional purposes to DJs, reviewers and the like. The artist is not paid a royalty on records given away for these promotional purposes, ie upon what might be called 'actual' free goods.

In North America, records are distributed on the basis that, say, for every ten albums distributed, nine are deemed to be sold and one given away for 'promotional purposes'. Sometimes two albums in ten are given away. In the case of singles, usually at least three singles in ten are given away. These 'freebies' are known not as 'actual' free goods but as 'automatic' free goods. Automatic free goods, of course, are merely a disguised discount. It would be just the same if all ten records were sold rather than nine but at a 10% discount. However, in the case of records given away free, the artist receives no royalty.

This is separate from the issue of the percentage of net sales, which attracts a royalty. If a US company pays a 16% royalty on 90% of net sales but gives away an average of 20% of its records as free goods and applies a 25% packaging allowance, the real rate of royalty is 16% x 90% x 80% x 75% – ie 8.64%. Artists are generally unable to do much about this.

3.6 WHAT RATES?

3.6.1   **UK Rates** – A new artist signing to a UK major would expect to receive between 15% and 20% of PPD (published price to dealers). However, there would usually be a number of embellishments to this. Again, let's assume a rate of 18%. This rate would apply for UK sales and is sometimes called the *headline rate*.

3.6.2   **Overseas Rates** – The artist should try to secure the same rate of royalty for the major overseas territories, but the 18% might reduce to say 16% for sales in major overseas markets, perhaps Germany, France, USA and Canada, Australia and Japan. Elsewhere, in the lesser markets, the rate might reduce to, say, 14%. The royalty would usually be inclusive of any royalty payable to a third-party producer. The subject of producers is dealt with more comprehensively in Chapter 5, but if we assume that the producer is paid 3% of dealer price, this would give a net rate for UK sales of 18% less 3%, making 15%. If the artist suffers territorial reductions, he should try to ensure that the producer accepts similar (*pro rata*) territorial reductions (so that if, in the major overseas territories, the artist receives a 16% rate rather than 18%, the producer should receive only $16/18$ of his UK rate for those territories).

Territorial reductions tend to be more dramatic under US contracts. If the 'headline' rate for US sales under a recording contract with a US major was 16% (and US recording contracts tend to provide for marginally lower rates than would usually apply under UK recording contracts), then very often the rate in the major overseas territories (including the UK) might be two-thirds of the US rate (ie 10.66%) and, in the remaining countries of the world, might be 50% of the US rate (ie 8%).

3.6.3   **Escalations** – The rates will often escalate automatically for later recordings. If the rate is 18% for the first album under a six-album deal, perhaps this will also apply for the second album but rise to 19% for the third and fourth albums, perhaps 20% for the fifth, and 21% for the sixth (with similar increases in relation to the overseas rates).

Very often (perhaps in addition to the automatic escalations) there may be sales-based escalations. For example, the 18% rate in the UK might increase to 19% on sales in excess of 300,000 copies and perhaps to 20% after 1,000,000 copies. Any escalation of this kind would normally apply only to the excess sales of that album and would not be retrospective. In some cases, the higher rate might automatically apply for all sales of the next and later albums. Escalations based on sales would normally work territory by territory, with different sales targets in each case.

3.6.4 **Format Reductions** – There are also likely to be format reductions. Singles might be at a reduced fixed rate of perhaps 12% or 13%. Alternatively, the rate for singles might be three percentage points less than the headline rate. When compact discs were first introduced, most record companies refused to issue records in this format unless the artist agreed to a reduced rate of royalty (usually 75% of the otherwise applicable rate). The (rather flimsy) justification given for this was that, as a new format, unit costs of production were high. Some companies even tried to plead a need for a 'break' in view of the research and development costs, but of course none of the record companies had to bear any of these costs (they were incurred by the hardware manufacturers). It is only comparatively recently that the reduced rate for CDs has tended to disappear from most contracts, although the reduced rate will continue indefinitely in relation to numerous back-catalogue items.

The CD 'rip-off' involved a double whammy in that, not only was the royalty rate reduced, but also the packaging allowance was increased, generally to 25%. Most artists and their advisers are now so relieved no longer to have to suffer a reduced rate that they accept the 25% packaging allowance without complaint (even though compact-disc duplicating costs are now minimal).

3.7 REAL ROYALTY RATE

One of the aims of the MMF is to hasten the demise of the misleading system by which record companies seek to confuse the royalty issue. One suggestion is that record companies should be compelled to state what the MMF would refer to as the RRR (Real Royalty Rate) in much the same way that lenders, when offering an interest rate, have to state the APR (Annual Percentage Rate). There is likely to be considerable resistance on the part of the government to bring in legislation to this effect, but it should be possible to achieve the same result by purely practical means. If it becomes common practice for artists and their advisers in discussions with record companies to talk in terms of the real royalty rate, the charade will become more transparent.

Contrary to popular belief, lawyers have no wish to perpetuate the current system. They would prefer to concentrate on the real issues. Moreover, more and more record company executives express dismay over the current system.

By RRR, the MMF means the rate of royalty obtained by expressing the amount in pence per unit which the artist actually receives, as a percentage of the dealer price (less VAT). This automatically takes into account packaging allowances, territorial and format reductions, the applicable percentage of net sales and all other accounting provisions in the agreement. Ideally, every record contract should specify the RRR for each format in each territory. None does at present, but BMG's initiative as referred to in Paragraph 3.2 above is to be applauded.

3.8 FURTHER REDUCTIONS

As we have seen, the real royalty rate will be only a fraction of the royalty rate apparently offered by the record company. The story doesn't end there. Further reductions will apply in the case of particular types of sale.

3.8.1   **Budget Sales** – The company will generally offer half-rate royalties on records sold at less than full price. Most labels have a published full-price category (which might have a published price to dealers in the case of a CD of £8.45), a separate mid-price category (which might have a published price to dealers in the case of CDs of £5.95) and a low-price or budget category (with a published price to dealers of perhaps £4.95 or less).

The costs of manufacturing and distributing low-price records are the same as for the full-price records, except that there may be a small saving on packaging costs. The company's margin will be considerably reduced. The company will argue that the artist's royalty should reduce in line with the reduction in the company's profit, and that this is not achieved simply by calculating the royalty on a lower sale price. The artist should investigate the company's pricing policies and ensure that the definitions of full price, mid price and budget price are sensible and do not allow room for abuse.

The company will usually wish to pay half-rate royalties on anything less than full price. One compromise is to accept three-quarter-rate royalties on mid-price sales and half rate only on genuine low price sales.

3.8.2   **Record Clubs** – A significant number, perhaps in the region of 15% to 30%, of total album sales by established artists are made through record clubs. Record-club sales attract half-rate royalties. Most contracts provide that, for example, no royalties are payable on records given away by the club to attract new members. However, record companies rarely conduct their own record-club operations. They merely grant manufacturing licences, or sell finished records, to the record clubs and allow them to get on with it. The company will not know whether the club has given away the records or sold them. The company will generally be paid for all records supplied to the club but, owing to the volumes involved, the clubs will receive substantial discounts. The company may only have to deliver large quantities of records to the club's fulfilment centre and will not have to worry about distributing those records to the shops.

The clubs can drive a hard bargain on discounts, so a reduced royalty rate may be justifiable. However, a 50% reduction almost certainly is not justifiable. Nevertheless, half-rate royalties on record-club sales remain standard.

3.8.3   **Compilations** – The compilation album market has grown steadily over the years. Most record companies now derive a substantial part of their income from compilation sales. At one time, artists and their advisers were sceptical about the benefits of compilation licensing. The concern is that, if a successful track is widely available on multi-artist compilations, the public may prefer to buy a compilation featuring the recording rather than the artist's own album. The contrary view is that exposure of an artist on compilations creates a greater awareness of that artist, and stimulates sales of the artist's own recordings. At one time, there was a general feeling that the widespread availability of an artist on compilations rather 'cheapened' the artist. Some still subscribe to this view, and there are major artists who still refuse to allow their recordings to be used on compilation albums.

The artist's record company may put together its own multi-artist compilation album, either entirely of its own artists or, more likely, a combination of its own artists together with repertoire licensed in from other record companies. In such cases, there is no convincing reason why the artist should not receive his full headline rate of royalty. This will be pro-rated between the number of tracks on the album. If the headline rate of royalty is 18% and the artist has only one of 20 tracks on the album, he might expect to receive $1/20$ of his normal rate, ie 0.9%, for the album. Nevertheless, the companies' standard position is to offer only a 50% rate in relation to compilation use. Again, assuming a headline rate of 18%, compilation use would therefore attract a pro-rata share of 9%, ie 0.45% on a 20-track album. The artist should resist any reduction in the headline rate for compilation use on the company's own releases.

The situation is different in the case of third-party compilations, which account for most compilation activity. In these cases, the company grants a licence to a compilations specialist in return for a royalty. If the royalty received by the company equates to the headline rate which it pays to its artist, the company will be left with nothing. The companies' standard position is therefore to offer the artist 50% of the headline rate. This is not necessarily fair to the artist. As we have seen, this may reduce the artist's rate to, say, 9%. At least in the case of first-rate current repertoire licensed for inclusion on something like the *Now That's What I Call Music* series, the company is likely to receive, say 20% or perhaps even 25%. If the company receives 25%, out of which it pays the artist 9% (which will be paid only if the artist has recouped), the company is earning nearly twice as much as the artist. The company will consider this to be entirely reasonable. After all, this means a ratio of nearly 2:1. The record company will claim that, in order to support its substantial overhead costs and the various A&R costs which have to be written off in respect of unsuccessful artists, it needs a ratio more in the region of 3:1 (see Paragraph 1.6 in this section)

The artist may reluctantly accept the 2:1 or 3:1 ratio on full-price sales (he has little choice) where the record company has a significant role to play and carries significant overhead costs in order to do its job. However, different considerations should perhaps apply where the company merely licenses its rights in relation to what is often referred to as *secondary marketing activities*.

An artist will sometimes succeed in securing 50% (or more) of the company's receipts. The contract might provide that the artist receives half-rate royalties or, if greater, half of the company's receipts. Alternatively (although this amounts to the same thing), the artist may receive his full rate of royalty or, if less, half of the company's receipts. In extreme cases, the artist may receive a share of any advances received by the record company from the licensee.

3.8.4   **TV Advertising** – In the early 1980s, record companies introduced half-rate royalties if the company paid for a television advertising campaign. They thought it unfair that the artist should benefit from the company effectively buying extra sales.

As time went by, artists' advisers found more sophisticated ways of limiting the impact of this. The reduction should apply only if the television advertising campaign is substantial. This has led to complex definitions of what is meant by 'substantial'. The reduction should only apply for a limited time, usually from the start of the campaign until the end of the next accounting period following the end of the campaign, or perhaps the accounting period after that. Sometimes, the company imposes a reduced royalty on all sales during the accounting period in which the campaign starts, even if that happens several months into the accounting period.

None of this solves the problem that the total reduction in royalty might work out at more than the cost of the campaign. The artist may end up paying (by way of a reduction in royalty) more than the entire cost of the campaign, with the company profiting from all the extra sales achieved. For a while, the companies argued that this was fair because television advertising campaigns are expensive and involve considerable risk. However, market research is now so sophisticated that any risks have been more or less removed. The record company will usually spend on TV advertising only if it is confident that additional sales will justify the cost. The trend is now for full royalties to be payable but for all or part of the costs of the campaign to be recoupable.

3.9 PERFORMANCE INCOME

Every time a record is broadcast or played in public, the broadcaster or venue owner needs to hold a licence from two distinct copyright owners: the Performing Right Society Limited (PRS), who grant licences on behalf of writers and publishers for use of copyright in the words and music; and Phonographic Performance Limited (PPL), who give consent on behalf of performers and record companies for use of copyright in the sound recording.

There are important differences between the way PRS and PPL operate. In order to understand these differences properly, a little history lesson is inevitable. Those interested only in the current position may skip the next few paragraphs.

Copyright law was slow to recognise the existence of rights in sound recordings. Although Thomas Edison applied for a patent for his sound-recording machine as early as 1877, sound-recording copyright was not recognised in English law until a case was decided in 1934. To this day, copyright in sound recordings lasts for only 50 years from the year of release, whereas musical and literary copyright lasts for the life of the creator plus 70 years.

Performers did not receive any right to control use of sound recordings on which they played until the Performers' Protection Act was passed in

1963. This act was supposed to give effect to the rights granted to performers by Article 12 of the Rome Convention of 1961, which the UK ratified in 1963. However, the law gave UK performers no right to income. Infringement of the Performers' Protection Act merely gave rise to criminal penalties.

In 1934, PPL agreed to pay featured performers 20% of the net income collected on behalf of its members, who were (and still are) exclusively record companies. This payment was made *ex gratia*, meaning that the performers had no legal right to demand it. In 1946, PPL agreed to pay a further 12.5% of its income *ex gratia* to the Musicians' Union, in recognition of the contributions of unknown session players. The UK government argued that these *ex gratia* arrangements complied with the Rome Convention.

The Musicians' Union made no attempt to distribute its 12.5% share of this income to the session players whose performances appeared on sound recordings. Instead, the money was paid into a special fund that would benefit musicians in general. Somewhat ironically, some of this income from sound recordings was used to finance the Musician' Union's Keep Music Live campaign.

In 1988, the Monopolies and Mergers Commission (MMC) investigated PPL's activities. It declared that the arrangements for the payment of performers were unsatisfactory and failed to meet the UK's obligations under the Rome Convention. The MMC recommended that performers be paid equitable remuneration in proportion to the use made of each recording in broadcast or public performance.

The most significant effect of the MMC's ruling was that PPL stopped paying 12.5% of its income to the Musicians' Union. PPL refused to pay until the Union could distribute income equitably to those individuals who had played on sound recordings. Finally, in 1994, PPL paid the Musicians' Union some £22 million in accumulated payments, which the Union distributed among its members.

In 1992, the EC Commission issued a Directive on Rental and Lending Rights and Piracy (92/100/EEC). The Directive also dealt with public performance income for sound recordings. Unlike Article 12 of the Rome Convention, the Directive gave performers a legal right to income from public performance of sound recordings. Article 8 of the Directive grants performers a right to a 'single equitable remuneration' paid by the user every time a sound recording is broadcast or played in public.

Most EC states passed laws granting such economic rights in the early

1960s. Nearly 40 years later, the UK has still not done so. The UK chose to enact the Directive not by an Act of Parliament but by means of a Statutory Instrument, the legislative equivalent of flat-pack furniture. This resulted in the Copyright and Related Rights Regulations 1996 (more than two years outside the deadline laid down in the Directive). Instead of granting performers a right which they could enforce separately against users, the Regulations give performers a right against copyright owners – in other words, PPL's members.

This is where the most significant differences between the PRS and PPL lie. Performers may not be members of PPL; PPL alone may negotiate with users; PPL alone may decide the division of the income it collects; PPL's members (record companies) may leave PPL on six months' notice or wind PPL up altogether, leaving performers to claim directly against their record company; PPL's members may license certain rights direct to users, as they have done with interactive rights. Without PPL's intervention between the user and the record companies, performance income is likely to be used to recoup advances.

The Copyright and Related Rights Regulations fail to implement the Directive because they do not ensure that performers receive the remuneration to which they are entitled.

Two organisations have been formed to look after performers' rights under the new legislation: the Performing Artists Media Rights Association (PAMRA) and the Association of United Recording Artists (AURA). PAMRA is backed, and to some extent directed, by the Musicians' Union, the actors' union Equity, record producers' association the Music Producers Guild (MPG), the Incorporated Society of Musicians and others. AURA is an independent organisation promoted initially by the International Managers' Forum.

The principal difference between AURA and PAMRA lies in the type of performer that each seeks to represent. AURA looks after featured performers, whereas PAMRA claims to represent all performers. However, since all PAMRA's members have equal voting rights and the vast majority are session players, PAMRA's emphasis is on the rights of non-featured players. This is hardly surprising, given the organisations which participate in PAMRA.

Whilst PAMRA administers only performance-income rights, AURA aims to collect related income such as CD rental and blank-tape levy, and to act as a lobbying and campaigning organisation on behalf of featured and, especially, contracted performers.

127

There is a further distinction between the associations in their attitudes to collection of performance income from overseas. AURA favours direct membership of overseas societies for its featured performer members. This allows performers and their advisers to negotiate directly with the society collecting income in the territory concerned. It also reduces administration costs by removing one tier of administration. The most significant disadvantage of this system is that certain funds of unattributable income (so-called 'black box' income) are accessible only to collecting societies and not to individuals. AURA's response to this is that the rules should be changed to allow individuals to claim a share of such income.

PAMRA discourages direct membership of overseas societies by depriving members who join overseas societies of their right to vote. PAMRA is a member of SCAPR, an informal international association of collecting societies. SCAPR lays down rules for its members concerning the exchange of performance income. One of these rules stipulates that SCAPR societies must distribute to their members 100% of the income they receive from overseas. SCAPR members meet their own administration costs by deductions from the money they send to overseas societies. The levels of these deductions are within the exclusive control of the society making the payment and are not disclosed. AURA believes that the lack of transparency in this system disguises inefficiency.

A far as UK income is concerned, featured performers may claim this direct from PPL by registering their details at the Performers' Registration Centre (PRC). However, many featured performers prefer to appoint either PAMRA or AURA to collect on their behalf. The cost of doing so is a flat rate of 15% for PAMRA members and a negotiable rate of 5–10% for AURA members. It seems that non-featured performers may not claim direct from PPL.

Before the Copyright and Related Rights Regulations were passed, 67.5% of PPL income went to record companies, 12.5% to the Musicians' Union and 20% to featured performers. Under the new law, PPL purports to pay 50% of its distributable income to performers, 32.5% of which goes to featured performers and 17.5% to session players. Income will in future be distributed on a track-by-track basis so that every performer's income should reflect the popularity of the tracks on which he/she played.

Where there are no session players, 100% of the distributable income will go to the featured performers on the track. Where there are session players, each session player's income is capped at a maximum of 3.5%. So where, for example, there are only two session players, only 7% of the possible 17.5% non-featured performers' income will be paid out to them. The distribution of the remaining 10.5% is still the subject of negotiation, with PAMRA arguing that it should be paid to session players on other tracks and AURA contending that it should be paid to the featured performers on the track.

Although PPL's decision to pay 50% of its net income to performers appears to be a concession, in reality performers are unlikely to receive any more income under the new system than they would have under the old. This is because of the treatment of US performers' income. Since the US does not recognise rights to income from the public performance and broadcast of sound recordings, US performers are not entitled to claim income from PPL for the use of their sound recordings in the UK. Under the old system, this income was simply shared between the record companies and the performers. Under the new system, however, PPL has decided that all US performers' income will go to the record companies. This is a direct result of the UK government's failure to implement the Directive on Rental and Lending Rights and Piracy.

PPL also refuses to pay performers any share of the income collected by its related company, Video Performance Limited (VPL), from the broadcast of videos. This is because PPL claims that videos are films. Since soundtracks (ie recordings of dialogue and sound effects) of films are exempt from the Regulations, PPL claims that sound recordings are exempted from the legislation when they are combined with images in videos. PPL also refuses to pay performers any share of the £3 million it collects from the sale of high-priced CDs which are licensed for public performance to aerobics instructors and the like, claiming that such income is collected for a dubbing service, and not for the public performance of sound recordings.

Contrary to European Court rulings which date from the mid-1970s, PPL has indicated that it will not accept direct claims from performers who are based outside the UK. In order to discharge its obligation to overseas performers, PPL has apparently paid all income due to overseas performers to PAMRA, who will deduct its administration costs from that income before paying it to the overseas collecting societies with which it has reciprocal arrangements. AURA will continue to insist that overseas featured performers should be permitted to claim direct from PPL.

The first distribution of income under the new law took place in 1999 for income relating to the year 1996–7. Income is now distributed regularly in November each year, a year in arrears. The interim distribution agreement reached between AURA, PAMRA and PPL applied only to the first two years' distributions. PAMRA entered into a renewal agreement with PPL in 2000 but, whilst invited to do so, AURA has so far refused.

3.10 OTHER USES

Record contracts usually contain provisions dealing with the artist's income from any use of the recordings beyond the manufacture and sale of records. Many agreements give the artist 50% of the company's net receipts from such uses. Those receipts are sometimes referred to as *flat-fee receipts*.

This might extend to any 'premium' use – ie the exploitation of the recordings in connection with another commercial product or service. For example, the record company may supply records to Kelloggs to give away free to anybody sending in a set number of tokens from Cornflakes packets. Kelloggs pay for the records even though they are then given away free. The artist should not accept that no royalties are paid on premium sales.

Sometimes the company offers half-rate royalties on premium sales, which might mean that an artist on a headline rate of 16% would receive 8% of whatever Kelloggs pays for the records. There seems to be little justification for this. A fairer system would be for the artist to receive a percentage (say 50%) of the company's receipts. As a precaution, the artist should always insist on a right of approval over premium use. This allows the artist to insist on full disclosure of the financial arrangements so that, if necessary, the royalty provisions may be varied before approval is granted.

The most typical example of flat-fee receipts is the income generated by the grant of synchronisation licences, ie the use of a recording in the soundtrack of a film or in an advertisement of some kind. Again, typically, the artist would expect to receive (or at least be credited with) 50% of the fee.

3.11 NEW FORMATS

When compact discs were first introduced, the record companies looked for ways of reducing their artist royalty liabilities (see Paragraph 3.6.4 in this section). They argued that compact discs were more expensive to manufacture than vinyl or cassette (which was probably true for a very short time when compact discs were first introduced and when they were manufactured and sold in relatively small numbers).

The most common device was to offer a royalty on compact discs equivalent in terms of 'pennies per unit' to the royalty on the sale of the equivalent vinyl disc version of the same record. In the event, the public wholeheartedly accepted the CD format and was persuaded to pay substantially more per unit than the vinyl or cassette equivalent. Nevertheless, for several years, all new contracts included provisions for reduced rate royalties in the case of compact discs. Sometimes the rate itself was lower (perhaps three-quarters of the otherwise applicable rate); sometimes the royalty was calculated on the vinyl or cassette price rather than the CD price; sometimes there was a higher packaging allowance. In the case of existing repertoire (which the record companies had acquired under the terms of contracts entered into before compact discs were contemplated), the record companies would usually refuse to release that repertoire in CD format unless and until the artist granted a royalty 'break' of some kind.

As a legacy of all of this, whilst full-rate royalties are now invariably paid for sales of compact discs, nevertheless a higher packaging allowance normally applies. Typically, there may be a packaging deduction of 20% for cassette sales but 25% for CD sales. There is a widespread feeling amongst managers and artists that they were out-manoeuvred by the record companies in relation to compact discs. For this reason, it is unlikely that the record companies will be given so easy a ride in relation to any new formats introduced in the future. Many new recording agreements define 'new technology' and provide for reduced-rate royalties.

Perhaps in the hope of pulling off a similar stunt, most contracts state that, if at any time records are sold in an as-yet-uninvented format, a reduced rate will apply. If pressed, most companies will accept that either this provision should be deleted altogether or that the reduced rate should apply for only a very limited period. This is sometimes linked to the point at which the format is no longer 'new'. This might be defined as the end of the accounting period during which sales in the new format first exceed a given percentage of total sales.

3.12 THE DIGITAL REVOLUTION

Technology is moving so fast that physical formats will be of less relevance in future. Digital technology enables the delivery of music in its state-of-the-art form by telephonic transfer. Records may be purchased over the internet.

The transaction may be effected over the internet and the record then sent by mail, but more frequently it is possible to purchase music which is delivered by direct download.

Some recording contracts are worded so that (intentionally or otherwise) any income from exploitation by means of digital transfer will fall to be dealt with under the secondary exploitation provisions so that, often, the record company will be obliged to pay one-half of its receipts to the artist.

The major record companies are unhappy about this position. Record companies will need, arguably, to continue to maintain a ratio of profits between the record company and the artist of something like 3:1. Without a profit ratio of this kind, there is the fear that the record companies will be unable to sustain their current overhead costs and the same level of investment in new talent. On the other hand, artists are unlikely to be impressed by the suggestion that most record companies will have little or nothing to do in terms of the physical manufacture and distribution of records but that nevertheless only, say, 25% of any income should be paid to the artist. Of course, by definition, a major record company is a company which owns or controls its own facilities for the manufacture and distribution of records, so if those facilities are no longer needed, there may no longer be any need in the new world order for major record companies. them.

4.0 the watershed

It is perhaps unsurprising that there is widespread cynicism about the current system. Many managers believe that recording contracts are laughable and not worth the paper they are written on. Managers from this school of thought concentrate on getting maximum possible advances as often as they can and pay little attention to the terms of the contract.

This is a short-sighted approach. Whilst a degree of cynicism is healthy, managers must pay attention to all of the provisions of any recording contract, not only during negotiations but at all times. As George Michael's court case has shown, recording contracts will generally be enforced by the courts. Most recording contracts contain the potential for artists to earn fabulous riches. It is a dreary task to argue about reduced royalties on budget sales and the like when the artist is concerned only with getting signed and into the studio, and when recoupment is a distant dream. But there is no point in approaching negotiations over any new recording contract on the assumption that the artist will not be successful. Sooner or later, if enough records are sold, the artist will recoup. This is a watershed, when royalties come gushing through. Suddenly, all those boring provisions have real and dramatic impact. The unfair terms which might with greater effort have been avoided will now stand out and mock the artist and his advisers.

5.0 accounting

5.1 ACCOUNTING PERIODS

The majors generally account to their recording artists twice a year. On sales for which the company is paid between 1 January and 30 June, the artist will usually receive a statement 90 days later, at the end of September. On sales for which the company is paid between 1 July and 31 December, the artist will receive a statement at the end of the following March.

Some record companies account for UK sales on the basis of sales information. These companies include on an accounting statement any sales notified during an accounting period. Other companies account only for sales for which the company has actually been paid. The busiest month of the year for record sales is December. The record company will probably not receive payment from its distributor for December sales until the following January. If the company accounts only for sales for which it has actually been paid, those sales will not appear on an accounting statement until the end of the following September.

There are more significant delays on overseas sales. Most companies receive accountings from overseas licensees every quarter. For example, for sales between 1 October and 31 December, the overseas licensee might account to the UK company in February. The sales will only appear on the artist's royalty statement delivered at the end of the following September (nearly 12 months later).

Some companies have even slower arrangements, partly for tax reasons. These companies might, for example, insist that all overseas licensees account to a particular group company which has a centralised accounting function.

That company subsequently accounts to each of the other companies in the group. For an artist signed to Warner Bros in London, Warner France will account to Warner International in London, which will then account to Warner Music UK. For an artist signed to one of the UK Universal Music companies, Universal France may, for example, account to Universal International in Holland, which would then account back to the UK operating company.

The artist should always check with his record company exactly how royalties are to be routed and what delays can be expected.

5.2 RESERVES

Most record companies insist upon provisions enabling them to make reserves against returns. Although a particular royalty statement will disclose a given number of sales, the record company will hold back the royalties in relation to a proportion of those sales in case the dealer returns some of the records.

In the UK and in most overseas territories, dealers are not usually allowed to return records unless they are faulty. In the case of the faulty record, the record company must replace this, and this should not impact upon the artist's royalty. In the UK, most distributors operate what is known as a 5% returns 'privilege' (see Paragraph 3.3 in this section), which means that the dealer may return up to 5% of any unsold stocks. It would therefore seem unreasonable for the record company to make a reserve of more than 5% (although, as explained in Paragraph 3.3, it is theoretically possible for an artist to suffer returns of more than 5% under the privilege scheme). In fact, in practice, most record companies do not impose a reserve at all on account of any 5% returns privilege or similar scheme.

The issue of reserves assumes more importance in the case of records distributed on a sale-or-return basis. In some territories (notably the USA and Canada), most records are sold on a 100% sale-or-return basis. In the UK and other territories, some records are distributed on this basis, but usually only when there is a special campaign involved. Many companies insist upon the right to maintain a reserve of, say, 25% but will agree that the reserve should apply only in the case of records sold on a sale-or-return basis. Most companies will agree that reserves should be liquidated either in the next accounting period (ie the reserve is then released after any royalties have been deducted in respect of records actually returned) or perhaps liquidated equally over two accounting periods.

Most UK record companies will accept that they may impose reserves only in respect of UK sales and that, in the case of overseas sales, they will not impose any reserves beyond those imposed upon the company by its overseas licensees. It is prudent to insist upon the disclosure of the relevant details. The most important territory in this respect is the USA and Canada. The artist should ascertain what reserves the company's North American licensee may impose against the company and over what period those reserves are to be liquidated.

5.3 WITHHOLDING TAXES

Most recording contracts include an express provision to the effect that the company may deduct from royalties and advances due to the artist any sums which the company is obliged by law to deduct by way of withholding tax. In the case of a UK company paying royalties to a UK resident, no tax is required to be withheld, so that withholding is generally only obviously an issue in the case of a record company and an artist situated in different territories.

If withholding tax does apply, then if a double-taxation treaty is in force between the two territories, the artist should be entitled to a tax credit against his own taxation liabilities. A provision should be inserted to the effect that the company must give the artist all reasonable assistance in obtaining such credit (this assistance would involve the supply of an appropriate certificate of deduction and dealing with any queries raised by the revenue authorities).

Sometimes, this will not be of any use to the artist because his tax affairs may be such that he has no (or insufficient) tax liabilities against which to set off the benefit of any tax credit. In these circumstances, if the record company has suffered withholding tax in respect of royalties received from its overseas licensees and has deducted a proportionate share of the withholding tax from the royalties payable to the artist but has then obtained the benefit of a tax credit, the company should, in fairness, pay back to the artist a proportionate share of that benefit.

In the case of some recording agreements, it may be worth the time and effort involved in investigating the record company's overseas licensing structure in order to ensure that the artist will not suffer unduly from withholding tax problems. At best, the artist will secure a provision to the effect that any foreign withholding tax will be ignored for the purposes of calculating the artist's royalties.

5.4 AUDIT RIGHTS

Most record companies will offer the artist a right of audit. If not, the principle of an audit right will never be resisted if the artist asks for this. However, the record company will seek to impose certain restrictions, so that, for example, audits may not be carried out more than once every, say, 12 months and may only be carried out by a reputable firm of chartered accountants. Most UK record company audits are carried out by one of the limited number of firms of accountants specialising in music industry royalty audit work.

Each audit will of course be different, but in the case of a relatively successful artist auditing a UK record company in relation to sales of records over a relatively successful period of, say, three years, then typically perhaps two or three auditors will be involved for perhaps a week at the offices of the record company. They will then prepare a report and then spend more time with the record company in an effort to clarify any areas of confusion.

Audits are therefore expensive. The auditors will normally try to spend only that amount of time which is likely to be justified by results, but typically an audit might cost between £5,000 and £10,000 or (in the case of a particularly successful artist where there have been numerous sales and where the amounts of money involved justify the accountants spending as much time as is needed) perhaps £15,000 and £30,000.

Some record-company personnel seem still to interpret a request for an audit as an allegation on the part of the artist that there has been some form of financial irregularity, but it is increasingly accepted that it is merely sensible and prudent on the part of any successful artist to carry out regular audits. As we have seen, the accounting function is a complex one, and mistakes – together with disagreements over points of interpretation of the relevant contractual terms – are therefore inevitable. Indeed, the more enlightened record companies welcome regular audits.

A successful artist should probably audit every two or three years (perhaps after each album cycle). The contract will usually state that all accounting statements are to be deemed accepted and no longer subject to any objection unless such objection is made within a specified period from when the statement was rendered (usually two, three or perhaps four years). If the artist does not carry out an audit within the prescribed objection period, he – or his lawyer or accountant – should write to the record company and secure an extension. Most record companies will readily agree to this rather than put pressure on the artist to carry out an audit before the expiry of the objection period.

Most companies will accept that, in the event of a discrepancy (but usually only if the discrepancy is, say, 5% or perhaps 10% or more of the sums properly payable), the record company will reimburse the reasonable costs of the audit. In most cases, the auditors will find a number of arithmetical errors which the company will readily accept and will also make a number of additional claims on behalf of the artist based upon how the contract should properly have been interpreted.

Royalty auditors have a reputation for sometimes making some rather extravagant claims and, typically, the auditors will prepare a report detailing numerous separate heads of claim. The aggregate claim will usually be a substantial sum in excess of the 5% or 10% limit, which may be specified in the contract as the amount of underpayment which triggers a liability on the part of the company to reimburse the audit costs. Accordingly, the report will include a claim not only for the aggregate unpaid royalties but also for the auditors' fees. This is then followed by a sometimes protracted negotiation, which will invariably result in the audit being settled on the basis of a round sum payment representing a fraction of the overall amount. If the settlement is higher than the amount of the audit fees then, from the artist's point of view, the exercise will have been worthwhile. It usually is.

PART 4: AFTER THE DEAL

1.0 contract administration

1.1 FILING

A recording contract is like a living thing. It tends to adapt and grow. Somebody needs to look after it. During the life of a recording contract, there will usually be 'side letters' adding to, or varying, the agreement. These might deal with the purchase of equipment, or tour support arrangements for various territories, or royalty breaks on campaigns in particular territories. Somebody (usually the lawyer) should be given housekeeping responsibilities. The housekeeper should maintain a file which will include the contract itself and any correspondence concerning it. In particular, it is sensible to fix to the contract all formal amendments together with copies of option notices.

1.2 DATES

Somebody has to keep an eye on any important dates. This might be the manager, the lawyer or the accountant. The main reason for carefully monitoring option dates and the like is to ensure that there is no delay in invoicing for any advance which is due. Record companies rarely pay advances unprompted, and if they are late in paying they will seldom agree to pay interest. It is also worth noting option dates in case the record company mistakenly fails to exercise an option in time. Mistakes do happen. Missing an option is the only cardinal sin in a Business Affairs department and is likely to lead to instant dismissal. A careful note should be made of exactly when masters are delivered.

2.0 renegotiation

2.1 WHEN?

The more cynical type of manager relies heavily on the fact that recording contracts are probably unenforceable and in any event will always be renegotiated in the event of success.

Basically, this is nonsense. Some years ago, similar cynics were to be found in record companies. They issued recording contracts which were quite unfair and which they assumed were probably unenforceable. Following any success, and sometimes even if there was only the smell of success, they were prepared to offer improvements to keep everybody happy.

The industry does not really work this way any more. If the record company is in profit, an aggressive manager can usually extract more advances on one pretext or another. However, such concessions would rarely come close to what is generally meant by a renegotiation.

2.2 HOW?

A proper renegotiation is difficult to achieve. Record companies are generally confident in the enforceability of their contracts. Whilst a record company will do what is necessary, within reason, to keep a successful artist happy, this rarely extends to giving away anything valuable. Accordingly, if a contract is to be renegotiated, it has to be a two-way street; the artist has to give something in return for the improvements he seeks.

The bulldozer or blackmailing approach to renegotiation involves explaining to the record company that the artist is desperately unhappy, for whatever reason. He cannot bring himself to finish recording the new album until something is done to make him happier. It is best to leave this approach quite late (preferably, until the album has already been scheduled for release and the record company has cleared its decks in anticipation of starting work on the album).

If this tactic fails (and it usually does, because the record company knows that, in fact, the artist is desperate to release the record), then probably the only thing the artist has to offer which the record company does not have already is the option to call for another album or two. This is why, during the negotiations over the original contract, so much significance attaches to the number of options. If the artist achieves success early on and is resentful about the terms of his deal, and if the company already has the right to call for another four or five albums, there is little incentive for the record company to renegotiate. The record company will probably not feel exposed, at least until the time when the penultimate album is delivered.

If the artist can manoeuvre himself into a strong enough position to renegotiate, he usually looks for higher royalties, more substantial advances (and perhaps a non-recoupable bonus payment as an additional reward for past success), the exclusion of long-form video rights, perhaps the exclusion of particular territories (usually North America if the performance there has been poor), the reversion at some point of the copyright in his masters (a particularly difficult nut to crack), and perhaps – in the case of a group – a specific solo recording commitment or the exclusion of solo recordings from the deal.

4 Enforceability Of Agreements

By Andrew Forbes

The enforceability of music-industry agreements is an emotive subject. The high-risk and speculative nature of the business leads those who invest in talent (ie record companies, music publishers and managers) to seek long-term, exclusive arrangements from their artists. The reason for this is obvious: if a substantial amount of money, time and energy is to be invested in an artist, the investor will obviously want to be sure that he'll be able to reap the rewards of this, should success follow.

This desire for protection by those who effectively work to build an artist's career has to be handled sensitively, particularly in view of the relative youth and lack of business experience evident in many artists. This, coupled with an artist's keen desire to find someone who can help them succeed, can create a situation ripe for exploitation by the unscrupulous.

It's for these reasons that the courts have seen a steady stream of cases in which artists seek to challenge the enforceability of agreements they've entered into with record companies, music publishers and managers. In general, the courts are extremely reluctant to interfere with contracts – the 'freedom to contract' on such terms as one wishes is one of the cornerstones of English contract law. However, the music industry has succeeded in making significant inroads in this respect by pursuing a range of potential rights which can be used to challenge the enforceability of an agreement. This is the subject of this chapter, which will cover three areas of law relevant to the enforceability of music-industry agreements: restraint of trade, undue influence and European Community law in the form of article 85 of the Treaty of Rome.

RESTRAINT OF TRADE

how the courts approach

THE POLICY BEHIND THE RESTRAINT OF TRADE DOCTRINE

The court doesn't interfere with bargains between artists and their management, publishing or record companies lightly. As Lord Reid stated in a case called *Esso* v *Harper*, 'In general, unless a contract is vitiated by duress, fraud or mistake, its terms will be enforced though unreasonable or even harsh and unconscionable... In the ordinary case, the court will not remake a contract.' Parties will generally be held to agreements that they enter into, no matter how unbalanced the terms may appear. You could agree to sell your house for £1 if you wished to; you'd be held to your bargain.

The doctrine of restraint of trade, however, is an exception to this approach which has been developed by the court. The rationale behind the formulation of the doctrine is to preserve the perceived public interest in free trade. It aims to achieve this by breaking down unreasonable contractual restrictions which seek to stifle competition. There is therefore a tension between the court's desire to uphold the freedom of parties to contract on whatever terms they consider appropriate and, on the other hand, to promote free trade.

It's important to bear in mind what exactly the court is doing when it applies restraint-of-trade principles to an agreement. It's generally accepted that the aim of the agreement is not to protect the weak and vulnerable from transactions which the court considers unfair – that is the role of the doctrine of *undue influence*, which is considered later in this chapter. However, in cases pertaining to the music industry, there's been a blurring of the distinction between restraint of trade and undue influence. Lord Diplock stated in *Schroeder* v *Macaulay* (1974) that the public policy behind restraint of trade was, in fact, the protection of those whose bargaining power is weak from being forced to enter into bargains that are unconscionable by those whose bargaining power is stronger. In the context of music-industry agreements, at least, this reflects the fact that both restraint of trade and undue influence are used to protect the interests of artists who enter into restrictive agreements when they're in a position of poor bargaining power.

THE NORDENFELT TEST

The essential mechanism which the court uses to determine whether a restriction is an unenforceable restraint of trade is what is known as the Nordenfelt test. This was set out by the House of Lords in its definitive analysis of the doctrine of restraint of trade in the case of *Nordenfelt* v *Maxim Nordenfelt Guns And Ammunition* (1894). Lord Macnaghten stated that 'all interference with individual liberty of action in trading, and all restraints of trade themselves, if there is nothing more, are contrary to public policy and void'. However, restraints may be justifiable if they are reasonable. Lord Macnaghten identified a two-stage approach to be applied, to the effect that a restriction will only be enforceable if such a restriction is both reasonable between the parties and it doesn't offend against public policy. These stages will be referred to from now on as the two limbs of the Nordenfelt test.

The Nordenfelt approach has been clarified in a number of subsequent cases. The last definitive statement concerning the way in which the doctrine applies to music-industry agreements was contained in *Schroeder* v *Macaulay*. In the well-known cases which have followed *Schroeder* (ie *Zang Tumb Tuum* v *Johnson* [1993, the *Frankie Goes To Hollywood* case], *Silvertone* v *Mountfield* [1993, the *Stone Roses* case], *Panayiotou* v *Sony Music* [1994, the *George Michael* case] and *William Nicholl* v *Shaun Ryder* [1998, the *Shaun Ryder* case]), the courts have merely been applying the principles stated in *Schroeder* rather than developing any new principles of law.

WHEN SHOULD THE TEST BE APPLIED?

Before applying the Nordenfelt test, the court must first decide whether the contract in question attracts the restraint-of-trade doctrine at all. There's no rigid definition to determine whether a contract will attract the doctrine; the court has stressed that the doctrine is 'to be applied to factual situations with a broad and flexible rule of reason'.

The most recent case, *George Michael*, clarified the approach to be taken. The doctrine only applies to contracts which are in restraint of trade in the sense that this is used 'as a term of art covering those contracts which are to be regarded as offending a rule of public policy'. There are two elements to this: the contract must be in restraint of trade as the term is used in ordinary parlance; and, if it is, the court must then consider whether there is some reason to exclude the contract from the application of the doctrine. The Nordenfelt test will only be applied if the contract passes this two-stage test. The court effectively defined the ambit of the doctrine by determining those situations that were covered by the doctrine rather than those which weren't.

In *George Michael*, the court held that the recording agreement between the artist and his record company was a 'compromise agreement' (ie an agreement settling a dispute). For reasons of public policy, the court considered compromise agreements to be beyond the scope of the doctrine of restraint of trade, and therefore decreed that, in this instance, the doctrine of restraint of trade didn't apply, and the artist's case fell at the first hurdle. The court nevertheless went on to express what its decision would have been if the doctrine had applied, providing further guidance on the way in which courts should approach the enforceability of music-industry agreements. What's clear from the case is that the court is willing, in principle, to apply the restraint-of-trade doctrine to recording, publishing and management agreements containing restrictions that are imposed on artists. them.

reasonableness between parties

If the court decides that the doctrine applies to a contract currently under consideration, it will then go on to apply the first limb of the Nordenfelt test – are the restrictions reasonable between the parties?

CONSIDERATIONS
The burden of proof is on the party seeking to enforce the contract (ie the manager, publisher or record company), who must show that the restrictions are reasonable between the parties. The restrictions are therefore presumed unreasonable unless the manager, publisher or record company can demonstrate the contrary.

In considering this, the court will look at two areas: whether the restrictions go further than providing adequate protection for the legitimate interests of the party in whose favour they are granted (ie the manager, publisher or record company), and whether they can be justified as being in the interests of the party restrained (ie the artist).

PROVIDING PROTECTION FOR THE RESTRICTING PARTY

Esso v *Harper* formulated a two-stage test to determine whether a situation attracted the doctrine. Firstly, what are the legitimate interests of the party seeking to enforce the contract, which it is entitled to protect? Secondly, are the restrictions more than adequate for that purpose? These are questions of fact depending on the business and circumstances of the case in question.

It's long been established that restrictions are examined as they would have applied to both parties at the date of formation of the contract. The court should consider from this standpoint what may happen under the contract rather than look at what actually has happened. However, the court made it clear in *George Michael* that a realistic approach should be taken, rather than a search for far-fetched effects which are divorced from reality.

The legitimate interests of a record company seeking to rely on restrictions contained in a recording agreement have been set out in *Frankie Goes To Hollywood* and *George Michael*, details of which appear later in this chapter. In *Frankie Goes To Hollywood*, the court wasn't particularly impressed by the legitimate interests raised, and thought that any validity that they might have possessed was outweighed by the one-sided bias of the contract. In *George Michael*, the court commented that all of the interests listed were valid aspirations for any record company, although some interests had more bearing on justifying the contract in question than others. The court thought that the restrictions in the contract went no further than was necessary to protect the record company's legitimate interests.

JUSTIFICATION OF RESTRICTIONS

The court will consider whether the restrictions were justified in view of the artist's interest in obtaining the benefit to him available under the contract in question, and will look at the net effect of the entire sweep of provisions in the contract. The aim is to balance the parties' interests – the artist will wish to obtain the benefit of the contract without restricting himself unduly while the manager, publisher or record company in question will want to maximise its own benefit under the contract. The exercise carried out by the court will be to balance the benefit of the transaction against the burden imposed. In *Stone Roses*, the court thought that the contract was so entirely one-sided and unfair that no competently advised artist in The Stone Roses' position would ever have agreed to sign it. However, note that, in *George Michael*, the court specifically stated that 'the restrictions contained in [the contract being considered] are both reasonably necessary for the protection of the legitimate interests of Sony Music and commensurate with the benefits secured to Mr Michael under it'.

Again, each decision will turn on the detail of the contract being considered and the facts of the particular case. However, it's possible to draw out various factors which the courts will take into account, which include the following.

GEOGRAPHICAL SCOPE OF RESTRICTIONS

The ambit justified in a particular case will depend on the nature of the business concerned. In view of the international nature of the music business, the courts are prepared to countenance worldwide restrictions in recording agreements, although they haven't fully considered whether there is a distinction to be drawn between recording agreements (in which international protection may properly be given to copyrights) and management agreements (in which this consideration will not apply).

DURATION

At the present time, there is no concrete ruling on the time-span of the contract. It's impossible to say, for example, that five years is fine but eight years is too long; the duration of each particular restriction must be considered in the context of the rest of the contract as a whole, including other provisions, such as amount of consideration required.

In *Frankie Goes To Hollywood*, the court thought that the possible eight- or nine-year duration of the contract was unreasonable, and that five years was too long in relation to the publishing agreement. It should be noted, however, that the court was clearly considering the cumulative effect of the restrictions in both agreements, such as that which demanded that the artists sign to sister record and publishing companies.

In *Stone Roses*, there was a potential period of seven years, or possibly even an indefinite period of duration, coupled with no release commitment. The court thought that this was unreasonable, and was particularly influenced by the fact that the band's career could have been 'sterilised' for this period.

In *George Michael*, duration was defined by the artist's obligation to deliver masters within various option periods, subject to a 15-year cap. In the context of the contract as a whole, the court didn't think that its potential duration was unreasonable.

In the context of a management contract, the court held in *Shaun Ryder* that a seven-year term (comprising an initial term of three years and two two-year options) was unreasonable. It also observed that it's usual in the music industry for an earnings target to be included in order to legitimise a further period subject to an option, and that it was unreasonable for an option period to be tied to an earnings target.

AMOUNT OF CONSIDERATION

The more money an artist receives under an agreement, the more extensive the restraints by which he can then expect to be bound. This was a major influence on the court in *George Michael* in deciding that the restrictions listed in the contract were reasonable.

BARGAINING POWER OF THE PARTIES

If one party exerts commercial strength over the other to take unconscionable advantage of the other's weakness, restrictions imposed as a result may well be unreasonable. To an extent, this blurs the distinction between restraint of trade and undue influence. In *Stone Roses*, the court emphasised the difference between the parties, in terms of experience and expertise, although in *George Michael* the court took the view that this was of only limited relevance.

BROAD APPROACH TO FAIRNESS

It's often argued that, as breaking new talent in the music industry is such a high-risk business, wide restrictions are justified, although this proposition wasn't accepted in *Frankie Goes To Hollywood*. However, it will form part of the factual matrix by which the court considers the restrictions in question, and the proposition will therefore have some relevance in the court's balancing of the parties' interests.

AVAILABILITY OF LEGAL ADVICE

The fact that an artist has taken expert independent legal advice won't of itself render restrictions reasonable (although it will assist a manager, publisher or record company in demonstrating that this is the case); the court must also ask itself in each case whether the contract was fair at the time that it was concluded. If legal advice from a lawyer experienced in matters concerning the music industry was unavailable, this may well be relevant to any consideration of inequality of bargaining power. In *Stone Roses*, for example, the court stressed that the knowledge of the industry lawyers would extend to the state of the market, an appreciation of the impact of various terms and the state of the law on entertainment contracts generally. The availability of expert independent legal advice is also an important factor in determining whether to apply the doctrine of undue influence.

RELEASE COMMITMENT

In the context of a recording agreement, the absence of an obligation to exploit the product of an artist's services may arouse the court's suspicions that the exclusive nature of a recording agreement could sterilise the artist's career, therefore increasing the likelihood of the court arriving at a finding of unreasonableness. In *Schroeder*, the court thought that some positive obligation on a publisher was necessary – maybe not as much as a positive commitment to publish the work of an unknown composer, but possibly a statement to the effect that the publisher would use their best endeavours to promote the composer's work. In *Frankie Goes To Hollywood*, the court was critical of the absolute discretion given to the record company, by which it could refuse to release records and yet still have the copyright in unreleased recordings assigned to it.

In *Stone Roses*, the record company wouldn't have been saved by an amendment which it had proposed, requiring it to allow a third party, 'chosen by mutual agreement', to release records if it had later declined to do so. In this case, there were still no guarantees in place to the effect that the records would ever be released.

In *George Michael*, the record company's only obligation was to release three singles in the UK and the US. However, if it didn't release albums in the UK, the artist could serve notice requiring release, and if this release wasn't carried out then the contract would terminate. Elsewhere, the artist compel the record company to enter into good-faith negotiations with third parties to license unreleased albums. The court took the view that there was no real risk that the record company wouldn't release the artist's records, and that to recognise any such risk would be a 'distortion of commercial reality'.

TERMINATION

If the manager, publisher or record company alone has the right to terminate an agreement, this could be viewed as having the effect of making restrictions unreasonable. In *Schroeder*, the publisher could terminate whenever it wished, but the composer had no right of termination by contract at all. This was also the case in *Frankie Goes To Hollywood* and *Stone Roses*.

RIGHTS OF CONSULTATION

In the context of a recording agreement, if the artist has a right of consultation concerning the choice of material to be exploited – the producer, the recording budget and the acceptance of masters, etc – this will improve the chances of the agreement being found to be enforceable. Compare *Frankie Goes To Hollywood* (in which the record company had the last word), *Stone Roses* (in which the artists had no artistic control whatsoever) and *George Michael* (in which the artist had wide artistic control).

LEAVING-MEMBER PROVISIONS

In the context of a recording agreement, these may be considered to unreasonably restrict the artist. For example, see *Frankie Goes To Hollywood*, in which a clause required both a leaving member's new band to be acceptable to the record company and to be procured to enter into an agreement on the same terms as the band, and also that any new member could only be allowed to join if approved by the record company and if he signed the same deal as the rest of the band. Although this issue may be relevant to management agreements, it's generally dealt with differently in those cases and is a point on which the courts have yet to provide guidance.

POST-TERMINATION PROVISIONS

In the case involving The Stone Roses, the court thought that the inclusion of a ten-year post-term restriction on re-recording in a recording agreement was excessive. In *George Michael*, the court took the view that a three-year restriction was reasonable, and was indeed usual in recording agreements. In *Shaun Ryder*, the court was strongly critical of a provision included in a management agreement which gave the manager a right to commission on an album both recorded and released after the end of the term of the management agreement. It observed that it could see no legitimate basis for this, and also stated that it wasn't persuaded that commissioning post-term indefinitely, at the full rate of commission, was reasonable.

UNLIMITED RIGHT OF ASSIGNMENT

In *Stone Roses*, the court was critical of the record company's right to assign its interest. In *George Michael*, however, it decided that the right of assignment involved a remote risk of detriment to the artist. This point may have some significance in relation to an agreement with a management company (rather than an individual) in which a right of assignment granted to the company isn't linked to an appropriate key-man provision.

PUBLIC POLICY

If the restrictions pass the first limb of the Nordenfelt test, the court should go on to consider the second limb: are the restrictions reasonable as a matter of public policy? The person challenging the contract (ie the artist) will have to shoulder the burden of proving that it's unreasonable on this basis. The restrictions will therefore be presumed to be reasonable on grounds of public policy unless the artist can demonstrate to the contrary.

Almost all cases concerning the enforceability of music-industry agreements are fought on the basis of reasonableness between the parties – ie the first limb of the Nordenfelt test, rather than the second. However, in practice it's very difficult to separate the two. It's in the public interest that contracts containing restrictions which are reasonable between the parties should thus be enforceable, and it's therefore difficult to envisage a situation in which the terms agreed by an artist are found to be reasonable between the parties and yet objectionable on grounds of public policy. An artist will consequently face considerable difficulties in satisfying the burden of proof under this limb of the Nordenfelt test once the manager, publisher or record company has demonstrated that the restrictions are reasonable between the parties. In *George Michael*, no grounds which pertained to the second limb of Nordenfelt were put forward by the artist. However, as noted above, the court relied on a consideration of public policy in deciding that the contract wouldn't attract the restraint-of-trade doctrine at all. them.

severance

THE DOCTRINE OF SEVERANCE
In those instances where a restriction is in fact a combination of several distinct promises, the court will be prepared to sever (ie strike out) those parts which it considers to be excessive in scope, the deletion of which will leave the remainder of the contract intact. However, any words which are to be removed must be 'clearly severable', which means that they must be independent of the rest of the clause in question and must be severable without their removal affecting the remaining part of the clause. For severance to be possible, there must be no need to add to or modify the remaining wording, the remaining terms must continue to be supported by adequate consideration and the character of the contract mustn't be changed by the removal of the wording in question so that it becomes wholly different to the contract into which the parties originally entered. This was stressed by the court in *Stone Roses*; the court would have changed the nature of the contract entirely if it had started introducing limitations, or if it had shortened the term of the contract (for example, by severing the last two option periods). In *Shaun Ryder*, the manager tried to shorten the term of the agreement by severing one of its two option periods, but the court wasn't prepared to accept this.

USE OF SEVERANCE CLAUSES
Parties who contract with artists often seek to use a clause which states that the parties agree to such modification of the contract as is necessary to render it valid and effective – ie inviting the court to sever objectionable clauses and leave the rest standing. While such clauses have received some support from the courts, there is a serious risk that they will be ineffective, as they amount to little more than an invitation to the court to rewrite the agreement if it's ever subject to litigation concerning its enforceability. They may also offend against the rule concerning certainty, in that the parties are agreeing to such terms as the court may consider enforceable at some time in the future. In *Stone Roses*, the court thought that this type of clause was objectionable on grounds of public policy, constituting an attempt by the record company to secure the enforcement of a contract which would otherwise be unenforceable.

effects of unreasonable restrictions

DIFFERENT TERMINOLOGY

Cases use various terms to describe the effects of contracts that constitute an unreasonable restraint of trade. They have variously been described as being 'void', 'voidable' or 'unenforceable'. The distinction is important, because if a contract is void it will, strictly speaking, be of no legal effect whatsoever. If it is voidable, it will be enforceable until a right of avoidance is exercised. If it is unenforceable, the contract will be valid in all respects, with the exception that one or both parties can't be sued over it.

UNPERFORMED OBLIGATIONS

In *Nordenfelt*, the court regarded offending restrictions as void, in line with the approach that the restrictions are to be considered at the date on which the contract was signed. However, the modern approach is that the obligations are unenforceable insofar as they remain unperformed (see *Esso* v *Harper*, *Schroeder* and *O'Sullivan* v *Management Agency and Music*, 1985 [the *Gilbert O'Sullivan* case]). This approach is open to criticism, in that the restraint is to be considered at the time at which the contract was signed, and also because it will allow the party seeking the restriction to obtain the contract's benefit up to the point at which the court determines that it's unenforceable. Nevertheless, this appears to be the current state of the law.

In the first-instance hearing in *George Michael*, the artist accepted the approach in *Schroeder*, although he reserved the right to argue on appeal that the agreement was void. The court's decision therefore didn't address this point.

UNDUE INFLUENCE

GENERAL APPROACH

Undue influence is a doctrine developed under what is known as the court's 'equitable jurisdiction', under which the aim is to achieve a level of fairness between parties to a dispute rather than the application of strict legal principles. The court will apply the principles of equity to set aside an unfair bargain. This is different to the doctrine of the restraint of trade in that, in this case, the court is concerned not with striking down clauses which amount to an unreasonable restraint of trade but instead with applying rules of justice to protect those in a weak and vulnerable position. Undue influence is based on a notion of moral reprehensibility rather than the unenforceability of unreasonable bargains in order to preserve free trade.

There are two categories of cases in which the court will set a transaction aside, as set out in the case of *Allcard v Skinner* (1887):

- Where influence was expressly used by one party to secure conclusion of an agreement (*express* or *actual* undue influence, where the court will strike the agreement down on the basis that it won't allow a person to benefit from their wrongful act);

- Where the relationship between the parties was such that a presumption of influence was raised (*presumed* undue influence, where the court will seek to prevent abuse of particular relationships on the basis of public policy).

In those cases which cover restraint of trade under music-industry agreements, we're generally dealing with the principles applicable to the second example here. The main music-industry precedents are *Gilbert O'Sullivan, Armatrading v Stone* (1984) and *Elton John v Richard Leon James* (1991, the *Elton John* case). The exertion of undue influence was also considered in *Shaun Ryder*, which was mentioned earlier in this chapter.

THE COURT'S APPROACH

An artist will need to prove two things to bring the presumption of undue influence into operation:

(i) That the relationship between the parties was such that the manager, publisher or record company was in a position to exert influence over the artist.

The court will consider the particular facts of each case to determine whether such a relationship exists (see *Joan Armatrading*). General guidance was given in a case called *Goldsworthy v Brickell* (1987), in which the court stated that it was necessary for there to be a degree of trust and confidence such that the party in whom it is focused is in a position to influence the other into effecting the transaction in question, either because they are the adviser of the other, they have become entrusted with the management of the affairs of the other, or for some other reason.

The relationship required has been found to exist in relation to a recording artist's manager and music publisher. In *Gilbert O'Sullivan*, the artist signed a management agreement with an individual who also controlled companies with whom the artist signed publishing and recording agreements. It was held that there was a fiduciary relationship between the companies and the artist, in view of the level of involvement which the former had in the management of the latter's career. This was sufficient for the artist to found a claim for undue influence. In the case of *Elton John*, the artist was unknown at the time of signing a publishing agreement and completely in awe of the publisher, who was a giant in music publishing. There was no negotiation, and the artist received no legal advice on the terms proposed. The artist had trusted that the publisher would treat him fairly on the basis of the publisher's stature in the industry.

It's interesting to note that, in *Shaun Ryder*, the manager didn't even attempt to dispute that the necessary relationship existed.

(ii) That the artist entered into a transaction which was so manifestly and unfairly disadvantageous to him that this couldn't be reasonably explained by the ordinary motives on which people ordinarily act.

It's necessary to show that the manager, publisher or record company has obtained an unfair advantage by acting in a morally reprehensible way. The court has stressed that this goes beyond showing that terms were objectively unreasonable. In *Elton John*, the artist was exclusively bound for a period of six years and assigned copyright in all of his output during this period to the publisher (even though there was no commitment on the part of the publisher to publish any of the artist's work). In exchange, the artist had a right to modest royalties. The court regarded this as an unfair bargain, even though the publisher had acted in good faith and had not intended to act unfairly regarding the terms imposed as the industry standard at the time.

In *Shaun Ryder*, the court identified one particular provision which, in its view, demonstrated manifest disadvantage to the artist. This was a clause entitling the manager to commission an album which was both recorded and released after the expiration of the term under the management agreement.

In the event that the artist proves that these two criteria have been met, the transaction will then be set aside unless the manager, publisher or record company can rebut the presumption of undue influence by proving that the artist was acting in circumstances which enabled him to exercise an independent will, free from the influence of the manager, publisher or record company, and that the artist had a full appreciation of what he was doing. The fact that an artist has had independent legal advice won't necessarily be sufficient to rebut the presumption, although this is likely to assist the manager, publisher or record company. It should also be noted that, if the artist misunderstands the advice, or is given possibly erroneous advice, the court won't set aside the agreement if he otherwise understood the nature of the transaction and acted with a free will. The manager, publisher or record company will be assisted in rebutting the presumption if it can show that the independent legal adviser used by the artist was expert in the negotiation of music-industry agreements.

In *Shaun Ryder*, the artist wasn't overtly pressurised to sign the management agreement, yet the court considered the following circumstances to show that the manager had failed to rebut the presumption of undue influence: the artist's lawyer had amended a draft of the management agreement proposed by the manager's lawyer; the manager took a draft which omitted those amendments to a studio to get the artist to sign it; and the manager knew that the artist had difficulty with paperwork and was likely to be under the influence of drugs, and hoped that the artist would simply sign it without consulting his lawyer further – which, in fact, he did.

FINDING UNDUE INFLUENCE

If a finding of undue influence has been established, the agreement will be held to be voidable (ie enforceable only until a right of avoidance is exercised). The artist will therefore be entitled to have the contract set aside and seek to be restored to his original position, and in principle the court will be prepared to order that this should happen. However, as undue influence is part of the court's equitable jurisdiction, the court will seek to obtain justice between the parties on the facts of the particular case. This may involve the manager, publisher or record company accounting to the artist for any profit obtained under the agreement, although in an appropriate case the court may permit retention of reasonable remuneration for work done. (See *Gilbert O'Sullivan*, in which the defendant was permitted to retain some profit to reflect its contribution to the artist's success.)

equitable defences

A claim for undue influence will be subject to defeat by various defences available under the court's equitable jurisdiction (known as *equitable defences*). The most relevant of these, for our purposes, are the defences of laches and acquiescence.

LACHES

Laches are essentially delays in the time it takes to prosecute a claim, such that it wouldn't be reasonable to allow the claim to be raised against the other party. If an artist delays in taking action once he becomes dissatisfied with their agreement, a defence may be available to the manager, publisher or record company on this basis. The artist will be at particular risk if he delays taking action once the agreement in question has expired (see *Elton John*).

ACQUIESCENCE

This is essentially what happens when a party to an agreement induces the other party – by its clear, unequivocal and deliberate conduct – to believe that the agreement won't be challenged. Conduct by an artist which indicates that he won't seek to challenge a manager, publisher or record agreement may provide a manager, publisher or record company with a defence on this ground.

THE TREATY OF ROME

Article 85 (1)

The Treaty Of Rome is a piece of European legislation which is applicable under English law. The provision which could potentially be used to seek to challenge the enforceability of music-industry agreements is Article 85 (1), which is aimed at promoting free trade within the European Community. The relevant wording from Article 85 (1) is as follows:

The following shall be prohibited as incompatible with the common market: all agreements between undertakings…which may affect trade between Member States and which have as their object or effect the prevention, restriction or distortion of competition within the common market…

MUSIC INDUSTRY AGREEMENTS

We don't yet have a case on the application of Article 85 (1) to a management or publishing agreement. Its application to a recording agreement, however, was considered in *George Michael*, although in that particular case the artist relied considerably on the evidence which he'd gathered in relation to his case on restraint of trade rather than producing any further evidence to support his case on Article 85. The court therefore made its decision in the absence of evidence directed to the various issues raised. The outcome of the case – ie that Article 85 didn't apply to the agreement in question and that, even if it had applied, the artist's claim on this basis would have failed – could well have been different if any evidence had been specifically provided to support the point.

The burden of proof will be on the artist to establish that the contract in question contravenes Article 85 (1). The artist will have to show:

(i)   That both he and the manager, publisher or record company are 'undertakings'.

The application of Article 85 (1) to performers' agreements was considered in the *Rai/Unitel* case (1978). It's clear that an artist will be an undertaking when he exploits his performances commercially. There was no dispute in *George Michael* that the artist was an undertaking.

(ii)   That the agreement may affect trade between member states of the Community.

Trade must be affected to an 'appreciable extent'. The contract must be considered in each case in its legal, economic and commercial context, which will require a detailed examination of the surrounding facts and, in particular, the operation of the market in question. It's important to note that, while under the restraint-of-trade doctrine a contract is examined as it applied on the date it was signed, Article 85 is perambulatory – the court will look at its effect in practice.

In *George Michael*, the court took the view that this was a preliminary requirement which the artist had to establish before looking at 'object' and 'effect' (see [iii] below).

It's important to consider the market which is being addressed when considering whether trade may be affected. In *George Michael*, two distinct markets were considered: the market for the artist's services themselves (the 'raw material') and the market for recordings of the artist's performances (the 'end product' of the artist's services). The court found that 'the market for the services of UK recording artists in the pop field…is a purely national and domestic market', and that 'there is no Community-wide market for the services of UK recording artists in the field of popular music, since…only in exceptional cases will UK recording artists sign to a non-UK recording company'. There was therefore no market (and no trade) between member states which could be affected by the agreement in question, and the artist's claim under Article 85 fell at this first hurdle.

157

The court nevertheless went on to consider whether (assuming that there was a Community-wide market for the UK artist's services) the agreement in question would have affected trade between member states. It held that it wouldn't, on a number of bases. As far as the 'raw material' was concerned, this was because there was insufficient evidence provided by the artist to show that trade would be affected in either a legal, commercial or economic context. In addition, the court had to look at the position in the market for the agreement in question. As the artist hadn't attempted to challenge a prior recording agreement by which he was bound, his claim on this point couldn't even get off the ground because, if the agreement in dispute hadn't existed, he would still have been restricted by the earlier agreement. With regard to the 'end product', there was no evidence of the record company's distribution system and the court therefore couldn't conclude that trade between member states would have been affected.

(iii)   That the agreement must have as its object or effect the prevention, restriction or distortion of competition within the common market. In considering the 'object', the court applies an objective test. It won't look at the intentions of either parties, but will instead try to discover whether, as a matter of fact, the agreement has an anti-competitive effect.

In *George Michael*, the court again went on to consider this aspect, even though it had already found that the artist would fail under Article 85. It held that the object was in fact the promotion of competition (ie the release of a new end product onto the market). The court thought that the artist's suggestion that the recording agreement was intended to prevent anyone from exploiting his recordings was a distortion of commercial reality.

The court should look at all of the surrounding circumstances in considering the *effect* of the agreement in question. There is a substantial overlap with the considerations in (ii) above.

The artist also failed on this ground in *George Michael*. This was on the basis that there was no market for raw material outside the UK, and that the restrictions on the exploitation of masters in the agreement were no more than was reasonable and didn't have an anti-competitive effect, and that, because Article 222 of The Treaty Of Rome excludes property ownership from the ambit of Article 85, the rules concerning competition wouldn't apply to the provisions relating to assignment of copyright in masters to the record company.

THE EFFECT OF ARTICLE 85

The agreement is rendered void automatically (see Article 85 [2]). In addition, there is a risk of substantial fines being imposed by the European Commission.

CLEARING AN AGREEMENT WITH THE EC

It's possible to apply to the Commission for a declaration that Article 85 doesn't apply to an agreement ('negative clearance') or to apply to the Commission for an exemption under Article 85 (3).

ENGLISH COURTS

Despite the decision in *George Michael*, it's clear that the court continues to regard recording contracts as agreements to which the principles of restraint of trade and undue influence are readily applicable. The balance between the interests of a record company and its artist therefore continues to be a very delicate one. Record companies can't rely on the sanctity of a contract which will apply to most of their contractual dealings with third parties, and they therefore make absolutely sure that, in each individual case, with each artist, every effort is made to ensure that they take no more protection than is adequate to safeguard their legitimate interests, and that any restrictions to which artists agree are commensurate with the benefits which they receive. It's undoubtedly the case that agreements with management and publishing companies containing restrictions will also continue to attract the attention of the courts, as has been demonstrated by the *Shaun Ryder* case. Again, a delicate balancing exercise of the parties' interests is required if the risk of a finding of restraint of trade or undue influence is to be minimised.

While there's a clear distinction between the principles of restraint of trade and undue influence, on occasion the courts use language more appropriate to the latter when discussing the former. We don't yet have a sufficient body of cases to see whether the courts are in fact using the restraint-of-trade doctrine to achieve the same end as undue influence (ie the protection of the weak). However, this is certainly consistent with the decisions to date. When young, inexperienced musicians have been involved, the courts have refused to enforce the agreements in question (see *Schroeder, Frankie Goes To*

Hollywood and *Stone Roses*). The case involving George Michael, on the other hand, involved an artist who had already achieved a considerable measure of success in his own right. The court appeared to have little sympathy for his position, and the agreement was thus held to be enforceable.

The availability of expert legal advice to the artist continues to be of great importance, in relation to the application of both restraint of trade and undue influence. If expert legal advice isn't provided, there will be a serious risk that agreements will be found to be unenforceable and voidable. The fact that the artist's lawyer's input was 'sidelined' in *Shaun Ryder* (ie the manager obtained the artist's signature on a contract which omitted the artist's lawyer's amendments) undoubtedly weighed against the manager.

Article 85 of The Treaty Of Rome may yet prove to be a potent weapon in the hands of artists. In *George Michael*, the court was presented with very little evidence on this issue. In this case, the court found that Article 85 didn't apply, as the specific market for the services of UK recording artists was limited to the UK. If evidence had been presented on this aspect, it could well have been demonstrated that this wasn't in fact the case; and if evidence had been presented on the further requirements of Article 85, it's possible that a claim under this could have been sustained.

PRACTICAL ASPECTS OF ENFORCEABILITY

In an ideal world, a manager, publisher or record company would have to regard the following with each contract signed. In practical terms, this is likely to be a counsel of perfection. They are, however, points worth bearing in mind.

- When a draft contract is prepared, ideally the manager, publisher or record company should be in a position to demonstrate that it has considered what it regards to be its legitimate interests, and has designed the restrictions contained in the contract to provide no more protection than is necessary to adequately safeguard these.

- It's important that draft contracts should be tailor made to each signing. If a smaller deal is proposed, more limited restrictions are likely to increase the manager's, publisher's or record company's chances of making them stick.

- The manager, publisher or record company runs a serious risk of a successful challenge to the contract if there is no negotiation of the main terms set out in it, or if the artist isn't represented by a lawyer with experience of the music industry.

- The agreement is more likely to be found to be valid and enforceable if the artist is given rights in relation to artistic matters.

- Post-termination provisions are very sensitive, particularly if they're likely to have the effect of sterilising an artist's career after termination has taken place.

the schedule

This section will investigate those legitimate interests which record companies seek to protect by use of restrictions in recording agreements in relation to those cases in which they became major factors.

THE FRANKIE GOES TO HOLLYWOOD CASE

- For every successful artist, there are a multitude of failures. It's therefore reasonable – and in the interests of everyone in the music business – that successful artists should be tied to their record companies so that the companies can over time be compensated for the costs of unsuccessful artists;

- The second record by an artist has much more chance of being successful if the first has been. The record company should therefore have the right to subsequent records in order to justify its investment in earlier ones.

THE GEORGE MICHAEL CASE

- The desire to sell as many records as possible;

- The desire to ensure that there's an even and adequate flow of product;

- The desire to be able to plan ahead;

161

- The desire to have proven successful product available for as long as possible;

- The desire and need to be able to compete on equal terms in an international environment against other record companies which have long-term signings;

- The desire to be known for continued high-calibre releases by long-term successful artists in order to maintain a reputation with consumers, dealers and new unsigned artists;

- The desire to maintain morale and enthusiasm amongst employees;

- The desire and need to recover the investment made in a particular artist;

- The desire to make a profit on that investment;

- The need to have sufficient product available to finance losses on unsuccessful product and the fixed costs of the infrastructure (including overheads);

- The desire to accumulate property rights as an asset;

- The desire to have a supply of successful product in the future at reasonable and predictable prices.

5 Producer Contracts

By Andrew Thompson

This chapter deals with the typical agreement between a major record company and a producer in relation to the production of a given number of tracks by a particular artist. It also looks briefly at the type of arrangements which may be made when a major record company is not involved.

In terms of the legal issues, a producer contract is more straightforward than a recording contract or a publishing contract. There is no exclusivity and there are no restraints. Essentially, the producer contract deals with what the producer has to do and what he should be paid. Nevertheless, in practice it is often hard to resolve these issues. It is therefore sometimes difficult to secure a signed contract. Whilst it is rare for a record company to put an artist in the recording studio without a signed recording contract, this cannot be said of producers, in that it is too often the case that producer contracts are only signed after the event.

PART 1: PRODUCERS

1.0 the problem of delay

1.1 CONFUSION

There are several reasons for the frequent delays in concluding deals for producers. One reason is poor communication between the A&R department of the record company and its Business Affairs department. The Business Affairs person may only come to hear of the deal after the pre-production work has started. Even if he is aware of the position, he may have difficulty in obtaining clear instructions from the A&R man as to what the producer is required to do and what he is to be paid. This is not necessarily due to the fault of the A&R man; there is often a reluctance on everybody's part to commit to (and define the parameters of) a particular project until the producer and the artist are seen to be able to work together effectively.

The position is sometimes made worse by poor communication between the producer, the record company and the artist. The preliminary discussions will concentrate upon artistic issues. In the case of most artists (and many A&R men) there is an in-built reluctance to discuss money or anything businesslike. Many producers suffer from the same malaise and tend to be shy (particularly when talking to artists) of raising the matter of their deals. Most such producers will engage a manager, and eventually there may be a businesslike discussion with the A&R man. As a result, the producer or his manager may think that he has agreed something in principle. Too often he will subsequently find that the business affairs man thinks otherwise.

1.2 INERTIA

It is important that any confusion is clarified at the earliest opportunity before this degenerates into a period of inertia so far as the deal making process is concerned. The risk of inertia arises partly because nobody (and this usually includes the producer) is prepared to treat the matter of the deal as one of priority. The producer is too busy building his relationship with the artist and in any event may well be in the studio day and night.

For the producer's lawyer, the producer's agreement is a dull affair when set against the excitement of a recording contract or publishing deal for a 'hot' artist. Similarly, the Business Affairs manager will view his batch of producer agreements as the most dreary part of his workload. The record-company executives may pester him as to why the latest hopeful has not yet signed his recording contract, but there is unlikely to be any internal pressure to deal with a producer agreement (other than in the rare event of a much needed producer refusing to work until his deal has been properly sorted out.) Moreover, there is no incentive for the record company to hurry because, generally, it will refuse to make any final payment until there is a signed contract. Part 2 discusses how best to overcome this inertia.

2.0 the role of the producer

2.1 THE SCAPEGOAT

The producer is the 'translator' of the artist's ideas. The artist may think that he is the best person to decide how to approach a particular recording but in many ways an artist may be too close to his art to do this. There is invariably great antipathy on the part of A&R departments towards the idea of artists producing themselves because this too often leads to over-indulgence. In one sense, therefore, the producer's role is to deal with any conflict of interest between the record company's commercial motives and the artist's creativity. This will often mean that the producer is on a hiding to nothing. He cannot please both the artist and the record company and, whatever goes wrong, he will always be the most convenient scapegoat.

2.2 PRE-PRODUCTION

Producers vary considerably in how they interpret their role and in what they actually do. Some producers may not wish to spend all day and night in the studio and may prefer to delegate some of the technical aspects of production to the technicians and engineers. This type of producer may be more interested in the process of the selection and rejection of songs and in how those songs should be arranged. He will be involved in rehearsal sessions and in the selection of the various backing musicians, etc. Some producers view this whole pre-production phase as the most crucial part of their responsibilities. However, most producers will accept that they should be in charge of the whole process in a hands-on sense and will wish to be in the studio at all times.

2.3 BUDGETARY CONTROL

The record company will invariably impose upon the producer responsibility for budgetary control. More mundanely, the producer will usually be responsible for booking the studio and for all of the form filling (including the Musicians' Union session forms and notifying the record company of the use of any samples).

2.4 SAMPLES

The record companies ensure that their position in relation to the use of samples is protected as fully as possible. The artist will be required in the recording contract to give certain warranties in relation to the use of samples. Separately, the record company will require additional protection in its contract with the producer. It will generally be the producer's responsibility to notify the record company immediately in the event of the use of any samples.

Sometimes, it will be the producer's responsibility to obtain clearance for the sample in question, although usually the record company will accept responsibility for obtaining clearances. Nevertheless, the record company will invariably insist that, for contractual purposes, a particular master will not be deemed to have been delivered until all necessary clearances are in place. This will often mean that the producer is in the hands of the record company in terms of when delivery is finally to be effected (if at all) so that any further advance due upon delivery may be paid. In order to overcome this difficulty, producers will sometimes prepare different versions of a track, ie one with the sample and one without

2.5 SONGWRITING

If the producer is crucially involved in the arrangements for a particular song, so that the recorded version of that song is substantially different from the original demo prepared by the songwriter, then arguably the final version will represent a new arrangement, and the producer (as the arranger) will have an interest in the copyright. For this reason, some producers insist upon being credited as a co-writer of the musical material.

Generally, this practice is frowned upon. The producer's advance and his royalty entitlement compensates the producer for all of his work, and whilst, arguably, that work may stray into the area of musical composition, nevertheless it is rarely accepted that the producer's involvement is such that he should be treated not only as the record producer but also as a co-writer/composer.

Sometimes, of course, the producer may have a genuine involvement in the songwriting. Either his songs will be recorded or he will co-write the material with the artist. In these circumstances, the producer will earn separately from the exploitation of the publishing rights in his contribution to the musical material.

In this event, there is one common pitfall which the producer should try to avoid. Most producer agreements contain controlled compositions clauses (see Chapter 2, Part 2, Section 8.0). As we have seen, the effect of controlled compositions provisions is generally to reduce a writer's income from mechanical royalties in respect of record sales in the USA and Canada. On occasions, the producer may succeed in deleting provisions of this kind, but this may simply have the effect of transferring the problem to the artist in that, if in the recording contract the controlled compositions provisions extend to any material written not only by the artist but also any producer, then if the producer succeeds in securing full mechanical royalties for himself, the reduction will instead be applied against the artist's share of the mechanical royalties.

2.6 MIXERS

Some producers are not really producers at all; instead, they belong to that special breed known as *mixers*. These people have little or no involvement with the artists, but they are technical wizards. They take the multitracks and remix them by whatever means to create a better (or at least different) sound.

All material needs to be mixed, so the mixing is simply one of many functions generally carried out by the producer. Some producers prefer to use a specialist mixer to carry out the mixing function, although usually the producer would wish to supervise this.

Sometimes the record company will be unhappy with the work done by the producer (and may therefore refuse to pay the advance due on delivery). In this case, rather than start again, the record company may decide to use the existing material but arrange for another producer or a specialist remixer to rework the existing material. On other occasions, there may be no criticism of the original producer but the record company may decide that, for marketing reasons, it requires a specialist remix of a particular track. In the case of dance music, in particular, several different remixes of the same basic track may be released.

2.7 DELIVERY STANDARD

Ultimately, the producer's responsibility will be to deliver finished recordings to the record company of a technically acceptable standard and, often, to a standard which is commercially acceptable to the record company. In fact, this is often the first area of controversy. Usually, all or part of the producer's advance will be deferred pending delivery of the masters. If the record company insists upon 'commercially' acceptable masters, then the producer will be nervous that at the end of the day the record company will decide that it does not like what it has been given and may, therefore, refuse to make payment.

Many producers are not prepared to accept this, but equally some record companies adamantly refuse to give up this protection. Some companies have a reputation for being difficult over the final payment and will refuse to make this unless and until the A&R department is 100% satisfied with the work. Accordingly, the argument over this issue may continue until the work has been completed. At that point, with luck, the record company will decide that it is happy with what has been done. An acknowledgement to this effect is then inserted in the contract, which is then signed and the advance is paid.

3.0 the record producer's rights

3.1 FINANCIAL ENTITLEMENT

The record company will usually take the convenient view that the producer has no rights in the recordings. It is precisely for this reason that the record company is rather relaxed about allowing the work to proceed despite the fact that there is no signed contract. As far as the record company is concerned, the producer has no rights other than the right to be paid for his work. This entitlement will be to receive such payment as may have been agreed. If there is confusion over what has been agreed, then nevertheless the producer is entitled to be paid on what is known as a *quantum meruit* basis – ie a fair and reasonable payment for the work done.

3.2 THE 'MAKER' OF THE RECORDINGS

As far as the record company is concerned, it is the maker of the recordings, and so is the owner of the copyright in those recordings. The record company does not require any performers consents from the producer because his 'performance' is not (usually) featured upon the recordings. Nor has the producer (usually) contributed to the writing and/or composing of the musical material featured upon the recordings, so the producer has no interest in that material.

Accordingly, the record company would argue, there is nothing the producer may do to prevent the company exploiting the material (beyond suing for payment). Any threat on the part of the producer to hold the company to ransom over his deal by threatening to make an application for an interlocutory injunction to prevent the release of the recordings is likely to be ineffective.

3.3 THE PRODUCER AS 'MAKER'

In fact, there is an argument to the effect that the producer does have an interest in the recordings so that the record company is perhaps being dangerously complacent.

Under the provisions of the Copyright Act 1956, the person owning the copyright in a recording was the person commissioning that recording. The position changed with the introduction of the Copyright Designs and Patents Act 1988, under which the owner of the copyright is defined as 'the person by whom the arrangements necessary for the making of the recording are undertaken'.

The following is an extract from the submissions by REPRO (the trade organisation then representing the interests of record producers but which was subsequently relaunched, in March 1999, as The Music Producers' Guild) made to the Monopolies and Mergers Commission in 1994 in relation to its enquiry into the supply in the UK of recorded music:

> We have recently taken the opinion of a leading QC who specialises in copyright law in order to determine the question of authorship of sound recordings which are subject to the 1988 Act. His unequivocal view is that a record producer is a person who undertakes the arrangements necessary for a recording to be made. If a record producer undertakes all of these arrangements alone then he or she is the sole author of the recording concerned. Where

those arrangements are undertaken jointly by the record company and the record producer authorship is shared between them. In any event, whenever a record producer is engaged by a record company he or she will always be at least joint owner. Section 11 of the 1988 Act provides that the author of a sound recording is the first owner of the copyright in that sound recording. In passing the 1988 Act Parliament also decided to drop the provisions in the 1956 Act which vested copyright in sound recordings in any person who commissioned their making. The fact that the record companies commission and pay for the making of sound recordings is now irrelevant to the question of ownership of copyright in recordings made after the introduction of the 1988 Act. It follows that under the new law record producers are at the very least one of the authors and first owners of the copyright in recordings produced by them.

3.4 ASSIGNMENT OF RIGHTS

A prudent record company would therefore ensure that, prior to commencement of recording, the producer made an unequivocal assignment in writing of his interest (if any) in the recordings. If the record companies were to recognise such a requirement, this might introduce a note of greater urgency into the whole negotiating process.

4.0 credit

This is usually of great importance to the producer. The form of credit should be agreed at the outset and an obligation should be imposed on the record company to ensure that all records bear the proper credit. The company may also be persuaded to feature the credit on paid advertising material. Sometimes a record company will accept that it may not engage another producer to carry out work on the recordings without the producer's prior consent. If there is no such restriction, the producer should insist upon being given a listening copy of any recording which features his work together with that of another producer, and he should have the right to insist, at his election, that his credit be removed.

PART 2: THE CONTRACT

1.0 the parties to the contract

1.1 UK AND US APPROACHES

Usually (although not always), the first contact with the producer is from the A&R man rather than from the artist or the artist's manager. It is usually the record company which pays all the recording costs, and of course the record company owns the recordings. Invariably, the form of contract is generated by the record company's Business Affairs person. The automatic assumption might, therefore, be that the producer will enter into a contract with the record company.

However, this is not necessarily so. The American record companies invariably refuse to enter into any contract with a producer; instead they insist that the artist or the artist's production company enters into the agreement. In this way, the record company shrugs off any responsibility for the producer and neatly sidesteps any potential contractual difficulties. With luck, the company will even be able to persuade the artist's lawyer to deal with the paperwork.

Fortunately, in the majority of cases, the UK record companies have not yet abdicated responsibility for producers in this way and are still prepared to contract with them direct.

1.2 DIRECT ACCOUNTING

The producer will always prefer to contract with the record company rather than the artist because this will improve his chances of being paid. This is not to suggest any dishonesty on the part of the artist; it is simply a question of cashflow and financial stability.

Also, a right of audit against an artist is more or less worthless. A right of audit needs to bring with it the right to inspect the record company's books and records of account. The problem is partially solved if the producer's agreement is with the artist (or some intermediary production company), but this is coupled with suitable direct accounting arrangements.

The producer should not be satisfied with a simple letter of direction from the artist to the record company requesting the company to pay the producer's royalties and to deduct them from any royalties payable to the artist. If the producer is to be properly protected, there needs in effect to be a separate contract between the producer and the record company. The best solution is a tri-partite agreement in the form of an irrevocable letter of instruction from the artist to the company countersigned by the producer but in which some 'consideration' is shown to move from the producer to the record company in order to create a legally binding commitment. The consideration might be the nominal sum of £1.

1.3 STANDARD FORMS

The MMF Producer Managers Group has introduced a preferred form of contract. The intention is that the various record companies should be persuaded to adopt this form of contract in an effort to reduce the delays and aggravations generally involved in agreeing a suitable form of contract on a case-by-case basis. In the case of many well-established producers, a form of contract will be agreed in relation to a particular project with each record company for whom the producer often undertakes work so that – again, as a shortcut – each time the producer undertakes work for the company in question, the same form of contract will be used as a template for the new deal (although the principal terms of this will vary case by case).

2.0 the deal memorandum

2.1 DRIVING THE DEAL

How does the producer overcome any preliminary confusion over his deal? He needs to know with certainty what he is to be paid, when he will be paid and by whom. In order to overcome the inertia which usually prevails, some strong-minded character has to get a grip of the deal and then needs to show some tenacity in driving that deal through. It is difficult and probably inappropriate for the producer to attempt to do this himself. The artist will usually be of no use. The artist's manager may go through the motions, but he has no authority to make any commitment on behalf of the record company.

The record company cannot be relied upon. The person to drive the deal is either the producer's manager (if he has one) or his lawyer.

2.2 PAYING THE LAWYER

If the task falls to the producer's lawyer, some thought should be given at the outset to the question of who pays the lawyer's fees. The record company will not contribute towards them. The producer will be liable for them in the first instance, but there should perhaps be an arrangement of some kind between the producer and his manager as to who bears the costs.

Arrangements between producers and their managers vary considerably. Often, the manager will charge 20% commission but will provide a complete service in the sense that the manager will not only secure the work and negotiate the principal terms but will also drive the deal through with minimal or even no involvement on the part of any outside lawyer. Other managers charge 20% but rely heavily upon a lawyer's input and agree to bear the legal fees out of the 20% commission. Others charge 10% (which is rare) or 15% but expect the producer to bear any legal fees.

What is fair and reasonable in a particular case will depend entirely upon the nature of the relationship and the value to the producer of the particular services provided. However, it would generally be unfair for a manager to charge a producer 20% commission but rely heavily upon the producer's lawyer to drive through the deal on the basis that the producer has to bear the legal fees in addition to the commission. For a lawyer, time is money, and if the lawyer is charged with the responsibility for negotiating the principal terms and/or of then driving the deal (rather than simply dealing at a gentlemanly pace with the paperwork), a lot of time will be needed and this will be expensive.

2.3 DISTRIBUTION OF THE DEAL MEMORANDUM

At the first available opportunity, the person charged with responsibility for the deal should issue a deal memorandum. At this stage, the lines of communication will still be tangled, and it is therefore important that everybody is provided with a copy of the deal. A copy should be sent to the artist's manager, possibly to the artist himself, certainly to the artist's lawyer, to the head of Business Affairs at the record company, to the A&R person responsible and probably to the managing director of the record company for good measure.

The trick is to secure agreement to the deal memorandum as quickly as possible so that based upon this the producer may commence work in the studio without undue risk. If, as is usual, the producer cannot be persuaded to hold back until there is clear agreement on all material terms before he starts work, then all the more reason to keep up the pressure to secure agreement to the principal terms of the deal before work progresses too far.

2.4 CONTENTS OF THE DEAL MEMORANDUM

For this reason, the memo should not be bogged down with detail, but it should cover all of the material terms together with those aspects of the deal which often prove controversial. It should, therefore, deal with the following points, the significance of which is more fully explained (where necessary) below:

2.4.1   The contract must be with the record company itself.

2.4.2   The number of tracks to be recorded.

2.4.3   The advance per track (or the overall advance for the entire project).

2.4.4   When the advances will be paid.

2.4.5   The rate of royalty together with any escalations in this rate and whether the royalty is to be calculated at that rate by reference to the dealer or retail price.

2.4.6   For clarification purposes, the royalty rate is to apply worldwide (if indeed this is the case) rather than be subject to the same *pro rata* territorial reductions suffered by the artist. Likewise format reductions.

2.4.7   The royalty is to be paid subject only to recoupment of the advance and is not to be subject to recoupment of any recording costs nor deferred pending such recoupment.

2.4.8   The recording budget should be specified, but it should be made clear that the producer will have no responsibility for any excess costs unless those costs have been incurred by reason of wilful neglect or default on the part of the producer.

2.4.9   The producer will require A-/B-side protection.

2.4.10   The royalty is not to be reduced by the amount of any royalty payable to any other producer or mixer engaged in relation to the recordings in question.

2.4.11   The credit requirements.

3.0 urgency

The producer may have to compromise on some of these issues, but if he is to secure his position in relation to them then he has to do so quickly. It is no good arguing any of these points after the work has been completed; the record company will simply dig in its heels.

When the deal memorandum is circulated, it should be accompanied by a request for copies of the relevant extracts from the artist's recording contract showing the detailed royalty calculation and payment provisions, but perhaps indicating that the producer will be willing to accept that his royalties will be calculated in the same manner, provided that the provisions are reasonable.

It is usually a mistake to relax and wait for a response to the memo; there very often will be no response within a sensible time frame. The next stage is to hound all of those concerned on the telephone. If there is both a lawyer and manager involved, they should both take part in this process.

PART 3: MONEY

1.O what is the producer worth?

1.1 BASIC CONCEPTS

The producer is generally entitled to a royalty so that his efforts will be rewarded according to the level of success achieved. The producer will rarely have any involvement in the promotion or marketing of the record, so the level of success is not within his control. The producer will invariably require a fee for his work which will usually be treated as an advance against his royalty entitlement.

Producer royalties range usually from 2% of the dealer price to 5% of the dealer price, with most producers being paid 3% or 4%. Most producers (like the rest of us) think they are underpaid. Some people think that producers are generally overpaid. It is certainly true that successful producers are very wealthy, but few would begrudge them their rewards. Sometimes, a producer will be persuaded to work on the basis that no royalty will be payable. This is rare and is generally restricted to the production of superstar artists.

Some superstars resent having to pay a substantial proportion of their royalty income to a producer in circumstances where the reputation of the artist is already established. The superstar may notice that his royalty earnings from his last album were, let's say, £4 million but that £1 million of this was paid to his producer. Having a superstar's ego, he will wonder whether the producer's input on the last album justified so high a reward. He may not want to pay the producer another £1 million for spending six weeks with him in the studio recording the next album. The superstar may remember that the producer was paid an advance of £50,000 for the previous album, and he may decide that on this occasion he will generously offer £250,000 (not bad for six weeks' work), but on the basis that this represents a buyout of all rights so that no further royalties will be payable.

Given that the artist is a superstar, no doubt the producer is also from the top drawer. He will be insulted by the suggestion that he should work on a record and have no royalty entitlement and will reject the proposal out of hand.

If the superstar persists and if the producer needs the £250,000 badly enough (perhaps he hasn't made a sufficient tax reserve in relation to earnings from the last album), the superstar may succeed.

1.2   ARTIST V PRODUCER

On balance, producers are probably valued more highly by record companies than by artists. Too often, artists end up resenting the amount the producer earns. If for example the gross artist royalty is 16%, and this is inclusive of a producer royalty of 4% (an example to which we will return later in this chapter), then, in the case of a solo artist, that artist will earn three times more than the producer (although the artist royalty will be available for recoupment of recording costs, whereas the producer's royalty probably will not). The solo artist may feel reasonably comfortable with this.

However, if we look at a four-member band, the producer's 4% will exceed the 3% available for each of the band members. Moreover, the band's work does not end once the recordings are completed. This may be followed by perhaps two years of hard slog by the band in terms of promotional work and touring. Also, of course, the band may have time to record only one album every two or three years; a producer may have time to produce perhaps three or four albums each year.

On the other hand, the producer might argue that his work helps to establish the artist's reputation and the artist is able to profit from this by the release of further material, whereas the producer derives no benefit from the artist's future activities (although producers have been known in extreme cases to ask for an override royalty on the artist's next album).

1.3 REMEMBER THAT THE ARTIST PAYS

The artist (or the artist's manager) should be aware of these issues and be diligent in negotiating the producer's deal. Too often, in a wave of enthusiasm for a particular producer, percentages are agreed in haste and with little thought. Still more dangerous is the tendency of record companies to secure the services of the producer and agree the terms of his deal with little involvement on the part of the artist. Ultimately (assuming recoupment is achieved), it is the artist's money generously being handed out by the record company to the producer. If the record company is determined to use a particular producer who insists upon a royalty of, say, 5%, on rare occasions the artist may be able to persuade the record company to make a contribution (so that perhaps of the 5% only 3% or 4% is deductible from the artist's gross royalty).

1.4 EUROPEAN APPROACH

European record companies (outside the UK) usually adopt a different approach. Often, the producer's deal is unrelated to the artist's deal – ie the artist's royalty payable under the recording contract tends not to be inclusive of the producer royalty, and the royalty payable to the producer tends not to be subject to recoupment of recording costs (although it seems that increasingly Germany is adopting the UK model). Nevertheless, the rates of royalty payable to producers in Europe tend to be similar to the rates which apply in the UK. European record companies generally adopt a more flexible approach than their UK counterparts and may sometimes be persuaded, for example, to allow the producer's lawyer to prepare the contract (a distinct advantage!) even sometimes contributing towards the legal fees.

2.0 royalties

2.1 ROYALTY RATES

Most producers used to command royalties of between 2% and 4% of the retail price. The most common rate was 3% of retail. Now that royalties are generally calculated by reference to the dealer price (see Chapter 2, Part 3, Paragraph 3.1), most producers command 3% or 4% (3% of retail roughly converts to 4% of dealer).

When negotiating his royalty rate, the producer should check that the royalties will be payable by reference to 100% of sales, and if not, the rate should be adjusted in order to take account of this. He should try to ensure that the agreed rate applies on all sales worldwide although he may have to suffer territorial reductions. If he is offered, say, 4% for UK sales and 3% elsewhere, he should reject this but perhaps be prepared to compromise on the basis that he will suffer the same *pro rata* reduction as the artist. If, for example, the artist's UK gross rate of royalty is 16% but elsewhere is 13%, the producer might accept 4% for UK sales and $^{13}/16$ of 4% in relation to foreign sales. The producer might also try for royalty escalations based upon sales targets of some kind (so that perhaps the 4% rate increases to 4.5% for sales in a particular territory in excess of the number of sales required in that territory to achieve perhaps gold or platinum status). As an alternative, the producer might benefit from a *pro rata* share of any royalty escalation enjoyed by the artist (although the record company and the artist will usually resist this).

2.2 METHOD OF CALCULATION

Most producers will accept that their royalty should be calculated at the agreed rate or rates in accordance with the same royalty calculation and payment provisions as apply between the record company and the artist concerned. Some producers refuse to accept this and insist upon the negotiations extending to a full-scale review of the detailed royalty calculation provisions.

There is some merit in this in the case of a sought-after producer engaged to produce a recent signing. The artist may not have been in a particularly strong negotiating position in relation to his recording contract. If the principle is accepted, then the person driving the deal for the producer should insist that he is given relevant extracts from the recording contract as quickly as possible so that these may be reviewed. If they contain provisions which are unfair or unusual, of course the producer should object to them.

2.3 A-SIDE PROTECTION

Most producers insist upon what is known as *A-side protection* so that in the case of a single record – if a track by the producer is featured as the A-side, the producer suffers no *pro rata* reduction in his royalty, even though he may not have produced the B-side. Sometimes the record company will accept this only on the basis that no royalty is payable to the producer if he has produced the B-side and not the A-side. A producer is normally reluctant to accept this but may do so if this is limited to those instances where the producer of the A-side also has B-side protection.

2.4 SECONDARY EXPLOITATION

Some record companies are careful to word their producer agreements so that the producer is entitled to a royalty only in relation to record sales, and so that nothing is payable in relation to any other form of exploitation. The producer should insist that he is also paid for any other exploitation.

Usually, the producer will accept a *pro rata* share of whatever is payable to the artist. For example, in the case of income from synchronisation licences, the record company is usually obliged to account to the artist for 50% of its receipts. Using our example of the 16% gross artist royalty and a 4% producer royalty, the producer should receive a one-quarter share of the 50% payable to the artist (ie 12.5% of the gross). The producer should ensure that his royalty entitlement extends not only to records in the usual sense but also to any videos or other audio-visual devices and to interactive formats.

Often, the producer will accept a *pro rata* share of whatever is payable to the artist in relation to the exploitation of audio-visual rights. It may be argued that this is inappropriate because the producer has been involved in only the audio element and not the visual element. On this basis, the producer's entitlement may be halved so that – again, using our example – the producer would be entitled to 12.5% of whatever is payable to the artist.

3.0 advances

3.1 SUCCESSFUL PRODUCERS

A successful producer may command an advance of £40,000 or £50,000 per album. Depending upon his working methods and the type of artist he works with, he may be able to complete, say, four album projects a year. He might therefore earn £200,000 per annum by way of advances (although this will be inclusive of any commission he has to pay, and he will have certain professional expenses, ie legal and accountancy fees).

Of course, in extreme cases a producer may be able to command far higher fees. A mid-range producer – ie a producer with a reasonably strong historical track record who is still in vogue because he has had one or two successful records in the last year or two – may command, say, £30,000–£40,000 per album and he may manage to complete three album projects per year, together with the odd track or two for other artists, and so he might gross perhaps £100,000–£125,000 per annum.

However, producers have to work hard for their money. They are under pressure to deliver the goods on time and within budget. Unfortunately, the creative process does not always work according to plan. They have to deal with temperamental artists and demanding A&R men and, quite likely, they will end up day and night in the studio. (This may explain why some producers have earned a great deal of money which has had to be used to finance expensive divorce settlements.)

Nevertheless, in most cases, once a producer is well established, his ability to command hefty advances is likely only to last for a few years and there is a natural temptation to 'make hay while the sun shines'. Producers are at the mercy of music trends, and often a producer is perceived to be only as good as the last album he produced.

3.2 LESS SUCCESSFUL PRODUCERS

A recognised producer who is not yet in the top league may command around £1,000 or £2,000 per track. Sometimes, a producer will be prepared to accept less than this if, for whatever reason, a limited budget is available and if the producer is particularly enthusiastic about the artist concerned.

3.3 MIXERS

A specialist mixer usually charges anything between £2,000 and £10,000 per track (usually inclusive of studio fees). High-profile remixers have been known to command as much as £20,000 for a single track.

A successful mixer will be offered more work than he is able to handle, even though he will often complete a particular mix within the space of one day (a day and a half per mix probably being the norm). If he is sufficiently in demand, he may also be able to secure a royalty entitlement, which will usually be 0.5% but might sometimes be a full 1%. A mixer brought in to mix an album would not usually secure a royalty entitlement. It is normally the specialist mixer – ie the club/dance remixer – who might insist upon a royalty entitlement. This might be offered for a 12" dance version, but some remixers will argue that their royalty entitlement should extend to any 7" version. Sometimes they will push for a co-production and/or co-publishing credit.

The record company will often insist that the original producer must accept a reduction in his royalty if the record company has to pay a royalty to a third-party producer or mixer. If the original producer is in a reasonably strong negotiating position, he should be able to resist this. As a compromise, he may accept that his royalty will be reduced if a third party is brought in to rework his material prior to its initial release, but he may insist that any special mixes for particular marketing purposes should be entirely at the record company's expense.

If the producer does have to accept a reduction, he would normally seek to limit this in some way. The reduction may be limited to, say, half of whatever is paid to the third party (so that the record company and the producer split the cost between them). Alternatively, the producer may accept that the entirety of the third-party royalty may be deducted from his royalty, provided that he receives at least half of his otherwise applicable royalty rate.

3.4 PER-TRACK ADVANCES

A producer will usually quote on a per-track basis. For example, he may ask for £4,000 per track. In the case of an album project, he may be asked to produce 13 or 14 tracks, and the compromise may be that he is paid only ten time his full per-track rate – ie £40,000 for the entire album irrespective of the number of tracks.

3.5 ADVANCE OR FEE?

Generally, the company will insist that the whole of any fee payable to the producer is treated as a recoupable advance. Sometimes, if the record company pleads poverty or for some other reason is not prepared to pay the producer's usual advance, it may be persuaded to treat the producer's fee (or perhaps 50% of this) as non-recoupable. This may be dressed up on the basis that the non-recoupable element is attributable perhaps to the producer's engineering services.

Likewise, if the producer also plays instruments on the recordings, he may be able to persuade the record company to treat part of the advance as a non-recoupable fee in respect of his playing services.

3.6 BONUS ADVANCES

The producer may be able to secure 'bonus' advances triggered perhaps by particular sales targets. This would normally simply improve the producer's cashflow in that (depending upon how the bonus is calculated) the bonus will often simply amount to an accelerated payment of royalties which may have accrued but are not yet due for payment.

3.7 PAYMENT SCHEDULE

Usually, one-half of any agreed advance is payable on commencement of the producer's services, with the balance payable upon completion. Nevertheless, most record companies refuse to make any payment until there is a signed contract. It is sometimes possible to accelerate payment of the final one-half of the advance so that perhaps 50% of this is payable upon completion of recording but prior to mixing, with the final balance payable only upon delivery of the finished and fully mixed masters. The producer should always resist any suggestion that part of the advance be delayed pending commercial release.

3.8 EXPENSES

The producer will usually expect his expenses to be reimbursed. He will often be entitled to a *per diem* payment to cover subsistence costs.

4.0 recoupment and deferment

4.1 UK AND US APPROACHES

Most UK record companies will agree to account to the producer for his royalty subject only to recoupment of his advance. Some follow the example of the US record companies, which invariably refuse to pay any producer royalties until the recording costs have been recouped. In the worst cases, the producer's royalty will actually be used towards recoupment of those costs. In most cases, however, the record company will simply agree to a deferral so that the producer's royalties will be paid calculated from the first record sold (subject, of course, to recoupment of the producer's advance), but only if sales are sufficient to enable the recording costs to be recouped from the artist's royalty.

4.2 EXAMPLE

By way of illustration, let's again assume a gross artist royalty of 16% inclusive of a 4% producer's royalty. Let's assume that the producer receives an advance of £20,000 but that there are additional recording costs of £100,000. What will be the position if the 16% gross royalty generates, say, £100,000 of royalties?

The 4% producer's royalty would be worth £25,000, so that after recoupment of his £20,000 advance, the producer at this stage is due a further £5,000 in royalties. However, if the contract provides that his royalties are to be deferred pending recoupment, no producer royalties will be payable until the recording costs, net of the producer's advance (ie £100,000, in this case), have been recouped from (usually) the net artist's royalty (ie 12%).

In this example, the net artist royalty so far amounts to only £75,000, so there is an unrecouped deficit of £25,000 (so no royalties will yet be payable to the producer).

If the next royalty statement discloses aggregate royalty income (calculated at the 16% gross rate) of £200,000, so that the producers 4% is at that stage worth £50,000, then the full £50,000 – less only the £20,000 advance – will then be payable because recoupment will by then have been achieved (ie the 12% net rate will have given rise to £150,000, which is therefore more than sufficient to recoup the £100,000 recording costs).

4.3 PITFALLS

If the producer is forced to accept deferment provisions of this nature, there are various pitfalls to be avoided. Firstly, he should ensure that he suffers only a deferment, and that his royalties may not actually be used to recoup a share of the recording costs. Secondly, for this purpose recoupment should either be calculated by reference to the net recording costs (after deduction of the producer's advance) from the net artist's royalty (as in the above example) or by reference to the gross recording costs (inclusive of the producer's advance) from the gross artist's royalty. Also, for the purposes of calculating recoupment, there should be a strict definition of recording costs. Most importantly, recoupment should not extend to any other costs which may be recoupable as between the record company and the artist (ie promotional video costs and tour-support payments).

5.0 accountings

5.1 METHOD

The producer will usually accept that he will be accounted to in the same manner and upon the same dates as the company accounts to the artist.

5.2 AUDIT RIGHTS

The producer should ensure that he has a suitable direct right of audit against the record company. Ideally, the record company should be obliged to reimburse the audit costs in the event of a discrepancy of some kind (perhaps where there is an underpayment of say 5% or 10% of the total amount properly payable in relation to the accounting periods under review).

As we saw back in Chapter 2 (Part 3, Paragraph 5.4), more and more recording artists undertake regular audits. However, the producer usually has a lesser financial interest than the artist. Given the considerable costs involved in undertaking a proper audit, producers tend to be reluctant to incur those costs, even if the contract provides that those costs are to be reimbursed in the event of a discrepancy.

In practice, the most sensible course is for the producer to maintain contact with the artist and to review from time to time with the artist whether they should jointly carry out an audit, with the artist and the producer contributing on a *pro rata* basis to the costs involved (to the extent that those costs cannot be recovered from the record company). In any event, it is worth trying for a provision to the effect that, if the artist carries out an audit as a result of which a settlement of some kind is made, the producer's royalty account should automatically be adjusted on the same basis.

PART 4: INDEPENDENT PRODUCTIONS

1.0 independent record companies

1.1 ROYALTY OR PROFIT SHARE?

A producer may have to accept that he will be paid on a rather different basis if he undertakes work for an independent record company or for a production company. The first difficulty is that independent companies generally do not have the same level of funding as the majors, so the producer may be squeezed harder as far as his advance is concerned. Many independent record companies have turned away from the traditional royalty system and instead pay their artists usually 50% of any net profits.

Although there is some logic in the artist and record company taking this joint-venture approach, it is less logical for the producer to be tied into this. The producer will have no involvement once his work in the studio is finished, and he will certainly have no control over what expenses are incurred. Usually, therefore, the producer will insist that his royalty is calculated in the normal way. In fact, if he has had to accept a reduction in his advance because of budgetary constraints, he may wish his royalty to be enhanced in some way to compensate for this.

1.2 WHAT PERCENTAGE OF PROFIT?

If the producer is nevertheless persuaded to accept a share of net profits, what percentage should apply? Our example of the 16% royalty under the traditional system inclusive of a 4% producer royalty gives a ratio of 3:1 – ie the artist's earnings are three times greater than the producer's earnings (although this doesn't take into account the fact that the artist suffers recoupment of recording costs from his share). If the gross royalty under the traditional system were at the higher end of the scale – at, say, 21% – then, in the case of a producer who would normally command a royalty of, say, 3%, the ratio increases to 6:1 in favour of the artist.

If the artist is to receive 50% of net profits, then logically the producer might ask for between one-sixth and one-third of the artist's 50% share. Although this does not affect the producer, the question then arises of whether the producer's share comes 'off the top', leaving the balance to be split equally between the record company and the artist (which is the more usual arrangement), or whether the artist's 50% share should be inclusive of the producer's share.

2.0 speculative work

2.1 BASIC PROTECTION

Sometimes the producer will be persuaded to carry out work on a speculative basis before an artist has even signed a record deal (the artist may have a manager or perhaps a publisher prepared to fund the costs involved). Ideally, the producer will nevertheless secure a fee of some kind, although sometimes he will be persuaded that there are no funds available for this purpose.

In order to protect his position, he should consider imposing a contractual obligation upon the artist to ensure that any record company which may become involved will account direct to the producer for royalties at an agreed rate, which should be fairly high in order to reflect the element of speculation and risk. The producer might insist that he owns the copyright in the recordings pending any record deal. Also, the producer should either impose a re-recording restriction upon the artist, or he should make it clear that his royalty is payable not only upon the recordings which he has produced but also upon any other recordings by the artist of the same songs.

2.2 STUDIO DEALS

Speculative work of this nature will often involve a studio deal of some kind. Sometimes, of course, the producer will have his own studio, or at least sufficient facilities to enable some quality demonstration recordings to be made. If the producer's own studio or facilities are used, he will need to factor this in when calculating what should be paid to him if and when the project is successful.

In other cases, the producer will carry out the work at a commercial studio but during 'down time'. Most commercial studios are prepared to offer a special deal of some kind for the use of their down time – ie those few hours (perhaps in the middle of the night) between bookings, when the studio might otherwise be idle. The deal might involve cut-price rates or, very often, no guaranteed payment but a royalty of some kind in the event that the recordings are commercially released.

In this situation, the producer may have to compete with the studio in protecting his own position. For example, the producer may not be able to own the copyright in the recordings because the studio will almost certainly insist upon owning the tapes, so that it may assign the copyright in the recordings to the record company when one is found in return for an agreement with that company for the payment of an override royalty and/or for the reimbursement of the studio costs.

Sometimes, the producer may work on a special project of this kind whilst at the same time working (in the same studio) for a fee-paying record company.

Arguments may then develop between the producer and the studio (and perhaps even the other artist/record company) as to whether or not the special project has made use of down time (which involves striking a deal of some kind with the studio) and/or whether work has been undertaken on the special project during time paid for but not used by the other artist (or the record company concerned).

The first rule for the producer, if he attempts to extract maximum advantage from the use of any commercial studio in this way, is to ensure that there is no ambiguity involved and that it is clearly understood that the producer will not be liable for any studio fees. If the studio requires a deal of some kind, the producer should ensure that the studio's deal is with the artist and not with the producer. He should secure his position with the artist separately.

6 Publishing Contracts

By Andrew Thompson

Whilst the recording contract is the principal means by which a recording artist pursues his trade if he writes and/or composes his own musical material, next in financial importance will be his publishing arrangements. Under the record deal, he will earn from the exploitation of the physical recordings; separately, he will also earn from the exploitation of his songs.

In the context of the music industry, 'publishing' refers the arrangements by which a song is exploited. When we refer to a publishing contract, we usually mean the agreement under which the writer agrees to write and/or compose material for his publisher. This is more accurately described as a songwriting agreement, or what the MCPS/PRS refers to as an ESA (Exclusive Songwriter Agreement). When a publisher enters into an agreement with another publisher (perhaps for the exploitation of particular songs overseas), that agreement is usually referred to as a *sub-publishing agreement*.

In Part 1 of this chapter, we consider whether a songwriter should enter into a publishing contract and, if so, when. Part 2 discusses the different types of publishing income and looks at how a particular deal may be valued. Part 3 looks more closely at a typical publishing contract. In Part 4 we briefly consider alternative contractual arrangements, and in Part V we review those factors which need to be borne in mind even after the deal is done.

PART 1: WHO NEEDS A PUBLISHER?

1.O the nature of a publishing contract

1.1 COPYRIGHT

In simple terms, a publishing contract involves the writer granting rights in his songs to the publisher in return for which the publisher collects all of the income from the exploitation of those songs and accounts to the writer for an agreed share of that income. Usually, the writer transfers to the publisher the copyright in his songs (although generally only for a limited period).

A song is generally a very precious and personal thing. Some writers have difficulty with the idea of giving their songs away. They prefer to retain ownership of their songs and make their own arrangements for the collection of any income. If the writer does not assign copyright to the publisher but merely grants a licence of some kind, the agreement probably would not be referred to as a publishing contract; it would instead be called an *administration agreement* or perhaps a *licensing agreement*. This area is investigated more carefully in Part 4.

1.2 THE PUBLISHER'S SERVICES

All publishers will emphasise a number of positive reasons why a writer should enter into a publishing contract. The publisher will claim that, with the various systems it has in place, it is better able to collect efficiently any available income than a writer operating on his own. Also, the publisher is more skilled at negotiating fees for the licensing of certain rights in the songs. The publisher will have a professional manager or a team of managers looking for additional ways in which to exploit the writer's material. He may be able to offer help and guidance, as far as songwriting is concerned (although this is now an old-fashioned concept and the publisher's creative involvement is usually limited to suggesting potential co-writers). He may also have facilities which the writer may use either at a subsidised cost or no cost at all (ie for recording demos) and may be prepared to invest in the writer's career by the payment of advances even before there is any sight of any publishing income from which to recoup those advances.. The funding supplied by the publisher may be vital during the early stages.

2.0 when should the deal be done?

2.1 SIGNIFICANCE OF THE RECORD DEAL

The conventional wisdom used to be (in the case of a singer/songwriter) that the publishing deal should be delayed until the record deal was in place. It is the record deal itself which gives value to the singer/songwriter's publishing rights, and there is a fear that, if the writer concludes a publishing deal before signing a record contract, he might sell himself short.

This view is no longer so common. Music publishers have become far more competitive. A publisher will often be the first to recognise (before any record company) a particular talent and may enthusiastically seek an involvement with the writer in the expectation of then being able to help secure a record deal. Some publishers will even finance master-quality recordings for independent release with a view to building up an artist to the point where a major record deal is achievable.

2.2 FUNDING

Publishers are skilled at selling themselves but, like all salesmen, they tend to make exaggerated claims. The plain fact is that, in the vast majority of cases, writers look to publishers for one overriding reason: money. If, in the case of a particular recording project, there is no difficulty in securing a record deal, then the prudent approach is probably to conclude that deal so that it may then be used to secure the best possible terms from a publisher. Otherwise, if reasonable terms are available from a publisher, there is no reason in principle why a publishing contract should not be concluded without delay.

3.0 the publisher

3.1 CHOICE OF PUBLISHER

As covered in Chapter 2, Part I, if there is competition between record companies for a particular artist, the choice of record company may prove difficult. If there is competition for a writer, the choice (at least for singer/songwriters) is more often determined simply by reference to the financial terms offered.

Some a singer/songwriters will be reluctant to sign a publishing deal with a publisher which is affiliated to their record company. Ordinarily, the accounting statements received from the publisher serve as a useful check upon the accountings received from the record company. If the record company and publishing company are related, there is a greater risk of concealment. However, this is more of a risk when signing to smaller companies – and even then, of course, most smaller publishers are entirely reputable. In the case of the major companies, the record and publishing arms are run entirely separately from each other.

3.2 EFFICIENCY OF ADMINISTRATION

Before concluding any deal, the writer should be satisfied that the publisher has efficient collection systems in place. Every publisher will say that his collection arrangements and accounting procedures are impeccable, so the writer should make other enquiries (perhaps of other writers signed to the publisher, and certainly of his professional advisers).

3.3 PROFESSIONAL MANAGEMENT

A songwriter who does not have a separate career as a recording artist and instead relies upon persuading other artists to record his songs and/or persuading television and film companies to commission his work is bound to attach more significance to the faith he has (or otherwise) in the particular personnel upon whom he relies to seek out commissions for him, to obtain covers and to introduce him to appropriate co-writers. As with every aspect of the music business, personal relationships count for a great deal.

PART 2: PUBLISHING INCOME

1.0 types of income

1.1 PERFORMANCE INCOME

In the UK, the PRS (Performing Right Society Limited) has a virtual monopoly in relation to performance income – ie the income generated by the public performance of musical works, whether on radio or television, in discothèques, restaurants or other places of entertainment, or in shops or any other public place. The PRS collects substantial licence fees and, after payment of its administration costs, divides up whatever is available for distribution between its various members.

Unless the writer is a member of PRS, he cannot participate in this income, and in order to be accepted as a member he has to assign to the PRS the performance right in all of his musical works. The PRS will then pay $6/12$ of any performance income attributable to the writer's songs direct to the writer (the PRS still thinks in terms of twelfths rather than decimals) and will pay the remaining $6/12$ to the publisher. If the writer does not have a publisher, the entirety of the performance income will be paid direct to him.

The manner in which the PRS calculates performance income for distribution to its members is complicated, but there are some specifics. For example, the current (April 2003) fee which the PRS will attribute to one minute of airplay on Radio 1 is £18.44. For one minute on BBC1, the fee is £45.85; for a minute on BBC 2, the fee is £43.33; and a minute on Capital FM is £2.32. These fees may appear small, but a successful single which enjoys considerable airplay will generate substantial performance income.

1.2 MECHANICAL ROYALTIES

In order to manufacture records, the record company requires a licence known as a *mechanical licence* from the owner of the song. Under the terms of the licence, mechanical royalties are payable at the statutory rate of 8.5% of the dealer price (for records manufactured in the UK). But what is the 8.5% mechanical royalty worth? In the case of a full-price CD album, the dealer price will be in the region of £8.89 excluding VAT, so that the 8.5% royalty is worth 75p.

Generally, the mechanical royalties are collected by the MCPS on behalf of its publisher members. The MCPS deducts commission at the rate of 4.75% in the case of mechanical royalties payable by the major record companies and those other record companies operating under what the MCPS refers to as its AP1 Scheme (which is intended for record companies with a proven track record) and 12.5% in all other cases.

1.3 SYNCHRONISATION FEES

The consent of the copyright owner is required for the use of a piece of music in a film. The consent is given in the form of what is called a *synchronisation licence* and the fees payable under the terms of that licence are referred to as *synchronisation fees*. Hence, a synchronisation fee is payable by an advertising agency for the use of a piece of music in a television advertisement, by a television company for the use of music to be broadcast on television and by a film company for the use of any music incorporated in a film.

Unlike performance income or mechanical royalty income (in relation to which neither the writer nor his publisher has any control over the method of calculation), synchronisation fees are freely negotiable so that the writer will rely upon his publisher to secure the best possible fee for each use. Even then, some uses are covered by what are known as *blanket licence agreements*, including for example any background music used on television which will be covered by the general licences granted periodically by the PRS/MCPS to the broadcasters.

1.4 PRINT INCOME

The most traditional form of music publishing is the printing of sheet music. Before records were available, publishers made their money by printing sheet music, for which there was a great demand. There has been something of a resurgence of sheet music sales (more for songbook compilations than single sheet music), and for some writers this is a material source of income.

2.0 the value of publishing income

2.1 PAST INCOME

It is impossible to know without a crystal ball how much money is likely to be generated from any particular publishing rights. The publisher will therefore agree to account to the writer for a given percentage of whatever is actually generated.

How does the publisher calculate what advances he is prepared to pay? If the deal relates to specific songs which have generated earnings in the past, it is a relatively simple task for the publisher to calculate the average annual earnings over the past few years and then decide how much to offer as an advance against anticipated future earnings. Past earnings are by no means a guarantee of future earnings (the profitability of a particular song will ordinarily decrease with the passage of time), but the publisher will make assumptions based upon what is planned in the marketplace.

2.2 FUTURE INCOME

But how does the publisher decide what to pay for a new writer – for instance, a singer/songwriter who has not previously released a record? The more sophisticated publisher will have the benefit of complex financial models which he will use to predict the speed and size of his return, but those models are only marginally more useful than the crystal ball because they depend upon the accuracy of numerous assumptions.

So, using a few crude rules of thumb, let's take a fanciful look at what the publishers might offer for a particular writer. We will take the example of a band which has just signed a record deal with a major record company which guarantees the release of an album. They intend to record only their own material. They do not co-write, so 100% of the publishing rights for the album is available.

2.3 THE PIGGYBACK APPROACH

The first publisher likes the setup. He knows the record company and he rates them highly. He also knows the record company paid the band £150,000 inclusive of costs. He has found out that this is a priority signing and that the record company intends to pull out all the stops. He decides that he is prepared to take a financial risk similar to the risk undertaken by the record company. He reckons they will make at least two promotional videos at an aggregate cost of £50,000 and he has heard that there is a commitment for independent promotion. He thinks that, after taking into account the band's advance, remixing costs, video costs, independent promotion costs and the like, the record company will be in for £300,000. He assumes that, after manufacturing and distribution costs (including mechanical royalties), the record company will make an average (over all formats) of £4 per unit on all UK sales (before paying artist royalties) and will receive a royalty of £1.50 per unit on overseas sales. He assumes the record company will take a long term view but he calculates that the record company will break even on 60,000 UK sales and 40,000 overseas sales. He calculates what income he might expect from those sales. After the MCPS has deducted its commission he still reckons on receiving, say, 60p per unit for the UK sales (averaged between cassette sales and CDs), giving rise to £36,000. After sub-publisher deductions, he reckons on 50p per unit for the overseas sales, so the company would gross another £20,000.

On top of the £56,000 gross mechanical royalties, he reckons there will be a fair amount of airplay generating more sales. He looks at his other comparable writers and discovers that their gross performance income is around 30% of their gross mechanical income. In this case, that would mean £16,800, but he will only receive $6/12$ of this.

All in all, if the record company breaks even, he reckons that by that stage he can expect at least £60,000. He is not too keen to pay out this much, because he knows he will have a long wait for the money to come through the pipeline. He decides to offer the band a 75/25 deal and to pay them £45,000 as an advance, but he will try and stagger payment so that £15,000 is payable now, £15,000 on UK release and £15,000 on US release. You never know, they just might go for it.

2.4 THE SCIENTIFIC APPROACH

The second publisher needs to build up his market share. He is in for taking a risk, but it has to be a calculated one. He knows there is competition to sign the band. The lawyer is already touting them around town. The band signed their record deal in a blaze of publicity. He knows he has to pay at least the going rate. He does not think that £50,000 on signing will be enough. He has pitched in at this level for several new bands this year, and every time he has lost out. He wants to offer £75,000 but he needs Board approval for this.

He gives the financial director some projections (similar to the first publisher) and asks him to work some figures. The financial director takes his laptop home and comes back the next day with the answer. He can offer £30,000 for the first album.

After lunch with the band's manager, the publisher calls in the financial director again. He has found out more about the band and he wants to revise the projections. He doubles the anticipated sales and asks the financial director to factor in the singles sales and some compilation income. Also, he has heard the remix of the first single and he wants to increase the projected performance income. He also wants to include a provision for some synchronisation income because the manager has told him that Disney want to use some of the music in their new film. The financial director reworks the figures and the next day the Board gives approval for £75,000.

2.5 THE MAVERICK APPROACH

The third publisher will kill for the band. He thinks they are the next big thing, and anyway, even if the band doesn't hold together, the main songwriter is a genuine talent. This publisher doesn't care what they cost. He will offer £100,000 and double it if he has to. He doesn't give a stuff about his Board because the company has already made £1,000,000 from his last year's signings and he has just signed a new three year employment contract at a huge salary with share options.

PART 3: THE CONTRACT

1.0 the term

1.1 CONTRACT PERIODS

Most contracts will run for a period of 12 months, but then the publisher will have a number of options to extend for a number of further successive periods of 12 months. Typically, the publisher will require two or three options so that the agreement runs for a total of three or four contract periods.

1.2 EXTENSIONS

If the publisher is prepared to pay an advance (and without this there would usually be little incentive to sign a long-term publishing deal), then the publisher will quite reasonably expect a minimum commitment of some kind from the writer (see Section 2.0 below). Each contract period will therefore be extended if necessary until a given period after the commitment has been met. The contract will usually enable the publisher to extend the relevant contract period until, say, three months after the commitment has been met (in order to give the publisher sufficient time to assess the position before deciding whether or not it wishes to exercise its option to continue into the next contract period).

In order to avoid restraint of trade problems most publishers are advised to put a limit on the period of extension of perhaps two or three years. In the case of a four-year deal, therefore, if there is a maximum period of extension of two years, each contract period will run for a maximum of three years, so that theoretically the contract might run for a maximum of 12 years.

1.3 EXCLUSIVITY

A publishing contract will invariably be exclusive so that the publisher will be entitled to all of the songs written and composed by the writer during the term of the contract. In addition, the publisher will expect to acquire any existing material (unless, of course, rights in that material have already been granted to another publisher). Sometimes, in order to prevent a writer holding back songs towards the end of the term of the contract, the publisher may insist that the contract also extends to any songs commenced during the term but only completed subsequently.

2.0 the minimum commitment

2.1 DELIVERY OR RELEASE?

In the case of an ordinary songwriter (as opposed to a singer/songwriter), the publisher may simply require a minimum number of songs to be completed and delivered. Nevertheless, if substantial advances are paid, then – notwithstanding the absence of a recording contract – the minimum commitment may be expressed in terms of a minimum number of songs which must be commercially released. Certainly in the case of a singer/songwriter the publisher will require a minimum number of songs to be released on record, and for this purpose the songs will often only qualify if they have been released by a major record company.

2.2 THE EXTENT OF THE COMMITMENT

It is important that the minimum commitment is realistic (ie achievable). For example, in the case of a singer/songwriter who co-writes all of his material and usually includes on his albums one or two songs written by other writers, the commitment should be for, say, 40% of an album (leaving room for him to write 50% of eight out of ten songs).

Sometimes the publisher may insist that the minimum commitment is only met when the minimum number of songs has been released by a major record company not only in the UK but perhaps also in one or more other specified overseas territories. Before agreeing to provisions of this nature, the writer should review his record contract and assess the likelihood of his being able to comply with the commitment within a reasonable period.

2.3 FAILURE TO COMPLY

If the commitment is not met, the extension provisions will apply. Also, the publisher may seek to reduce the writer's advance if the commitment is not met in full. For example, the contract may specify that the writer must procure the release of an album which has been written by the writer as to at least

90%. However, the contract may be structured so that the commitment will be deemed to have been met provided at least 50% of the album has been written by the writer (ie so that the extension provisions no longer apply) but so that the advance is reduced – for example, if 50% of the album qualified, five-ninths of the advance would be paid, and if 70% of the album qualified, seven-ninths of the advance would be paid.

3.0 territory

3.1 OVERSEAS EXPLOITATION
Most publishing agreements are worldwide, so that the publisher will enjoy rights in the songs in question throughout the world. Most of the major publishers have affiliated companies in all of the important territories. The independent publishers have appropriate sub-publishing arrangements in place throughout the world. Generally, therefore, all reputable publishers are in a position to exploit songs on a worldwide basis.

3.2 LIMITED TERRITORY
Some publishing agreements are restricted to a limited territory. As discussed in Chapter 2, Part 2, Section 3.0, a number of practical problems arise when recording arrangements are made on a territory-by-territory basis. However, those practical considerations do not arise in the case of publishing arrangements.

3.3 PROS AND CONS
A UK publisher may be prepared to pay higher advances for worldwide rights than the writer is able to achieve by securing individual advances for each territory. The UK publisher would then have the protection that income from all territories throughout the world will be available for recoupment purposes (which therefore spreads the publisher's risk).

Conversely, the advantage for the writer of entering into territory-by-territory deals is that, if there is particular success in one territory, then once the advance for that territory has been recouped, royalties will immediately begin to flow (ie those royalties will not be available to recoup advances paid for other territories). Another benefit is that the writer may expect to receive his overseas royalties more quickly than if they were routed back through a UK publisher.

On the other hand, if a number of deals are entered into rather than one worldwide deal, this is likely to increase the legal fees payable by the writer and, of course, the writer (or his manager) will have to monitor and liaise with a number of different companies. In some overseas territories, it is common practice to incentivise a record company by granting publishing rights to a publisher affiliated with the record company. Accordingly, if an artist controls his own recordings and licenses these throughout the world on a territory-by-territory basis, it might make sense to deal with any available publishing rights in the same manner. However, territory-by-territory publishing deals are generally unpopular, and the typical UK writer (certainly a singer/ songwriter) prefers to conclude a worldwide deal with a UK publisher.

4.0 advances

4.1 RELEVANT FACTORS

For most writers, the advances are critical, and yet advances vary dramatically. A would-be recording artist struggling to find a record deal but able to attract publisher interest may be pleased to secure an advance on signing a publishing deal of £10,000 and perhaps less, since this may provide vital funding at a time when the artist is struggling to keep his project together. If he has secured a valuable recording contract, he might expect ten times as much.

Various factors will affect what the publisher is prepared to pay. Part 2 of this chapter discussed publishers vary in their approaches, such as the piggyback approach, the more scientific approach and what the maverick approach. Of course, none of these is quite real. The publisher will make an assessment of the writer's talent. If there is an element of competition for the writer, the level of any advance will largely be dictated by market forces. Otherwise, the most crucial factor is likely to be what the writer needs and how little he is prepared to accept. The publisher will assess the entire setup, including the proven abilities and track record not only of the writer but also of those close to him, including the management team. If a record deal is not yet in place, the publisher's assessment of what should be risked by way of an advance payment will depend largely upon what record deal the publisher believes may be achieved.

4.2 PAYMENT SCHEDULE

Having agreed an advance, the publisher will try to reduce its risk by spreading payment. The suggestion may be that 25% of the advance for the first album is payable upon signature, a further 25% upon commencement of recording, a further 25% upon UK release and perhaps a final 25% only upon release in the US or some other specified overseas territory.

4.3 DEFERRED ADVANCES

If a singer/songwriter signs a publishing deal before a record deal is in place, there will probably be only a relatively modest advance upon signing. However, this will usually be followed by a more significant advance upon signature of a record deal with a major record company (with a further advance usually payable upon release of the first album).

4.4 OPTION ADVANCES

As far as any option periods are concerned, typically the advance for each period will be calculated in accordance with a formula (often two-thirds of the royalty earnings from the previous album) but subject to a minimum and a maximum payment. The minimum payment will usually be not less than the advance for the first album, and the maximum figure is often double the minimum figure.

For example, in the case of a four-album deal, if there is an advance of £75,000 for the first album, the advances for the subsequent albums might be calculated in accordance with a formula but subject to a minimum payment of perhaps £75,000 again for the second album (and a maximum of £150,000), with perhaps a minimum of £100,000 (maximum £200,000) for the third album and perhaps a minimum of £125,000 (maximum £250,000) for the fourth.

Alternatively, the option advances are sometimes fixed amounts (rather than calculated in accordance with a royalty earnings formula) with generous increments, but so that in each case the option advances may be reduced by the amount of any unrecouped balance. On this basis, if the advance for the first album is £75,000, the publisher might agree advances of £100,000, £150,000 and £200,000 respectively for three option albums. Using this example, if the first album is disappointing and generates only £25,000 in royalties (leaving an unrecouped balance of £50,000 from the initial £75,000 advance), the publisher might exercise its option to continue with a second album upon payment of a reduced advance (ie £50,000 being the £100,000 agreed for the second album less the £50,000 unrecouped balance).

5.0 royalties

5.1 RATES OF ROYALTY

Traditionally, publishers accounted to their writers for 50% of their income. A 50/50 split is still more or less standard in the case of television and film companies when commissioning writers to compose music for a specific use. However, a songwriter would now generally expect something far better (usually falling within the range of 60% to 80%). A singer/songwriter – whose own efforts will generate most of the publishing income – would expect to receive royalties at the top end of the scale, usually 75% or 80%, while royalties of 85% or 90% are sometimes payable. However, there is an obvious correlation between the royalty rate and the amount of any advance payable so that for example a publisher prepared to pay a writer an advance of £100,000 against a royalty of 75% of the publisher's receipts might be prepared to increase the 75% to, say, 85% or even 90%, but only on the basis that perhaps no advance is payable. An 85% or 90% royalty will more often be seen in the context of administration arrangements (see Part 4 of this chapter).

Under a typical publishing contract, a new writer would often expect to achieve a 75/25 royalty split. He may be persuaded to accept a royalty of, say, 70/30 in relation to the songs delivered during the initial contract period, but if the publisher exercises the first of its options, there will be a 75/25 split. The 75/25 split might therefore apply for the second and third contract periods. If the publisher has an option for a fourth contract period, this may be granted only on the basis that at that stage the split increases to 80/20.

If the royalty rate is 75% then, in the case of performance income, the writer will receive 50% (or what the PRS prefers to refer to as $^6/_{12}$) direct from the PRS. The remaining $^6/12$ will be paid to the publisher, but the writer will require 50% of this (so that overall he receives 75% of the gross performance income). However, his 50% share of the publisher's $^6/12$ will be available to the publisher to apply towards recoupment of any advance. As far as mechanical and synchronisation income is concerned, the writer will receive 75% of what the publisher receives (although the reader is advised to look at Paragraph 5.3 below to determine what is meant by 'receipts' for this purpose).

In the case of sheet-music sales, the publisher will generally licence sheet music rights to a third party and will simply pay the writer 75% of its receipts pursuant to any such licence. If the publisher itself publishes the music in sheet form, the contract will usually provide that the publisher will pay the writer between 10% and 15% of the retail selling price.

5.2 REDUCED ROYALTIES FOR COVERS

Publishers will often seek a reduction in the rate of royalty in relation to income derived from cover recordings. If we again assume that the basic split is 75/25, the publisher may insist that a split of say 60/40 applies in the case of income from covers. This is a dubious practice, but it is quite common. Here, the term *cover recording* refers to a recording by an artist of somebody else's song, so in our example the writer would receive 75% of the income generated by his own recordings of his songs but perhaps only 60% of the income generated from other recordings of those songs.

The task of collecting the income from a cover is no different from the task of collecting the income from the writer's own recordings, so this in itself does not justify the income being treated in a different manner. The publisher will argue that a reduction in royalty is justified because of the input of its professional manager or managers in securing the cover in question. The vast majority of covers happen because the recording artist concerned makes a unilateral decision to record a new version and the first the publisher will know about this is when the artist's record company applies for a mechanical licence.

To be fair, most publishers will therefore accept that the reduced rate should apply only for covers which have been obtained as a result of the direct efforts of the publisher. Even in these cases, however, the practice of paying a reduced royalty is a questionable one. All publishing contracts will contain an express provision to the effect that the publisher must use all reasonable endeavours to exploit the songs in question. It is therefore difficult for the publisher to argue that, if it achieves some success in doing what it is obliged to do, it should be more handsomely rewarded.

The only logical argument in favour of the publisher (using the same example) is that the basic rate should be 60/40, but if the writer secures any exploitation himself (in particular by means of his own recordings), then in relation to those recordings the split should increase to 75/25. Obviously, this amounts to the same thing, but it might be more palatable for the writer if the contract were presented in this way.

What is clear is that a pure songwriter (who does not have a recording career) should not be fooled into thinking that he has a 75/25 deal if this provides for a 60/40 split in relation to covers. Clearly, he has a 60/40 deal.

5.3 METHOD OF CALCULATION

Royalties are either calculated on what is known as a 'receipts' basis or upon what is know as an 'at source' basis. This has particular relevance in relation to overseas income.

An overseas sub-publisher (whether affiliated to the UK publisher or not) will naturally be entitled to retain part of the income arising in its territory before remitting the balance to the UK publisher. Usually, the sub-publisher will be entitled to deduct 10% or 15%. However, in some cases (particularly with the smaller independent publishers), the UK publisher may have negotiated a substantial advance from the overseas sub-publisher (in which the writer will not share) on the basis that the overseas sub-publisher is entitled to as much as, say, 25%.

If we look again at our example of a publishing agreement providing for a 75/25 split, then if we assume that the publisher's overseas sub-publishers are each entitled to retain 20%, it follows that the UK publisher will receive 80% of any foreign income. If the writer's publishing agreement is a receipts deal, he will receive 75% of 80% of foreign income, 60% of the gross. If the deal is 'at source', he will receive 75% of the gross (ie for every £100 arising in the territory concerned, the sub-publisher will retain £20, remitting £80 back to the UK publisher, who will then account to the writer for £75, retaining a margin of only £5).

Most publishing contracts – certainly those with the major publishers –

are now at-source deals. Some publishers try to draw a distinction between major territories and minor territories and calculate royalties at source in the major territories (which might be defined as those territories where the publisher concerned has its own affiliated sub-publishers) but account for royalties only on a receipts basis in relation to the minor territories.

If the writer has to accept a receipts deal, then a cap of some kind should be imposed so that, perhaps, a maximum sub-publisher deduction of, say, 15% might be imposed. If, for example, the publisher actually suffers a 25% deduction, then for every £100 which arises in the territory concerned, £75 will be remitted to the UK publisher, but out of this the publisher will have to pay the writer 75% of £85 (ie £63.75).

The writer should also ensure that there is no double deduction in relation to locally originated covers. What happens, for example, if the sub-publisher in France procures a local cover recording? Again, let's assume that the writer's deal is 75/25 but reducing to 60/40 in the case of income from cover recordings. If the writer's royalties are to be calculated at source, his entitlement will be clear – ie 60% of the income arising at source. If, however, the writer's royalties are calculated on a receipts basis, problems will arise if the foreign sub-publisher is entitled to deduct, say, 20%, in ordinary circumstances, but maybe 40% in the case of a locally originated cover (which is not uncommon). If there is no cap on the sub-publisher deductions, the writer would be entitled to 60% of 60% (36%) of the income arising at source. This is unfair, and the writer should instead require his full 75% of the UK publisher's 60% share (ie 45% of the income arising at source) or the cover rate (ie 60%, but calculated upon deemed receipts of 80%, which would give the writer 48% of the income arising at source).

6.0 accountings

6.1 STATEMENTS

Most publishers will account to the writer on a semi-annual basis usually within 90 days, so that, for the six-month period ending on 30 June in each year, a statement will be delivered at the end of September, and for the six-month period ending on 31 December, a statement will be delivered at the end of the following March. The writer will, of course, receive his share of performance income direct from the PRS, who account quarterly, although there are only two main distributions in each year.

6.2 DELAYS

We have seen (Chapter 2, Part 3, Section 5.0) that, in the case of a record deal, there may be lengthy delays before royalties (particularly in relation to foreign sales) actually come through the pipeline. Publishing income is prone to still longer delays, mainly as a result of the inefficiencies of the various collection societies.

The record company in the territory concerned will pay mechanical royalties to the local mechanical copyright collection society. In turn, the local society will then pay the UK publisher's sub-publisher. The sub-publisher should then pay the UK publisher, although it is important for the writer to establish that the UK publisher's sub-publishing arrangements are structured so that the UK publisher will receive accountings direct from the overseas sub-publisher (ie so that no unnecessary link has been added to the chain).

By way of example, in relation to records sold in Germany, the German record company for a record sold in December may account to GEMA (the German collection society) only in January the following year. GEMA account quarterly within 30 days, so the payment would fall within the first quarter of the year and be due for payment by GEMA to the local sub-publisher in April. If the German sub-publisher accounts to the UK publisher on a quarterly basis, the money (having been received during the second quarter) will be due within, say, 60 days of the end of that quarter, so the UK publisher would receive payment at the end of August. If the UK publisher accounts to the writer semi-annually, payment would not be due until the end of March the following year (a total period, since the income, arose of some 16 months). Inefficiencies and delays often result in a period of perhaps two years or more before foreign royalties finally work their way through the system.

6.3 AUDITS

The writer should ensure that he has appropriate rights of audit. An audit of a publishing company tends to be far less complicated than a record company audit, but nevertheless it is prudent to carry out an audit periodically. If a writer's royalty account is unrecouped so that the audit is unlikely to give rise to any additional payment, it may be sensible to delay carrying out the audit. The writer should be careful not to fall foul of restrictions in the agreement to the effect that accounting statements are to be deemed accepted and no longer subject to any objection after a given period (usually two or three years). Generally, it is a simple matter to persuade the publisher to extend any objection period to allow any audit to be deferred.

7.0 retention period

Under a typical publishing contract the publisher will acquire the copyright in the songs in question. Sometimes, the writer may retain the copyright and instead grant the publisher an exclusive licence. This effectively places the publisher in no worse a position, because an exclusive licensee of copyright has the same rights as the copyright owner. As a rule, however, the publisher will wish to own the copyright and be able to register the copyright in the publisher's own name.

Traditionally, the publisher insisted upon owning the copyright outright – ie for the full period of copyright (currently the life of the writer plus a further 70 years thereafter). Some publishers still insist upon owning songs for the full period of copyright, but this is generally restricted to those cases where a publisher commissions a writer to compose music for a specific purpose (ie for a film or television programme). In the case of a singer/songwriter signing a typical publishing contract, he would expect to assign the copyright in his songs to the publisher for only a limited period (ie the term of the agreement, which as we have seen will generally be three or four years but may be extended if necessary until fulfilment of the minimum commitment) and then for a further period.

This tends to be one of the more controversial areas in any negotiation. In the 1980s, competition was so fierce that publishers were persuaded to accept very limited retention periods – ie perhaps the term plus five years, or even less in extreme cases. A retention period of the term plus seven to ten years was quite common.

Towards the latter part of the 1980s, there was a great deal of activity in the sale of various music catalogues. Many of those catalogues were sold for stunningly high prices. The reason for this was that the catalogues contained successful songs, or 'standards', which were owned by the publisher concerned for the life of copyright and from which it was clear that income would continue to accrue for many years to come. As a result, the trend in relation to retention periods was reversed, and ever since then, publishers, having relearned the lesson of the value of copyright, now fight hard for longer retention periods.

The publishers have lost too much ground to be able to claw their way back to the full period of copyright, but a typical new deal now will provide for a retention period of the term plus a further period of between 10 and 20 years. Sometimes, in return for the writer agreeing to a longer retention period, the publisher may be persuaded to improve the royalties – perhaps from 75/25 to 85/15 – in relation to income received after the expiration of a given number of years. The publisher might even be persuaded to pay a further advance at some point. For example, perhaps the writer will agree to a retention period of the term plus 15 years, provided that, at the end of seven years after the term, the publisher pays a further advance equal to perhaps three or four times the average annual royalty earnings over the preceding three years. (This is not a standard formula by any means; it is one example of the many compromises which may be reached during the negotiations in relation to the retention period.)

8.0 rights

As the owner of the copyright in the songs, the publisher will have the exclusive right to control their use (even to the exclusion of the writer). As we have seen, the copyright will not extend to the performing right in the work, because this right will have been assigned by the writer to the PRS by virtue of his PRS membership. In fact, in practice the publisher will have only limited control over the songs. For example, any third party wishing to record one of the songs will be entitled to do so as of right under the terms of the compulsory mechanical licensing system which operates in a substantially similar form in all of the major territories in the world. However, as far as other forms of exploitation are concerned, the writer will often wish to impose various contractual restrictions upon the publisher. The publisher will usually require the writer to waive his 'moral rights' (ie the right of the writer to be identified as the author of the work, together with his right to object to any derogatory treatment of the work).

Nevertheless, the publisher will usually accept contractual restrictions to the effect that the writer will be given appropriate credit and that there will be no adaptations or arrangements of the songs without the writer's consent, and perhaps that no synchronisation licences should be granted without the writer's approval. Sometimes, the writer may wish to impose an obligation on the publisher to grant synchronisation licences to third parties upon such terms as the writer may specify. This is designed to overcome the danger of the writer requiring his song to be used for a particular purpose but the publisher refusing to grant a licence (the publisher may be dissatisfied with the financial proposals and may not wish to set a precedent).

9.0 exploitation

All publishing agreements include a provision to the effect that the publisher must use reasonable endeavours to exploit the songs. However, if the publisher fails to exploit a particular song within a particular period (perhaps prior to two years following the expiration of the term of perhaps a period of two years commencing with delivery of the song in question), machinery will be available to the writer to require (perhaps after what is know as a *cure period*) all rights in the song in question to be re-assigned to him, irrespective of the duration of the retention period, so that he may seek to exploit them by other means.

The primary reason for the inclusion of provisions of this nature is to protect the publisher from any claim to the effect that the agreement may be unenforceable by reason of constituting an unreasonable restraint of trade. (The courts would not be prepared to enforce an agreement under which a publisher is theoretically able to hold a writer to an exclusive contract for a lengthy period but then refuse to exploit his work.)

10.0 warranties

Publishing contracts generally contain a number of warranties on the part of the writer. Perhaps the most significant of these is the warranty to the effect that all of the compositions will be original and will not infringe the rights of any third party.

There is an increasing number of copyright disputes. Many of the disputes arise from the current fashion for 'sampling' so that, if a singer/songwriter wishes to incorporate a sample of any kind into a recording, it is vital that he immediately seeks advice and ensures that any necessary clearances are obtained. Given the risk of copyright disputes, it may be prudent for a writer to enter into any publishing contract through a limited company so that by virtue of an employment agreement of some kind the writer assigns to his company the copyright in his songs. If disaster does occur, he will at least be protected from personal bankruptcy. The writer should also consider taking out insurance against copyright claims.

11.0 group provisions

In the case of a group, the publisher will require all of the members of the group to sign the publishing contract, notwithstanding the fact that it may be anticipated that one member only of the group will be writing the songs. This is simply a security measure on the part of the publisher. Obviously, this will not be possible if one of the group members is already a party to a publishing contract of some kind, but in that event, this is bound to impact upon the financial terms of the deal.

In the case of a group, the publishing contract will contain complex leaving-members provisions. The important point for the writers to bear in mind is that, if one of them should leave the group and if the publisher should elect to continue with that leaving member, he should have a separate contract which stands on its own, as far as the minimum commitment is concerned (so that the duration of his contract is not governed by the fulfilment of the group commitment). Also, the leaving-member provisions need to deal sensibly with the issue of cross-recoupment. The same principles apply here as with any recording contract (see Chapter 2, Part 2, Section 7.0).

PART 4: CONTRACTUAL ARRANGEMENTS

The writer may not wish to give away his songs, and he may therefore choose not to enter into a publishing contract at all. Nevertheless, some arrangements must be made to collect his publishing income. The basic choices are, firstly, to join the PRS and the MCPS and do nothing further; secondly, to employ somebody direct to administer the songs for him; or, thirdly, to enter into an administration agreement with a third-party administrator.

1.0 reliance upon the PRS/MCPS

Both organisations have international relationships so that a writer may wonder why he should bother to make any other arrangements. Why not simply wait for the monies earned overseas to flow through via the appropriate organisation?

There are two main problems here. The first is that the system itself is not particularly efficient. Neither the PRS nor the MCPS automatically notifies its affiliated societies of its claim to royalties. They will, however, make such requests by a system of international 'fiches' in response to the copyright owner's request. This system is not wholly computerised, and there is some doubt about whether the overseas societies will always act on the notifications. Worse still, there may be local covers of which the copyright owner is unaware and which, therefore, are never notified.

The other problem is that, even if the societies manage to collect the funds in the first place, there is a significant delay in the remittance of those funds. The theory is that if, instead, the writer were to be represented by a publisher in the relevant overseas territory, then that overseas publisher would be charged with the responsibility of registering its interest and ensuring that the local collection society makes payment direct to that publisher. Because the local publisher has a vested interest, it seems that this generally results in the funds being paid through rather more efficiently than is the case where the local society is left of its own volition to pass funds back to PRS/MCPS. Moreover, there is not necessarily as significant a saving involved in relying upon the PRS/MCPS because two sets of commission will be charged (ie the overseas society will deduct its commission before accounting to the PRS/MCPS and the PRS/MCPS will then deduct its own commission before accounting on to the owner of the copyright).

2.0 self-administration

Self-administration is the process of exploiting copyright without appointing a publisher (and, through that publisher, various overseas sub-publishers) but instead by becoming a member of the local collection societies. In most major territories, this is now a reasonably simple procedure, although it is often helpful to employ an agent in the local territory to deal with the formalities. However, it is not possible to join directly in Japan, and it is still difficult in Italy. In theory, there should be no obstructions in Italy, but one of the Italian society's rules is that you need to produce 200 copies of a booklet which includes 20 Italian compositions which are to be published by the person wishing to join. A few of these booklets are given to the local society but the rest have no practical use and are usually destroyed. The aim behind this is to prove that the applicant is a *bona fide* publisher.

There are significant advantages in the self-administration approach. The first is that the copyright owner will bear the commission only of the local society and will not bear additional commission of a UK collection society or sub-publisher. The second is that the copyright owner will receive any applicable funds immediately those funds are distributed by the local society and there will be no further delay whilst the funds are processed by a third party. Thirdly, membership of the local societies will normally bring with it the privilege of qualifying for a share of 'black box' income.

So called 'black box' income is mainly comprised of income obtained by the local societies by virtue of various blanket licensing agreements under which, for example, perhaps a television company pays a substantial fee for the privilege of performing all the musical works controlled by the society in question. Blanket licences of this kind are issued in the UK, but the PRS, for example, has a reasonably sophisticated system which enables it to identify particular uses so that the PRS's income may be distributed sensibly between the specific titles controlled by the PRS.

Many overseas countries (most notably Italy) are far less sophisticated so that the societies end up with vast amounts of money which they are unable or unwilling to attribute to any particular song. This money (or part of it) is therefore distributed between its various publisher members (and those publisher members generally retain their share in any black-box distribution for their own use and benefit without sharing this with their writers.) The publisher member's entitlement to a share of black-box income usually increases with the length of time the publisher has been a member.

One disadvantage of self-administration is that the societies do not generally pay advances. Moreover, it is the publisher's responsibility to notify the local societies of the compositions in respect of which it wishes the society to make claims and the publisher is responsible for checking its own statements. To undertake these tasks effectively, the publisher needs to have a reasonably sophisticated administrative system and thus may have to maintain a higher overhead cost than would otherwise be the case. Further, under self-administered arrangements, there will be no local promotion of the catalogue. One way around this would be to hire one or more people to undertake specific promotional tasks, but the writer would need to assess whether the cost of doing this means that he is able still to justify direct membership or whether he would be better off paying commission to a sub-publisher.

In view of the complexities involved, only a very successful writer with a considerable turnover would normally consider self-administration.

3.0 appointing an administrator

Accordingly, if the writer wishes to avoid entering into a publishing contract of the traditional sort, and if he is prepared neither simply to rely upon his PRS/MCPS membership nor make his own administration arrangements, the most sensible solution is to enter into an administration agreement of some kind with a third party.

Administration agreements are not dissimilar to publishing agreements but the publisher will generally offer no professional management services. Instead, the publisher's responsibilities will be limited to purely administrative services – ie registering the songs and collecting the money. Generally, no advance will be payable, but the royalties will be higher (perhaps an 85/15 split or even 90/10).

Also, given the absence of any advance, administration agreements tend not to be for a lengthy fixed term. Usually, they will continue at least for a year (to save the bother of the publisher setting everything up only to find that the writer then wishes to terminate the arrangements), but thereafter the arrangement would usually be terminable by either party upon reasonable notice (perhaps three months). The publisher would administer the songs in the writer's name. For instance, if the writer is Joe Bloggs, the songs might be registered under the name Joe Bloggs Music.

PART 5: AFTER THE DEAL

As with a recording contract, life does not come to an end once the contract has been signed. Here are some practical points for writers to bear in mind.

LEAD SHEETS AND DEMOS

As soon as a song has been completed, it should be delivered to the publisher in the form of a lead sheet or perhaps a demonstration tape, or at the very least a lyric sheet. Delivery will be particularly significant if this triggers the payment of an advance or if the date of delivery impacts upon the publisher's option date. In any event, as soon as a song has been delivered, there is immediately additional evidence of its existence which may be significant in the event of any subsequent copyright dispute.

SINGLE-SONG ASSIGNMENT

Most publishing agreements impose an obligation on the writer to execute a short form assignment in relation to each particular song. (The publisher may need this in certain territories for registration purposes.)

RELEASES

The writer should ensure that his publisher receives copies of all records (ie singles, albums, videos, etc) which are released featuring any of his songs. This will help the publisher track the royalty income.

COLLABORATIONS

If the writer co-writes, this is likely to have implications under the publishing contract. The writer may be under a contractual obligation to use all reasonable endeavours to ensure that his co-writer assigns his interest in the song in question to the same publisher.

Also, of course, co-writing will invariably have implications as far as the minimum commitment is concerned. When two or more people collaborate in writing a song, this is usually on the basis that they will be deemed to have contributed to the overall musical work in equal shares. The writer should ensure that the arrangements are understood by everybody before the work begins. In the unfortunate event of a dispute over the proportionate shares the publisher may be able to assist in resolving that dispute. If not, the PRS has its own procedures for this.

SAMPLES

A writer should never make use of samples in a work without obtaining clearance (not a 'nod and a wink', but a proper written clearance). The sooner the writer notifies both his record company and the publisher of the intended use, the better.

GROUP CHANGES

In the case of a publishing agreement entered into by a group, any change in line-up will have contractual ramifications. There will almost certainly be an obligation on the group to notify the publisher immediately any changes occur, but even before doing this the writers should consult their solicitor.

LIKENESSES AND BIOGRAPHIES

Many writers will have a right of approval over the use by the publisher of any autobiographical material and/or photographs and likenesses. In any event, the best way to deal with this in practice is for the writer to deliver approved materials from time to time.

THE PRS

If this has not already been done, any writer signing a publishing contract must ensure that he joins the PRS without delay. The publisher will be able to arrange this on the writer's behalf. As a PRS member, the writer is entitled to designate whether the PRS should appoint either ASCAP or BMI (the major USA performing right societies) to represent the writer's songs in the USA. A particularly prudent writer will wish to meet the UK representatives of both organisations before making a choice. Sometimes a choice is not available because the UK publisher will insist upon nominating one or the other.

CONSENTS

From time to time, the writer may be asked by the publisher to give consent to a particular matter – ie perhaps a synchronisation licence or an adaptation or arrangement of some kind. The writer should not give approval without first insisting upon being provided with full details of the financial implications.

EXPLOITATION

As we have seen, the publisher is under an obligation to exploit the writer's songs. If the writer delivers a song which he does not intend to record himself, he should try to bring some pressure to bear upon the publisher to make an effort to find some other use for the song. Moreover, the writer should not lose sight of the machinery in the contract which enables the writer in certain circumstances to require unexploited songs to be reassigned to him.

ACCOUNTINGS

Invariably, the first few accounting statements received by the writer will not be accompanied by a cheque because the writer's account will remain unrecouped (this state of affairs will often continue for an extended period, and in many cases indefinitely). This does not mean that the statements may be discarded. The writer should always ensure that the publisher accounts promptly on the due date and those statements should always be checked. If the writer is unwilling to do so or does not feel adequately qualified for this purpose, the manager or lawyer should check them for any obvious errors. Statements should then be referred to the writer's accountant and the accountant should be reminded to check any objection periods in the publishing agreement to ensure that no audit rights are lost.

CONCERT APPEARANCES

Every time the writer performs a concert, he must ensure that the proper PRS returns are made. Performance fees will be payable by the promoter via the PRS. In fact, as a result of the recent investigation into the PRS by the Monopolies and Mergers Commission, the PRS's monopoly position has been dented in a few respects, and one example of this is that a PRS member may now elect to collect performance fees in relation to his own live performances direct from the promoter. There are complications involved in this, and few PRS members have so far taken advantage of this.

The promoter is obliged to pay 3% of the gross box office receipts. In rough terms, a full house at a smaller recognised venue might trigger a payment of around £500. A full house at Wembley Stadium might trigger a payment more in the region of £100,000. Remember that one half of the performance fees will be paid direct to the writer and the balance to the writer's publisher. The PRS is able to administer these arrangements under its 'fast track' procedures, but it requires two standard forms to be filed with the PRS no later than 30 days after each concert – one form signed by the band or its management and the other by the promoter. Similar rules apply outside the UK.

ADVANCES

The writer should make careful note of the provisions in the publishing contract relating to the payment of advances. Often, those provisions are complex, so some effort may be required to calculate exactly when advances are due. If, as often happens, the writer fails to spot that a particular advance is due, some publishers will delay payment. No doubt the advance will eventually be paid, but the publisher is unlikely to agree to pay any interest on the late payment.

One other point to bear in mind is that, if the royalty account is fully recouped, publishers sometimes try to accelerate payment of a particular advance so that payment is made immediately prior to the accounting date (which then enables the publisher immediately to recoup the advance from the royalties due on that accounting date).

COVERS

If the writer has had to accept reduced royalties in relation to cover recordings, the publisher will probably have been persuaded to exclude for this purpose any covers actually procured by the writer. In this event, if the writer has introduced one of his songs to another recording artist or producer (however tenuously), then he should ensure that the publisher is aware of this.

TERMINATION DATES

The writer should monitor any relevant dates. For example, the writer should be aware of the last date upon which the publisher is entitled to exercise any option. The writer may wish to involve his solicitor in monitoring any relevant dates. Often, it is not a simple matter to calculate the option date, and the publisher may make a mistake. If the publisher fails to exercise an option properly, this will mean that the writer is free of contract (although many publishing agreements now include failsafe provisions whereby, if the publisher fails to exercise an option, the writer must serve an option warning notice giving the publisher a few more days in which to do so).

The writer must also monitor the expiration date of the retention period. Far too often, writers forget (or perhaps never knew in the first place) when their publishing deals expire. The effect of this is that publishers will generally continue to exploit a catalogue of songs until such time as they are told that they no longer have authority to do so. Unless there are specific provisions dealing with this in the contract, the implication will be that the publisher has been allowed to 'hold over' on the same terms as before. This may enable a publisher to continue to deduct a substantial commission despite the fact that, if the writer were alert to the position, he may have been able to secure an advance and/or better royalties or perhaps withdraw the songs from the publisher altogether and enter into more cost effective administration arrangements.

EXTRA FUNDING

Some publishers are prepared (in the case of writers with recording contracts) to pay towards tour support or for independent promotion or poster campaigns and the like (although it is generally difficult to persuade publishers to do so). If a publisher is persuaded to make such payments, the publisher will normally insist that those payments are fully recoupable from royalties. The writer is probably better advised to persuade the record company to bear such costs even though, likewise, the record company will want to recoup them. Publishing deals generally recoup more quickly than recording deals, and for this reason it may be preferable to load as much recoupment as possible onto the record company account so that the publishing royalties begin to flow as quickly as possible.

Also, in the case of a group, unless all of the group members contribute to the writing in equal shares, the recoupment of what are essentially record-company costs from publishing royalties will merely serve to exacerbate the complexities of recoupment (given the imbalances which will arise between the band members) and may fan the flames of a potential dispute between the band members.

PROFESSIONAL ADVICE

The writer must consult a solicitor at the earliest possible stage in any negotiations over a publishing contract. It would be prudent for the writer also to consult his accountant before rather than after the event.

7 Agents

By Martin Hopewell And Jef Hanlon

The role of the agent is to represent the artist in the field of live performance and to seek suitable engagements for the artist to perform in front of an audience or on TV or radio. The agent not only seeks to secure engagements at the best possible fee for the artist but, ideally, also takes into account whether the engagement is constructively contributing to the furthering of the artist's career and the increasing of his prestige. Many agents have also recently become responsible for bringing offers of sponsorship to artists from commercial entities wishing to identify or ingratiate themselves with the artist's following, in return for fees payable to the artist for his association or identification with a product or service.

the role of the agent

The agent is effectively a valve between the hundreds of thousands of acts and the limited worldwide body of promoters, whether they be promoters of concert venues, festivals, clubs or colleges. Take away the agent and there would be chaos, and promoters would be overwhelmed with calls from artists or their managers. Modern management is complex and covers many diverse areas, and as the agent is an expert in arranging live performances the manager will often delegate his responsibility in this area to him. The agent is seen as the intermediary between the promoter and the artist, although as he's representing the artist he's more often seen as a kind of referee who wears one of the teams' colours. He's often required to explain the position held by each side to the other, and he must therefore understand what makes both sides tick as well as take into account the needs of both.

TYPES OF AGENT

The classic perception of the agent is historically 'Mr 10%', the cigar-chewing loudmouth who would sell his granny if the price was right. He is, in fact, a rarity today, and most modern agents – especially those dealing in contemporary music – do far better business by retaining a reasonable (if not friendly) relationship with promoters, and indeed many pride themselves on a hard-earned reputation for fair dealing. Although sharks undoubtedly still exist, they're mostly relegated to the periphery of the business. These unscrupulous types are rarely the exclusive representatives of some artists, and are usually fairly easy to spot because they tend to act as bookers rather than as artists' agency representatives. These bookers are invariably more interested in either buying the artist for the lowest possible fee or selling him to a promoter for the highest possible amount, often with scant regard to the technical staging requirements and whether the performance is constructive and positive for the artist's career.

THE SKILLS REQUIRED

To fulfil his responsibilities to his clients, the agent needs to be able to perform a multitude of tasks. An agent must be a negotiator, and in theory he must negotiate the best possible deal for the artist, in terms of both fees and in furthering the artist's career. However, in practice the agent also has to consider the welfare of the promoter in a world in which acts come and go but in which promoters are usually still there in the future, when they may be needed to take a risk on staging shows for new emerging acts. At the negotiating table, the ability to shout loudly and sell hard isn't usually as important in obtaining the best deal as having a high level of technical awareness of the way in which deals operate, or of commanding an understanding of such subtleties as arranging the artist's billing, which must be of a style and size agreeable to the artist on all advertising for the engagement, particularly on those occasions when more than one artist is appearing at the same location on the same show.

Another important function of an agent is that of spokesman for the act in the live music business, and he should attempt to reflect the attitudes and wishes of the artist as accurately as possible in order to ensure that the final show is as close as possible to that which the artist would have set up himself. He must also be an expert at logistics, be able to plan the most effective route for a tour and be aware of the production and travel limitations, types of venue and the technical limitations of each.

He must also carry out administration, preparing and issuing engagement contracts. These are effectively not only the information summary on the event and the functions that both the promoter and the artist are expected to fulfil, but also the binding document that ties each party to their side of the deal. He will also monitor ticket sales, organise schedules of payments, receive and hold deposits and provide the promoter with the details of immigration and work permits concerning the artist's travelling party. He might also make available any information relevant to minimising withholding tax, and will send out artwork, logos, photos and any other publicity material needed to advertise the contracted engagement.

As the middleman, the agent also acts as an information centre. He's often the best contact person for all parties with an interest in the performance, and he will liaise with the production personnel working for the act, the promoter, the local record company, the public relations company, the accountant and any other interested parties. Most agencies have stockpiled large collections of data over the years on everything from venues and the technical specifications of festivals to the murky personal histories of promoters. Information is the key to setting up successful shows and tours.

As well as this, the agent must also play the role of accountant. It's the agent's role to carry out pre-show financial projections of income versus costs and after-show 'final settlements', in which percentage deals are involved, as well as to provide practical advice on dealing with the vagaries of 'foreign-artist tax' and to play the international currency game. However, most agents will recommend that the artist's official accountant is also consulted, if only to have someone available as a scapegoat if it all goes horribly wrong!

THE AGENT'S REPUTATION

An agent is often considered to be only as good and as influential as the acts he represents. Therefore, if the agent fails to adopt the additional role of talent scout, and simply relaxes on the strength of a couple of currently successful acts, he'll find himself with a lot of time on his hands when those acts decide to stop touring or split up. Agents need to keep petrol running through the engine and ensure that there's a steady stream of new acts always waiting to be developed through the agency system, finding space on stages that wouldn't otherwise have been available in order to expose those new acts and nurture them into becoming the superstars of tomorrow.

The agent's influence and power plays an essential part in his ability to package acts together in joint shows, tours or festivals. It's common knowledge that, if an agent represents a very popular act, he's more likely to be able to persuade promoters to provide solo shows or opening-act slots for the lesser-known artists that he represents.

One of the more unnatural but most frequent things that an agent has to do is to say 'No' and turn down offers from prospective promoters. This he may do for a number of reasons: the inquiring promoter may not be considered suitable to promote the act; the act may be nabbed by another promotion company; or the act simply may not be available on the date required. This is a role for which no commission can ever be calculated, but it's an essential requirement for an agent solely representing an artist.

COMMISSION

Historically, the agent's commission is 10% of the artist's engagement fee, although there are many variations to this arrangement. It's not unusual for new acts to be asked to pay 15%, for example, as their commissionable fees are so much lower than those of established acts, and the agent's costs won't decrease if a smaller show is negotiated. A compromise is often reached here whereby the agent sets up a sliding-scale commission rate, in which commissions decrease as fees rise – for example, 15% up to £2,000, 12.5% on fees from £2,000 to £5,000 and 10% on all fees exceeding this. This arrangement avoids unpleasant renegotiating later, as long as the scale is reasonable in the first place. Very large acts can often negotiate commission rates that are even lower, although 5% is generally accepted as rock bottom. This isn't unreasonable when you consider that large stadium tours can produce commissionable income in the region of millions of pounds, particularly in cases where the agent can't claim to have been involved in the development of the act to a level of high income. On the other hand, at the point at which this sort of money is being made by him, the artist is normally in a position to be able to afford to pay high bills. However, few major acts would ever see the merit in this argument. It's also worth noting that an agent's commission is fully tax deductible under all known tax regimes around the world.

All agents will expect to be entitled to commission from any promoters with whom they've previously secured an engagement for the artist. The length of activity for this right of re-engagement is normally at least one year from the date of the first engagement which the agent secured with the promoter. Artists and their managers must acknowledge that they can't expect an agent to use his contacts and experience to introduce them to viable promoters and then, once the introduction has been effected, that it would be appropriate for them to deal directly with the promoter and cut the agent out of the relationship. Agents will rigidly enforce this principle and their rights to commission on re-engagements.

AGENCY AGREEMENTS

An old and thorny source of disagreement between agents and their artists is the subject of agency agreements. These consist of contracts between the two parties that lay down the terms and conditions under which their working relationship will operate. Unlike recording, publishing or even performance contracts, the agency agreement rarely involves a financial inducement for the artist to sign it, and many managers believe that it will unfairly tie their artist with a single agent for an unreasonable period of time and at a set commission rate which they might otherwise wish to renegotiate later. Because the question normally arises at an early stage of the artist's live career, at a point at which income is low and the agent's job is at its toughest, most agents feel that they need some sort of commitment from the artist that will protect them in more successful times when the agent ceases to be the hero of the hour and becomes viewed more as the guy who takes 10% of the money for making a few phone calls. Unless everyone is very lucky, they will argue, and it'll normally take most of the three to five years (comprising the term of the agent's contract) for the act's income to reach a level at which the agent can expect a reasonable return on his time and effort.

CHOOSING AN AGENT

Most artists tend to arrive on a particular agent's roster after being recommended, or through existing relationships. Along with these introductions, it's fairly easy to ask around and research the reputations of various agents. Many acts try to gauge the skill of the agent by the acts which they already represent and the nature of their touring strategies, the theory being that, if they could do that for other acts, they could do the same thing for the aspiring artist. This is probably a reasonable assumption, although it makes no account of how much the other acts and their managers have planned their own live careers, or of another important factor:plain old luck. As a result, agents often develop 'boutique rosters' of similar artists, and a snowball effect comes into play as other acts join the family. Several agents have built remarkable careers from having stumbled by accident on a particular act which has then acted as a magnet for others, irrespective of the skill of the agent.

LARGE AGENCIES

The size of the agency is probably nowhere near as important as other important criteria, such as enthusiasm, experience, commitment and business acumen, but it's true that, for an agent to be able to perform his responsibilities accurately, he must be in command of the relevant information, and the larger organisations are certainly in a position to provide a larger net with which to gather data. These agencies are also usually able to apply more leverage to secure shows and packaging because of the way in which promoters rely on the continued goodwill shown by agencies that represent large artist rosters. An agent that represents a large number of artists, however, can get rather stretched when large numbers of them decide to tour at the same time. The personal attention from the head of the agency at the start of a relationship can gradually turn into a dialogue with the office junior booker when things get busy, or the artist's career may not ignite quite as quickly as he'd hoped.

It's true, of course, that a successful agent will be earning a reasonable income, but also that the agent – unlike the publisher or record company – only makes money from an act that's actually touring. A famous band on the roster can look very decorative, but this is of no use if it never plays live, and as soon as it quits touring or splits up the agent's income stops altogether. In addition, most large offices cost hundreds of thousands of pounds a year to run, which adds up to a lot of ten percents to meet the bill! It's not surprising, therefore, that the number of people who have become very fat cats out of careers in agency alone is extremely small. Most of the people currently filling agents' chairs started their careers just wanting to get into the music business, found an opening in agency and simply stuck to it. Many others have used a grounding in working at an agency as a qualification to help them move into management or a career in a record company. Some have even been tempted into the high-risk world of concert promotion.

CODES OF OPERATION

Up until 1995, in order to run an employment agency in the UK, it was necessary for an agent to hold a licence issued by the government. Things have now changed, however, and this is no longer the case. The operation of employment agencies is now controlled by the Employment Agencies Act of 1976, which is now being thoroughly policed and enforced by the Employment Agencies Standards section of the Department of Trade and Industry. Under the terms of the Act, any breaches that lead to the prosecution of an agent are considered to be criminal rather than civil offences, and therefore most agents are meticulous in making sure that they work within the parameters set out by the Act. There are certain procedures that an agent must follow under the Act, and the most important points are as follows:

- He must maintain a clients bank account in a manner which is entirely separate from his own agency's account in order to receive money due to his artists. This makes it clear that the money held by the agent, or passed through his clients account, is in fact the artists' money and not earnings for the agency. A bonded account is most desirable, from the artist's point of view, but not a legal requirement.

- Under the terms of the Act, an agent must pay any monies that he collects on behalf of the artist to him within ten days of receiving it, unless the artist specifically asks the agent, in writing, to hold his money for a longer period of time.

- An agent should, by law, present the artist with a written copy of the terms of business setting out what the agent intends to charge the artist and expects from the artist in return for securing engagements for the artist. This can take effect on the artist signing a sole agency contract with the agent at the beginning of their relationship, but if a written contract doesn't exist then the agent should – again, by law – provide written terms of business to the artist for every contract of engagement presented to the artist. It's essential that the artist is clearly notified in writing of the rate of commission which the agent will be charging with respect to any and all future engagements.

• It's important to point out and always remember that the agent earning commission from the artist is never a party to the contract negotiated for an engagement, and is therefore not legally liable for the fulfilment of that contract by the parties entering into the contract – ie the artist (employee) and the promoter (employer).

Ultimately, the more one discovers about the function of an artist's agent and the more one appreciates the degree of knowledge, experience and skills needed to succeed in this field, it's probably fair to say that the stereotypical image of the agent as a shark is very outdated. The only real similarity between an agent and a shark is their mutual need to keep moving in order to survive.

8 Live Performance

By Rusty Hannan, Jef Hanlon And Terry O'Brien

Touring will be an important element in the careers of most artists, and therefore in those of most managers. Once the manager has decided that the time is right to tour, he must start to draw together a team of specialists in each area of expertise required to ensure that the tour runs smoothly.

There are four scales of touring, in terms of venue size:

- A small club tour, promotion or personal appearance;

- A small venue, club or college tour;

- A theatre/concert-hall tour;

- An arena tour.

Obviously, the arrangements will vary enormously, in terms of supporting personnel, equipment and the amount of planning necessary, according to the size of the tour.

key personnel

The first port of call is the artist's agent, whose role is discussed in more detail in the previous chapter. The agent will use his understanding of the venues and the types of music appropriate for those venues, as well as his expertise in judging the best price to ask for a performance in those venues. He will also assemble and hold dates in a viable schedule. It will then be the responsibility of the agent to contact and secure the services of the promoters in all territories. It's most likely that the agent will be involved no matter what the scale of the tour.

THE PROMOTER

The promoter will be responsible for providing the venue for each show, for advertising and marketing the sale of tickets, for supplying the artist's rider requirements, for ensuring the safety of both the public and the artist during the course of the gig and for conforming with licensing regulations. For small-club and small-venue tours, it's likely that a different promoter will be involved with each show. For a theatre/concert tour, things could be arranged so that one promoter catered for an entire national tour, or the tour could be split between several regional promoters. For an arena tour in the UK, one promoter will almost invariably promote all dates, with the possible exception of shows in Scotland and Ireland, which are sometimes given to promoters based in those countries.

THE TOUR MANAGER

The tour manager will be brought in as soon as the dates are confirmed. It'll be his responsibility to supervise the engagement of the crew, and he'll also start to look at the financing by getting quotes and budgeting for costs. He'll also advance the tour to ensure that the items specified in the rider to the contract and all other production requirements are available and will be provided, and that, if any of these are impossible to obtain, a suitable compromise can be found to enable the show to be performed. While on tour, he'll manage the tour crew as well as liaise with the local crew and technical personnel. Careful and realistic planning by all involved should keep costs to a minimum, but often tour support from the artist's record company will be needed in order to allow the tour to proceed, and the manager will need to negotiate the basis on which this money is given, how much the record company will contribute and the proportion of this sum which is recoupable. The tour manager is usually responsible for handling and collecting money on tour and settling the show with the promoter, which involves receiving payment under the terms of the contract along with paying any running expenses and collecting receipts for cash payments etc, organising and supervising travel arrangements and arranging accommodation.

If the tour is a small-club promotional tour, the function of the tour manager is fulfilled by the manager or, alternatively, by somebody who is also able to supervise sound mixing and basic lighting, and who can probably also drive the tour vehicle. This would usually mean that the tour party would comprise the artists and one other person.

On a small-venue tour – and depending on the complexity of the act's technical needs – the supporting tour personnel will usually consist of a tour manager and possibly someone who can supervise sound, lighting and backline, either of whom will probably double up as a driver.

On larger tours, in addition to dealing with the artist's needs and comfort, the tour manager will also be responsible for supervising guest lists, dealing with press and media enquiries or interviews, liaising with the tour sponsors (if they are present) and ensuring that any promotional materials (such as banners, etc) are displayed as promised under the sponsorship deal. He should also make sure that an accurate PRS return is completed and given to the promoter to ensure that the songwriters of the material performed during the tour receive their due income, which – in theatres, concert halls, arenas and stadia – is a percentage of the box-office takings. This can amount to a very substantial sum of money.

THE SOUND ENGINEER

The sound engineer will probably be the second man on the team after the tour manager. On the two smaller levels of touring, he'll provide the channel listings for the venues to make sure that they have the right mixing console and equipment, and he'll also operate the desk during the show. On the larger tours he'll draw up the specification for a sound system of a size and power suitable for those venues, and in liaison with the tour manager and production manager he'll submit this as the basis for obtaining a price quotation from a company which will provide the public-address system and the crew for the tour.

Unlike the front-of-house sound engineer, who mixes the audio for the general public, the monitor engineer mixes the on-stage sound for the performers, who all have individual audio requirements, including individual mixes through their on-stage monitors. The monitor engineer and mixing console will be positioned stage left in close proximity to the performers so that they can communicate easily throughout the performance. A dedicated monitor engineer is usually employed at the theatre/concert-hall level of touring, and is definitely required for performances in arenas and stadia.

THE PRODUCTION MANAGER

A production manager will only be employed for shows big enough to require a skilled person to direct the technical side, so his involvement is usually limited to theatre, concert-hall or arena shows. His function is first that of an overall crew boss, co-ordinating the activities of the sub-contracted PA, lighting rental, trucking and catering companies, and he'll work closely with the tour manager in establishing costs, scheduling, loading in, soundchecking and local crew-call times. He'll also deal with the technical advance of the venues in order to establish that the basic facilities – such as stage size, electrical supply, over-stage loading points, number of dressing rooms, kitchen and catering areas, parking spaces for the tour trucks and buses and extras such as forklift trucks and cherry-pickers – are all of sufficient size and quantity to satisfy the needs of the touring production. He'll also liaise with the musicians for the supply of their backline equipment requirements. All of these facilities and requirements generate a cost factor, and therefore constant communication with the tour manager and (if applicable) tour accountant is essential in order to keep these costs within the limitations of the budget.

The quantity of crew will depend on the type and size of the show. If the artist is performing in small night clubs and college bars, only one person may be needed fulfil the roles of sound engineer, driver and backline technician. However, if the artist is playing a major arena, a crew of over 50 people may be required.

THE BACKLINE TECHNICIANS

Backline refers to the equipment and instruments that are used by the musicians for the performance, and this includes guitars, keyboards, amplifiers and stands, etc. Backline technicians are responsible for all of the instruments, amplifiers, equipment and the stage set, and often comprise a guitar technician, drum technician and stagehand-cum-carpenter. It's their responsibility to supervise the unloading of the backline equipment from the truck and to set it up on stage; to make sure that the equipment is in perfect working order; to have instruments tuned; and to fit new strings and drumheads, if required. Usually, they'll also ensure that there are towels, water and set-lists on the stage, and will help the artist if strings break or equipment fails during the show. Additionally, they'll look after the maintenance, operation and erection of the stage set.

THE MUSICIANS

Depending on the type of band, a leader or musical director may be required to arrange the score and find backing musicians for the tour. There are various agencies that provide session musicians for tours where the artist doesn't have regularly used musicians at his disposal, and at this point it's important to consider backline requirements. It's important to know the backline that the musicians are supplying before the tour, so that any extras can be hired, and it often needs to be ascertained who is supplying the instruments. A musician should come fully equipped with personal gear, unless he's required to play an unusual instrument. For example, a guitarist should come with a guitar and an amplifier, but it may be necessary to hire a mandolin if it appears on one song. It's also worth noting that strings, drum sticks and skins and gaffa tape are all classed as consumables, and are therefore considered to be tour costs.

THE LIGHTING DIRECTOR

On large shows, a lighting director will be appointed to put together a lighting plot, rigging plot and equipment list, on which the lighting budget will be based. He'll tailor the lighting – and possibly special effects, such as lasers or pyrotechnics – to enhance the performance and ensure that the show is as visually appealing as possible, and he'll also operate the lighting control board and cue spotlight operators during the show. This will require discussions with the artist at rehearsals to determine specific cues or effects, and as always the lighting director's specifications will be passed via the production and tour managers, who will oversee the costings and logistical requirements, such as what truck space and local crew loaders will be required.

At small venues, lighting and an operator are usually provided if desired. If the budget is limited, it may be wise to spend cash on a sound engineer rather than on a lighting technician, as a lighting technician probably won't know the equipment as well as the local operator. However, if one is available, the artist's own lighting technician could either telephone or visit the venues in advance and ask for specific lighting equipment to be made available, or – if the budget allows – he could travel on the tour to supervise and cue the house operator, which will certainly improve the appearance of the show.

THE ACCOUNTANT

The accountant will require the finalised budget, and if payments are to be dealt with through him it may be necessary to produce a payment schedule with purchase order numbers. The payment schedules will outline when payments are to be made to the various staff on the road, which tend to be staggered throughout the course of the tour. Payments out must be co-ordinated with payments in to make sure that cashflow problems don't arise. The accountant will help overcome monetary problems, such as withholding tax, and will ensure that tax exemption forms – such as the E101 form necessary for touring in Europe – are completed. On smaller tours, the function of the accountant is often fulfilled by the artist's management, while on very large arena tours a dedicated tour accountant usually travels with the tour to deal with all financial matters as they arise.

With the team in place, there will be many areas of the tour which need to be planned and overseen in order to ensure that no problems occur, either before the tour begins or on the road.

other resources

THE RIDER

The manager – along with the agent – needs to draft a rider to the standard contract that will inform the promoter of what he's obliged to provide at the venue, in terms of facilities, supplies and services, so that the artist can perform the show.

REHEARSALS FOR TOURING

Rehearsals must be booked, along with venues for performances. There are three types of rehearsal that are generally required – band/music rehearsals, dance choreography rehearsals and production rehearsals – and there are many facilities that can provide these. The first two are self explanatory, while production rehearsals will be required for extremely large shows and constitute a time allocated as a technical period for lighting directors, technicians and set carpenters to iron out any problems before the tour begins. The band will probably arrive on the penultimate day of production rehearsals for a practice show run-through with the crew. Ideally, production rehearsals will be at the venue in which the artist will perform the first show of the tour, for ease and cost-effectiveness. Or, alternatively, a venue of similar size will be used, so that all of the elements of the show can be run exactly as they would be for the public performances.

GROUND TRANSPORTATION

Transportation for the artist, crew and equipment will need to be booked and co-ordinated. If the artist is performing personal appearances at night clubs, and needs just a couple of singers and dancers, it makes sense to hire a people carrier, as these are roomy and ideal for getting around quickly. However, if the band are musicians and are carrying backline, the ideal vehicle for the touring party would be what's known as a splitter van. These are mostly converted self-drive vehicles which have been split or divided in some way in order to allow more room for the storage of equipment at the back and space for a lounge and basic living quarters at the front, including such essentials as a TV and video. When a tour increases in size, or if great distances are involved, it becomes necessary to have a number of sleeper coaches included in the entourage, equipped with bunks and lounges, and to allow both the crew and the artists to sleep while travelling overnight between venues.

FLIGHTS

If necessary, flights and hotels will usually be booked with a specialist music travel company, who will hopefully understand the need to keep costs to a minimum but who will also understand the often very specific needs of artists and their touring parties. With local flights, it's important to check that all flightcases that are carrying equipment and stage costumes will fit into the holds of smaller aircraft before booking the flight, and the airline should be given advance notice of the weight and dimensions of the flightcases to be checked in over and above personal luggage.

TRUCKING

If the tour is providing its own production at all shows, trucks will invariably be required. It's important to note that only companies that hire trucks for the music industry should be used, as they will provide air-ride trailers, which protect the expensive and delicate equipment being transported. It also means that the drivers will understand the importance of getting to the next show, whatever it takes. It's important to note that trucks can't travel at the same speed as buses, and this must be taken into account when working out logistics and distances. It's also important to note that both PSV coaches and HGV trucks all carry a tachograph, which records the distances and hours driven by the drivers and the amount and length of the breaks they take. Vehicles governed by tachographs are subject to random checks by traffic police, and there are very strict laws governing the hours which the drivers of these vehicles can stay behind the wheel and the amount of rest periods they must take. If the distances and time available between shows is such that the drivers will infringe these regulations, a second driver must also be hired.

the stage set

ESSENTIALS
The stage set will also be transported in the trucks. Not every band requires an elaborate set, but even a drum riser needs to be calculated into the budget. The set will be of the mobile variety made by a company specialising in tour sets rather than a fixed set of the kind used for television and theatre. A tour set must be easily and quickly dismantled, and must therefore be built from materials that are sturdy, light, compact, and which fold up so that they take up as little space as possible in the trucks. There's a lot to consider in this respect, and a good set carpenter is worth his weight in gold. Included within the set will be the drapes and backcloths used in the show, and sometimes hydraulic equipment to lift platforms or staircases.

COSTUMES AND PROPS
If the artist wears stage clothes or costumes, an adapted flightcase is usually carried as a wardrobe in which to transport and store them. Sometimes, if clothes are a major part of the presentation, a full-time wardrobe person is employed to clean, maintain and be responsible for the stage garments. If any specific props are used, these are usually looked after and maintained by either the wardrobe person or the backline crew.

SPECIAL EFFECTS

Special effects, such as pyrotechnics, are usually referred to as simply 'specials'. They're often very expensive, and it will therefore be important to know if they are to be used at an early stage in the planning stages, so that they can be included in the budget. The use of pyrotechnics, lasers and strobes are governed by licensing laws, and normally advance notice of their use is required by the local authority health and safety inspectors and fire brigade. These officials will often attend the venue on the day of the show to check and approve the installation and operation of these effects and make sure that the public isn't in danger. They will have the power to prevent the effects from being used, if they think that they could be a danger to the audience, artists or crew, and should therefore be treated with respect and consulted in advance whenever possible. In order for pyrotechnics to be used in Europe, they'll need to be installed by a licensed technician who has an official permit.

VIDEO

On a tour, the term 'video' refers to any projection and video used in a performance. Most artists will be unable to use this until they experience megastardom, not so much due to the cost (although it is expensive) but rather due to the size of the venue needed to accommodate it, although the fixed screens now installed in many larger venues means that video is increasingly used on major tours. The pictures projected for the video can be either pre-recorded and edited tape for effects, live pictures from cameras or a mixture of both.

CATERING

Feeding crew and artists on a major tour can be a huge undertaking, which is made more difficult if some members of the team have dietary requirements that only specialist tour caterers will understand and be equipped to accommodate. A catering company is hired on bigger tours, where the crew are unable to leave the venue and the band aren't able to move around easily in public. The caterers will travel on the crew buses, and their equipment will be transported on the production trucks, along with the lights and sound equipment. If the tour isn't large enough to justify the expense of hiring a tour catering company, the crew will usually be given a per diem (a small daily payment to cover expenses, including those meals not provided with the accommodation).

security

PASSES

Passes play an important part of a tour's security and will be used to prevent any unauthorised person from going backstage. The ultimate backstage pass is the laminate, which predictably consists of a laminated pass with a photo and which is supplied to tour personnel with a lanyard to wear around their necks. These will almost certainly allow access to all areas, including the onstage and backstage areas and the dressing rooms.

However, on some tours an escort pass is issued, which allows access to dressing rooms only and is given only to the tour manager, the security staff, any wardrobe personnel and the person responsible for dressing-room catering. This allows the artists an extra level of privacy and security.

Day passes – also known as 'stickies' – will be given to visitors such as the press, the staff of the record company, local crew, the families of the artists or crew and any special guests. Depending on the access requirements of the visitor, the day pass may give access to all areas at all times, only certain areas or even backstage access after the show has finished. The colours of the day passes will change each day in an effort to prevent them from being re-used.

SIGNAGE

On larger tours, it's common practice to use pre-printed backstage signs to indicate direction to the stage, dressing rooms, dining room, production office and other areas in order to help people those people unfamiliar with the venue find their way quickly and efficiently around the backstage area.

ITINERARY

It's customary to produce an itinerary for every tour. This is a schedule for everyone, including the management personnel, the record company and touring personnel, and contains dates, venues, times and other useful contact information. This constitutes the touring bible, and it must never be misplaced, because all of the information contained within it is confidential.

SPRING TOUR 1999

DATE: **MONDAY 30TH MARCH**
TRAVEL: **ZENITH**
    211 AVENUE JEAN JAURES
    75019
    PARIS

TEL: **00 33 (0) 1 42 45 91 48**
FAX: **00 33 (0) 1 42 01 42 49**
CAP: **6000**

PLACE: **PARIS**
PROD: **00 33 (0) 1 42 45 99 5**
FAX/PROD: **00 33 (0) 1 42 45 99 5**
LOAD IN: **10.00AM (APPROX)**
S/C: **4.00PM**
DOORS: **6.00PM**

SUPPORT: **7.00PM**

MAIN: **8.00PM**

LOCAL PROMOTER: **PARIS PROMOTIONS**
    PARIS

TEL: **00 33 (0) 1 44 92 45 48**
FAX: **00 33 (0) 1 46 06 38 73**

CONTACT: **PASCAL**

PROD: **00 33 (0) 1 44 92 45 45**
FAX: **00 33 (0) 1 46 06 38 79**

AFTER-SHOW TRAVEL:
ALL BUSES O/N DRIVE PARIS–LONDON APPROX 300 MILES 10 HRS
BAND ARRIVE 10.00AM, HAMMERSMITH APOLLO
CREW ARRIVE MID–DAY, KINGS CROSS STATION

HOTEL: **HILTON**
    106 RUE ST EMILLION
    PARIS

TEL: **00 33 (0) 1 34 56 87**
FAX: **00 33 (0) 1 54 98 21**

ROOM SERVICE: **24HR**

FACILITIES: **SAUNA/DISCO/PUB**

HOTEL: **NO HOTEL**

TEL:
FAX:

ROOM SERVICE:

FACILITIES:

ADDITIONAL INFORMATION:
NOTE: LAST DAY FOR HANDING IN PASSPORTS FOR VISA APPLICATIONS

An example of a typical tour checklist

TOUR CHECKLIST

BAND	TOUR		DATE	
ITEM	**PERIOD**	**QUOTE**	**TO DO**	**DONE**
TOUR/CONTACTS				
AGENT				
PROMOTER				
VENUE				
TERRITORIES/RIDER				
TOUR ACCOUNTANT				
PERSONNEL				
MUSICAL DIRECTOR (MD)				
CHOREOGRAPHER/DANCERS				
TOUR MANAGER (TM)				
PRODUCTION MANAGER (PM)				
SOUND ENGINEER/FOH				
LIGHTING DIRECTOR (LD)				
BACKLINE TECHNICIANS/CREW				
CATERING				
SET CARPENTERS				
DRIVERS/TRUCKS & BUSES				
STAGE REQUIREMENTS				
SOUND EQUIPMENT				
MONITORS/IN-EAR MONITORS				
LIGHTING				
SET/HYDRAULICS/DRAPES				
VIDEO PROJECTION				
SPECIAL FX/PYROS				
STAGE PROPS/COSTUMES				
BACKLINE INSTRUMENTS				
TRANSPORT/TRAVEL				
HOTEL/QTY				
BUSES				
SPLITTER VAN				
FLIGHTS				
TRUCKS				
ADDITIONAL				
REHEARSALS/MUSIC/DANCE				
REHEARSALS/PRODUCTION				
CATERING				
ITINERARIES/PASSES				
MERCHANDISING				
PROMOTION				
RADIO/TV				
POSTERS/FLYERS				
MEET & GREETS				
SPONSORSHIP/BUY-ON FEE				
LEGAL				
BUDGET/FLOAT/PER DIEMS				
TOUR SUPPORT				
PUBLIC LIABILITY INSURANCE				
PERFORMANCE INSURANCE				
EMPLOYER'S/EQUIPMENT INSURANCE				

An example of a typical tour checklist

VENUE CHECKLIST

BAND		PERIOD	
VENUE		SHOW DATE	
ADDRESS		CAPACITY	
		LOAD-IN	
		DOORS	
TELEPHONE		SOUNDCHECK	
FAX		SUPPORT	
PRODUCTION TEL		MAIN	
PRODUCTION FAX		CURFEW	
CONTACT			
PROMOTER		TELEPHONE	
PROMOTER'S REP		FAX	
		MOBILE	
DRESSING ROOMS		PRODUCTION OFFICE	
ITEM		**ITEM**	
STAGE SIZE	W: D: H:		
CLEARANCE			
STAGE TYPE		PROSCENIUM ARCH	
PA WINGS		SIGHT LINES	
FOH POSITION		CRASH BARRIER	
LOAD-IN ACCESS		MASKING	
POWER LIGHTS		POWER SOUND	
FORK-LIFT		CHERRY-PICKER	
SET		RISERS/MARLEY	
PYROS/SMOKE		LICENCE/BY-LAWS	
DRY ICE/LASERS		SPECIAL EFFECTS	
LAND-LINE POWER		PARKING PERMITS	
FERRIES		TOLLS	
TOWELS		LAUNDRY/DRY CLEANING	
RUNNER		ELECTRICIAN	
FORK-LIFT DRIVER		RIGGER	
SECURITY		RED CROSS	
WARDROBE PERSON		WARDROBE CASES	
VISAS/WORK PERMITS		PASSPORT PHOTOS	
FIRE CURTAIN		SAFETY CERTIFICATE	
TICKETS SOLD		TICKET PRICE	
EXPENDITURE		INCOME	
WITHHOLDING TAX		PRS	
BROADCAST FEE		AGENT'S/PROMOTER'S FEE	
GUARANTEE/ADVANCE		COLLECTION	
TOTAL EXPENDITURE		TOTAL INCOME	
SHEET NUMBER:			

An example of a typical venue checklist

INSURANCE

It's of paramount importance that the risks involved in touring and performing shows are covered by insurance, and there are several specialist insurance brokers who deal with the touring industry and understand its idiosyncrasies. The insurance necessary to cover a tour can be covered by three categories:

- Public, products and employers liability cover, which covers liability for claims issued by the public or for those issued by people employed by the tour – a variety of insurance essential for absolutely all levels of touring activity;

- Equipment and personal possessions insurance, which should normally be taken out by individual musicians in respect of their instruments, although it's normal for rental companies to insist that the hirer takes out insurance to cover damage or theft to the equipment;

- Contingency insurance. This is insurance against cancellation, which can cover expenses incurred on the tour and, if required, it can assure payment of the artist's fees (including percentage payments), depending on the level of cover that is initially taken out.

paperwork

CARNET

This is a document that lists the goods transported in the trucks, such as instruments, amplifiers, sound, lighting and stage equipment, and specifies their monetary value and their countries of origin. It's an essential document for tours which span a number of countries, and is usually issued by a chamber of commerce in the town or city in which the tour production originates. A bond is deposited with this chamber of commerce to cover the value of the equipment, which in effect signifies the intention of the people transporting it to use it on the tour, but also affirms that they will return it to its original point of departure and not sell or dispose of any of it in any countries along the way. The possession of a carnet simplifies the acquiring of customs clearances at the borders of countries, and in effect means that all that's required is a customs officer's stamp on the carnet on entry and departure from their country in order to verify that the items of equipment have been checked in and out, therefore reassuring the individual customs authority that the touring company harbours no intent to import the equipment on a permanent basis with a view to selling it to a resident of that country, and that the importation is purely temporary for the purposes of presenting the shows and will be followed by the equipment's immediate exportation on completion of the shows, and ultimately by return to its country of origin. If you're in possession of this document, it means that you'll be able to avoid the charging of import taxes or duties on equipment and instruments, and it's absolutely essential for an international tour.

POST-PRODUCTION

On completion of the tour, it's the tour manager's responsibility to liaise with each member of the crew and to arrange that all of the items that have been carried on the tour are returned to their owners or stored in the artist's warehouse space, and especially to ensure that rental equipment is returned promptly and not left running up unnecessary rental charges. If a carnet is being used, the stamped copies – together with the rest of the paperwork – should be returned to the relevant authority from which they were issued, and the deposited bond will then be released. The tour manager should then work through the paperwork and check all of the invoices and budgeted bills. For those bills that haven't been budgeted, he should be able to explain to the artist and its management why such overages have occurred. The tour manager should be able to produce a complete set of show settlements which have been agreed with the promoters, and should ideally produce a summary of the number of people attending each show relative to the capacity of the venue, the relevant paperwork recording the guest lists and the number of complimentary tickets issued (whether or not these tickets were picked up), press items such as the names and contact details of those journalists who have either interviewed the artist or reviewed the show, and signed waiver forms submitted by the photographers who have taken pictures of the shows. He should also produce a set of accounts and receipts justifying all cash payments made by him during the tour.

Touring is a vital element of any artist's career. If a team of experienced and skilful professionals are employed, the complex business of planning and executing a tour will run smoothly, the shows will be visually appealing and they will provide the artists with the best possible conditions to reproduce their music for the audience, allowing them a chance to present themselves to their fans in a first-hand capacity, and – through a professionally and creatively presented live show – develop that all-important relationship with those fans that will help them achieve commercial success.

9 Press And PR

By Bernard Doherty

The job of a band's publicist can appear to be among the easiest and most attractive in the music business, because there seems to be so much scope for mixing work and having a good time, and the job doesn't require special academic achievements. However, the ability to think on your feet is essential.

The publicist has regular access to artists, and therefore has ample opportunity to observe their work at close quarters. For some people, this may be an appealing bonus; but an awe-struck, star-gazing publicist who wants to hang with the band is more of an all-round liability than an asset! Although it's true that many PR people in the industry have the opportunity to work directly and closely with the bands that they represent, the job is particularly demanding in a number of ways, and also has a great deal of stress and tension attached to it.

THE PUBLICIST'S ROLE

THE WORKING DAY

The publicist's average working day may begin at home with an unexpected phone call about a breaking news story in which one of his clients plays some part, and he'll then make the necessary calls to the management personnel. Instead of heading for the office, he must then change the day's timetable to accommodate the event, and meetings and other routine affairs are postponed so that he has time to deal with the new emergency.

Otherwise, the day that gets under way without such surprises may start with a skim-read of the morning tabloids, in which most music stories break.

The mix of the routine day's work might include phone calls to clients and journalists, either to talk about specific plans or merely to stay in touch; a drink with a useful media contact; a session of press interviews for an artist who has something new to promote; and an appointment at a photographer's studio to supervise the shooting of some new publicity pictures. There could also be a meeting to attend with record-company people in order to lay down the foundations of a new album or tour PR project. The variations on this theme are endless, and as a rule almost always mean a long and busy working day.

The publicist needs to have a nose for sniffing out a promising news story, a well-developed sense of loyalty and discretion, a genuine devotion to the job, a willingness to work very unsociable hours and a broad spread of skills and capabilities, some of which need to be almost instinctive while others are far from easy to learn and can't be acquired from any textbook or solely from a university or college course.

WHERE TO START

Extremely few independent music publicists set themselves up in business without previous PR experience, and the most usual place to acquire this experience is in the press office of a record company.

There are equal opportunities for women and men in the field of public relations. In fact, if there is an element of discrimination, it may very well favour women, and indeed some employers and some clients insist that, all other things being equal, women tend to make more persuasive (and therefore more successful) publicists, whether dealing with male or female journalists.

Broadly speaking, the role of the music business publicist is much the same whether the service is performed as an in-house employee or as an outside independent consultant. Part of the job's appeal is that it's comprised of so many individual activities, and the work is seldom repetitious. Each day's activities differ from those of previous days.

WHO EMPLOYS PUBLICISTS?

Artists in all sectors of the music business can benefit from press and publicity representation. The launch of an unknown newcomer needs the boost of added publicity to increase public awareness of a first record release or any initial public performances. The well-established box-office success and chart-topping recording star with a limited amount of time to spend on interviews and photo sessions needs the expert advice of a publicist concerning which editorial opportunities to take and which to turn down with the minimum loss of goodwill. The greater the artist's celebrity, the more the publicist's role includes an element of protection against unfavourable stories. It's naïve to believe that all publicity is good publicity, or to underestimate the damage that can be done to an artist's reputation when bad press is printed in the media.

In the music business, the largest employers of PR services are the record companies, many of which have their own in-house press offices run by a team of publicists and their assistants. Medium-sized and smaller record companies may not operate a full-blown department, but instead simply employ one or two publicists. Others who hire full-time publicists – or who retain the non-exclusive services of independent PR consultants – include music publishers, artists' managers and agents, independent record producers and recording studios, music-industry associations, concert-tour promoters and music-video production companies and their distributors. Out-of-house publicists – whether self-employed individuals or those who are part of a consultancy – may be retained on a year-round basis or periodically drawn when a client wants a short burst of PR activity in order to assist in the promotion and marketing of a product, which could be an album, a tour or a video.

Whatever the specific line of business in which the publicist's employer or a client is engaged, an artist or a roster of artists will be at the core of most PR campaigns. Without waiting for others to act on their behalf, individual artists often feel that their careers might benefit from the attention of a publicity consultant, and they will approach an independent publicist directly. Such deals can be on a short-term, single-campaign basis, or they can run for an open-ended period of time. As a rule, if both parties are getting along well, the publicist will hope to keep the account running indefinitely. The clout of the independent consultant is linked intrinsically to the strength of his client roster, and to the attractiveness of the names of those represented in the eyes of reporters.

WHAT SKILLS ARE NEEDED?

Previous journalistic experience is a great asset to anyone contemplating a career in PR, although not all journalists have the vocational inclination or the right temperament to move into PR. In theory, at least, a journalist who has had regular dealings with publicists should be better equipped to move from one end of the process to the other.

The publicist must be articulate, he must have a fairly large vocabulary, and he must also be a willing and able communicator, with an instinctive flair for spotting the makings of an interesting news story or an eye-catching picture. From the ragged jumble of biographical data or a heap of photographer's contact sheets, the publicist should be capable of picking out the tiniest speck of information which might be turned into some sort of media opportunity.

A DEDICATED PROFESSION

Office hours? Forget them! Early in the morning, breakfast TV and radio reporters and evening newspaper journalists working on first editions may have urgent need to reach a publicist. Similarly, people writing for final editions of morning papers often work through until midnight or later. PR work is therefore not for the person looking for a nine-to-five job. The responsible publicist or delegated deputy has a duty to remain available to the media 24 hours a day. To be unobtainable during the breaking of a news story concerning a client or employer can be a disaster.

areas of responsibility

ACTING AS A SOURCE OF INFORMATION

It's a basic function of the publicist to be thoroughly informed about the activities of the bands he represents. Accurate, adequate and up-to-date written information should be available to the media on request, and journalists should be able to acquire answers to questions promptly.

PUTTING OUT THE NEWS

The publicist needs to know how to construct an instantly attractive news release, sometimes creating a good story from less-than-attractive raw material, putting the vital facts at the top of the copy and the background information lower down. Brevity is as important as accuracy. News – real news – should be delivered by the fastest possible and most efficient method, preferably by fax or e-mail.

IMAGE BUILDING

Whether acting individually as head of a small independent PR consultancy or within a team of full-time marketing and promotional executives at a major record company, the publicist is directly concerned with image creation and revision. This can involve the design or improvement of a company's overall public image (with the introduction of fresh corporate livery and logo) or the professional image of an artist. It can be a fascinating challenge for the publicist to start from scratch on the creation, development and establishment of a new artist's image prior to a launch. The image of an artist is projected not only via a style of music but also by his appearance and personality.

Areas which a publicist is likely to cover include the definition of an artist's musical style, his visual image for photo sessions and public appearances and live performances (grooming, hair, clothing) and a choice of the most suitable media for the occasion (which publications or programmes to go for and which to treat as a lower priority, or even to simply avoid). A publicist may also become involved in redefining an established artist's image, particularly to coincide with a change of career direction.

PROMOTION AND PROTECTION

Positive promotion of the employer's or client's activities in the public marketplace is the top priority of the publicist. However, there are times in which a reverse strategy needs to be applied, and in these cases a different approach comes into play. Such occasions arise when there is a call for damage limitation over a story which threatens to spoil the image of an artist. A publicist's protective know-how can be employed in putting the best possible face on an unfavourable story, perhaps by countering quickly with something positive, and can also mean calling in favours from friendly media contacts. This is the area in which a publicist's diplomatic skills come into play, and the strength and level of his relationships with media people is very important.

STIMULATING MEDIA INTEREST

Mutual trust between a journalist and a publicist is the best basis for successful business. Schmoozing with media contacts in order to develop or consolidate relationships is fine, but the wise publicist delays hard-sell discussion of specific stories until another occasion rather than pushing specific stories. Many prefer to avoid hard-sell tactics altogether, knowing that there are few people who journalists dislike more intensely than the time-consuming, ear-bending publicist who hopes that sheer brute-force verbal assault will compensate for a weak case. The publicist's task is to present the facts in a persuasive way, but not to press a case too zealously or aggressively and therefore cause irritation.

SETTING UP INTERVIEWS

As a routine part of the job, a publicist arranges media interviews for clients and employers. Most of these will involve artists, and a necessary part of the publicists job is linking each interview with the most suitable journalist and offering potential interviewers a mutually appropriate (and sometimes exclusive) angle. Popular artists will be in such media demand that some interview requests will have to be turned down, although on the other hand some unknown newcomers or rising stars will need the publicist's extra push. Often the two extremes can meet at the middle, when a little subtle leverage is brought into play by the publicist.

ARRANGING PHOTOGRAPHY

As with writers and broadcasting journalists, photographers fall into two categories: freelance and staff. Among the freelancers are those who specialise in specific areas, such as album-sleeve photography. When pictures of an artist are being taken to accompany a particular article, the publicist may be less able to select a photographer by name, because the decision will be taken by the journalist or picture editor. Otherwise, it's up to the publicist to learn which photographers work best with which artists, and a good rapport between the two should produce substantially better pictures. Past experience will help the publicist to choose the best photographer for each different situation.

TRAVELLING

The frequency of a publicist's out-of-town trips will vary hugely according to the jobs in hand. A major artist on the road for a large series of concerts may require on-site PR services at each new leg of the tour in order to handle media interviews and to set up press conferences. The publicist should be prepared to travel sometimes, often at short notice, in order to accompany an important journalist to a gig and occasionally to cope with an unexpected surge of media interest – negative or positive – somewhere on the road.

RECEPTIONS AND CONFERENCES

Media receptions are held to launch publicity campaigns and are used to introduce new artists, sometimes with a showcase performance. Few such events are expected to generate immediate media headlines, and are arranged more to create general goodwill and prepare the way for more specific media situations at a later time.

Press conferences are more formal, and should involve the announcement of some sort of news. Typically, they are based on the distribution of a press release and a live question-and-answer session in which the concerned parties face rows of journalists and their photographers from behind a table. As a rule, the publicist acts as a moderator, controlling the flow of questioning.

ways into the business

ACADEMIC TUITION

At the time of writing, ten universities and colleges throughout England, Scotland and the Republic of Ireland offer courses in public relations or communication and issue degrees and diplomas recognised by the London-based Institute of Public Relations for purposes of membership. Such courses theoretically provide a sound fundamental knowledge of PR machinery, although not of its practical application within the music business. Students often gain mid-course hands-on experience by offering their (unpaid) services to a suitable company (in this case a record-company press office or an independent publicist's consultancy) during their long vacations.

JOURNALISTIC EXPERIENCE

Working for a local home-town newspaper or broadcaster can be a useful starting point, particularly if the chance exists to review concerts or records. A journalist receives press releases from publicists and learns to separate the useful and informative material from the badly written or badly targeted stuff, which can be a very valuable experience. Would-be publicists unable to find a job on a newspaper or a radio station can still submit reviews and other articles on music topics to feature editors and programme producers on a freelance basis. Even if they fail to be published, the writing experience will still be worthwhile.

EXPERIENCE IN THE MUSIC INDUSTRY

Juniors in the press office of a record company can pick up a lot of useful knowledge of the industry, and some are even lucky enough to fill in for more senior people from time to time. The would-be publicist learns from what goes on here, and isn't afraid to put forward ideas.

Only after accumulating sufficient qualifications by way of academic achievement and/or useful work experience should anyone contemplate applying for a publicist's job, probably with a record company. Smaller independent companies will take much less in the way of academic achievement if aspects of a candidate's personality seem to be right for the job. At this stage, timidity, uncertainty, hesitation or an inability to communicate your own best features will go against you. Moderate self-confidence, self-salesmanship, a controlled sense of humour, some intelligently inquisitive questions about the work you might be doing and a show of interest in the label's artists will go down well. Most importantly of all, the would-be publicist should demonstrate his knowledge of the media to the interviewers, and it's essential that he should know his subject: music in all its contemporary guises.

10 Managing Merchandising

By Andy Allen, Steve Brickle And Jef Hanlon

There are only two reasons to get involved in music merchandising: to maximise on the potential revenue involved, and to heighten public awareness of your band by ensuring that their logo or image is prevalent in the marketplace, on T-shirts, posters or chewing gum. The fact that you can persuade people to pay for the privilege of becoming a walking billboard or to pay to allow their walls to become a marketing tool featuring that same logo or image for your band is something that most managers will obviously find attractive. How one maximises the revenue and enhances the market impact will vary from band to band, depending on the type of the band and the size of its audience. Metal? Pop? Dance? Mainstream? Marketing for bands of each of these genres will require a different approach.

Sales of merchandise can be broken down into two main areas: sales at concerts and sales through retail, e-commerce, mail order and any licensing or sub-licensing. This latter category covers everything, including sales of shirts in record stores, sales of posters, badges, patches, and in fact anything that will benefit from association with your client's logo, image or endorsement. Fan-club direct sales also fall into this category.

tour merchandise

When first starting on a commercial career, one of the first things a band should consider is whether or not it's a worthwhile exercise to print some shirts to sell at their gigs. It's probably wise that a manager should refrain from this temptation until the demand is there, as the initial euphoria from being supported by a following of a few friends can lead to disappointing sales and, worse, the incurring of a debt before the band has even reached the bottom rung of the commercial ladder. As time passes, however, and the demand for merchandising increases, it will be necessary to make a decision on how best to arrange this. There are three options outlined here that you may wish to pursue.

SUPPLY-ONLY DEAL

Strike up a relationship with a merchandiser and operate on a supply-only basis. This deal requires you to accept the merchandise and then admit responsibility for the sales. You can either appoint someone to sell for you [from past experience this will normally end up being you] or can strike up a deal which, and involves the venue supplying personnel, who will check in and then sell the merchandise. You may encounter concession-hall fees or site-rental fees, but these are usually only charged at larger venues. With regard to a concession fee site, at the end of the show, the staff will return whatever stock is left over along with the cash they've taken, minus their percentage, which is generally 25% of cash taken, plus VAT, although at some larger venues they can charge more. This figure is calculated on the retail price, which means that the artist will actually be charged 29.38% of the net (plus VAT) or 25% of the gross (plus VAT). Although this has been a contentious issue in the industry for a long time, it appears that this arrangement will remain just the way it is for the foreseeable future.

ROYALTY-RATE DEAL

In a royalty-rate deal, the rate is calculated on gross sales. It's important to note, however, that gross sales are considered to be the retail price less taxes (ie VAT), and on some occasions the concession fee from a venue is also deducted before the royalty rate is calculated. The royalty rate is usually in the region of 25% to 35%, but – depending on how large an artist you manage – you may be able to negotiate a better rate, should the tour generate a higher income, or even to have an increase written into the deal, depending on performance of the tour. A merchandiser will generally offer a lower rate in foreign territories, which usually tends to be 75–80% of the domestic rate.

SPLIT-PROFIT DEAL

This deal is organised by the merchandiser responsible for the supply and sale of products on tour and for then analysing the figures at the tour's conclusion. Once calculated, an agreed split of the profits can be anywhere between 65/35 and, in extreme cases, 90/10. Generally, however, the average split is calculated between 75/25 and 80/20, in favour of the artist. It should be noted, however, that the merchandiser may take an administration fee, based on gross sales.

RETAIL

A merchandiser will generally sell your T-shirts, sweatshirts, caps and other merchandise to a specialist music merchandise wholesaler. (The royalty rates for merchandising span from 12% to 25% of wholesale.) Furthermore, they will attempt to procure licensing deals with other non-clothing merchandisers to merchandise other goods – for example, posters and badges. In consideration, they will take a percentage of roughly 20%. The agreed royalty rate will be generally 10% to 15% of wholesale.

E-commerce or mail-order will result in the receipt of approximately 20%-23% of gross sales. With foreign royalties, once again this will be approximately 80% of the UK rates.

Whether you arrive at separate tour and retail deals, or a combined one, there are a few points which are very important to remember:

- The artist should approve all designs and items of merchandise, and if the funds are available then the artwork should be copyrighted and trademarked;

- There should be a restriction of sell-off rights, which is important when the term comes to an end and there is excess stock left over. The merchandiser should try at some point (approximately three months before) to sell this stock, but the stock must then be destroyed or bought back;

- All sub-licensing deals need to be approved by the artist;

- Should an advance be received, it must be determined whether or not there will be cross-collateralisation on the tour and retail agreements;

- Deals operate either under a time limit or until the advance is recouped.
  However, there must be some contract term or time period stated to this
  effect in the contract, or it isn't legal.

ADVANCES

On occasions an artist can attain an advance from merchandisers, but these
agreements will require that the money is paid back if recoupment doesn't
occur. Merchandisers will build various contingency plans to safeguard their
investment, should the tour not take place or be unsuccessful, and there will
be various other clauses included – for instance, that the tour must take place
over a specified amount of time, or that a minimum number of paying clients
will be attending the shows.

As you can see, there are a variety of ways in which to put together a deal,
and the set-up depends on the requirements of the artist.

11 Insurance

By Martin Goebbels

Yes, it's accepted that insurance has the tag of being the world's most boring subject, but in all honesty, and to be fair to the insurance profession, this is often the fault of individuals who frankly don't want to pay any attention to the subject, want to minimise on the insurance that they buy, consider it an unnecessary expense and yet expect full and immediate payment as soon as there is a claim.

The whole subject, however, can be made far simpler than anticipated, and the first step in doing so would be to find a specialist broker for the entertainment industry, who would then:

- Fully understand your needs;

- Talk the same language;

- Know the relevant questions to ask;

- Be able to be relied on to provide the correct advice or reminders as and when policies become necessary;

- Never 'sell' policies to you that may not be needed but would instead offer the right guidance at the right time.

Don't ever be too shy to ask questions – no query is ever too silly or naive!

What follows is a brief résumé of some of the different types of insurance available and is intended to put into simplistic form the basic details of cover without getting bogged down in the nitty-gritty. It will hopefully provide the basis from which to consider your options.

the role of an insurance broker

It's important to understand the difference between an insurance broker and an insurance company/underwriter. It is the insurance company/ underwriter that takes all of the financial risk and dictates many of the terms and conditions, as well as the premiums. The insurance broker's role is to act on the client's behalf at all times, offering advice as well as obtaining the best deal, after having shopped around the various insurers that he feels would best suit his client's needs.

Whilst the broker will receive his fee from the insurance companies, it's imperative for you to feel that he's working on your behalf, and you must therefore be comfortable that he's not simply intending to make a fast buck. A reputable broker should be looking to build a long-term relationship with a client, and would therefore realise that, by not offering the most competitive premiums and the widest cover, he will end up conducting only a short-term business relationship.

In fact, it would be wise to incorporate an insurance broker as part of your team, in the same way that you would hire an accountant or a lawyer. Many people are apprehensive when it comes to talking to insurance brokers and historically keep them at arm's length, whereas if you liaise with them in the most open manner they will ultimately provide you with the widest cover and the least problems in the event of a claim being made – and let's face it, that's why you buy insurance.

Any broker who is experienced in dealing with the entertainment industry will not only share the ultimate confidentiality of a client but will also know when to disclose the correct and relevant information to an insurance company.

Obviously, the most important shop window for any insurance deal is the claim settlement, and again this is where a broker should come into his own, offering guidance and advice when presenting a claim to insurers and monitoring its progress until the point of settlement. However, most brokers will justifiably point out that, if it turns out that any information has been withheld by a client when a policy is placed – whether this is security details, the true value of sums insured, details of previous claims, etc – this will only cause major problems when a claim is made and may well invalidate a policy.

On many types of policy, these days it's common practice for insurers to use a loss adjuster, or claims assessor, whose role is to serve as an independent body, collating information and presenting facts to insurers. In many people's opinion, he acts more like a private investigator, with the sole intention of voiding or reducing any claim. In truth, however, this is not the case, and if a policy has been placed, and a subsequent claim has been presented in an honest and open manner, he won't represent a threat. Again, a broker should work with the client at this time, and if required he should attend any necessary meetings with the loss adjuster.

Unfortunately, no broker or insurer can guarantee a time frame for the settlement of a claim, and it's probably unfair to expect a claim to be settled within a few days, as they will both require certain information (receipts, back-up documentation, etc).

Finally, many insurance companies will come and go – particularly in the entertainment industry – depending on claims experience, and a reputable broker will monitor this and find the most suitable insurer for his client's particular needs.

It's not uncommon for some insurers to enter into the placement of policies for the music industry, sensing glamour and tinsel and something to impress the children, but soon back off once they realise that claims can still be made by even the most famous personalities! Most insurers won't allow dealings directly with the public and obviously won't be able to offer specialist advice, and therefore many of today's 'direct to the public' insurers aren't recommended for the sometimes peculiar needs of the entertainment business.

As a final word of warning on this subject, on the more regular policies, such as household and motor insurance, it should never be recommended not to fully disclose a policy-holder's true occupation – for example, 'engineer' isn't an adequate description for a rigger, nor is 'publisher' a suitable description for a renowned singer/songwriter.

To lie or be hazy on any information is a false economy and means in reality that you'll be wasting money on buying a product that will be of no use when claiming.

policies to be considered

EQUIPMENT
This covers the band's equipment and any stage, scenery, set and props, as well as stage clothing and costumes (which may need to be noted separately). All policies will exclude mysterious disappearances (you will need to provide physical proof of any theft) or material damage to any equipment, as insurers will balk at a claim presented to them by a client who hasn't checked his equipment for some time and seems to be a few items lighter than he was when he last looked. Always keep insurers updated on regular storage location details, and ensure that your total amount insured is adequate. It's imperative to report any losses to the police or local authorities (airlines, carriers, etc) within 24 hours of any loss.

EMPLOYER'S/PUBLIC LIABILITY
Employer's liability is a legal requirement for any employer. It covers legal liability for any accidents or injuries happening to any employees in connection with their work. Public liability, meanwhile (which isn't a legal requirement but is highly recommended in these litigious days), covers the policy-holder's legal liability for any accident or injury to any third parties or any damage to third-party property. (Promoters and venues would also have to have their own policies, but these wouldn't cover the band's risk.) It is also recommended that a manager or management company is added as an additional policy-holder to an artist's policy (normally this shouldn't incur any extra charge) in order to ensure the widest cover.

CANCELLATION/NON-APPEARANCE
This policy can cover your costs and/or loss of profit (plus merchandise and sponsorship, if required) in the event of a show or number of shows being cancelled due to reasons beyond your control. This can – and should – include record-company support, which would generally be recoupable from future income.

Examples of cancellations range from illness, injuries (including to principal performers and backing musicians and should be extended to include their respective families, which may be charged additionally), adverse weather, transport delays and periods of national mourning. The principal exclusions are breach of contract, lack of ticket sales and other financial causes.

This policy should also provide cover in respect of a show being cancelled due to adverse weather. It's possible that you may still be paid the fee by the promoter if this was the case, but if the show was a loss-making venture, from the band's point of view, the shortfall in costs would be picked up by insurers, as would the guarantee, if this had to be returned to the promoter. Additionally, any extra expenses incurred in making alternative arrangements in order to proceed with a show would be borne by insurers, provided that these expenses weren't greater than that involved with cancelling the show in the first place.

CANCELLATION (RECORDING TIME)

This policy would cover your costs and expenses incurred should you have to cancel recording time due to reasons beyond your artist's control. This would particularly relate to illness, but in view of various storm damage and flood incidents in recent winters it would also apply if the studio became unusable for these reasons and you ended up having to make alternative arrangements at additional expense.

Should you be a studio owner yourself, the same cover can apply to protect your income or your additional costs incurred by having to rent an alternative studio rather than use your own.

TOUR CASH

This covers the cash float carried by the tour manager or by any authorised representatives of the policy holder. The principal exclusions here are as follows:

- Losses that occur while not being in the policy holder's personal possession or in a locked safe;

- Mysterious disappearances;

- Losses not reported to the police within 24 hours.

TRAVEL INSURANCE
This can be arranged either on a short-term or annual basis to cover emergency medical expenses, personal luggage and personal cash, as well as other fringe benefits, whilst travelling either on business or pleasure. Annual policies are highly recommended, as they work out to be much cheaper and the terms of cover are far wider. It is vital to ensure repatriation to the UK is included within the policy.

NB: Do be wary of policies offered by airlines and credit-card companies, as they often carry restrictions, particularly relating to the entertainment industry, and they may only be in force when their own card or airline is used.

PERSONAL ACCIDENT
This covers accidental death and/or permanent disablement from the insured person's normal occupation. The policy can be taken out by the artist, the manager, the record company, publishers, etc. It can cater for a manager's investment in the band, but it should also be considered by the band members as a way of covering their fellow band members if it's considered that they would suffer severe financial loss if anything happened to any one of them – particularly the songwriters.

CONFIDENTIAL PROGRAMME
This is a policy designed for record companies, publishers and managers who need to protect their investments in their artists through insurance but are unable to obtain suitable medical information or do not wish their insured artists to be aware that they have arranged the insurance. To take out such a policy, they need only fill in a very brief proposal form. However, there is a condition that the insured person cannot be aware of the existence of the policy. The policy was designed by Robertson Taylor many years ago to cater for the needs of record companies, publishers and managers who may have a particular problem with having medicals undertaken by an insured person.

MASTER TAPES
Not so relevant these, this would cover re-recording costs incurred in the event of any recorded material (audio or visual) or photographic material being lost or damaged.

OFFICE INSURANCE

This is a standard package to cover office contents, liability, office cash, etc. This may need to be looked at separately, even if the office is set up at home, as household policies will not cover professional office use. Make sure that any laptops and mobile phones are covered while you're away from the office.

HOUSEHOLD

This covers your building or home contents, with consideration to extend the policy to include items – particularly clothing, computers, mobile phones, jewellery, cash, etc – while you're away from home. Don't assume that your policy will automatically include musical equipment (or home studios), as standard exclusions on general policies will not provide cover for professional equipment.

MOTOR

This policy covers either cars or commercial vehicles and, if necessary, can be arranged on a short-term basis, although comparatively speaking this always proves very expensive.

12 Band Agreements

By Rupert Sprawson

In terms of legislation, the Partnership Act of 1890 has withstood the test of time. For over a century of enormous social and economic change, it has remained the foundation upon which many business relationships have flourished. However, the application of the Act to the relationship between band members is often either ignored or dealt with inadequately, as has been highlighted in the recent court battles between the former members of both The Smiths and Spandau Ballet.

Put simply, a partnership arises when individuals carry on business together with a view to making a profit. In the context of bands, this normally happens when band members start performing, recording or writing together. In the absence of an agreement between band members, the Partnership Act will determine the rights and liabilities between the partners and against third parties. Although the agreement need not necessarily be in writing, it can be hard (and sometimes impossible) to prove the existence or terms of an oral agreement. This point was illustrated in the Smiths case, referred to below.

The implications of relying on the Act are as follows:

- Actions by one band member in the course of carrying on the band's business will bind all of the members. For example, all members will be individually liable (on a joint and several basis) for the cost of hiring equipment, even if that equipment was hired by only one member. This principle even extends to the actions of a band's employees, if a hire company can reasonably be expected to assume that the employee was acting with the band's authority. However, if one member finds that he's had to foot a bill for more than his share of a partnership debt, he's entitled to reimbursement from his other partners;

- Each member is entitled to share equally in the capital and profits of the band, and must contribute equally to the losses;

- A member will continue to remain liable even after he has left the group where a liability has arisen as a result of actions or omissions of other members while the leaving member was still with the group;

- Members cannot be expelled from the partnership, but the partnership can be dissolved by a member on notice. (This need not necessarily be in writing);

- A member must account to the partnership for any profits made by him from any activity connected to the partnership, including any activity competing with that carried on by the partnership. This arguably means that any solo projects or session work carried out by a member would have to be accounted to the partnership.

It's for these and other reasons that careful and practical consideration must be given to the rights and liabilities of each individual member and towards each other. The following list of issues should be addressed when a band first start performing or writing together.

COMMUNICATION

The effective running of a band requires good communication between the band's members and their manager. It's sensible for the partnership agreement to include a provision for regular meetings, including meetings with the manager.

PROFITS

This can often be a source of great tension, as demonstrated in recent court cases involving the former members of The Smiths and Spandau Ballet. Issues which can result in intense rivalry, and even open conflict, include each individual's contribution to the group (by way of ownership of instruments) and songwriting and/or a band member's public perception thereof (ie who is the driving force behind album sales). A member may also be pursuing a solo career.

If the scope of the partnership doesn't encompass songwriting, each songwriting member of the band is entitled by right to all of the 'composer's share' of publishing income generated by his songs. However, it's common for a proportion of this income to be distributed to the other members of the band in recognition of their contribution as performers and as helping to generate income for those songs. They may also have contributed – albeit indirectly – by adding a riff or by encouraging the songwriter's creative ability. If there is a material contribution to a song, the contributors may also be entitled to claim that they are co-writers. The not-uncommon practice of registering a non-contributing member as a co-writer is not to be encouraged, however; it can lead to problems with publishers, can lead to unexpected problems at a later date and may be fraudulent.

The conflicts which can arise were all too clearly seen when, in the Smiths case, Johnny Marr and Morrissey contended that Mike Joyce and Andy Rourke were each entitled to only 10% of the band's profits. Marr and Morrissey supported their case by relying on various conversations, extracts from the band's accounts and evidence from their accountant. The court didn't accept the evidence of Marr and Morrissey or their accountant, and went as far as to state that Morrissey's evidence was 'devious and truculent', deciding in the end that Joyce (Rourke had previously settled) was entitled to a 25% share of the band's profits (ie an equal share). Marr's and Morrissey's appeal was unsuccessful.

In the case involving the former members of Spandau Ballet, Tony Hadley, John Keeble and Steve Norman argued that they were still entitled to share in Gary Kemp's songwriting income, although he had stopped paying them a share many years before. They argued that there had been a binding agreement for him to keep paying this income to them, although their contribution to Kemp's songwriting had been negligible. The judge found Kemp's version of events the more satisfactory of the two, and didn't accept that there had been an element of 'offer' and 'acceptance' to form a binding contract. The claim failed.

EXPENSES

Normally, these are shared in the same proportion in which group income is shared. However, there may be grey areas that need to be discussed – for example, a band member who decides to spend money in areas totally unconnected to the band's activities or decides to take his partner or a relative on tour should be expected to personally meet any such costs. A band member may also want to travel more economically than the other band members. Should he therefore benefit from the resulting savings? These issues must be discussed and dealt with appropriately.

If a partner incurs an expense outside of the normal business of the partnership, he would probably not bind the partnership in any event and this expense should fall to him personally.

EQUIPMENT

Any decision to sell or acquire equipment using band funds which is intended to be owned jointly by the band should be a joint decision. On the other hand, if a member has paid for equipment personally, he can take it with him when he leaves. If the band wishes to retain the equipment, one way of doing so would be to pay any outstanding balance and give the leaving member his proportion of this money. Where there is a hire purchase arrangement, one of the members may have to act as a nominee for the purposes of owning and purchasing the equipment. In these situations, care must be taken to protect the nominee from any liability that he may suffer individually (ie if a hire-purchase company seeks to recover an outstanding debt from the nominee).

GROUP NAME/MERCHANDISING

In many cases, the band's name can be the partnership's most valuable asset. Merchandising and sponsorship income – whereby a band's name and image are licensed or a product is endorsed – can constitute a valuable source of income. The Spice Girls are a good example of a group who have capitalised on their image and created a strong and recognisable brand. A band's image – insofar as it is distinctive, distinguishing its products and services from those of others and indicating their source of origin – can possibly be protected by registering it as a trademark. Even without the protection of a trademark, bands can protect their names against unauthorised use by others under the law of passing off, although this can be more difficult than bringing an action for the infringement of a registered trade mark.

Unless the band's name is that of one of its members, or is owned by one member as an asset, it will be owned equally by the members partnership.

This can lead to competing claims when a band splits up. If one member owns the rights to a name, he will continue to be allowed to use the name after the band has split up. However, its continued use may end up confusing the public, who may associate this use with the band prior to its break-up. Any such use could also lead to a passing off action, if such use leads to confusion and causes damage to the original band's goodwill or finances.

A similar problem arose in a recent appeal against a decision to dismiss an application to invalidate a trademark registration in the name of 'Saxon'. The mark was registered by two former members of the heavy metal band. The appeal was brought by Peter Byford, who was in the original lineup and had continued to perform with the band through its various manifestations over the years.

The proprietors of the trade mark performed in a number of bands since they had left the original line-up, including 'Graham Oliver's Saxon' and 'Oliver/Dawson Saxon'. The band had never had a partnership agreement.

The trademark owners argued that as original members of the band, they as former partners, were entitled to use the name 'Saxon', an asset of the original partnership.

The judge disagreed. He said that the former members did not own the name or the goodwill or any part of it and definitely in the case of one of the ex-members, had abandoned any interest in the original partnership's trading style and the goodwill generated in the name. The judge went on to add that if any of the former members performed under the name 'Saxon' they could be sued for passing off by the band in respect of its most recent use of the name and the goodwill. The original partnership could also bring proceedings against the use of the name by a former member. The appeal was successful and the application was allowed.

These problems could have been avoided if the original band had entered into a partnership agreement which had expressly provided for the partnership to continue on the departure of one or more members and confirmed the right of the continuing and expressly limited the right of departing members to make use of the partnership name and goodwill.

The use of the name, therefore, must be dealt with at an early stage. If a band splits up into competing factions, one practical solution may be to allow the faction consisting of the majority of band members to use the name. Where there is a deadlock, any decision could be made by an 'independent' third party. Where one member of a band owns the rights in a name, it's possible to provide a mechanism whereby, when the band splits up, the member in question must license the name to members of the band who wish to continue using it, in return for a royalty.

LEAVING AND NEW MEMBERS

In the absence of an agreement, changes in the line-up of a band are subject to a unanimous decision. However, there may be situations in which the band feels that any such decision can be taken by a majority decision. This must be dealt with in the partnership agreement.

Any new member joining the band must be careful about what liabilities he is inheriting from those leaving the band. In the absence of any written agreement, a new member won't take over the liability of his predecessor. However, by becoming party to an agreement which may relate to albums and other product on which the new member's predecessor performed or was involved with (ie a settlement agreement), he may find himself carrying burdens from the past. A new member should seek proper legal advice.

A leaving member will continue to be paid royalties and a share of advances on albums and other tracks on which he has performed, but he shouldn't continue to receive a share of any merchandising income, because it relies on future participation as a member of the band.

Sometimes a member may leave just before an album is recorded but after he has received a share of the album advance. This is particularly unfair when the other members must continue to record, tour and generally support the album. Therefore, it would be prudent to agree in writing that, for example, a member isn't entitled to a share of any advance unless he has remained with the band for a period of time and performed on a minimum number of tracks on any forthcoming album. Also, on receiving notice of his intention to leave, a band must also consider forthcoming tours and gigs which would be prejudiced with the departure of that member.

When a member leaves, all accounts should be brought up to date and the proportion of any income due to him checked and paid. The member will need to be released from all liabilities and will have to indemnify the partnership from any liabilities that they may incur as a result of any improper or unlawful behaviour on his part.

It's usual under a recording and/or publishing agreement for the publisher

269

or record company to sign a leaving member under an exclusive agreement similar to the existing one. In these cases, their accounts will need to be separated out, uncrossed, and those recording costs already incurred will have to be pro rated for the purposes of recoupment.

CONFLICT OF INTEREST

In advising a band it is vital to ascertain from the members of the band whether or not an arrangement or agreement they are about to enter into properly reflects each of their positions. Where an arrangement clearly favours some members over others then a conflict of interest may arise where all the members of the band are represented by one solicitor. In such circumstances those members of the band who are adversely affected by the arrangement must be advised to take independent legal advice.

The issue of conflict recently arose in a an action brought by the former drummer of Oasis, Anthony McCarroll, against the band's solicitors at the time their record deal was signed with Sony in 1993.

The effect of that agreement was that the name 'Oasis' was owned by the Gallagher brothers and left Mccarroll vulnerable to instant dismissal without compensation. McCarroll argued that the band's solicitor was negligent and that if he had been properly advised he would have taken independent legal advice and secured written terms of partnership which would have protected him from the risk of being summarily expelled.

McCarroll was unsuccessful in his claim, although on completely different grounds, it being decided that the claim had not been brought within the statutory time limits.

The case highlights the steps which must be taken to ensure that each member of a band is fully aware of arrangements which may adversely affect him and benefit the others. Where no consensus is reached then a dissenting partner must be given the opportunity of obtaining independent legal advice.

OTHER MATTERS TO CONSIDER

The following areas must also be considered:

- The appointment of a bank and the opening of a bank account;
- The choice of band members to be signatories on the account;
- The appointment of accountants;

- The appointment of solicitors;
- The appointment of manager;
- Whether there is to be unanimous consent for issues such as loans;
- Creative decisions;
- Changes in the group name;
- The appointment and dismissal of members;
- The purchase of equipment;
- The procedure when entering into recording and/or publishing agreements.

LIMITED COMPANIES

Although the administration and running of a company is more burdensome and expensive than running a partnership, the security that a shareholder receives and the attraction of limited liability may make it a preferred vehicle to carry the band's activities. Taxation will be one of your main considerations in deciding whether a limited company should be formed, and the advice of the band's accountant should be sought before any such move is contemplated. It may be more suitable for just the band's publishing and, in some cases, its touring activities to be channelled through a limited company, but again proper professional advice must be sought. In some cases, each individual band member establishes his own service company. (It's worth noting that the accounts and directors' details of a limited company must be filed with Companies House, and that these are open to public inspection.)

LIMITED LIABILITY PARTNERSHIPS

This new form of business organisation was created by the Limited Liability Partnerships Act of 2000. An LLP is designed to be a hybrid between a conventional partnership and a limited company. The Act LLP itself is a separate legal entity, and its benefit is that its members enjoy limited liability. Although the filing requirements are the same as those for a limited company, the Act doesn't impose a structure to determine the management of an LLP. For tax purposes, LLPs are treated as ordinary partnerships, with the partners being liable to pay tax under Schedule D for their share of any profits. As with normal partnerships, the Limited Liability Partnership Act imposes implied terms in the absence of an agreement.

CONCLUSION

When bands seek legal advice, they tend to focus on their dealings with third parties, such as record companies and publishers. However, they frequently ignore the relationship between themselves and how this should be governed and regulated. All too often one hears the phrase, 'We're all mates and we trust each other.' However, money, success, creative tensions and egos can all play a part in undermining any notion of mutual trust and confidence which may exist at the outset of band members' relationships with one another. Ignorance is no defence, though, and issues shouldn't be left to chance and the rigidities of English partnership law.

As with any creative relationship, there will be driving forces within the band and members will have varying degrees of talent and temperament. Although a partnership agreement may not be able to deal with personality conflicts and irreconcilable creative differences, it will help create a more structured and secure environment and preclude the need (as happened in the Smiths case) to rely on an elderly statute in the light of difficult and often conflicting evidence.

13 Information And Communication Technology

By Nigel Parker

To many people, the term information and communication technology (ICT) means the internet and little else. It's true that the internet plays a crucial role, but in truth it's only one aspect of the much broader trend of convergence. Convergence describes the process whereby the telecommunications, broadcasting and computer industries are moving closer to one another, and the theory is that they will ultimately merge seamlessly together, driven by technology and consumer demand.

Digital technology has given these industries previously unimaginable capacity to deliver information in digital form to consumers at home, in the workplace and – through portable communications devices – while on the move. The speed of technological development has created a dynamic and, at times, frenzied commercial atmosphere as entrepreneurs struggle to find profitable applications for the researchers' inventions. Whilst 1999 was full of stories of instant internet millionaires and billionaires, 2000 was dominated by the bursting of the 'dotcom' bubble.

One telling indication of the speed and severity of the shake-down which has taken place during 2000 is the fate of the 17 dotcom companies which took TV advertising during coverage of that year's US Super Bowl, which is about the most expensive TV advertising in the world. Of the 17 companies, ten were no longer in business and only three were still taking advertising in early 2001.

In such a rapidly moving world, it would be impossible to make a work which is intended to be current for one year as up to the minute as a newspaper article. Therefore, this chapter attempts to look at the longer-term issues and trends in the field of ICT and, in particular, their bearing on the music industry. Its aim is to give managers a basic understanding of the commercial and legal issues which the new environment has thrown up and some responses to them.

THE DIGITAL INFRASTRUCTURE

The vast sums which have been spent researching and developing the digital distribution infrastructure dwarf the record industry. This difference in scale can be hard to appreciate from the perspective of an artist, but in political and economic terms it is crucial. For example, the only major record company quoted on the UK stock market, EMI, has a market value approximately one-twentieth the size of BT, which is only one of a number of UK-quoted telecommunications companies. As a further example of the size of these companies, at one point in the '80s Nippon Telecom, the Japanese telephone operator, had a market capitalisation greater than the whole of the German stock market.

In order to obtain a return on their huge investments in the new infrastructure, companies such as BT, Orange, AOL, Ericsson and Vodafone must first persuade consumers to accept and use the new technologies. They and their online business customers must then develop products and services which can be sold profitably to consumers through the new media. The process of converting on-line surfers into paying customers is known as *monetising*, and is the Holy Grail for all online traders. In other words, everyone is looking for digital information that customers are prepared to pay for – or *content*, as it has come to be known.

Competition law prevents infrastructure companies from simply buying up significant content providers (for example, see Rupert Murdoch's failed attempt to acquire Manchester United Football Club), so the infrastructure companies have used their scale and their very significant lobbying budgets to wield enormous political influence at a national, European and global level. Their principal aim is to ensure that copyright and e-commerce laws obstruct distribution as little as possible.

In the context of the EU Copyright Harmonisation Directive and E-commerce Directive, the companies have strenuously lobbied the EU to excuse online distributors from liability for distributing material which infringes copyright. As an illustration of their political influence, the UK Department of Trade and Industry has about 150 full-time employees working in the telecoms sector and not one employee with full-time responsibility for the music industry.

CONTENT AND THE INFORMATION SOCIETY

The term 'content' is indicative of the technocratic mindset which is currently driving the online revolution. Infrastructure development is led by technology rather than by consumers. Consumers don't set out to buy an undifferentiated commodity called content any more than they set out to buy consumer goods in general. When a consumer buys a fridge, it's because they need a fridge – a television isn't an acceptable substitute. Similarly, for consumers of music, not only is Westlife not a substitute for Funkadelic or Nine Inch Nails, it isn't even a substitute for Boyzone.

Many of those who work in the creative industries object to the use of the term 'content' to describe what they produce. It's true that digitisation allows us to homogenise Picasso, Spielberg, Rachmaninov, The Rolling Stones, US nuclear secrets and more or less anything into a series of zeros and ones, but this doesn't mean that anything which can be digitised becomes mere 'information' and, by implication, a commodity in the public domain.

Those who advocate the economic benefits of the 'information society' stress the importance of the freest possible flow of information. This overlooks the fact that the most valuable 'information' is created – often at great expense – and therefore owned by someone. Use of this intellectual property without the owner's consent or control damages the economic interests not only of the rights owner but of all of us who live in developed Western economies, which depend on the orderly commercial exploitation of creativity in order to maintain their high standard of living.

The term *information society* stresses the point of view of the distributor of information at the expense of the creator. The term 'information' should properly be used exclusively to describe true public-domain information of the kind disseminated in newspapers. If intellectual property – such as copyright, patent, trade mark, design, confidential information and expertise – is treated as mere information, the internet represents the greatest possible threat to the preservation of our place in the global economy.

The failure to grasp the unique aesthetic, personal nature of music is not altogether surprising in organisations which are used to selling simple commodities, such as telephone time. However, if these companies treat music as a commodity, merely as a subset within 'content' or 'information', the infrastructure providers are missing an opportunity to earn much greater long-term profits. There is more to be gained from co-operating with the music industry – which has a long history of marketing music successfully – than from treating it as an adversary.

OPPORTUNITIES FOR MUSIC

The music business is uniquely placed both to benefit and to suffer from the explosion in demand for content on the converging services. Music can be delivered electronically, its perceived cultural and economic value is high and it can be turned into digital data files small enough to be sent between computers cost-effectively. Only a few years ago, computer experts were predicting that it would never be possible to exchange digital data through existing phone lines at speeds that would make the downloading of music viable. Now we know otherwise.

The speed of technological change is so fast that there is a danger of allowing transient developments and temporary problems to obscure the longer-term trends. Recent events suggest that all new technology is likely to prove intermediate, and consumers are wary of paying out to acquire obsolescent technology. For example, take-up of ISDN lines from BT was hampered by the imminent arrival of the much cheaper ADSL technology. WAP phones have also failed to sell as quickly as had been hoped, largely owing to the impending introduction of improved technologies such as Bluetooth and increased memory chips for the next generation of mobile phones.

ICT - THE ARTISTS' PERSPECTIVE

It's clear that the new ICT allows artists and their consumers to communicate with each other in new ways. In particular, many artists see the internet as a way of bypassing the stranglehold which major record and publishing companies have on the distribution of music and a way of allowing them to access their fans directly. This process has been dubbed *disintermediation* (ie cutting out the middle-man). However, the internet has spawned a new distribution network which has taken over some of the roles of the traditional record industry, a process called *re-intermediation*.

For some artists, ICT is a weapon against their old foe, the record industry. Whilst the new environment has some advantages for certain types of artists at particular points in their careers, these are far from decisive or universal. The vast majority of new artists will still spend much of their careers dealing with record and publishing companies, to say nothing of those who are already under contract with record and publishing companies for the foreseeable future. It's true that ICT has given rise to new areas of disagreement and negotiation between the record industry and its artists. More significantly, however, it has exposed huge areas of common ground, especially concerning the extent of copyright and the means by which it can be licensed to users.

ICT - THE RECORD COMPANIES' PERSPECTIVE

Record companies have seemingly been slow to embrace ICT. Many commentators have ascribed this apparent reluctance to their supposed incompetence or lack of understanding of the new technologies. In truth, however, the record companies have little incentive to hurry. Although many records are exchanged between users over the internet without payment of royalties, thereby depriving the record companies of income, sales of CDs globally have held up remarkably well, even in the US, where internet use has been the highest. Private copying has always been an irritation to the industry, and the record companies have wisely concentrated their initial efforts on dealing with commercial piracy and lobbying for strong copyright laws.

There is no benefit to the record industry in embracing new technology unless it can increase its income by doing so. This requires a secure method of delivery and payment for music. To this end, the record industry spent hundreds of millions of dollars developing a system known as SDMI (Secure Digital Music Initiative). The encryption incorporated within this system was supposed to be so effective that the industry offered a reward of $100,000 to anyone who could crack it. Within a few days of its launch, several claimants for the reward had come forward. This is clearly a major embarrassment, although not a terminal setback.

The delay in developing SDMI – and in searching for a substitute – has skewed the marketplace, since it is virtually impossible to buy authorised music from major artists on the internet. EMI's attempt to release 40 or so albums on the internet in a secure format was foiled when all of the albums were found to be available free of charge on the MP3 format within a few hours. So far, unauthorised users have so far had a relatively free ride, but other systems of secure delivery and payment will be developed (although the technology will probably not be owned by the record industry). Billing and security techniques already adopted by the credit-card and telephone companies have obvious applications in this area, and the systems that they use are likely to form the basis of the commercial online delivery of music.

The record companies' attitude to the internet has also been misinterpreted by those who see the litigation against MP3.com and other unauthorised sites as naïve and hopeless. The genie is out of the bottle, it is said, and there is nothing that the record industry can do to put it back. There are many who believe that copyright law simply doesn't (or shouldn't) apply to the internet, or that any application is only theoretical, since in practice music is exchanged freely on the internet without payment. These views betray a touching naïveté of their own, as well as demonstrate a lack of experience in the litigious nature of the entertainment industries. Have these people never heard the saying, where there's a hit there's a writ?

Even if the aim of litigation isn't to put MP3.com and others out of business altogether, which is doubtful, and even if that aim hasn't been realised, the record industry nevertheless gains many advantages from such court actions. By forcing the major commercial suppliers of music on the internet to spend money on litigation, and by exposing them to the risk of enormous damages, the record industry deters other potential competitors from entering the market and increases the likelihood that MP3.com and others will agree to pay a reasonable licence fee for the music they supply, as indicated by BMG's agreement to license MP3.com. Just as with MTV (which was also in a long-running dispute with the record industry over copyright), eventually other record companies are likely to follow BMG's lead and reach agreements with MP3.com.

As the 19th-century German General Von Clausewitz observed, 'War is diplomacy carried on by other means.' The litigation is simply part of a negotiation between the record industry and internet music suppliers. Far from needing to eradicate these businesses altogether, the record industry wants to transform them into new avenues of authorised distribution. Eventually, it will be easier to buy than to steal, and most consumers will take the line of least resistance, even if they have to pay for it.

ICT – THE NEW USERS' PERSPECTIVE

From MP3.com's point of view, paying a licence fee to the record industry in exchange for legitimacy and co-operation would be a reasonable commercial outcome of the litigation. At worst, the litigation represents MP3.com's bid to drive down the price it ultimately has to pay. At best, the company may succeed in establishing that it isn't infringing copyright, although this seems unlikely. Above all, the litigation isn't a sign that things aren't working. Quite the reverse, in fact; it's a sign that – in the virtual world, as in the real world – the normal rules of business apply. It's business as usual.

Proponents of the new technologies point to the internet as being a marvellous promotional tool for the record industry, and some statistics would seem to support this view, in the current state of the market. However, if one thing is certain, it's that the market will change. As the new technologies gain greater public acceptance – especially among older, more affluent consumers – sales of physical sound carriers will inevitably decline. As these sales of physical objects are replaced by the online delivery of music and – with the advent of broadband technology – TV and film, there will be a pressing need to replace the lost income with licensing income.

An identical argument has been used in the past by radio and television broadcasters (most recently by MTV in relation to music videos) to justify making no, or only nominal, payments for airplay. As past experience shows, it is inequitable to lay down the laws which are to govern a market over the long term at a time when the market is immature. With this in mind, the record companies' policy of delaying the introduction of licensed online music, coupled with the long delay in completing the European Copyright Harmonisation Directive, is likely to benefit the music industry and artists alike.

The music and broadcasting industries are often described as being symbiotic, but this is obviously untrue. Whilst the music industry could survive without music radio (albeit in a markedly different form), music radio would disappear altogether without the music industry.

More recently, the same description has been applied, with even greater inaccuracy, to the relationship between the music industry and online distribution, especially via the internet. The truth is that the music industry has no need of the internet; it functions perfectly well without it. In contrast, it's clear that, for the internet to have any long-term commercial potential, it desperately needs the products of the music and the film industries, if only because they are the only consumer goods that can be delivered online.

Furthermore, online delivery has far greater potential to damage the record industry by being a substitute for the sales of physical sound carriers than the traditional forms of radio and TV broadcast. The most important issue facing the music industry now is how online delivery of music should be licensed, and at what price.

THE IMPOSSIBLE DREAM

One of the enduring myths that have grown up around the new technologies is embodied in the following quotation from a lobbying document prepared by British Telecom entitled 'The EU Copyright Directive – Essential Facts And FAQs': 'The internet is enabling SMEs and individuals to enter and compete in markets from which they have traditionally been excluded.' Here is the age-old dream that technology will help the little guy compete on the same terms as the big corporations, rather implausibly styling BT as the little guy's best friend. In the real world, this won't happen.

Why not? Well, there are a number of reasons. Consider these recent results from Forrester Research in the US: the top 50 internet sites take 95% of all advertising revenue; 80% of Mexican internet consumers buy from US sites; local businesses will lose 6% of their business in one year to national businesses as a direct result of online trade. Combined with this, shopping online from people you never see or even speak to can be disorienting, especially following widespread publicity questioning the security of disclosing personal details online. More than ever, consumers want the reassurance of dealing with brand names that they know and trust.

BARRIERS TO COMPETITION

Absolutely anyone can set up a web site selling goods or services, and it's much less expensive than opening a high-street store. The problem is that it's too easy. Entering the market by opening your doors for online business is only the first step; if you want to compete and make money, you have to let potential customers know that you're there and persuade them that it's safe to buy from you. That's the hard part.

The MMF encountered similar arguments when it appeared at the Monopolies and Mergers Commission's inquiry into the supply of recorded music in 1995. The MMC declared that it was easy to make a record and set up a record company, and wrongly concluded from this that there were no real barriers to entry into the record market. Here, again, there was a confusion between entering a market and being able to compete effectively in it.

Making a record and getting it into record stores isn't the most difficult job. The real problem is in letting people know that the record is available and in persuading them to buy it. For this, you need airplay, and this is where we enter the Catch 22 world of the charts. To get airplay, you need to be in the charts; to get in the charts, you need airplay. This is where the majors really flex their muscles. They can afford to promote their artists with pluggers, massive ad campaigns and by giving away huge quantities of singles to retailers. Smaller independent labels simply can't afford this level of promotional activity, and so can't begin to compete for the attention of audiences.

The world won't change just because an indie or an artist chooses to do business online. New internet businesses have bankrupted themselves by spending fortunes on traditional TV and poster ad campaigns in an effort to drum up traffic. Even internet enthusiasts are recognising the problem of 'background noise' (the difficulty of making your voice heard above all the other people who are trying to make a fortune from online trade).

For established artists with a recognisable name, the internet is a fantastic opportunity. This is especially true for the droves of former stars who can still sell, say, 10,000 to 200,000 albums. No longer of interest to major record companies, the internet will put them in direct touch with their fans and will allow them to make a reasonable living, and perhaps a very good one. Stiff Little Fingers are now making more money from selling records on their own label through their web site – especially in the US – than they ever did during their heyday in the late '70s, and Marillion famously financed the recording of an album by selling advance copies to their fans.

However, the cost of establishing a name via the net is astronomical. Many companies with a multi-million-dollar capital value have never made a profit, and are unlikely to do so in the foreseeable future, if ever. Without the backing of major investors, most of the new online businesses would never have got started and couldn't have continued in business for more than a few weeks. The entrepreneurs who set up these companies raise money by offering shares to the major investment banks, venture capitalists and multinational media and telecoms companies. They are usually prohibited from selling their own shares until their company is in profit, and so, in order to unlock their capital, they either have to float their companies on the stock exchange, making them targets for take-over, or sell out to the existing major shareholders.

Major corporations already have substantial stakes in many of the so-called SMEs doing business on the net. As in any financial market, the chances are that the most successful companies will eventually be bought by the most dominant companies – Murdoch, Microsoft, BT, AOL Time Warner, AT&T, Nippon Telecom and the like.

ARTIST WEB SITES - PRACTICAL AND COMMERCIAL ASPECTS

Although the internet is no magical solution to an artist's problems, an online presence is now an essential part of any artist's long-term business plan. The direct relationship between artists and their fans that is made possible by the web has many commercial advantages. Most significantly, it allows artists to generate income independently of recording and publishing agreements. It also gives artists a continuous public presence which isn't tied to album releases or tours and is under the artist's exclusive editorial control, allowing artists to profit directly from their celebrity. Rights to artists' names, likenesses and biographical material are likely to become a significant battleground between artists and record companies.

Building an attractive web site isn't just a matter of keeping fans happy. A well-run web site can become a commercial asset in itself, generating profits from sponsorship, co-operative marketing, mailing-list sales and advertising, quite apart from any merchandise which may be sold from it. One of the key factors in taking advantage of these opportunities is the site's 'stickiness' (a term used by web entrepreneurs to indicate the length of time that the average visitor spends on the site).

Unlike making an album, creating a web site isn't a matter of working hard until it's finished and then putting it out; a good web site is never finished, and running an artist web site is a full-time activity. Not long ago, many artists were proud that they updated their web sites once a month. This now seems hopelessly infrequent, and new material must be fed into sites on at least a weekly basis, if not daily, in order to keep fans coming back for more. Music fans are notoriously dedicated, and – provided that the material is available – they will happily spend hours online finding out more about their chosen artists.

The cost of establishing and maintaining an attractive web site is very significant. For an established artist, this may run to many hundreds of thousands of pounds. Also, in addition to the financial investment, artists must be prepared to devote considerable personal time and effort towards making the site appealing to fans. This might involve preparing exclusive interviews, backstage video access on tours, regular video diaries and messages to fans. Journalistic quality is crucial when preparing material for inclusion on the web site; fans will pay for high-quality, interesting, insightful material, but they won't buy bland press releases or material that can be obtained elsewhere free of charge.

It's also important to allow fans to participate in building the site. Competitions, chatrooms (for instance, the Stiff Little Fingers web site includes a virtual pub), exclusive fan-club concerts and similar initiatives make fans feel involved and help to make a web site sticky without necessarily requiring large financial investment from the artist. Many fans have computer expertise which they are happy to use for their artist's benefit, and artists can save money by 'adopting' unofficial web sites.

The most basic function of a web site is to keep fans informed about the artist's forthcoming releases and tours. The second most important function of a web site is to provide a vehicle to sell artist-related merchandise, including sound recordings. The physical process of despatching goods and banking payments can be sub-contracted to a third party. At present, for most artists, the sale of recordings will be conducted via a simple CD mail-order facility, which may be administered by a fulfilment house when the scale of the operation justifies it.

Direct downloads from artist web sites will soon be more commonplace as secure online payment and delivery systems become more established. Some artists, such as David Bowie, have already adopted a subscription model, allowing fans access to all of their new recordings in exchange for a regular payment. Even signed artists may sell copies of their recordings from their web sites, although some record companies are sensitive about this issue and will try to insist on a degree of control over their artists' sales.

ARTIST WEB SITES - LEGAL CONSIDERATIONS

When considering the legal position of artists in the light of ICT, it's helpful to distinguish both between the promotional and the commercial use of artist web sites and between signed and unsigned artists.

For unsigned artists, there is a wide range of sites that are based on different business models offering publicity and, in some cases, income from sales. Few artists are likely to generate significant income from such sites in the foreseeable future, and they should be regarded as a useful addition to, rather than a substitute for, conventional methods of finding recording and publishing deals.

For signed artists, the first issue to consider is whether the publisher or record company has the right to distribute the artist's work online and, if so, on what basis the artist is to be paid. In most cases, the wording of the agreements will at least give the record or publishing company a strongly arguable case that online rights belong to them rather than to the artist. Most agreements grant an outright assignment (in the case of recording agreements) or licence (in the case of publishing agreements) of the artist's entire copyright to the company concerned.

As the law currently stands, it would seem that the online use of copyright material doesn't involve the creation or use of a new legal right. Accordingly, online use will be deemed to be included in copyright assignments from artists. Some US artists are reportedly taking legal action in order to establish that contracts signed before the introduction of online technology can't be deemed to transfer such rights. Much would depend on the exact construction of the specific wording of any given contract, but such actions would be of little benefit in the UK. Most contracts, in addition to assigning the entire copyright, specifically assign rights to exploitation 'by any means now known or hereafter devised', or some such form of words. It's therefore unlikely that many UK artists will succeed in establishing that online rights aren't included in their assignments to their record and publishing companies. If you're in any doubt about whether a particular combination of words covers the online use of copyright, you should of course seek expert legal advice.

The basis on which recording artists should be paid for the online use of their work is more uncertain. In some cases, the artist might be entitled to payment under the 'flat-fee' or 'other income' provisions of the recording agreement – usually split 50/50 – rather than on the much lower conventional royalty basis. This may depend on whether the online use is characterised as a download (equivalent to a sale) or as streaming (equivalent to a broadcast). Again, the position will vary from artist to artist, and each agreement will need to be analysed carefully in order that the specific terms may be determined.

A further issue which has aroused considerable controversy is the record companies' right to artist web sites. In the absence of an agreement granting such rights to the company, in the vast majority of cases such rights belong automatically to the artist. Many record companies are seeking to control their artists' web sites, and there are many ways in which an artist may qualify the acceptance of such demands short of an outright refusal.

If a record company insists on controlling a web site, artists should absolutely insist that rights to the web site revert to the artist without payment on termination of the recording agreement. The record company's control should also be conditional on the company meeting in full the agreed costs of not only setting up the web site but also of running it. Such expenses shouldn't be treated as an advance, however, and they certainly shouldn't be recouped from the artist's royalty account if the web site is owned or controlled by the company. If control of the web site is to be shared, it might be appropriate to share the expenses.

An agreement should also be reached concerning the division of any income derived from the web site. Just as an artist wouldn't allow a record company to participate in income from sales of tour tickets or merchandise, record companies shouldn't normally receive a share of online sales income, except in respect of sound recordings. The artist should also look for exclusive ownership of the user data collected from the web site.

14 Mediation

By Dennis Muirhead And Harry Hodgkin

WHAT IS MEDIATION?

Quite simply, mediation is a way of resolving disputes without the need to go to court. If both parties in a dispute agree to mediation, then a trained mediator – who is always an impartial third party, skilled in the type of dispute that has arisen – guides the parties to a settlement on which they both agree. The mediator does not impose a decision or attempt to judge the merits of the case. The mediator's aim is to assist the parties equally and neutrally to a resolution.

WHY IS MEDIATION NOT USED IN EVERY CASE?

The difficult bit about mediation is actually getting both parties to agree that mediation is a good idea in the first place. Many disputes in the music industry inevitably become very personal, and the common-law legal system is geared to a combative approach – finding fault, picking holes, showing blame or error. People are all too often not inclined, by the very nature of the process, to settle, even when it is in their personal, career or commercial interests. They want their day in court. They want to show the other party that they were in the wrong. The only beneficiaries of this process are generally the parties' lawyers.

HOW DOES MEDIATION OVERCOME THIS?

Mediation looks at the common ground, the positive aspects and finds the best resolution for both parties. It identifies the risks both parties have in litigation and encourages them to assess the strengths and weaknesses of their case. It looks to the longer term and can explore the interests of the parties, both individually and together. Mediation can be (and is) used before or during the litigation process.

HOW DOES IT WORK?

Mediation requires the consent of all parties concerned, but if one or more have not indicated willingness, it's possible to approach a mediation provider so that he may help negotiate that initial agreement. The choice of mediator is important – it is generally best left to the mediation organisation to recommend a trained mediator with the relevant experience and, usually, knowledge of the subject.

At an agreed time and venue, the mediator listens, allows the parties to express their feelings, explores underlying issues, challenging and encouraging where necessary. The mediator spends time with each party, both in joint session and in private meetings (sometimes called 'caucus'), helping each party to focus on their interests and the interests of the other parties, rather than what they may perceive as their legal 'rights'.

In commercial or contractual disputes, the mediator will explore the early part of the relationship, drawing out what it was that caused them to work together initially and what caused the breakdown in trust or confidence between the parties. The mediator will help the parties to examine areas of possible agreement as well as disagreement. Experience, skill and training are essential in this process.

The mediator will also help each party to examine their own resolve, testing out their belief in the true strength of their own case and their resolve to fight rather than settle.

MEDIATION IS PRIVATE, CONFIDENTIAL AND WITHOUT PREJUDICE

Some of this process can be difficult, if not painful, for some parties, and for this reason the mediator will never test parties or try to expose weaknesses in a case in joint session, only ever in private.

All the discussions are completely confidential – the mediator will not repeat or imply to another party anything that one party has said unless or until the mediator has been given express permission to do so. This confidentiality allows the parties to trust the mediator so that they can discuss openly all aspects of their case.

Mediators and their providing organisations recognise the key importance of absolute confidentiality and discretion. Details of mediations, arbitrations or settlements are never given by mediators. The parties may disclose them only if that is agreed within the terms of the settlement. This is an important facet of music industry mediation.

Eventually, by spending time shuttling between the parties, the mediator can help the parties to understand their own and each other's positions in a way quite different to that of the traditional adversarial case and, in over 80% of civil cases, reach an agreement on the day.

If no agreement is reached, the parties are not in any way bound by what has been discussed. The discussions are expressly without prejudice and may not be referred to in court. This confidentially is enshrined in a written mediation accord which the parties are required to sign before the mediation.

If the parties settle the matter, the mediator will help them to draw up an agreement. This agreement becomes binding only once it has been drawn up and signed by the parties. If the agreement is not honoured, it may be enforced contractually or preferably by a further mediation. Most agreements are honoured, though, precisely because the parties have worked hard to achieve a settlement and upon terms that were always within their control, unlike an imposed court decision.

WHY MEDIATE?

There are plenty of very good reasons, such as:

- The outcome of mediation is always within the control of the parties. With the help of the mediator, they decide for themselves upon a settlement they can live with.

- Parties in mediation avoid the uncertainty and dissatisfaction often experienced in court or at arbitration, where they have little choice but to accept the judgment, which may disappoint.

- Mediation resolves disputes fast, usually within a day, and can be arranged in days or weeks, and can last for as long as the parties want, ignoring conventional court hours.

- Mediation is very significantly less expensive than litigation, because months or years of litigation are avoided, as are the consequent fees of lawyers and experts. Parties may, of course (and generally do), have legal or other advisors present during the mediation if they wish.

- Mediation is voluntary – any party may withdraw at any time.

- The Mediation can take place at any time – it is not limited to ordinary working days or hours. If it suits the parties to negotiate over a weekend, then that is when it happens.

- There is strict confidentiality and neutrality.

- The parties often find that, at the end of the process, new common goals are established which sometimes allow for a full or partial reconciliation or restoration of common production, recording, performance or other aims.

Mediation is a key part of the civil court procedural reforms introduced by The Lord Chief Justice Lord Woolf. In the UK, the recently established Civil Mediation Council – chaired by Sir Brian Neill – is a useful impartial contact with a good knowledge of the music industry. For further information, contact the address below:

> *The Secretary*
> *Civil Mediation Council*
> *12 Bloomsbury Square*
> *London WC1A 2LP*
> *Tel: (+44) (0)18 2344 2671*
> *Fax: 0870 094 0605*
> *Email: alto@clara.net*

Appendix 1: Societies

AIM

The Association of Independent Music is a non-profit making trade body established in 1998 by UK independent record labels to represent the independent record sector across the UK in all genres. It has over 700 members, all of whom are UK-based independent record labels or distributors.

AIM represents the UK independent record sector, a quarter of the UK market, among both industry and government. AIM also plays a key role in industry-wide initiatives such as the Music Industry Mentoring Scheme.

> *Association of Independent Music*
> *Lamb House*
> *Church Street*
> *London W4 2PD*
> *UK*
> *Tel: + 44 (0)20 89945599*
> *Fax: + 44 (0)20 89945222*
> *Web: www.musicindie.org*
> *Email: info@musicindie.com*

ASCAP

The American Society of Composers, Authors and Publishers is the oldest performing rights organisation in the US, representing over four million copyrighted works. ASCAP generates the highest annual distributions to its members (2002 distribution totalled more than $587 million) while its operating costs remain the lowest in the US at 14.8%.

The society was founded in 1914 by a small group of songwriters and publishers to protect the rights of its members by licensing and collecting royalties for the public performance of their copyrighted musical works. Today, ASCAP boasts more than 150,000 members and represents the music of more than 200,000 foreign writers and publishers through agreements with over 60 performing rights organisations worldwide.

ADVANTAGES

ASCAP is the only true membership society among US performing rights organisations, and is the only US society governed by a board of directors consisting entirely of composers, lyricists and publishers, who are elected by the members. Members have a strong voice in the operation of their society, and can participate in any of the annual open membership meetings held in the three major US music centres: Los Angeles, Nashville and New York.

ASCAP is owned by the people who create music – writers and publishers – and is the only US performing rights organisation whose financial records are open to the public. Fair and equal treatment is a hallmark of membership; every penny they collect, less operating costs, is distributed to their members. Writers and publishers sign identical contracts, with the right to resign every year of the contract. ASCAP is also the only society that determines royalties objectively over the life of copyright.

The ASCAP web site (http://www.ascap.com) is a convenient gateway to ASCAP, providing news of events and workshops, along with other information. Also available for access on the web is ACE (ASCAP Clearance Express), which provides quick, easy and continuous access to ASCAP title, writer and publisher information.

ASCAP Atlanta
PMB 400
541 Tenth Street NW
Atlanta
GA 30318
Tel: (+1) 404 351 1224

Fax: (+1) 404 351 1252
Web: www.ascap.com

ASCAP Chicago
1608 N Milwaukee
Suite 1007
Chicago
IL 60647
Tel: (+1) 773 394 4286
Fax: (+1) 773 394 5639

ASCAP London
8 Cork Street
London
W1X 1PB
Tel: (+44) (0)20 7439 0909
Fax: (+44) (0)20 7434 0073

ASCAP Los Angeles
7920 W Sunset Boulevard
3rd Floor
Los Angeles
CA 90046
Tel: (+1) 323 883 1000
Fax: (+1) 323 883 1049

ASCAP Miami
420 Lincoln Road
Suite 385
Miami Beach
FLA 33139
Tel: (+1) 305 673 3446
Fax: (+1) 302 673 2446

ASCAP Nashville
Two Music Square West

Nashville
TN 37203
Tel: (+1) 615 742 5000
Fax: (+1) 615 742 5020

ASCAP New York
1 Lincoln Plaza
New York
NY 10023
Tel: (+1) 212 621 6000 (admin)/212 621 6240 (membership)
Fax: (+1) 212 724 9064

ASCAP Puerto Rico
Calle Boris 1542
Local A
Urb Belisa
Rio Piedras
Puerto Rico 00927
Tel: (+1) 787 281 0782
Fax: (+1) 787 767 2805

AURA

The Association of United Recording Artists was set up by the MMF in 1995 to safeguard the interests of artists. It is now a stand-alone, non-profit-making organisation run for the good of its membership, which consists primarily of featured recording artists.

Its initial mandate covered the then newly established Public Performance Right. The EC Directive requires that all relevant parties receive an equitable share of income derived from public performance of a sound recording. AURA's initial activity was the successful negotiation with PPL and PAMRA over the distribution policy of PPL money. AURA's unswerving and consistent position has led to featured performers having a greater and more equitable share of performance income compared with non-featured (or session) players.

Along with the other performer organisations (the Musicians' Union, MPG, PAMRA and Equity), AURA has joined forces with PPL in a group called the Performers' Forum. The Performers' Forum is the template for a joint society in the UK. As a result, AURA already has a director representing the performer organisations on the PPL board.

The Performers' Forum is now turning its attention to the proper collection of overseas performer income. This will have a considerable impact on performers, in terms of the future income they receive from their recordings. Of course, the degree of influence that AURA will be able to exert will depend on the level of support available.

AURA is an association – not a union – that represents primarily featured recording artists and producers. It does not limit the terms on which artists do business. The organisation helps its members in a variety of ways by representing their point of view in discussions with industry bodies, both within the UK and abroad, and with local, national, European and other international governments.

For further information, contact the general secretary, Peter Horrey, at the address below:

AURA (Head Office)
1 York St
London W1U 6PA
Tel: (+44) (0)870 8505 200
Fax: (+44) (0)870 8505 201
Email: info@aurauk.com
Web: www.aurauk.com

BMI

Broadcast Music Incorporated is an American performing rights organisation representing more than 300,000 US and foreign songwriters and composers and US publishers. The company collects licence fees on behalf of those

American creators it represents, as well as for the thousands of creators from around the world who have chosen to be represented by BMI in the US. The fees exacted for the public performance of its repertoire, consisting of more than three million compositions – including performances featured on radio airplay, TV broadcast and cable TV transmission, as well as live and recorded performances by all other users of music – are distributed in the form of royalties to the appropriate writers of the songs and owners of the copyright.

BMI's list of affiliates is unsurpassed. Among the songwriters it represents are many classic songwriters in different musical genres. It was founded in 1940 as a non-profit-making corporation whose aim was to provide performing rights representation for those songwriters and composers who were ineligible for protection from the older American performing rights societies. BMI offered first-time representation to songwriters of blues, jazz, R&B, gospel, folk, country, Spanish-language music and other types of American music. As several of these musical trends converged to produce rock 'n' roll, BMI became the pre-eminent performing rights organisation in the country to represent songwriters of this new genre. The organisation quickly made reciprocal agreements with its sister performing rights organisations around the world to license its repertoire.

BMI's pop, rock, R&B, country and jazz repertoire is extensive. A listing of the Top 100 singles of the rock era by *Rolling Stone* magazine showed that BMI represents 75% of these works. More than 75% of the inductees into the Rock 'n' Roll Hall of Fame are represented by BMI, as are more than 80% of the inductees in the Country Music Hall of Fame and more than 90% of those honoured with Pioneer Awards by the Rhythm and Blues Foundation. For further information, contact Phil Graham at the address below:

> *BMI Atlanta*
> *3340 Peachtree Road NE*
> *Suite 570*
> *Atlanta, GA 30326*
> *Tel: (+1) 404 816 5670*
> *Fax: (+1) 404 816 5670*
> *Email: atlanta@bmi.com*
> *Web: www.bmi.com*

BMI London
84 Harley House
Marylebone Road
London
NW1 5HN
Tel: (+44) (0)20 7486 2036
Fax: (+44) (0)20 7224 1046
Email: london@bmi.com

BMI Los Angeles
8730 Sunset Boulevard
Third Floor West
Los Angeles, CA 90069
Tel: (+1) 310 659 9109
Fax: (+1) 310 657 6947
Email: losangeles@bmi.com

BMI Miami
5201 Blue Lagoon Drive
Suite 310
Miami, FL 33126
Tel: (+1) 305 266 3636
Fax: (+1) 305 266 2442
Email: miami@bmi.com

BMI Nashville
10 Music Square East
Nashville, TN 37203
Tel: (+1) 615 401 2000
Fax: (+1) 615 401 2707
Email: nashville@bmi.com

BMI New York
320 West 57th Street
New York, NY 10019
Tel: (+1) 212 586 2000

Fax: (+1) 212 245 8986
Email: newyork@bmi.com

BMR

British Music Rights Limited was established at the end of September 1996 to promote, protect and develop the interests of music creators and publishers and to demonstrate the value of the British musical heritage in today's society. BMR seeks to influence the formulation of national and international policies and to initiate and respond to legislative measures and technological developments that may affect the creative and rights-owning interests that it represents. BMR seeks to underline the economic and artistic importance of the work of creators and publishers, with emphasis on the consequent commercial, cultural, educational and social benefits of their efforts.

MEMBERSHIP OF BMR
Some members of BMR include the Music Publishers' Association, the Alliance of Composers' Organisations (including the Alliance of Professional Composers, the Composers' Guild of Great Britain and the British Academy of Songwriters, Composers and Authors), the Performing Right Society and the MCPS. For more information, contact the director general, Francis Lowe, at the address below:

British Music House
26 Berners Street
London
W1P 3LR
Tel: (+44) (0)20 7306 4446
Fax: (+44) (0)20 7306 4449
Web: www.bmr.org

BPI

The economic success of the British record industry is undeniable. Retail sales of CDs, cassettes and LPs in the UK now total more than £1.6 billion, while physical exports and invisible earnings exceed £1 billion each year. Equally important is the recognition of the vital role that music plays in everyday life and in reflecting Britain's contemporary culture.

The BPI is the trade association for record companies in the UK. It boasts over 200 members, including all of the major record companies, as well as many small independents. Each member company, regardless of its size, has a single vote. Together, member companies account for over 90% of UK record sales.

The BPI exists to protect the interests of its members in all areas of activity. Much of the work is unseen, involving lobbying in Westminster and Brussels, working with government departments and protecting the industry by negotiation and, if necessary, litigation. An important element of the BPI's work involves liaising with other media, providing press information and promoting the record industry in general. The BPI also recognises that the growth in multimedia applications provides exciting opportunities for the music industry, but it's keen to ensure that the rights of its members are protected. Whenever a recording is used in a multimedia product, a licence must first be obtained from the record company that owns its copyright.

As well as providing services for its members, the BPI also provides a forum and an environment in which members can actively participate in the industry's future development. Through their involvement in committees, the representatives of record companies can take part in discussions with the retail sector, and can also play an important role in negotiations to help ensure that future legislation takes account of their interests.

Through its charity, the Brit Trust, the BPI supports the Brit School for Performing Arts in Croydon and other educational institutions and charities.

BENEFITS OF MEMBERSHIP

Membership of the BPI carries with it automatic entitlement to a number of benefits: the legal department provides advice for members and negotiates on their behalf with other music-industry bodies; members can obtain sponsorship for attendance at international trade fairs, such as MIDEM, MIDEM Asia and PopKomm; and the anti-piracy unit takes action on behalf of members to protect their rights from counterfeiting and other abuses of copyright. The BPI maintains an extensive specialist library, and the research department also provides members with a wide range of statistical and other market data. Also, CIN chart information is available at a discounted price. Members receive priority bookings for events such as the Brit Awards, and they are also entitled to claim BPI-certified awards.

For further information, contact:

Riverside Building
County Hall
Westminster Bridge Road
London
SE1 7JA
Tel: (+44) (0)20 7287 4422
Fax: (+44) (0)20 7287 2252
Web: www.bpi.co.uk

IFPI

The International Federation of the Phonographic Industry represents some 1,100 record producers in over 70 countries around the world, including independent producers and the six major record companies: BMG, EMI Music, MCA, Polygram, Sony and Time Warner. National groups representing the local record companies are officially recognised by the Federation in 41 countries, and the RIAA (Recording Industry Association of America) and PLAPE (Federation Latinoamericana de Productores de Fonograms y Videogramas) are also counted among its affiliates.

IFPI's Secretariat is located in London and is responsible for central co-ordination and research, while the federation's Brussels-based European office deals with issues concerning the EU and EFTA. IFPI also has other regional offices in Warsaw, Moscow, Hong Kong, China, Seoul, Kuala Lumpur, Singapore, Bangkok and Jakarta.

IFPI'S ROLE

The recording industry's commercial success depends on its ability to invest time and money in nurturing new talent, and in order to make this practical artists must receive remuneration for its works. One of the aims of IFPI is to ensure that the recording industry is able to realise its full potential throughout the world, and in order to achieve this the Federation governs a number of activities in several areas, including those listed below.

promoting national legislation and international conventions

To protect its members' rights, IFPI campaigns for the introduction, improvement and enforcement of copyright and other rights legislation at national, European and international levels, voicing its members' concerns and representing their interests in negotiations for new legislation.

new technologies

IFPI is involved in the development of technical solutions for combating piracy, such as SID (Source Identification) codes, and also strives to discover solutions which will allow the industry to collect remuneration for its work in both the digital and analogue domain, such as the ISRC (International Standard Recording Code).

providing information

IFPI provides a wide range of information and statistical analyses on the recording industry, including statistics on legitimate and pirate sales, reports on emerging markets and technical issues and updates on legislative issues. It's also the Federation's role to inform the media – through press releases and press briefings – of any developments in the recording industry.

MEMBERSHIP OF IFPI

Any company or firm which produces sound recordings which are then made available to the public in reasonable quantities is eligible for membership. Others closely connected with the production or distribution of sound recordings may also be admitted. For further information, contact:

IFPI Secretariat
54 Regent Street

London
W1R 5PJ
Tel: (+44) (0)20 7434 3521
Fax: (+44) (0)20 7439 9166
Web: www.ifpi.com

MCPS

As an agent, the Mechanical Copyright Protection Society represents thousands of composers and music publishers. It exists to ensure that the recordings of its members' works are properly authorised and commercially rewarded. Incorporated in 1924, it has been a subsidiary of the MPA since 1976. Its board of directors consists of 12 music publishers and four composers, and these composers represent the various UK composers' bodies. Acting on behalf of its members, the MCPS negotiates agreements with those who wish to record music, ensuring that the owners of the copyrights are rewarded for the use of their music.

The mechanical right is defined as the right to record a piece of music, and by law anyone who records a copyrighted musical work must obtain the permission of the copyright owner, who is then entitled to receive a royalty. The MCPS collects royalties from record, video, broadcasting, multimedia and independent production companies, along with many other organisations, who are obliged to pay whenever they use a work controlled by an MCPS member.

MEMBERSHIP OF THE MCPS

The MCPS has no formal membership criteria, but it does expect prospective members (publishers or composers) to have had – or to expect to have – works commercially recorded in some form. It's only necessary to join if mechanical royalties are being generated. If you have a publishing deal which includes all of your compositions, membership is probably not necessary, as it's likely that the publisher will be a member. However, if your musical works remain unpublished, and are likely to be recorded and released by someone other than yourself, you should consider joining the society.

The MCPS doesn't charge a fee for membership, but instead extracts a commission on any royalties distributed to its members. The commission rates vary, depending on the source of the income, and currently range from 4.75% to 12.5%. (The average in 1995 was 6.68% of total distributions.) The last few years have seen a consistent growth in the royalty income collected and distributed by the society – 1995 saw distributions rise to £137.4 million, with a budgeted distribution for 1996 in excess of £140 million. The MCPS also has reciprocal agreements with societies in other countries, thus enabling it to protect its members' works in a worldwide capacity.

For further information, contact the society's corporate communications department, who can give general information on the services provided by the society as well as advice on other matters relating to copyright. A wide range of literature is also available on request. Enquiries should be addressed to:

> *Elgar House*
> *41 Streatham High Road*
> *London*
> *SW16 1ER*
> *Tel: (+44) (0)20 8664 4400*
> *Fax: (+44) (0)20 8769 8792*
> *Web: www.mcps.co.uk*

MPA

Established in 1881, the Music Publishers' Association has always encouraged greater professionalism within its membership. It publishes a wide range of recommendations, advice and information on legal, commercial and general matters for the music publishing industry, along with a wealth of material used in training courses and seminars.

PRINCIPAL OBJECTIVES

The aims of the MPA for the foreseeable future include the following:

- To promote and protect the interests of music publishers;

- To provide a forum to discuss mutual problems;

- To support the MCPS as a wholly-owned subsidiary company of the MPA;

- To originate and promote improvements in the law regarding music copyright and other topics of concern to music publishers;
- To assist publishers and their composers in maximising their income;

- To help combat resistance to paying for the use of copyrighted music;

- To improve communication and encourage active participation;

- To obtain feedback on important issues;

- To educate the public concerning the role of the music publisher;

- To underline the importance and value of copyright;

- To emphasise the illegality of copyright infringement and pursue offenders;

- To campaign for greater professionalism within the industry.

The MPA – a non-profit-making company, limited by guarantee – is controlled by its articles of association and governed by an elected council of popular and classical (standard) publishers. Day-to-day business is administered by the association secretary, his assistant and other staff. There are also specialist sub-committees which deal with specific interests.

For further details, contact Sarah Faulder at the address below:

MPA
3rd Floor Strandgate
18-20 York Buildings
London
WC2N 6JU
Tel: (+44) (0)20 7839 7779
Fax: (+44) (0)20 7839 7776
Web: www.mpa.org

MPG

The Music Producers' Guild promotes and represents all individuals in the music-production and -recording professions. It is a professional organisation that embodies collective and individual creative contributions to the production and recording of all genres of music- and media-related activities.

As an independent and democratic organisation, MPG members include producers, engineers, mixers, remixers, programmers, students and trainees, those involved in multimedia and any other individual involved in the creative process. It aims to be a non-discriminatory, representative body with an effective and transparent infrastructure in line with other music industry bodies and seeks to set and maintain the highest standards and values of our professions.

Central to the MPG philosophy are subsidiary Special Interest Groups as a 'melting pot' for ideas. These SIGs focus like-minded individuals in generating constructive activities that offer support within and direction to the MPG, as well as those outside the organisation.

> *The Music Producers Guild*
> *PO Box 32*
> *Harrow*
> *HA2 7ZX*
> *Tel: (+44) (0)20 7371 8888*
> *Fax: (+44) (0)20 7371 8887*
> *Email: office@mpg.org.uk*
> *Web: www.mpg.org.uk*

Musicians' Union

The MU represents musicians and protects their interests, and negotiates with the record companies and the BPI in terms of payments to musicians for various endeavours, including recording and promotional work. It also establishes rates of payment with broadcasters for the appearances of musicians on radio and television, and also offers legal advice for artist members and competitive equipment insurance. Its suggested rates for someone performing as a session musician, a live performer or in a number of other capacities are published in a book of guidelines.

The union also acts as a collecting agency, recouping funds payable to its members, and offers legal and business advice for contracts and disputes. It publishes a monthly members' magazine, The Musician, along with directories of its members and a wealth of material on issues concerning musicians.

For further information, contact:

The Musicians' Union
60-62 Clapham Road
London
SW9 0JJ
Tel: (+44) (0)20 7582 5566
Fax: (+44) (0)20 7582 9805
Web: www.musiciansunion.org.uk

PPL

Founded in 1934, Phonographic Performance Limited is a non-profit-making organisation established by British record companies, and its aim is to control the broadcasting and public use of their recordings and to issue licences for those purposes. Members of PPL include over 1,900 companies, ranging from multinationals to small specialist producers, who together control 5,000 record labels. All radio and TV broadcasters in the UK pay annual blanket licence fees to PPL. In addition, tens of thousands of licences are issued annually to such public performance venues as discos, clubs, dance halls and jukebox operators.

The newest forms of use for PPL material include Discline telephone services (previously run by British Telecom and now run by private enterprise service providers) and those background music services supplied by specialist satellite services. In addition, PPL will also be licensing the new generation of post-deregulation broadcasters, including satellite and community radio companies.

Wherever possible, PPL negotiates its conditions and fees with national bodies representing the various types of user. It negotiates on the basis that higher fees should be paid by those who derive most commercial benefit from recordings. Therefore, radio stations, discos and jukebox operators should expect to pay more than theatres, shops or cinemas.

PPL income is distributed to its member record companies, to individual recording artists and to session musicians, and this distribution takes place on a regular basis. The amount required to be paid to each company and recording artist is calculated by examining a list of detailed returns provided by broadcasters and by a sample of public performance venues. The rate per unit of time is the same for every member, whether large or small.

In December 1997, the PRC (Performer Registration Centre) – a division within PPL's distribution department – was set up to issue each performer with a PID (Performer Identification) number, which assists in the administration of performers' new statutory rights under the recent changes to UK copyright legislation.

For further information, contact:

> *PPL*
> *1 Upper James Street*
> *London*
> *W1R 3HG*
> *Tel: (+44) (0)20 7534 1000*
> *Fax: (+44) (0)20 7534 1111*
> *Web: www.ppluk.com/www.royaltiesreunited.co.uk*

PRS

Collective administration of rights has long been the bedrock on which the careers of composers and authors have been built. This fact – first recognised in Europe around a century ago – continues to be recognised globally as new copyright laws are developed and enacted in emerging territories.

Until composers, authors and music publishers came together to join forces and exercise their rights through societies such as the Performing Right Society, there was very little that the individual creator could do to collect what he was rightfully due from performances of his copyrighted works. The words 'rightfully due' are important here, particularly in today's world, where increasingly easy access to music in a proliferating variety of forms reinforces the public's long-preferred misconception that musical performance belongs to everyone and no one, and that it should therefore be free.

The right of composers and authors (and the music publishers to whom they assign their creative output) to control and be rewarded for public performance was protected by the 1911 Copyright Act in the UK, and has continued to be protected by the 1956 and 1988 Acts. Set up in 1914, the PRS is the UK association of composers, lyricists and publishers. Membership currently totals approximately 35,000, including more than 31,000 composers and lyricists and around 2,650 music publishers. The society is a commercial but non-profit-making company, and is limited by guarantee.

The essential function of the PRS has always been to achieve collectively what creators can't effectively do for themselves – that is, to administer the non-dramatic performing and broadcasting rights in their copyrighted musical works. In those cases where the use of music can be more easily controlled by writers and their publishers or agents – in plays, opera and ballet, for example – the PRS has generally not been required to control and administer the performing right. For many composers whose music may be broadcast or performed in public thousands of times daily throughout the world, it's still impossible or intolerably costly to give personal permission to each would-be music user and then to collect the appropriate fee.

The PRS's policies and administration are controlled by an elected board of non-executive directors, guided by a chairman and two deputy chairmen. The council is divided evenly between composers and publishers, and each half is then broadly divided between classical and non-classical interests. In line with recommendations suggested in the society's Corporate Governance Report, the board now also includes as executive directors the chief executive officer of the MCPS/PRS music alliance and its director of membership, and has also appointed two external directors.

The PRS has always played an important international role through its position as a greatly respected member of CISAC, and also through its reciprocal links with other societies worldwide, including those societies which it has helped to found in emerging countries. Further information about the society can be obtained from John Sweeney at the address below:

PRS
29-33 Berners Street
London
W1P 4AA
Tel: (+44) (0)20 7580 5544
Fax: (+44) (0)20 7306 4050
Web: www.prs.co.uk

SESAC

SESAC, the smallest US performing rights organisation, has recently garnered international recognition by broadening its focus from primarily European- and gospel-music copyrights to include every mainstream musical genre. With its list of affiliates, SESAC has transformed the way in which performing rights societies in the US conduct business by being the first US performing rights organisation to use state-of-the-art broadcast data systems technology for monitoring broadcasts and distributing royalties.

In 1996, SESAC began using BDS (Broadcast Data System) to track more than 8.3 million hours of radio airplay, including formats such as Top 40, adult contemporary, country, modern rock, rhythm and blues, AAA and AOR. SESAC affiliates, therefore, enjoy the advantage of receiving royalties based on the most monitored airplay in the US. They are also paid quickly, with a gap of only one calendar quarter between performance and payment. SESAC's rapid payment schedule means that SESAC songwriters and publishers are paid up to two quarters faster than with other US performing rights societies.

European writers and publishers interested in learning more about SESAC should contact Wayne Bickerton, director of international affairs, by phone or by fax. Alternatively, he can be reached at the following addresses:

SESAC
6 Kenrick Place
London
W1H 3FF
Tel: (+44) (0)20 7486 9994
Fax: (+44) (0)20 7486 9929

SESAC International
55 Music Square
East Nashville, TN 37203
Tel: (+1) 615 320 0055
Fax: (+1) 615 329 9627

Web: www.sesac.com

Key To Appendix 2

For aid of reference, the International Directory of Managers has been arranged alphabetically. The country in which each manager is based is represented by a margin abbreviation, as shown below:

AUS – Australia
BRA – Brazil
CAN – Canada
DEN – Denmark
FIN – Finland
FRA – France
NLD – Netherlands
NOR – Norway
NZ – New Zealand
TUR – Turkey
UK – United Kingdom
USA – Unites States of America
UZB – Uzbekhistan

Appendix 2
International Directory Of Managers

NOR **TORILL AAS**
Continental
PO Box 110, Smestad
Oslo 0309
Tel: (+47) 22062770
Fax: (+47) 22062771
torill.aas@powertech.no
www.continentalmusic.net
ROSTER: Secret Garden, Leif
Ove Andsnes, Herborg Kraakevik,
Espen Lind, Trondheim
Soloists

AUS **SCOTT ADAM**
Scott Adam Management
PO Box 8332
Perth Business Centre
Western Australia 6849
Tel: (+61) (0)8 9202 4816
Fax: (+61) (0)8 9202 4815
Mobile: (+61) (0)419 047 427
Email: scott@qstik.com.au
Website: www.qstik.com.au
ROSTER: Matthew de la Hunty;
Moriarty

SWE **ANDERS ADIS ADAMSSON**
Massive Management
Simrishamnsgatan 70
214 23 Malmö
Tel: (+46) 40 971 671
Mobile: (+46) 707 77 57 58
adis@massivemanagement.net
www.massivemanagement.net

ROSTER: Air Bureau

CHRIS ADSHEAD **UK**
Me 2 Management
105 Canelot Studios
222 Kensal Rd
London
W10 5BN
Tel: (+44) (0)20 8960 8060
Fax: (+44) (0)20 8960 2525
cadshead@hotmail.com

SEAN AGNEW **US**
Blue Metallic Entertainment Group
LLC
2835 Aurora Ave, Suite 115, #203
Naperville, IL
60540
Tel: (+1) 877-667-2696
Fax: (+1) 877-667-2696
sean@bluemetallicmedia.com
www.bluemetallic.com
ROSTER: Aruna, David Phiele

JANNE AIRO **FIN**
2x4 Music Oy
Teiskontie 17 A 14
FIN-33500 Tampere
Tel: (+358) 50 3450777
Fax: (+358) 3 2557039/(+358) 50
3450777
janne.airo@2x4music.com
www.2x4music.com
ROSTER: Del Buzz, Blake

AUS ANTHONY AITKEN
Revolution Entertainment Group
1606 Chambers Flat Road
Chambers Flat
QLD 4133
Tel: (+61) (0)7 32970351
Fax: (+61) (0)7 32970953
Email: anthony@revolution-
entertainment.com
Website: www.revolution-
entertainment.com
ROSTER: Antiskeptic
www.antiskeptic.com.au

AUS JANE ALLAN
Artsend Productions
39 Westbury Rd
Launceston 7249
Tel: (+61) (0)3-63434156
Mobile: (+61) (0)421 581487
Email: artsend@tassie.net.au
Website: www.mp3.com/wavecage
ROSTER: Wavecage, Darren Lucas,
Jane Allan

UK ANDY ALLEN
Offside Management
Unit 9 Ground Floor
Blenheim Court
62 Brewery Road
London
N7 9NY
Tel: (+44) (0)20 7700 2662
Fax: (+44) (0)20 7700 2882
andy@bsimerch.com
ROSTER: Swervedriver (band), The
Crocketts (band) Toshack Highway
(band), Adam Franklin (film score
songwriter)

CAN KIRBY ALLEN
SoloStar Records Inc
17 Appleby Rd
Brampton
Ontario L6T 2S7
Tel: (+1) 905 790 1272

Fax: (+1) 905 790 1272
kirbyallen@hotmail.com

ATTILA AMBRUS CAN
ATH Entertainment
246 Scott St
Fort Frances
Ontario P9A 1G7
Tel: (+1) 807 274 0660
Fax: (+1) 807 274 0660
athent@jam21.net
ROSTER: Blinki

STEVE ANCLIFFE UK
Big Blue Music
113a Churchill Rd
London
NW2 5EH
Tel: (+44) (0)20 8452 7106
steve@bigbluevu.com
www.bigbluevu.com
ROSTER: Phoebe (artist), Tom
Ritchie (artist), Leighton Jones
(artist)

KENNETH ANDERSEN NOR
Vox Management
Kampensgate 51
4024 Stavanger
Tel: (+47) 51919200
Fax: (+47) 90020401
kenneth@voxmanagement.no
www.voxmanagement.no
ROSTER: Thomas Dybdahl,
Helldorado

GUY ANDERSON UK
ASM Ltd
42 City Business Centre
Lower Road
Rotherhithe
London
SE16 2XB
Tel: (+44) (0)20 7740 1600
Fax: (+44) (0)20 7740 1700
guy@mission-control.co.uk

ROSTER: Rat Pack (artist/producer), Harry (artist)

UK ELIZABETH ANDREWS
15 Hawthorn Hill
Letchworth
Herts
SG6 4HF
Tel: (+44) (0)1462 685 333
Fax: (+44) (0)1462 685 333
lizzie@music-consultancy.fsbusiness.co.uk
ROSTER: unnamed (band)

UK CLIFF ANGOL
Euro Entertainment & Management (EEM)
26 Morden Way
Sutton
Surrey
SM3 9PH
Tel: (+44) (0)20 8641 3054
Fax: (+44) (0)20 8641 3054
euroents.man@vizzavi.net
ROSTER: Lakeshore Drive (band)

UK KOFI ANKRAH
Genuine Article Entertainment
74 Cardigan Close
Cippenham
Slough
Berkshire
SL1 5HB
Tel: (+44) (0)1753 534125
kofi.ankrah@talk21.com
www.thegenuinegroup.com
ROSTER: Caji (artist/songwriter), Scanky The Ashante (artist), Soundscape (producer), The Monarchy (band), Emma Ray (artist/songwriter)

UK DAVE ARCARI
Buzz Artist Management
14 Corsiehill Rd
Perth
PH2 7BZ

Tel: (+44) (0)1738 638140
Fax: (+44) (0)1738 638140
dave@thebuzzgroup.co.uk
www.thebuzzgroup.co.uk
ROSTER: Radiotones (band), Tenesee Kait (band)

TERRY ARMSTRONG UK
Armstrong Academy Artist Management Ltd
Triple A Multimedia Group Ltd
GMC Studio
Hollingbourne
Kent
ME17 1UQ
Tel: (+44) (0)1622 880599
Fax: (+44) (0)1622 880020
terry@triple-a.uk.com
www.triple-a.uk.com
ROSTER: Danny Litchfield (artist), Felon (artist), Hussey (artist)

JOHN ARNISON UK
J Management
55 Loudoun Road
St Johns Wood
London
NW8 0DL
Tel: (+44) (0)20 7604 3633
Fax: (+44) (0)20 7604 3639
john@jmanagement.co.uk
ROSTER: Gabrielle, Aswad, Rozanna, Jay Smith

SUSAN ARNISON UK
Air Edel Copyrights Ltd
18 Rodmarton Street
London
W1H 3FW
Tel: (+44) (0)20 7486 6466
Fax: (+44) (0)20 7224 0344
susan@air-edel.co.uk
ROSTER: Thomas Morse (artist/songwriter), Sam Babenia (songwriter), James Shearman (songwriter), Paul Gabrowsky

UK NICK ASHTON-HART
Subversive Management
PO Box 32160
London
N4 2XY
Tel: (+44) (0)20 8800 1011
Fax: (+44) (0)20 7681-3135
nashton@subversive-music.com
ROSTER: UK Subs, Charlie Harper,
Nick Baroque

UK RICHARD ASKEW
RMP Management Services
4 The Drive
Hove
BN3 3JA
Tel: (+44) (0)1273 725 462
richard@razcal.net
www.razcal.net
ROSTER: Cinnamon (band),
Container (band), Waxed Apple
(band)

UK MIKE AUDLEY
Taste Media Ltd
263 Putney Bridge Road
London
SW15 2PU
Tel: (+44) (0)20 8780 3311
Fax: (+44) (0)20 8785 9894
safta@tastemedia.com
www.tastemedia.com
ROSTER: Muse (band, Mushroom)
Vega4 (band, Taste Media), Serafin
(band, Taste Media), One Minute
Silence (band, Taste Media)

FRA CLAUDE GUYOT
Fair
15 rue Henry Monnier
75009 Paris
Tel: (+33) 1487 84610
Fax: (+33) 1487 84611

FIN TIMO, ISOMÄKI
Extra Large Music Ltd

Kauppakatu 10, Tampere
FIN-33210
Tel: (+358) 3 2232242
Fax: (+358) 3 2127257
timo.isomaki@xlmusic.net
www.xlmusic.net
ROSTER: Päivi Lepistö

DE QUINCEY BAILEY   UK
Quintessential Music
PO Box 546
Bromley
Kent
BR2 ORS
Tel: (+44) (0)20 8402 1984
Fax: (+44) (0)20 8325 0708
urban_music@msn.com
ROSTER: Ricky Turner-Brown
(Suburban Soul Production), Ayoka
(artist), Buckle (artist), Fleur de Lys
(artist)

YVONNE BAILEY   UK
J Management
55 Loudoun Road
St Johns Wood
London
NW8 ODL
Tel: (+44) (0)20 7604 3633
Fax: (+44) (0)20 7604 3639
info@blujay.co.uk
ROSTER: Aswad, Rozanna, Gabrielle,
Jay Smith

RALPH BAKER   UK
Equator Music
17 Hereford Mansions
Hereford Road
London
W2 5BA
Tel: (+44) (0)20 7727 5858
Fax: (+44) (0)20 7229 5934
ralphb@equatormusic.com
ROSTER: Jeff Beck (artist), Tony
Iommi (artist)

UK **THERESA BAMPTON-CLARE**
Prophet Music
147 Drummond Street
London
NW1 2PB
Tel: (+44) (0)20 7383 5003
Fax: (+44) (0)20 7383 5004
info@prophetmusic.co.uk
www.prophetmusic.co.uk
ROSTER: Andrew Skeet
(artist/songwriter), Millennia Strings
(band), The Orchestra (band), Spacer
(Luke Gordon), The Twenty Jackies
(band), Hornographie (band), Riz
Maslen (artist/ songwriter)

FRA **JULIEN BANES**
La Ouache Production
5 rue Bugeaud
29200 Brest
Tel: (+33) 143590145
Mobile: (+33) 6 10 32 83 77
laouache.banes@wanadoo.fr
ROSTER: Matmatah, Svinkels, Alfa
Jet

UK **CYNTHIA BARNACHEA**
CNR Management
PO Box 894
Woking
Surrey
GU21 8ZJ
Tel: (+44) (0)1483 480694
Fax: (+44) (0)1483 473100
cbarnachea@yahoo.com
ROSTER: Draven (band)

UK **STEPHEN BARNES**
SBM
50 Cavendish Drive
Leytonstone
London
E11 1DL
Tel: (+44) (0)20 7837 6597
Fax: (+44) (0)20 7923 5564
stephenbarnes@upshotcom.com

ROSTER: Carl Mann
(artist/songwriter), The Measures
(band)

MICHAEL BARNETT **UK**
Farguard Ltd
21 Broughton Rd
Banbury
Oxfordshire
OX16 9QB
Tel: (+44) (0)1295 264436
Fax: (+44) (0)1295 266411
farguard@onetel.net.uk
ROSTER: Percy (band, Mook/Ten)

BEN BARRETT **UK**
Mondo Management/IHT Records
Unit 2D
Clapham North Arts Centre
26-32 Voltaire Rd
London
SW4 6DH
Tel: (+44) (0)20 7720 7411
Fax: (+44) (0)20 7720 8095
ben@ihtrecords.com
Rotser: David Gray (artist, IHT/East
West/RCA), Orbital (band, London
WEA), Tennason (HTI), Adam Snyder
(HTI), Damien Rice (DRM/HTI)

DAVE BARRIE **AUS**
Platform Management
5 Kalinga St
Clayfield
QLD 4011
Telephone: (+61) (0)7 3357 9911
Mobile: (+61) (0)421 382 501
Email: management@platformsix.com
Web: www.platformsix.com
ROSTER: Platform Six

TAHIR BASHEER **UK**
Sheridans
14 Red Lion Square
London
WC1R 4QL

Tel: (+44) (0)20 7774 9444
Fax: (+44) (0)20 7841 1391

UK   **PAUL BASSETT**
Mathe-Matic Management
101 Clubgarden Road
London
S11 8BW
Tel: (+44) (0)7866 762191
pauljamesbassett@hotmail.com
ROSTER: Texas Pete (band)

FRA   **BERNARD BATZEN**
Open Bar
14 rue Bleue
75009 Paris
Tel: (+33) 1 44 79 95 54
Mobile: (+33) 6 08 71 94 42
Fax: (+33) 1 44 79 00 34
bernard@azimuthprod.com
www.azimuthprod.com,
www.lesmediterraneennes.fr
ROSTER: Sawt el Atlas, Cyrius

GER   **BARBARA BAUER**
Konzertbüro Richard Weber
Hauptstr 66
77652 Offenburg
Tel: (+49) 0781/72041
Fax: (+49) 0781/23406
konzertbuero.weber@baden-online.de
www.ivan-rebroff.de
ROSTER: Ivan Rebroff

DEN   **JESPER BAY**
Musicmatters ApS
Kong Valdemarsvej 28-B
DK-2840
Holte
Tel: (+45) 2323 4686
Fax: (+45) 2323 4680
jesper@musicmatters.dk
www.musicmatters.dk
ROSTER: Ann-Louise (artist), Bliss
(artist), Doublestar (artist), Maria
Montell (artist), Andy Roda (artist),

Morten Woods, Halfdan E (producer)

PETER BAYLISS   **AUS**
Company Sunflower Entertainment
179 Mouat Street
Lyneham
ACT 2602
Tel: (+61) (0)26257 0875
Fax: (+61) (0)26257 0875
Mobile: (+61) (0)418 458457
Email: sunflowerent@hotmail.com
Web: www.sunflowerent.com
ROSTER: Quick 50, Redletter, Beanort

PETER 'SKIP' BEAUMONT-   **AUS**
EDMONDS
Company Cranium Management
PO Box 240
Annandale
NSW 2038
Telephone: (+61) (0)2 9660 6444
Fax: (+61) (0)2 9660 8111
Email: cranium@smartchat.net.au
ROSTER: Mental As Anything, Adam
Harvey, Dog Trumpet, David Mason-
Cox, Martin Plaza And The Lost
Vegans

JAKE BEAUMONT-NESBITT   **UK**
Clownfish
The Garage
61 Moriatry Close
London
N7 OEF
Tel: (+44) (0)20 7609 7501
Rockers@clownfish.net
www.clownfish.net
ROSTER: Louis Shaw (artist), The
Sone Motif (band), The Dead on
Holiday (band)

DAN BECK   **USA**
Accelerated Development, Inc
265 Morris Avenue
Rockville Centre, NY
11570

Tel: (+1) 516-764-0724
Fax: (+1) 516-764-0778
adinorth@aol.com

UK CARL BEDWARD
Anger Management
PO Box 6105
Birmingham
B43 6NZ
Tel: (+44) (0)121 357 3338
Fax: (+44) (0)121 580 2643
anger.1965@virgin.net
ROSTER: Shamefaced (band)

AUS LINCOLN BEECROFT
Smash It Up
PO Box 593
Turramurra
NSW 2073
Tel: (+61) (0)2 9436 0346
Mobile: (+61) (0)402 901 789
Email: smashitup@bigpond.com
ROSTER: Outfit

NLD ALEXANDER BEETS
Maxanter Muziekproducties
Hamersveldseweg 22B
3833 GP Leusden
Tel: (+32) 33 455 71 99
Fax: (+32) 33 455 71 55
info@maxanter.nl
www.maxanter.nl
ROSTER: Rita Reys, Eddie Conard

AUS MARIA BENARDIS
In Step In Time Management
PO Box 1292
Double Bay
NSW 1360
Tel: (+61) (0)2 9310 3433
Mobile: (+61) (0)418 73 73 11
Fax: (+61) (0)2 9310 3803
Email: maria@instepintime.com.au
www.instepintime.com.au

SWE GILLIS BENGTSSON

SwingKids Productions
Långlandia 2a
414 53 Gothenburg
Tel: (+46) 31 24 41 99
Mobile: (+46) 739 22 90 26
gillis@uscb-allstars.com
ROSTER: USCB Allstars, Jaqee

ALAN BENNETT **UK**
LnB Entertainments Ltd
Room 5170
The Heath Business Park
Runcorn
Cheshire
WA7 4QF
Tel: (+44) (0)8707 567390
Fax: (+44) (0)8707 567391
alan@lnb-entertainments.co.uk
www.lnb-entertainments.co.uk
ROSTER: Heidi (artist/
songwriter), Rachael Marie (artist),
Lowensa (band), Daniel James (artist),
Angel Lazelle (artist/songwriter)

ANNETTE BENNETT **UK**
Saphron Management
36 Belgrave Rd
London
E17 8QE
Tel: (+44) (0)20 85217764
Saphron@msn.com
ROSTER: Joy Silva

PAUL BENNEY **UK**
Daddy Management
15 Holywell Row
London
EC2A 4JB
Tel: (+44) (0)20 7684 5229
Fax: (+44) (0)20 7684 5230
paul@daddymanagement.net
www.daddymanagement.net
ROSTER: Dave Clarke (artist,
Skint/BMG Publishing), FC Kahuna
(band, City Rockers), Ralph
Lawson (producer, 20:20 Vision),

Justin Robertson (artist, Bugged Out Recordings), Phil Kieran (artist)

UK LINDY BENSON

Shamrock Music Ltd
9 Thornton Place
London
W1H 1FG
Tel: (+44) (0)20 7935 9719
Fax: (+44) (0)20 7935 0241
lindy@celtus.demon.co.uk
www.folking.com/celtus
ROSTER: Celtus (band), Unloaded

AUS KERRY BERGH

Bergh & Associates
23 Santa Cruz Parkway
Secret Harbour
WA 6173
Tel: +61 (0)8 9524 8529
Fax: +61 (0)8 9524 8529
Mobile: +61 (0)402 786 597
Email: kbergh@iprimus.com.au
ROSTER: Fallen Idol

USA BARRY BERGMAN

Barry Bergman Management
350 East 30th St, Suite 4D
New York, NY
10016
Tel: (+1) 212-213-8787
Fax: (+1) 212-213-9797
barrybergman@earthlink.net
ROSTER: Billy Harvey, Marc Ribler

UK MATT BIFFA

AE Copyrights Ltd
18 Rodmarton Street
London
W1H 3FW
Tel: (+44) (0)20 7486 6466
Fax: (+44) (0)20 7224 0344
matt@air-edel.co.uk
ROSTER: Anne Dudley (artist/songwriter), Hans Zimmer

(songwriter), Thomas Morse (artist/songwriter), Sam Babenia (songwriter), James Shearman (songwriter)

VIE BILLUPS UK

VF Management International
Phoenix Sound
Engineers Way
Wembley
Middlesex
HA9 0ET
Tel: (+44) (0)20 8733 8185(6)
Fax: (+44) (0)20 8733 8199
info@vfmanagementinternational.com
ROSTER: Rube, Hands Off, Leslie Loh, Tee Morris, Taofeeq Sanusi, Oliver, Flirtations, Pearly Gates

JEFF BIRNBAUM US

Relentless Management
140 Riverside Drive, Suite 9N
New York, NY
10024-2605
Tel: (+1) 212-496-1813
jeffb@relentlessmgt.com
ROSTER: Mama Zeus, Chris Ford

MICHAEL BISPING GER

Mad Music Management
Rahlstedter Str 92A
22393 Hamburg
Tel: (+49) 40 6756900
Fax: (+49) 40 67569930
michael@madmusicmanagement.com
www.madmusicmanagement.com
ROSTER: Russ Ballard (worldwide), Ezio (worldwide), The Jezuz Nut (worldwide)

JAKA BIZILJ UK

Star Entertainment International Ltd
Rivington House
Suite 202
82 Great Eastern St
London
EC2A 3JF

Tel: (+44) (0)20 7613 5790
Fax: (+44) (0)20 7613 5562
jaka@star-entertainment-intl.co.uk
www.magicofthedance.com
ROSTER: Magic of the Dance (Irish
Dance production), The Black Gospel
Singers, Wilhelm Keitel (conductor),
Enzio Maria Tise (artist)

UK **STEWART BLACK**
Blagg Management
10 Ramsden Road
Doncaster
South Yorkshire
DN4 0BN
Tel: (+44) (0)1302 326553
Fax: (+44) (0)1302 325434
info@thesugarcaneclub.co.uk
www.thesugarcaneclub.co.uk
ROSTER: The Carousels (band)

UK **SCOTT BLAND**
62 Kiniver Drive
Glasgow
G15 6RF
Tel: (+44) (0)141 944 8316
scott.bland@btopenworld.com
ROSTER: Streetside (band)

UK **NICK BLANKS**
Rick Lowe Management
4 Sycamore Close
Bourne Ends
Bucks
SL8 5UT
Tel: (+44) (0)1628 810836
Fax: (+44) (0)7966 406344
nicholas.b@whsmithnet.co.uk
ROSTER: Michael Groth (songwriter,
MCS), Nicky Rubin (songwriter,
MCS)

UK **ANNA BLIGHTMAN**
Unique Corp Ltd
15 Shaftesbury Centre
85 Barlby Road

London
W10 6BN
Tel: (+44) (0)20 8964 9333
Fax: (+44) (0)20 8964 9888
annabunique@aol.com
ROSTER: Jamie West (artist)

MISJA BLIX DEN
Zoobaba Booking/Management
Osteraagade 2, 1
Aalborg
DK-9000
Tel: (+45) 9634 5034
Fax: (+45) 9634 5035
misja@zoobaba.dk
Alex Nyborg Trio, Allan Olsen, Bjørn
Berge, Bjørn Eidsvåg, C21, Ester
Brohus, Great Big Sea, James
Sampson, Mike Tramp, Razz, Runrig,
Savage Affair, Åge Aleksandersen

ROGER BOLTON UK
Release Records.co.uk
1 The Lodge
High St
Avebury
SN8 1RF
Tel: (+44) (0)1672 539696
Fax: (+44) (0)1672 539638
roger@releaserecords.co.uk
www.releaserecords.co.uk
ROSTER: Incision (band,
Recognition/Universal), Nubium (
Band), Fold (band)

JACK BOOKBINDER USA
Fun Palace Entertainment
PO Box 20806
Columbus Circle Station
New York, NY
10023
Tel: (+1) 212 489 2425
Fax: (+1) 212 333 7226
funpalace@walrus.com
www.funpalaceentertainment.com
ROSTER: The AM, Blackbeetle, The

319

Quiet, Road Recovery, Sandy Bell

USA SCOTT BOOKER
Hellfire Enterprises Ltd
PO Box 75995
Oklahoma City, OK
73147
Tel: (+1) 405 524 0094
Hellfiremgt@aol.com
The Flaming Lips

UK MATT BOOTH
Crazeltown
6 Lansdown Road
Redland
Bristol
BS6 6NS
Tel: (+44) (0)117 946 7718
Fax: (+44) (0)117 946 7718
matt@crazeltown.com
www.crazeltown.com
ROSTER: Dust (band)

FRA VIRGINIE BORGEAUD
Double V
2 rue Navarin
75009 Paris
Tel: (+33) 140164652
Fax: (+33) 140164724
doublev@club-internet.fr
ROSTER: Indochine, Pierre-Henry,
David Halliday…

FRA PATRICE BOUCHON
Ivoire Musique
Bp 1323
06006 Nice Cedex 01
Tel: (+33) 492098085
Mobile: +33610309131
Fax: (+33) 492098092
patrice@ivoiremusic.com
www.ivoiremusic.com
ROSTER: Ivoire, Mal D'azur

FRA SEBASTIEN BOUREL
35 rue de L'amiral Mouchez

75013 Paris
Tel: (+33) 153802860
Mobile: (+33) 6 07 08 17 75
bourel.s@wanadoo.fr
ROSTER: Julie Bourel, Midoli

ANDRÉ BOURGEOIS   CAN
Instinct Artist Management
1436 Highway 202
Gore
Nova Scotia B0N 1P0
Tel: (+1) 902 632 2149
Fax: (+1) 902 632 2468
andre@instinctartistmanagement.com
www.macmastermusic.com
ROSTER: Natalie MacMaster, The
Ennis Sisters, Robert Michaels

GRAHAM BOWES   UK
Desilu Records Ltd
6 Rookwood Park
Horsham
West Sussex
RH12 1UB
Tel: (+44) (0)1403 240272
Fax: (+44) (0)1403 263008
gbowes@desilurecords.com
www.desilurecords.com
ROSTER: Nicolas Cabrera
(artist/songwriter, Desilu Records)

LOUISE BOWOLIN   CAN
The Rock Empire
RR#1
Malakwa
British Columbia V0E 2J0
Tel: (+1) 250 836 2187
Fax: (+1) 250 836-2182
lbowolin@telus.net
ROSTER: Robin Brock

PAUL BOWREY   UK
PJ Music Management/Shmusicmusic
156a High St
London
Colney

Herts
AL2 1QF
Tel: (+44) (0)1727 827017
Fax: (+44) (0)1727 827017
pjmusic@ukonline.co.uk
www.shmusicmusic
Rostser: Headrush (band), Tony
Morgan (artist), Lucy (artist), Bernie
Devine (songwriter)

UK   JOHN BOYER
Bigg Music Management
Station Studios
91 Station Road
London
N11 1QH
Tel: (+44) (0)20 8361 8114
Fax: (+44) (0)20 83618114
bigg.music@virgin.net
www.stationstudios.co.uk
ROSTER: Freakee Deakee

AUS   ROBERT BOYNTON
R&D Management
1 Marissa Close
Mansfield
QLD 4122
Tel: (+61) (0)7 3219 2993
Mobile: (+61) (0)402 353 697
Email: rdmanagement@tpg.com.au
ROSTER: DJ/Producer Indelible
(drum and bass)

UK   BARBARA BRACEGIRDLE
Modena Records
15 The Lagger
Chalfont St Giles
Bucks
HP8 4DG
Tel: (+44) (0)1494 872 372
Fax: (+44) (0)1494 872 372
barbara@modenarecords.com
ROSTER: Chicane (dance artist/
composer), Disco Citizens (dance
artist/composer), Tomski (dance
artist/composer)

HEATH BRADBY   AUS
Naked Ape Management
PO Box 1551
Fremantle
WA 6959
Tel: (+61) (0)89 433 6333
Fax: (+61) (0)89 433 6444
Mobile: (+61) (0)412 249 979
Email: heath@nakedapemgt.com
Website: www.nakedapemgt.com
ROSTER: Jebediah, Rhibosome, El
Horizonte, Bob Evans

CHRIS BRADFORD   UK
Burning Candle
151 Bookerhill Road
High Wycombe
HP12 4EU
Tel: (+44) (0)1494 445673
Fax: (+44) (0)1628 488003
Mobile: (+44) (0)7767 388373
burningcandle@ukgateway.net
ROSTER: Lease of Life (band),
Undercover (band), Permission To Land

KEITH BRADLEY   UK
Twenty First Artists
1 Blythe Road
London
W14 OHG
Tel: (+44) (0)20 7348 4800
Fax: (+44) (0)20 7348 4801
ROSTER: Elton John (Mercury), Mis-
Teeq (Telstar), Luan Parle (Sony),
James Blunt (TBO), Phil Ramone
(producer)

JAMIE BRAMMAH   AUS
Jamestar Management Pty Ltd
PO Box 5884
Brisbane
QLD 4101
Telephone: (+61) (0)7 3342 7456
Fax: (+61) (0)7 3342 7457
Mobile: (+61) (0)409 627 945
Email: jamie@jamestar.com

Website: www.jamestar.com
ROSTER: Isaac James, Sally
Hollingdale, Steven Jaymes, Uke Boy

CAN BERNIE BREEN
Bernie Breen Management
13 Blackburn Street
Third Floor
Toronto
Ontario M4M 2B3
Tel: (+1) 416 461 9969
Fax: (+1) 416 461 0589
mail@berniebreen.com
www.berniebreen.com
ROSTER: Alexandra Slate, Big Wreck,
Colin Cripps, Headstones

AUS NATHAN BRENNER
Ideal Management
51 Kooyong Rd
Caulfield Nth
VIC 3161
Tel: (+61) (0)3 9509 7575
Fax: (+61) (0)3 9509 7575
Mobile: (+61) (0)412 16 16 92
Email: nathanb@ozonline.com.au
ROSTER: George Dreyfus, The Elks,
Self, Emma Grant.

UK COLIN BREWER
Fox Records Ltd
62 Lake Rise
Romford
Essex
RM1 4EE
Tel: (+44) (0)1708 760 544
Fax: (+44) (0)1708 760 563
foxrecords@talk21.com
ROSTER: Carla Stephens, Lisa
Andreas, Route 66, Ben Franco

UK JONATHAN BRIGDEN
Prophet Music
147 Drummond Street
London
NW1 2PB

Tel: (+44) (0)20 7383 5003
Fax: (+44) (0)20 7383 5004
jon@prophetmusic.co.uk
www.prophetmusic.co.uk
ROSTER: Andrew Skeet
(artist/songwriter), Millennia Strings
(band), The Orchestra (band), Spacer
(Luke Gordon), The Twenty Jackies
(band), Hornographie (band), Riz
Maslen (artist/songwriter)

MAGGIE BRITTON AUS
Telephone: (+61) (0)7 55 611 778
Fax: (+61) (0)7 55 611 779
Mobile: (+61) (0)412 757 337
Email: info@maggiebritton.com
Web: www.maggiebritton.com
ROSTER: Jason Lee Scott, Lesia

CAROLYN BRONSON USA
5975 Copper Leaf Lane
Naples, FL
34116
Tel: (+1) 239-352-2201
Kafrances@aol.com

QUENTIN BROWN AUS
Genshen Management
PO Box 7165
East Brisbane
QLD 4169
Telephone: (+61) (0)7 3891 2860
Mobile: (+61) (0)408 069 756
Email: genshen@hotmail.com
Website: www.genshen.net
ROSTER: Genshen

MARLON BROWN UK
B'Sharp Management
287 Olney Road
London SE17 3HS
Tel: (+44) (0)7956 411664
newbran@hotmail.com
ROSTER: Alex Cartana (artist, EMI),
CNN (artist), Beat Down Production
(producer)

UK **NICK BROWN**
Deluxe Artist & Label Management
PO Box 5753
Nottingham
NG2 7WN
Tel: (+44) (0)115 914 1429
Fax: (+44) (0)115 914 1429
ngb@deluxeaudio.com
www.deluxeaudio.com
ROSTER: Phats And Small (band,
Skint/Sony), Charles Webster
(producer, Peacefrog), Presence (band),
Sophie Moleta (artist/songwriter,
BMG France)

FRA **ANNE BRUGIERE**
L'asticot
12 Villa Salamandre
92700 Colombes
Mobile: (+33) 6 12 51 44 12
abrugiere@club-internet.fr
ROSTER: Antoine Sahler, Stephane
Cade

NOR **EIVIND BRYDOY**
Next to Management
Karl Johansgate 5
Oslo 0154
Tel: (+47) 24145500
Fax: (+47) 24145501
Mobile: (+47) 95766850
eivind@nextto.no
www.nextto.no
ROSTER: Björn Berge, Kaizers
Orchestra, Noora, Samsaya

UK **NEIL BUCKLE**
Justice Promotions
66 Allerdean Close
West Denton Park
Newcastle Upon Tyne
NE15 8XW
Tel: (+44) (0)191 267 5089
ROSTER: Deb Fairs (solo rap artist)

UK **STEPHEN BUDD**

Stephen Budd Management
109x Regents Park Road
London
NW1 8UR
Tel: (+44) (0)20 7916 3303
Fax: (+44) (0)20 7916 3302
StephenBudd@record-producers.com
www.record-producers.com
ROSTER:
PRODUCERS/REMIXERS/
ENGINEERS: Andy Hughes, Arthur
Baker, Audio Drive, Ben Mitchell,
Benoit, Carsten Kroeyer, Cathy B,
Charlie Rapino, Chris Kimsey, Dan
Frampon, Darren Allison, Dave
Anderton, Dom T, Goatboy, Greg
Fitzgerald & Tom Nichols, Greg
Haver, Ian Grimble, James Hallawell,
John Brough, Jon Kelly, K-Warren,
Mark McGuire, Mark Wallis, Martyn
Ware, Mick Glossop, Nigel Butler,
Oskar Paul, Rafe McKenna, Rick
Nowels, Rob Playford, Robin Smith,
Steve Levine, Steve Lyon, Teo Miller,
Tore Johannson

DENNY BURGESS **AUS**
Denny Burgess Management
2/2 Rawson St
Newtown
NSW 2042
Tel: (+61) (0)2 9519 3978
Fax: (+61) (0)2 9516 4960
Mobile: (+61) (0)419 481 449
Email: regalrecords@bigpond.com
Web: www.air.org.au/search.asp
ROSTER: Rob Nobilia, Wizard,
Blackboard Jungle, Good Time
Charlie

RICHARD BURGESS **USA**
Burgess World Co
PO Box 646
Mayo, MD
21106-0646
Tel: (+1) 410-798-7798

Fax: (+1) 410-798-0099
burgess@compuserve.com

UK NICK BURNE
NJB Management
Montpellier House
Suffolk Place
Cheltenham
Cheltenham
GL50 2QG
Tel: (+44) (0)7712 648826
info@littledyna.com
ROSTER: Little Dyna (artist)

UK NIAMH BYRNE
CMO Management (Int) Ltd
Westbourne Studios
Studio 223
242 Acklam Road
London
W10 5JJ
Tel: (+44) (0)20 7524 7700
Fax: (+44) (0)20 7524 7701
niamh@cmomanagement.co.uk
ROSTER: Blur (band, EMI), Elastica
(band), Midge Ure (artist, BMG),
Morcheeba (band, China/Warners),
Ooberman(band), Gorillaz (band,
EMI Records), Fionn Regan
(singer/songwriter), Turin Brakes
(band, Source Records), Siobhan
Donoghay (singer, London Records),
Jamie Hewlett (artist)

FRA DIDIER CAGE
16 rue Jean Say
94120 Fontenay Sous Bois
Tel: (+33) 33665091789
Mobile: (+33) 664738180
Fax: (+33) 142939147
didiercage@hotmail.com
ROSTER: Quentin Lamotta

UK NICOLA CAIRNCROSS
ArtistManager.com
32 St Michaels Road

Worthing
West Sussex
BN11 4RY
Tel: (+44) (0)1903 522712
Fax: (+44) (0)1903 210068
nicola@artistmanager.com
www.artistmanager.com
ROSTER: DK21 (R&B duo)

AIDHEAN CAMPBELL   UK
104 Wightman Road
London
N4 1RN
Tel: (+44) (0)20 8340 1622
aidheancampbell@yahoo.co.uk
ROSTER: Tom Ollerton (artist), Kicks
(band)

BARRY CAMPBELL   UK
7HZ Management
3 Harvard Road
Isleworth
Middlesex
TW7 4PA
Tel: (+44) (0)20 8847 3556
Fax: (+44) (0)20 8232 8717
barry@7hz.co.uk
ROSTER: Neil Davidge (producer,
BMG), Pocket Angel
(artist/songwriter)

ELEENA CANN   AUS
Cat Scratch Promotions
PO Box 587
Leichhardt
NSW 2040
Tel: (+61) (0)403 294273
Email: miasma_music@hotmail.com
ROSTER: Women Of Troy,
NineTimesOver, Tom 'G' (Miasma),
Anne O'Reilly

SCOTT CAPEN   USA
Music 1 Management
PO Box 193427
San Francisco, CA

94119-3427
Tel: (+1) 510-207-6207
scapen@music1management.com
www.Music1management.com
ROSTER: 2Bucks Short, Mnemonic, 2
Way Radio

UK   KATE CARLISLE
TKR Management
47 Stanley Road
Peacehaven
East Sussex
BN10 7SP
Tel: (+44) (0)1273 587129
Fax: (+44) (0)1273 589469
tkrproductions@aol.com
ROSTER: Chantelle (artist), Matthew
Mitchell (artist)

UK   CHARLIE CARNE
Yellocello
49 Windmill Road
London
W4 1RN
Tel: (+44) (0)20 8742 2001
Fax: (+44) (0)7092 227632
charlie@yelloccllo.com
www.emporium.org
ROSTER: Brian Lock, Julian 'Bev'
Moore, Lawrence Oakley

UK   JOANNA CARR
PO BOX 28742
London
E18 2WJ
Tel: (+44) (0)20 8988 1114
gorerotted@btconnect.com
ROSTER: Gorerotted (band)

CAN   SHAUNA DE CARTIER
World Leader Pretend Inc
Box 98038
970 Queen St E
Toronto
Ontario M4M 1J0
Tel: (+1) 416 465 2459

Fax: (+1) 416 406 6608
sdecartier@earthlink.net
ROSTER: Captain Tractor, Veal, Luke
Doucet, Martin Tielli

SUSAN DE CARTIER   CAN
Starfish Entertaiment
906-A Logan Ave
Toronto
Ontario M4K 3E4
Tel: (+1) 416 588 3329
Fax: (+1) 416 588 2842
susan@bluerodeo.com
www.bluerodeo.com
ROSTER: Blue Rodeo, Jim Cuddy,
The Swallows

RICHARD CARTWRIGHT   AUS
Platinum Entertainment Pty Ltd
11/66-70 Constitution Road
Meadowbank
NSW 2114
Tel: (+61) (0)2 9807 1367
Fax: (+61) (0)2 9419 5157
Mobile: (+61) (0)407 778533
Email: rscartwright@bigpond.com
Website: www.cherrypickers.com.au
ROSTER: Cherrypickers, Craig
Csongrady, twelve at dawn

SUE CAVENDISH   UK
Active Management
54 Boileau Road
London
SW13 9BL
Tel: (+44) (0)20 8748 9951
Fax: (+44) (0)20 8741 7886`
suecavendish@compuserve.com
www.netrhythms.co.uk
ROSTER: David Hughes (acoustic
singer/songwriter), Paul Wood
(singer/songwriter

TERENCE CEDAR   UK
Catchwise Management
68 Princes Square

325

London
W2 4 NY
Tel: (+44) (0)20 7243 8220
ask_terry@hotmail.com
ROSTER: Ultra-Violet (band)

NLD SPIROS CHALOS
SilvaScreen Management & Productie
    BV
Naarderweg 16
1217 GL Hilversum
Tel: (+35) 628 88 88
Fax: (+35) 628 80 00
Spiros@SilvaScreen.tv
www.silvascreen.tv
Sonja Silva, Winston Post, Denise van
Rijswijk, Yorick Bakker, Seth
Kamphuijs, Kim-Lian van der Meij,
Sander Foppele, Touriya Haoud,
Mohammed Chaara, Sylvie Meis,
Todd Rotondi, Cyrille Carreon

AUS MICHELLE CHANDLER
Girls 2 Productions
PO Box 23
Montrose 3765
Tel: (+61) (0)3 9761 8015
Fax: (+61) (0)3 9728 3610
Mobile: (+61) (0)400 757 447
Email: mchandler@wild.net.au
Web: www.michellechandler.wild.net.au
ROSTER: Michelle Chandler, Denise
Smith, Girls 2, Sigi Gabrie, Christina
Green

NOR CHARLIE CHARLTON
Interceptor
98 White Lion Street
London
N1 9PF
Tel: (+44) (0)20 7278 8001
Fax: (+44) (0)20 7713 6298
charlie@interceptor.co.uk
ROSTER: Suede (band)

NOR OLIVIER CHASTAN

Arobas Entertainment Group
17 West 89th Street, Suite 4R
New York, NY
10024-2074

RICK CHAZAN   **AUS**
The Boat People Management
PO Box 159, Kenmore, QLD 4069
Telephone: (+61) (0)7 3878 4600
Fax: (+61) (0)7 3878 8336
Mobile: (+61) (0)412 721 417
Email: rick@herbalcreations.com.au
Website: www.theboaties.com
ROSTER: The Boat People

VINCENT CHEVRET   **FRA**
Chukchuka
3 rue Eugene Varlin, Appartement 102
93170 Bagnolet
chukchuka@netcourrier.com
ROSTER: Naab, Al & Adil

ANGELA CHIEW   **AUS**
Whipsmart
PO Box 3125
Unley
South Australia 5061
Tel: (+61) (0)8 8357 0101
Fax: (+61) (0)8 8239 0689
Mobile: (+61) (0)8 403 435 762
Email: whipsmart@chariot.net.au
ROSTER: Bergerac, Brer Mouse

TIANI CHILLEMI   **AUS**
Tall Poppy Agency
2/7 Ross Street
Glebe
NSW 2037
Tel: (+61) (0)2 9552 2779
Fax: (+61) (0)2 9552 2779
Mobile: (+61) (0)415822343
Email: music@tallpoppyagency.com
Web: www.tallpoppyagency.com

HELEN CHILMAN   **AUS**
Wash Records

416/18 Maloney St
Eastlakes
NSW 2018
Tel: (+61) (0)2 9667 2113
Mobile: (+61) (0)412 038 960
Email: helen@washrecords.com.au
Website: www.washrecords.com.au
ROSTER: Dappled Cities Fly

USA **THOMAS CHINN**
Salt-H2O Entertainment, Inc
1216 Danbury Court
Nashville, TN
37214
Tel: (+1) 615 883 8339
thomaschinn@comcast.net

FRA **CEDRIC CLAQUIN**
Aïlassam
118 Av Roger Salengro
13003 Marseille
Tel: (+33) 491081343
Mobile: (+33) 6 14 42 31 60
cedrick2@club-internet.fr
ROSTER: K2R Ridim, Raspigaous

UK **TIM CLARK**
IE Music Ltd
111 Frithville Gardens
London
W12 7JG
Tel: (+44) (0)20 8600 3400
Fax: (+44) (0)20 8600 3401
tc@iemusic.co.uk
ROSTER: Robbie Williams, Sia,
Archive, Craig Armstrong

USA **VICKI CLARK**
Clark Management Company
3156 Foothill Blvd
Glendale, CA
91214
Tel: (+1) (818) 240-5808
Fax: (+1) (818) 790-8997
iampuresuccess@hotmail.com

ANNE CLAVERIE **FRA**
Absolute Management
135 Avenue Parmentier
75011 Paris
Tel: (+33) 1 47 00 79 79
Mobile: (+33) 6 62 55 02 00
claverieanne@hotmail.com
ROSTER: Les Valentins

CATHERINE CLOHERTY **UK**
Nomadic Music
Units 18 A & B
Farm Lane Trading Estate
101 Farm Lane
Fulham
London
SW6 1QJ
Tel: (+44) (0)20 7381 6298
Fax: (+44) (0)20 7385 6105
catherine@nomadicmusic.net
www.nomadicmusic.net

JULIAN CLOSE **UK**
Silent Records
The Townhouse
150 Goldhawk Road
London
W12 8HH
Tel: (+44) (0)20 8742 9755
Fax: (+44) (0)20 8743 5624
julian.close@silentrecords.com
www.silentrecords.com
ROSTER: Maria Wilson (artist,
Telstar)

LEE CODRINGTON **UK**
East Side Management
30 Villiers Close
London
E10 5HH
Tel: (+44) (0)20 8279 0959
Fax: (+44) (0)20 8279 0959
lee.codrington@eastside-records.co.uk

BRUNO COLLETTE **FRA**
Cosa Music

23 rue des Tilleuls
14760 Brettevilles / Odon
Mobile: (+33) 609712686
bruno.collette@wanadoo.fr
ROSTER: Positive Radical Sound (PRS)

AUS **ROBERT COLLINGS**
L38 Group
Level 4
45 Clarence Street
Sydney
NSW 1213
Tel: (+61) (0)2 9455 9517
Fax: (+61) (0)2 9335 7775
Email: management@L38.biz
Website: www.L38.biz
ROSTER: Debra Dicembre, Nadya
Golski, Nadya Giga And Their 101
Candles Orchestra
(Represents Asia/Pacific interests of
Los Angeles ON MUSIC)

UK **AMANDA COLLINS**
Furious? Records
PO Box 40
Arundel
BN18 OUQ
Tel: (+44) (0)1243 558444
Fax: (+44) (0)1243 558455
amanda@furiousrecords.co.uk
ROSTER: Delirious? (band, Delirious?
Records)

UK **JAMES COLLINS**
Collins Long Solicitors
24 Pepper St
London
SE1 0EB
Tel: (+44) (0)20 7401 9800
Fax: (+44) (0)20 7401 9850
info@collinslong.com

UK **JONATHAN COLLINS**
Profundo Music
1 Holyoake Walk
London

N2 OJX
Fax: (+44) (0)20 8444 0013
Fax: (+44) (0)20 8444 0069
jcollinsco@aol.com

PATRICIA COLLINS **UK**
Level 7 & Bare Bones Studio
The Milton Room
Lindham Court
Starey Close
Milton Ernest
Bedford
MK44 1RX
Tel: (+44) (0)1234 828839
Fax: (+44) (0)7803 542764
pixink1@globalnet.com

TIM COLLINS **UK**
Mission Impossible Management
#2 2nd Floor
Enterprise Point
Melbourne St
Brighton
BN2 3LH
Tel: (+44) (0)1273 677 476
ROSTER: The Jellys (band)

DENNIS COLLOPY **UK**
Menace Management Ltd
2 Park Rd
Radlett
Herts
WD7 8EQ
Tel: (+44) (0)1923 853 789
Fax: (+44) (0)1923 853 318
menacemusicmanagement@
      btopenworld.com
ROSTER: Lisa Millett (artist,
Defected), Neil Halstead (artist, 4AD),
Mojave 3 (band, 4AD), Steve Edwards
(artist, Virgin/Skunt), Charles Webster
(artist/producer, Pagan/Peacefrog),
Presence (artist, Pagan), Rachel
Goswell (artist, 4AD), Matt Aitken
(producer/songwriter), Gary Benson
(producer/songwriter), Kenreay

(producer), The Electric Company
(artist), Ciro Sasso (producer), Dean
Hover (producer)

UK   GAIL COLSON
Gailforce Management ltd
24 Ives Street
London
SW3 2ND
Tel: (+44) (0)20 7584 5977
Fax: (+44) (0)20 7838 0351
gail@gailforcemanagement.co.uk
ROSTER: Peter Hammill (artist),
Chrissie Hynde (artist), Stephen Street
(producer), Mike Edwards (artist),
Pretenders (band)

UK   KIERON CONCANNON
FDM Records
15 Woodcote Road
Leamington Spa
CV32 6PZ
Tel: (+44) (0)1926 833 460
Fax: (+44) (0)1926 426 393
kieron.concannon@btinternet.com
ROSTER: Nizlopi (artist)

UK   SAMANTHA COOKE
Deluxxe Management
95b Embleton Road
Ladywell
London
SE13 7DQ
Tel: (+44) (0)7957 623038
cookesam@hotmail.com
ROSTER: A Girl Called Eddy
(artist/songwriter, BMG/ Setanta),
Eliza New Man (artist/songwriter)

UK   ALEX COOPER
Kyboside Ltd
8 Evening Court
Newmarket Road
Cambridge
CB5 8EA
Tel: (+44) (0)1223 314857

Fax: (+44) (0)1223 311078
alexcoop10@aol.com
ROSTER: Katrina and the Waves
(band, EMI Music Publishing), Mike
Nocito (producer), Vince de la Cruz
(producer), Poser (band), Tracy (artist)

CHRISTINE COOREY   UK
9 Wyndham Street
London
W1H 1DB
Tel: (+44) (0)20 8600 9208
c_coorey@hotmail.com
ROSTER: The Dilaters (band)

**FRANK 'SUPERFRANK'   USA
COPSIDAS**
Intrigue Music Management, Inc
224 SE 9th Street
Fort Lauderdale, FL
33316
Tel: (+1) 954 712 4500
SuperFrank@intriguemusic.com

ANTONIO COREA   AUS
TheTalent Scout
41 Gillam Drive
Kelmscott
Perth
WA 6111
Phone: (+61) (0)418 945501
Email: antonio @thetalentscout.tv
Website: TheTalentscout.tv
ROSTER: The Thunder from Down
Under, Hypercentre.

TESSA CORNER   UK
19 Market Close
Poole
BH15 1NQ
Tel: (+44) (0)1202 770714
Fax: (+44) (0)1202 770714
tessa@streetscene.org.uk
ROSTER: Xtian Navarro (artist),
Damaged Gods (band)

UK **FRANCESCO CORRADINI**
3 Devonshire Mews North
London
W1G 7BJ
Tel: (+44) (0)20 7323 1632
Fax: (+44) (0)20 7323 1632
srs.uk@talk21.com
Lukee (artist/songwriter)

UK **LUCA CORRADINI**
3 Devonshire Mews North
London
W1G 7BJ
Tel: (+44) (0)20 7323 1632
phat-gecko@talk21.com
ROSTER: Soho Electric
(artist/songwriter)

UK **CAROL CRABTREE**
Solar Management Ltd
42-48 Charlbert Street
London
NW8 7BU
Tel: (+44) (0)20 7722 4175
Fax: (+44) (0)20 7722 4072
info@solarmanagement.co.uk
www.solarmanagement.co.uk
ROSTER: Zero 7 (band), Jimmy
Sommerville (artist), Nigel Godrich
(producer), Dave Eringa (producer),
Stephen Hague (producer), Sally
Herbert (songwriter), Yo Yo
(songwriter), Graeme Stewart
(producer)

FRA **MALCOLM CRESPIN**
Submusic
14 rue du Groupe Manouchian / 17
    rue Henri Monnier
75009 Paris (Adresse de Facturation)
75020 Paris
Tel: (+33) 1 40 30 00 03
Mobile: (+33) 6 20 32 90 71
malcolm.submusic@ifrance.com
ROSTER: Shin, Louis, Activity, Mister
Zabu

STEVE CROSBY **UK**
Steve Crosby Management Ltd
Unit 220
Canalot Production Studios
222 Kensal Road
London
W10 5BN
Tel: (+44) (0)20 8962 0000
Fax: (+44) (0)20 8962 0011
steve@soundslikeahit.com
www.soundslikeahit.com
ROSTER: Scooch (band, Parlophone),
Divas (band), Russ Spencer (artist),
Whitney And Fornara (artists),
Honeytrap (band), Kickstart (band)

JULIE CROTHALL **UK**
Diamond Artist Management
Hatch Farm Studios
Hatch Farm
Chertsey Road
Addlestone
KT15 2EH
Tel: (+44) (0)1232 831677
Fax: (+44) (0)1932 831725
julie@diamondartistmanagement.com
www.diamondartistmanagement.com
ROSTER: 3rd Edge (band)

NEIL CRUICKSHANK **NZ**
Tangata Records Ltd
PO Box 33-063
Petone
Wellington 6008
Tel: (+64) 4 9393 844
Fax: (+64) 4 9393 843
Email: info@tangata.co.nz
Website: www.tangata.co.nz
ROSTER: Moana, Ruia, WVVLC,
Soul Paua, Iwi, Psparx

JANE CUDWORTH **UK**
Siren Music Management
7a Shanklin Road
Brighton
East Sussex

330

BN2 3LP
Tel: (+44) (0)1273 673 432
Fax: (+44) (0)1273 673 432
jane_cudworth@btopenworld.com

AUS BILL CULLEN

One Louder Entertainment
PO Box 989
Darlinghurst
Sydney
NSW 1300
Tel: (+61) (0)2 9380 9011
Fax: (+61) (0)2 9380 9866
Email: hq@onelouder.com.au
Web: www.onelouder.com.au
ROSTER: Alex Lloyd, Amiel, george,
Shane Nicholson, Elixir

AUS MARSHALL CULLEN

MC Management
PO Box 920
Rozelle
NSW 2039
Tel: (+61) (0)2 95551710
Fax: (+61) (0)2 95552710
Mobile: (+61) (0)416 143030
Email: marshall@damiengerard.com
Web: www.damiengerard.com
ROSTER: NOOGIE (universal), Once
Upon A Time (Interscope), Angelik
(Foghorn/MGM), Arcade
(Foghorn/MGM), SULO
(Razorblade), Grow Your Own Series
(Foghorn/MGM)

UK DAVE CUMMING

Sugar Loaf Management
29 Brunswick Court
The Albany
Albany Park Road
Kingston
Surrey
KT2 5SR
Tel: (+44) (0)20 8333 6401
Fax: (+44) (0)870 056 1643
dave071@btclick.com

DEE CURTIS   UK

152a Howard Road
London
E17 4SQ
Tel: (+44) (0)208 520 3975
Fax: (+44) (0)208 520 3975
citizenk@ukf.net
ROSTER: Citizen K (band)

JOE D'AMBROSIO   USA

Joe D'Ambrosio Management, Inc
c/o Star Management Group
1311 Mamaroneck Ave, Suite 220
White Plains, NY
10602
Tel: (+1) 914-422-0022
Fax: (+1) 914-517-5055
info@jdmanagement.com
www.jdmanagement.com
ROSTER: Mark Bacino, Fuller, One
Found Day

MARC D'AZZO   UK

56 Church Walk
Thames Ditton
KT7 0NW
Tel: (+44) (0)7676 736 309
marc.d'azzo@virgin.net
ROSTER: Joshua (artist/songwriter
[Publishing]), Dee-Dee
(singer/songwriter/producer)

MARK DALE   UK

Dizzy Height
20 Coniston Close
Grove Park
Chiswick
London
W4 3UG
Tel: (+44) (0)20 8747 4681
Fax: (+44) (0)20 8747 4681
markdale@hotmail.com
ROSTER: Charlotte Kelly (artist)

ANDI DALEY   UK

Scout It Out Management

Flat 3
57 Strathblaine Road
Clapham Junction
London
SW11 1RG
Tel: (+44) (0)7950910142
Fax: (+44) (0)20 7738 1454
andio@tinyworld.co.uk

UK **MO DAMPHA**
A-Freak Entertainment
16 Missenden House
Roland Way
London
SE17 2HS
Tel: (+44) (0)20 7703 2577
Fax: (+44) (0)7790 882 898
modampha@hotmail.com
ROSTER: MC RB (artist), Aylesbury
Allstars (artist), MC Para D (artist),
DJ Ross Young (producer), DJ Martell
(producer), Drop Squad (artist)

FRA **RODOLPHE DARDALHON**
Kulturart
23 rue D Artois
75008 Paris
Mobile: (+33) 6 86 67 41 11
Fax: (+33) 1 40 76 05 28
rodolphe@orange.fr
www.kulturart.com
ROSTER: Nolderise, Jérôme Attal,
Sapho, Néry, Polo

UK **ROSIE DARKIN**
Engine Room
12 Ninhams Wood
Orpington
Kent BR6 8NJ
Tel: (+44) (0)1689 852 453
r_darkin@hotmail.com
ROSTER: Lee Miller
(artist/songwriter)

UK **TOBY DARLING**
Toby Darling Limited

7 Merchants Place
Upper Brook St
Winchester
SO23 8HW
Tel: (+44) (0)1962 860537
Fax: (+44) (0)1962 860942
tobydarling@hotmail.com
www.tobydarling.com
ROSTER: Jody (singer/songwriter)

CHARLOTTE DARNAL **FRA**
Tabata Tour Sarl
9 rue Francoeur
75018 Paris
Mobile: (+33) 6 11 32 72 24
Fax: (+33) 1 42 62 24 84
tabata@easynet.fr
ROSTER: P 18, Jil Caplan

JACKIE DAVIDSON **UK**
Jackie Davidson Management Ltd
Gardiner House
3-9 Broomhill Road,
London
SW18 4JQ
Tel: (+44) (0)20 8870 8744
Fax: (+44) (0)20 8874 1578
jackiedvn@aol.com
ROSTER: Ali (artist/songwriter),
Wayne Hector (songwriter), Madasun
(artists), Mickey P (producer/
songwriter), Rap Walters
(producer/songwriter

NATHAN DAVIES **UK**
42 Wylde Green Rd
Sutton Coldfield
West Midlands
B72 1HD
Tel: (+44) (0)121 686 5705
Fax: (+44) (0)777 591 4057
myst@mystvibe.com
ROSTER: Myst (band)

SUE DAVIES **UK**
HEC Organisation

PO Box 184
West End
Woking
Surrey
GU24 9YY
Tel: (+44) (0)20 8200 4488
Fax: (+44) (0)1276 858785
suedavies@shakinstevens.com
www.shakinstevens.com
ROSTER: Shakin' Stevens (artist)

UK ALISTAIR DAVIS
112 Wellesley Road
Chiswick
London
W4 3AP
Tel: (+44) (0)7956 468118

UK PHIL DAVIS
Not Them Limited
246 Hawthorn Rd
Bognor Regis
West Sussex
PO21 2UP
Tel: (+44) (0)1243 866021
phil.davis@notthem.com
www.notthem.com
ROSTER: Urbanswallow (band),
Maximum high (band), Lando (band)

AUS JAMES DAWSON
Lükstat
PO Box 3685
Marsfield 2212
Mobile: (+61) (0)418 684 180
Email: dawsonjp@bigpond.com
Website: www.lukstat.com
ROSTER: Lükstat, Roan, Dawler

UK CICELY DAYES
Future Formulas
11 Florence Rd
London
SE14 6TW
Tel: (+44) (0)20 86919071
Fax: (+44) (0)20 8691 0446

cic@futureformulas.com
www.futureformulas.com
ROSTER: Ellie Lawson (artist), Dave
Harewood (artist), Ekiti Son
(artist/producer)

LEANNE DE SOUZA   AUS
Buzz Office
PO Box 393
Paddington
QLD 4064
Tel: (+61) (0)7 3369 5158
Fax: (+61) (0)7 3369 5128
Mobile: (+61) (0)412 622 881
Email: leanne@buzzoffice.com.au
Web: www.buzzoffice.com.au
ROSTER: Stringmansassy

DEBBIE DENNIS   CAN
Shensei Mei Inc
124 Nelson Circle
Newmarket
Ontario L3X 1R3
Tel: (+1) 416 566 3886
Fax: (+1) 905 853 5485
serialjoe@rogers.com
www.serialjoe.com
ROSTER: Serial Joe, Jaclyn &
Cassandra, Jessie Weafer

PAUL DEVANEY   UK
Jude Street Management
15 St Jude Street
London
N16 8JU
Tel: (+44) (0)20 7923 1362
paul@judest.com
www.blufftoni.com
ROSTER: Blufftoni (band)

BROOKES DIAMOND   CAN
Brookes Diamond Productions
24 Rockwood
Halifax
Nova Scotia B3N 1X5
Tel: (+1) 902 492 4436

Fax: (+1) 902 492 8383
brookes@brookesdiamondproductions
    .com
www.brookesdiamondproductions.com
ROSTER: Bruce Guthro, Aselin
Debison

FRA PATRICE DIAW
United Publishing
18 rue Godot de Mauroy
75005 Paris
Tel: (+33) 147428334
Mobile: (+33) 609880581
patrice.diaw@wanadoo.fr
ROSTER: Fuko

UK NATALIE DICKENS
Tonic Music
3, 51–3 Rupert St
London
W1V 7HW
Tel: (+44) (0)20 7434 2979
Fax: (+44) (0)20 7434 2979
natalie.tonicmusic@virgin.net

UK PETER DICKSON
No Bad Records
Hayfield Cottage
Glenfarg
Pertshire
Scotland
PH2 9QH
Tel: (+44) (0)1577 830431
peter@nobadrecords.co.uk
www.nobadrecords.co.uk
ROSTER: Range#Eleven (band)

NLD KOOS VAN DIJK
PO Box 59559
1040 LB Amsterdam
Tel: (+32) 20 623 37 66
Fax: (+32) 20 623 31 42
sue@brood.nl
www.brood.nl
ROSTER: Herman Brood, Ellen ten
Damme

CHARLIE DILKS   NOR
MINE
Ture Nermans Gränd 6
112 37 Stockholm
Tel: (+46) 8 653 21 71
Mobile: (+46) 735 80 96 02
charlie@mineonline.net
www.mineonline.net
ROSTER: The Klerks, Morland,
Casino

MARIE DIMBERG   NOR
DD Management Consulting
Lilla Nygatan 19
Stockholm
SE-11128
Sweden
Tel: (+46) 8 440 4595
Fax: (+46) 8 440 4594
marie@dimberg.com
ROSTER: Peter Jöback (artist,
Sony), Roxette (band)
(EMI)

TANSY DIPLOCK   UK
dBM Ltd
8 The Glasshouse
49A Goldhawk Road
London
W12 8QP
Tel: (+44) (0)20 8222 6628
Fax: (+44) (0)20 8222 6629
tansy@dbmltd.co.uk
ROSTER: Jennifer Hatt
(artist)

JEREMY DIXON   UK
Thatsrocknroll.com
5 St Johns Street
Reading
RG1 4EH
Tel: (+44) (0)118 950 7763
Fax: (+44) (0)118 956 0982
jeremy@thatsrocknroll.com
www.thatsrocknroll.com
ROSTER: Monarchy (band)

AUS DMAND PTY LTD
PO Box 648
Fortitude Valley
QLD 4006
Telephone: (+61) (0)7 3256 0233
Fax: (+61) (0)7 3256 0450
Email: info@dmand.com.au
Web: www.dmand.com.au
ROSTER: The Ten Tenors, The
Disables, Andrew Langford

FRA OLIVIER DONATO
Acapulco Productions
5 rue des Tanneries
78200 Mantes-la-Joile
Mobile: (+33) 683290965
acapulcoprod@hotmail.com
ROSTER: Digital, Severine Clair

AUS KEVIN DONNELLY
The Donnelly Factor
PO Box 407
Greenwood
Western Australia 6924
Tel: (+61) (0)403 133 703
Fax: (+61) (0)8 9409 8749
Email: donnellyfactor@hotmail.com
Website: www.donnellyfactor.com
ROSTER: Kevin Donnelly, Sloof, The
Rubbishmen, Jimmi Luxa

AUS GREGG DONOVAN
Step2 Artist Management
Suite 1
30 Eastern Ave
Dover Heights
NSW 2030
Tel: (+61) (0)2 9337 5722
Fax: (+61) (0)2 9337 4695
Email: step2@ozEmail.com.au
ROSTER: Grinspoon, Tapered Edges

AUS JOAN DOUGLAS
The Pub Management
Box 7068
MSW

Tamworth
NSW 2348
Tel: (+61) (0)2 6765 4875 office
Mob: (+61) (0)417 233713
Fax: (+61) (0)2 6762 4304
Email: joandouglas@thepub.com.au
Website: www.thepub.com.au
ROSTER: Felicity, Feral Swing Katz,
The Baileys, Aleyce Simmonds, Aaron
Bolton

JEANNE DOWNS   UK
Smudge Productions Ltd
PO Box 110
East Horsley
Surrey
KT24 5XT
Tel: (+44) (0)1372 650606
Fax: (+44) (0)1372 459876
jeanne@smudgeproductions.co.uk
ROSTER: Cookie (band), Manuka
(artist/songwriter), Aron Friedman
(producer), Leah (artist)

EIBHLIN DOYLE   UK
19 Bradley House
Raymouth Road
London
SE16 2DL
Tel: (+44) (0)20 7231 7226
eibh@ntlworld.com

JURGEN DRAMM   UK
BMP
206 Riverbank House
1 Putney Bridge Approach
London
SW6 3JD
Tel: (+44) (0)20 7371 0022
Fax: (+44) (0)20 7371 0099
ripe@compuserve.com
CJ Nelson (artist)

NAOMI DRENT   AUS
LIVEFEED Management
PO Box 350

Newtown
NSW 2042
Tel: (+61) (0)403 463871
Mobile: (+61) (0)403 463871
Email: info@livefeed.com.au
Web: www.livefeed.com.au
ROSTER: Andy Clockwise

AUS DON ELFORD
Ion Music Pty Ltd
6 Mulvey Place
Canberra
ACT 2904
Mobile: (+61) (0)418 622 666
Email: donelford@bigpond.com
Website: www.iononline.net
ROSTER: ion

UK ROSEMARY EMERY
BHP
2 College Square
Llanelli
South Wales
SA15 1DT
Tel: (+44) (0)1554 777 657
Fax: (+44) (0)1554 777 634
ukbhp@aol.com
ROSTER: Katherine Crowe (artist,
songwriter), Andrew Mark Jones
(artist, songwriter), Raisinskin
(band)

UK DAVID ENTHOVEN
IE Music Ltd
111 Frithville Gardens
London
W12 7JG
Tel: (+44) (0)20 8600 3400
Fax: (+44) (0)20 8600 3401
de@iemusic.co.uk
ROSTER: Robbie Williams, Sia,
Archive, Craig Armstrong

UK MARCUS EPSTEIN
Faceless Management
46 The Lawns

Hatch End
Pinner
Middlesex
HA5 4Bl
Tel: (+44) (0)20 428 1594
mre7@le.ac.uk
ROSTER: Mr E (artist/songwriter)

ANDERS ERIKSSON   SWE
A Eriksson Music AB
Box 34024
100 26 Stockholm
Telephone: (+46) 8 618 03 66
Mobile: (+46) 708 61 02 61
anders@eriksson-music.com
www.eriksson-music.com
ROSTER: Paatos, Wilson Pickett,
Spyro Gyra, Jerry Douglas, Maxi
Priest, Mountain

WIVI ERIKSSON   NOR
The Managemment
Walhallavägen 50
114 23 Stockholm
Tel: (+46) 8 673 24 70
Fax: (+46) 8 673 24 71
Mobile: (+46) 733 61 21 01
wivi.eriksson@themanagement.nu
www.themanagement.nu
ROSTER: Fredrik Kempe, Dilba,
Lambretta

ROBIN ESROCK   CAN
Watchdog Management
#200, 1505 West 2nd Ave
Vancouver
British Columbia V6G 2R1
Tel: (+1) 604 734 5945
Fax: (+1) 604 732 0922
robin@slfa.com
www.slfa.com/watchdog
ROSTER: Sondre Lerche, Kyprios,
Day Theory

GRAHAM ESSON   UK
Secretion Music

PO Box 167
Worcester Park
London
KT4 8UF
Tel: (+44) (0)20 8296 0992
Fax: (+44) (0)20 8330 5738
admin@secretionmusic.com
www.secretionmusic.com
ROSTER: Steranko (band),
Yusuf (band), Mean Mr
Mustard (band), Pheramone
(band), Dust (band), Somnium
(band)

FRA VALERIE ETIENNE
Cle de Scene
7 Impasse des Jardiniers
75011 Paris
Tel: (+33) 1 43 56 19 77
Mobile: (+33) 6 60 73 09 13
Fax: (+33) 1 43 56 19 77
valerie.etienne@free.fr
ROSTER: Eux

UK JENNIE EVANS
Stackridge Ltd
The Old Manse
Bath Rd
Beckington
Somerset
BA3 6SW
Tel: (+44) (0)1373 830806
Fax: (+44) (0)1373 831401
jennie@stackridge.com
www.stackridge.com
ROSTER: Stackridge (band)

AUS LOUISE EVANS
Flat 1
16 Victoria Square
Penarth
Vale Of Glamorgan
CF64 3EJ
Wales
Tel: (+44) (0)29 20 653335
info@sub-lime.net

www.sub-lime.net
ROSTER: Transposer (band),
Nathaniel Shelley (songwriter)

DARRYL FELLOWS   AUS
NOLABEL Management
23 Bareena St
Canley Vale
NSW 2166
Tel: (+61) (0)2 9728 2916
Mobile: (+61) (0)401 352 462
Email: nolabel@bigpond.com
ROSTER: Asymmetric

COLETTE FENLON BYATT   UK
CFM Management
24-26 Hope Street
Liverpool
L1 9BX
Tel: (+44) (0)151 707 7703
collettefenlon@btopenworld.com
ROSTER: Jennifer Ellison (artist,
Warner EastWest)

KEITH FERGUSON   UK
Kingston Management
PO Box 1172
Kingston Upon Thames
Surrey
KT1 2ZD
Tel: (+44) (0)20 8546 6463
Fax: (+44) (0)20 8546 6463
keith.ferguson@ukonline.co.uk
www.alexanderdgreat.com
ROSTER: Alexander D Great
(artist/songwriter)

STEVE FERNIE   UK
East Central One Ltd.
1 York Street
London
W1U 6PA
Tel: (+44) (0)20 7486 2248
Fax: (+44) (0)20 7486 8515
steve@eastcentralone.com
www.eastcentralone.com

ROSTER: Messenger (artist)

UK **ARMANDO FERRARI**
Stylus Automatic
27 Klinside Rd
Paisley
PA1 1RQ
Tel: (+44) (0)141 887 3235
Fax: (+44) (0)141 581 9867
stylusautomatic@hotmail.com
www.stylus-automatic.com.uk
ROSTER: Stylus Automatic (band)

UK **TIM FERRONE**
Slikcuts Productions
6 Cavalier Court
1 Berrylands
Surbiton
Surrey
KT5 8JD
Tel: (+44) (0)7703 284160
slikcuts@hotmail.com
ROSTER: Magic Eye (band, Serious),
Pixie (producer), Hannah Thomas
(artist), Hunpafunk (producer), Rosco
(band)

UK **GRAHAM FILMER**
16 Cheriton Road
Winchester
SO22 5EF
Tel: (+44) (0)7747 032005
grahamfilmer@btopenworld.com
ROSTER: Headstand (band)

UK **KINGSLEY FITZGERALD**
3rd Element Music
68 Himley Road
London
SW17 9AW
Tel: (+44) (0)20 8682 0243
ROSTER: Eye-sis (artist/songwriter)

CAN **LARRY FITZPATRICK**
Celtic Stone
#210, 365 Roncesvalles Ave

Toronto
Ontario M6R 2M8
Tel: (+1) 416 516 1319
Fax: (+1) 416 516 1237
lpfitzp@sympatico.ca
ROSTER: David Wilcox

STEINAR FJELD **NOR**
Steinar Fjeld Management
Prinsensgate 6
Oslo 0152
Tel: (+47) 22424850
Fax: (+47) 22424851
steinar.fjeld@oslove.com
www.oslove.com
ROSTER: Vincens

HEIDI FLEMING **CAN**
Fleming Artists Management
4102 St-Urbain St
Montréal
Quebec H2W 1V3
Tel: (+1) 514 844 7393
Fax: (+1) 514 844 5093
famgroup@videotron.ca
www.flemingartistsmanagement.qc.ca
ROSTER: Susie Arioli Swing Band,
Penny Lang, Trio François Bourrassa,
André Leroux

JULIE FLETCHER **UK**
7HZ Management
3 Harvard Road
Isleworth
Middlesex
TW7 4PA
Tel: (+44) (0)20 8847 3556
Fax: (+44) (0)20 8232 8717
Julie@7hz.co.uk
ROSTER: Neil Davidge (producer,
BMG), Pocket Angel
(artist/songwriter)

TOMMY FLOYD **CAN**
Outlaw Entertainment International
101-1001 W Broadway

Dept 400
Vancouver
British Columbia V6H 4E4
Tel: (+1) 604 878 1494
Fax: (+1) 604 878 1495
info@outlawentertainment.com
www.outlawentertainment.com
ROSTER: American Dog, Keith
County

UK RICHIE FOLKES

Creation Management Ltd
2 Berkley Grove
Primrose Hill
London
NW1 8XY
Tel: (+44) (0)20 7483 2541
Fax: (+44) (0)20 7722 8412
thefox@dial.pipex.com
ROSTER: Mew (band, Sony), The D4
(band, Infectious), Kathryn Williams
(artist, EastWest), Kill City (band,
Poptones)

UK NICK FORD

Madrigal Music – Artist Management
And Promotion
Guy Hall
Awre
Gloucestershire
GL14 1EL
Tel: (+44) (0)1594 510 512
Fax: (+44) (0)1594 510 512
madrigalmusic@genie.co.uk
ROSTER: Anastasia (band), Cindy
Stratton (artist), Ben Demidecki
(artist), Freefall (band), Peter Dorrian
(artist), Kathy September (artist)

UK PAUL FOREMAN

Paul Foreman Management
1 Lysander Drive
Ipswich
IP3 9TL
Tel: (+44) (0)147 372 1378
p.foreman@btinternet.com

ROSTER: Jacquiline Stubs
(artist/songwriter)

ROLAND FORSTER GER

Künstleragentur
Sonnenstr 16
80331 München
Tel: (+49) (0)89 6208180
Fax: (+49) (0)89 62081850
roland-forster@t-online.de
www.roland-forster.de
ROSTER: Ottfried Fischer, Sissi
Perlinger, Klaus Peter Schreiner,
Dietrich 'Piano' Paul

CHARLES FOSKETT UK

Shmusicmusic Production &
   Management
Great Northern Villa
86 Great Northen Rd
Dunstable
Bedfordshire
LU5 4BT
Tel: (+44) (0)1582 609720
Fax: (+44) (0)1582 668211
charles.foskett@ntlworld.com
www.shmusicmusic.com
ROSTER: Lauren D Field (artist),
Damien Paul (artist), Michael Carter
(artist)

COLLEEN FOSTER UK

Stagecoach Theatre Arts
53 Magazine Road
Ashford
Kent
TN24 8NR
Tel: (+44) (0)1233 611 696
Fax: (+44) (0)1233 611 696
cofost@netscape.net
ROSTER: Penny Foster
(singer/songwriter)

TOM FRANKLAND UK

Ace Of Diamonds/Ace High Group
6 Hillside

Lancaster
LA1 1YH
Tel: (+44) (0)1524 382097
aceofdiamondsmanagement@
    hotmail.com

NLD PATRICK VAN FREDERIKSLUST
Magic Bus Management
PO Box 47861
2504 CD Den Haag
Tel: (+32) 70 356 96 83
Fax: (+32) 70 356 96 88
magicmailbus@planet.nl
www.magicbusmanagement.nl
ROSTER: Grof Geschut, Van Katoen, Postmen

UK SALLY FREEMAN
Bedouin Records
Units 18a & b
Farm Lane Trading Estate
101 Farm Lane
London
SW6 1QJ
Tel: (+44) (0)20 7386 2400
Fax: (+44) (0)20 7385 6105
sally@saharasound.com

FRA STEPHANIE DE FREITAS
Open Bar
17 rue Burq
75018 Paris
Mobile: (+33) 624562944
sdf5@wanadoo.fr
ROSTER: La Rue Ketanou

SWE HANSI FRIBERG
United Stage Management Group
    AB
Box 11029
100 61 Stockholm
Tel: (+46) 8 555 70 000
Mobile: (+46) 704 40 85 10
hansi@blackstarmanagement.com
www.blackstarmanagement.com

ROSTER: Sahara Hotnights, Marit Bergman, Isolation Years, Randy, Emmon

MICHAEL FULLER UK
3rd Element Music
13 Himley Road
London
SW17 9AR
Tel: (+44) (0)20 8682 0243
mfuller@3rdelementmusic.com
ROSTER: Eye-sis (artist/songwriter)

GABRIEL'S DAY UK
48 Broadley Terrace
London NW1 6LG
Telephone: (+44) (0) 870 262 6121
Website: www.gabrielsday.com
ROSTER: Gabriel's Day

KAREN GAFURDJANOV UZB
Guli-Bonu Producer Center
Bobur Str 20
Room 207
Tashkent
700100
Uzbekhistan
Tel: (+99 8712) 552 458
Fax: (+99 8712) 552 458
gulnara@albatros.uz
www.karen.uz
ROSTER: Karen (artist), Abbos (band), Nargiza (artist)

JASON GANNER UK
Diamond Artist Management
Hatch Farm Studios
Hatch Farm
Chertsey Road
Addlestone
KT15 2EH
Tel: (+44) (0)1232 831677
Fax: (+44) (0)1932 831725
info@diamondartistmanagement.com
www.diamondartistmanagement.com
ROSTER: 3rd Edge (band)

CAN **BARRY GARBER**
IMC
#200, 1445 Lambert Close
Montréal
Quebec H3H 1Z5
Tel: (+1) 514 939 0100
Fax: (+1) 514 931 9246
barry@garberimc.com
www.garberimc.com
ROSTER: The Corrs, Human Nature,
Tina Arena, Patrick Bruel, David
Hallyday, Notre Dame de Paris,
Deborah Cox, Antoine Sicotte, Sonia
Benezra, Gabrielle Destroismaisons,
Cindy, Matt Laurent

NOR **TOM GARRETSON**
Wildstar World
Grefsenkollveien 5a L390
Oslo 0490
Tel: (+47) 22 15 66 95
Fax: (+1) 3608387823
Mobile: (+47) 48145048
wildstar@sensewave.com
www.wildstarworld.com
ROSTER: Silje Nergaard, Lydia Lunch

USA **STEPHEN BOND GARVAN**
Garvan Media, Management &
Marketing
7919 Fairfax Court
Niwot, CO
80503
Tel: (+1) 303 652 3489
Fax: (+1) 303 652 3610
steve@garvanmanagement.com
ROSTER: Katoorah Jayne, Radio
Junkies, Walt Wilkins, Michael Kelsh,
Tom Roznowski, ELK

UK **GUY GAUSDEN**
26 Straightsmouth
London
SE10 9LB
Tel: (+44) (0)20 8269 4550
Fax: (+44) (0)20 8269 0808

guy@13artists.com
ROSTER: Saint Rose (artist),
Harrington (artist/songwriter)

MARILYN GAYLE **UK**
Sowelu Management
101 Kennington Lane
Kennington
London
SE11 4HQ
Tel: (+44) (0)20 7735 1833
marilyngayle@onetel.net.uk
ROSTER: Sol@r (band), Vertigo
(band), Prestige (band)

MELANIE GAYLE **UK**
MTG Management & Promotions
38 Chambers Lane
Willesden
London
NW10 2RJ
Tel: (+44) (0)20 7461 0624
melanie.gayle@ntlworld.com
http.smilerecordsuk,iuma.com
ROSTER: Myster?ous
(artist/songwriter), MC SmartGuy
(artist/songwriter), Shook (artist), Pure
Affection (artist), J Dawg (artist),
CaraMel G (artist)

ANTHONY GEORGIOU **UK**
Montana Artist Management
130b Loudoun Rd
London
NW8 OND
Tel: (+44) (0)20 7722 7670
tony.montanamgt@virgin.net
ROSTER: Katanya Pier Louis (artist),
Damien Townsend (artist), Tony
Georgiou (artist)

THIERRY GERARDOT **FRA**
Gt Production
12 rue des Lilas
21110 Genlis
Tel: (+33) 380379258

Mobile: (+33) 608657124
info@gt-productions.com
ROSTER: Eva Marcha, Vladimir
Cosma

UK ANDREW GILDERT

AJG Management
Linstock House
Linstock
Carlisle
CA6 4PY
Tel: (+44) (0)1228 521902
andyjgildert@aol.com
ROSTER: Laine (artist/songwriter)

UK JOHN GLOVER

Blueprint Management
PO Box 593
Woking
GU23 7YF
Tel: (+44) (0)1483 715336/7
Fax: (+44) (0)1483 757490
blueprint@lineone.net
ROSTER: Tony Hadley (artist), Pete
Cox (artist), Go West (band), Ritchie
Neville, Kenny Thomas, Alison
Limerick (artist)

FRA DAMIEN GODET

29 rue D'orfeuil
28100 Dreux
Tel: (+33) 237426018
Mobile: (+33) 663572755
damiengodet@wanadoo.fr
ROSTER: Armazem

UK SIMON GOFFE

Heavyweight Management
33 Sunnymead Road
London
SW15 5HY
Tel: (+44) (0)208 878 0800
Fax: (+44) (0)208 878 3080
simon@heavyweightman.com
www.heavyweightman.com
ROSTER: Roni Size (artist), The

Freestylers (artist), Us 3 (band), Skitz
(artist), Adam Freeland (artist),
Dynamite MC (artist), Krust (artist),
Die (artist)

JUSTIN GOLDBERG USA

Measurement Arts, LLC
2934 1/2 Beverly Glen Circle, PMB
295
Los Angeles, CA
90077
Tel: (+1) 310 283 7131
Fax: (+1) 310 474 8333
MeasArts@aol.com

JACOB GOLDING UK

Flying Man Music Management
15 Ashford Road
Wilmslow
Manchester
SK9 1QD
Tel: (+44) (0)7930 345 312
Fax: (+44) (0)1625 582 517
jacobg@zoom.co.uk

MIKE GORMLEY USA

LA Personal Development
4215 Coldwater Canyon
Garden Suite
Studio City, CA
91604
Tel: (+1) 818 980 7159
Fax: (+1) 818 980 0054
lapersdev@yahoo.com
www.radioplayers.com/lapd/LAPD_
    home.htm
ROSTER: Lowen And Navarro, Paul
Schwartz, Anne McCue, 20 Second
Cycle, Clair Marlo, Carter Larsen,
Alex Baker

EVITA GOUAMENE FRA

Association MCs
C/O Mme Gouamene,
159 rue St Pierre
13005 Marseille

Tel: (+33) 491428359
Mobile: (+33) 664776165
mcstyle@wanadoo.fr
ROSTER: Sly Asher, Ra Syn

NOR NLD
Massif Music Management
PO Box 424
5000 AK Tilburg
email.govaert@massifmusic.com
www.massifmusic.com
ROSTER: Danny Vera, IM, Krezip,
La Flor Azul

UK CAROLINE GRACEY
Solar Management Ltd
42-48 Charlbert Street
London
NW8 7BU
Tel: (+44) (0)20 7722 4175
Fax: (+44) (0)20 7722 4072
info@solarmanagement.co.uk
www.solarmanagement.co.uk
ROSTER: Zero 7 (band), Jimmy
Sommerville (artist), Nigel Godrich
(producer), Dave Eringa (producer),
Stephen Hague (producer), Sally
Herbert (songwriter), Yo Yo
(songwriter), Graeme Stewart
(producer)

USA STEPHANIE GRANADER
SG Artist Management
1206 Bomar
Houston, TX
77006
Tel: (+1) 713 526 9663
sgranader@aol.com

AUS PAUL GRANT
Executive Producer
(Da Vinci) Entertainment Pty Ltd
Adaminaby
Snowy Mountains
NSW 2630
Mobile: (+61) (0)413 07 8436

Email: paulgrant@davinci-ent.com
Website: www.davinci-ent.com
ROSTER: Hope www.hopemusic.tv

JIMMIE GRAY UK
Sujiro Productions Ltd
65A Beresford Road
London
N5 2HR
Tel: (+44) (0)20 7354 0841
Fax: (+44) (0)20 7503 6457
sujiro.gray@btinternet.com

PAUL GRAY UK
Mischief Music
31 Axminster Road
Penylan
Cardiff
CF23 5AR
Tel: (+44) (0)2920 405902
Fax: (+44) (0)2920 405902
paul.gray@ntlworld.com

CRISPIN GREEN UK
Green Design
44 Croft Close
Chislehurst
Kent
BR7 6EY
Tel: (+44) (0)20 8249 4193
cgreen@greendesignweb.com
www.greendesignweb.com
ROSTER: Anthony Q (artist/songwriter)

HOWIE GREEN USA
Intrigue Music Management, Inc
224 SE 9th Street
Fort Lauderdale, FL
33316
Tel: (+1) 954 712 4500
hg@intriguemusic.com

STEPHEN GREEN AUS
Fireball Management
PO Box 30
Chermside South

QLD 4032
Tel: (+61) (0)7 3861 4534
Mobile: (+61) (0)412 321 368
Email: info@fireball.com.au
Website: www.fireball.com.au
ROSTER: Her Majesty's Finest,
Jasper's Dilemma

UK **HELEN GREGORIOS-PIPPAS**
Squeaky Records Ltd
85 Cardiff Place
Bassingbourn, Royston
Herts
SG8 5LR
Tel: (+44) (0)1763 243603
Fax: (+44) (0)1763 245623
helen@squeakyrecords.com
www.squeakyrecords.com
ROSTER: Sophie Agapios (artist)

UK **LISA GRIFFITH-JONES**
D&L Music Management
107 Crofton Road
Camberwell
SE5 8LZ
Tel: (+44) (0)20 7703 4339
ROSTER: Zemriel (artist)

UK **ADRIAN GRIFFITH**
72 Russell Road
Walton On Thames
KT12 2LA
Tel: (+44) (0)1932 232 474
adrian.griffith@bmn-systems.com
www.nermal.net
ROSTER: Nermal (band)

UK **RICHARD GRIFFITHS**
Modest! Management
Matrix Studios 2-3
91 Peterborough Road
London
SW6 3BW
Tel: (+44) (0)20 7384 6410
Fax: (+44) (0)20 7384 6411
rgriffiths@modestmanagement.com

ANDREA GRIMSHAW **AUS**
iNdiePe Promotions
21 Cambridge St
West Leederville 6007
Tel: (+61) (0)8 9382 1658
Mobile: (+61) (0)439 945 698
Email: orbytal@eftel.com
ROSTER: Ten Speed Racer,
Heathcliffe

MARCEL DE GROOT **NLD**
BOO!
Veenendaalkade 380
2547 BA Den Haag
Tel: (+32) 70 329 01 38
marcel@boolive.com
www.boolive.com
ROSTER: BOO!

SOPHIE GROS **FRA**
Louma
52 Av de la Republique
94120 Fontenay Sous Bois
Tel: (+33) 143942767
Mobile: (+33) 613071932
assolouma@tiscali.fr
ROSTER: Tyken Jah Fakoly

JULIAN GRUHL **CAN**
Coalition Entertainment
202-10271 Yonge St
Richmond Hill
Ontario L4C 3B5
Tel: (+1) 905 508-0025
Fax: (+1) 905 508-0403
julian@coalitionent.com
www.coalitionent.com
ROSTER: Melanie's Loveseat

MATTHEW GUGGISBERG **AUS**
Red Shift Artists Pty Ltd.
PO Box 3040
Alice Springs
NT 0870
Tel: (+61) (0)8 89 533222
Fax: (+61) (0)8 89 533233

Mobile: (+61) (0)417 891 331
Email: matthew@redshiftartists.com
Website: www.redshiftartists.com
ROSTER: NoKTuRNL
(www.nokturnl.com)

UK WILSON HAAGENS
PPM Management
Ingersol House
9 Kingsway
Covent Garden
London
WC2B 6XF
Tel: (+44) (0)20 7240 3432
tufnut@btinternet.com
ROSTER: Sweet Vendetta (band), Dax
(artist)

UK STEPHEN HALEY
Vision Management
7 Zetland Rd
Bristol
BS6 7AG
Tel: (+44) (0)117 909 9955
Fax: (+44) (0)117 909 9956
steve@visionuk.fsnet.co.uk
ROSTER: Monk And Canatella
(artist/songwriter), Virginia
(artist/songwriter), Static (band),
Finger (band)

UK JOAD HALL
69 Hamilton Terrace
St John's Wood
London
NW8 9QX
Tel: (+44) (0)20 8962 8692
Fax: (+44) (0)20 8962 8692
joadbhall@hotmail.com
ROSTER: Salamander Pets (band)

UK GEORGE HAMILTON
Xposure Management
Beechwood
St Marks Road
Bracknell

Berkshire
RG42 4AN
Tel: (+44) (0)134 440 9084
george@x-m.biz
http://www.x-m.biz
ROSTER: Moss Gospel Company
(band)

BRIGITTE HANDLEY AUS
1/5 Monash Parade
Dee Why
NSW 2099
Tel: (+61) (0)2 9981 1275
Fax: (+61) (0)2 9981 1275
Mobile: (+61) (0)416 1959 52
Email: rockafilly@hotmail.com
Web: www.brigittehandley.com
ROSTER: Brigitte Handley

JEF HANLON UK
Jef Hanlon Management
1 York Street
London
W1U 6PA
Tel: (+44) (0)20 7487 2558
Fax: (+44) (0)20 7487 2584
jhanlon@agents-uk.com

ANDERS HANNEGÅRD SWE
The Managemment
Walhallavägen 50
114 23 Stockholm
Tel: (+46) 8 673 24 70
Fax: (+46) 8 673 24 71
Mobile: +46 708 899 11 10
anders.hannegard@themanagement
.nu
www.themanagement.nu
ROSTER: Fredrik Kempe, Dilba,
Lambretta

LAUREN HARMSWORTH AUS
Harmsworth Productions
PO Box 2513
Fitzroy
VIC 3056

Tel: (+61) (0)403 924 692
Email: info@thebroke.com.au
Website: www.thebroke.com.au
ROSTER: The Broke

UK JON HARRIS

Number 9 Management &
   Promotions Agency
67 Mayfield Rd
South Croydon
Surrey
CR2 0BJ
Tel: (+44) (0)20 8657 4083
Fax: (+44) (0)20 8657 4083
jon.harris@number-9.co.uk
www.number-9.co.uk
ROSTER: Cayenne (band), Yookay
(band), Payback (band)

UK KEITH HARRIS

Keith Harris Music Ltd
PO Box 2290
Maidenhead
Berkshire
SL6 6WA
Tel: (+44) (0)1628 674422
Fax: (+44) (0)1628 631379
keith@keithharris.plus.com
ROSTER: Lynden David-Hall
(singer/songwriter), Elroy 'Spoonface'
Powell (singer/songwriter), Lain Gray
(artist)

UK STEPHEN HARRISON

Steve Harrison Management
10-12 Hightown
Sandbach
Cheshire
CW11 1AE
Tel: (+44) (0)1270 750448
Fax: (+44) (0)1270 750449
steve@shmanagement.co.uk
www.shmanagement.co.uk
ROSTER: The Charlatans (band,
Universal/Island), Alfie (band,
Parlophone), The Rain Band (band,

Universal Records, The Wandering
Step

ROSIE HARTNELL   UK

Hartfelt Management
2 Matthews Road
Greenford
Middlesex
UB6 0SG
Tel: (+44) (0)20 8931 0413
rosie_hartnell@hotmail.com

PAUL HARVEY   UK

Blue Aura Management
6 Cinnamon Gardens
Guildford
Surrey
GU2 9YZ
Tel: (+44) (0)1483 237 603
Fax: (+44) (0)1483 237 603
paul@blueaura.co.uk
www.blueaura.co.uk
ROSTER: FUME (band), Heckler
(band), Katja

RAE HARVEY   AUS

Crucial Music
PO Box 255
Chelsea
VIC 3196
Tel: (+61) (0)3 9772 5499
Fax: (+61) (0)3 9772 7599
Email: rae@thelivingend.com
Web: www.thelivingend.com
ROSTER: The Living End

MICHAEL HAUSMAN   USA

Michael Hausman Artist Management
511 Avenue of the Americas, #197
New York, NY
10011
Tel: (+1) 212 505 1943
Fax: (+1) 212 505 1127
michaelhausman@earthlink.net
ROSTER: Aimee Mann, Michael
Penn, Pete Droge, Marc Cohn

UK DAVE HAYNES
Inspirit Music
150 Desborough Rd
High Wycombe
Bucks
HP11 2QA
Tel: (+44) (0)1494 538 111
Fax: (+44) (0)1494 514452
dave@inspiritmusic.com
www.inspiritmusic.com
ROSTER: Specimen A (band), Kamini
(artist), Soul Sista (band)

UK MANDY HAYNES
Covetous Corner
Hudnall Common
Little Gaddesden
Herts
HP4 1QW
Tel: (+44) (0)1442 842039
Fax: (+44) (0)1442 842082
mandy@haynesco.fsnet.co.uk
ROSTER: Robert Hart
(artist/songwriter)

AUS PAULINE HEALY
Well Heeled Management
PO Box 34
Kerrimuir
VIC 3129
Mobile: (+61) (0)419327294
Fax: (+61) (0)3 9890 0834
Email: paulinehealy@bigpond.com
Website: www.fezperez.com
ROSTER: Fez Perez, Matt
Black/Fireballs

AUS LEE HEATHER
Sounds For Space
PO Box 2014
Lygon Street North
East Brunswick
VIC 3057
Tel: (+61) (0)3 9387 8003
Mobile: (+61) (0)438 092
539

soundsforspace@bigpond.com.au
ROSTER: Orisha, Emah Fox

STEVE HEAVER   **UK**
CMO Management (Int) Ltd
Westbourne Studios
Studio 223
242 Acklam Road
London
W10 5JJ
Tel: (+44) (0)20 7524 7700
Fax: (+44) (0)20 7524 7701
steve@cmomanagement.co.uk
ROSTER: Blur (band, EMI), Elastica
(band), Midge Ure (artist, BMG),
Morcheeba (band, China/Warners),
Ooberman(band), Gorillaz (band,
EMI Records), Fionn Regan
(singer/songwriter), Turin Brakes
(band, Source Records), Siobhan
Donoghay (singer, London Records),
Jamie Hewlett (artist)

CHRISTIAN HEE   **FRA**
Transformances
3 rue des Fatrives
57630 Vic Sur Seille
Tel: (+33) 387011666
Mobile: (+33) 687281190
Fax: (+33) 387011666
contact@alcaz.net
ROSTER: Alcaz'

GLENN HELMOT   **AUS**
Secret Agent
PO Box 77
Park Orchards
VIC 3114
Tel: (+61) (0)3 9872 6949
Fax: (+61) (0)3 9872 6949
Mobile: (+61) (0)418 582 083
Email: helmot@bigpond.com
ROSTER: Ross Helmot

SAM HEMPHILL   **AUS**
NOISE

PO Box 369
Fortitude Valley
QLD 4006
Tel: (+61) (0)413 889 846
Fax: (+61) (0)7 3870 0384
Mobile: (+61) (0)413 889 846
Email: sam@noisemanagement.net
Website: www.noisemanagement.net
ROSTER: The Buzzeddie Family,
Nemo, Katie's Birthday, Kindling On,
The Embers

UK   NICK HENDY
GPS Music Management
4 Argyll Place
Ryde
Isle Of Wight
PO33 3BX
Tel: (+44) (0)1983 567103
Fax: (+44) (0)1983 567103
NickHendyGPsMgt@aol.com
ROSTER: Gweido (rock/funk
band)

AUS   MATTHEW HENNESSY
598 Canning St
Carlton North
VIC 3054
Tel: (+61) (0)3 9381 4548
Mobile: (+61) (0)425 769 637
Email: matthue@bigpond.com
Web: www.thebrownhornet.com,
www.megabias.com
ROSTER: The Brown Hornet,
MegaBias, Velure

AUS   MATT HIGH
Future Seal Corporation
PO Box 12255
A'Beckett Street Post Office
Melbourne
VIC 8006
Tel: (+61) (0)3 9645 8388
Email: matthigh@mira.net
Web: www.augie-march.com
ROSTER: Augie March

BORIS HILBERT   **GER**
BO Unterhaltungsproduktion EK
Kurze Mühren 1 - Spitalerhof
20095 Hamburg
Tel: (+49) (0)40 39902525
Fax: (+49) (0)40 39902527
office@bo-up.de
www.bo-up.de
ROSTER: Dinner For 3, The Divas,
The Golden Spaceriders

CELIA HIRSCHMAN   **USA**
Downtown Marketing
67 East 11th St, #517
New York, NY
10003
Tel: (+1) 212 979 9392
Fax: (+1) 212 979 0026
Celiahman@aol.com

LORI HIRST   **CAN**
Hirst Artist Management
1100 Davis Dr
Unit 31
Newmarket
Ontario L3Y 7V1
Tel: (+1) 416 414 5848
Fax: (+) 905 952 0013
lhirst@sympatico.ca
www.theawesometeam.com
ROSTER: The Awesome Team

NICK HOBBS   **TUR**
Charmenko-Pozitif
Kavala Apt 1/4
Oba Sokak
Cihangir
Istanbul
80060
Turkey
Tel: (+90) 212 252 5167 ext 135 or 13
Fax: (+90) 212 245 4176
nick@charmenko.net
www.charmenko.net
ROSTER: Adi Lukovac & Ornamenti,
Birdpen, Laibach, Spearmint

UK LYNDA HODGES
Elwood Entertainment
12 Langton Close
Woking
Surrey
GU21 3QJ
Tel: (+44) (0)1483 724 740
lyndahodges@aol.com
ROSTER: David Burnett
(singer/songwriter)

FRA CATHERINE HOFFMAN-BISMUTH
In Touch With Music
8 Chemin de la Maree
95685 Montlignon
Tel: (+33) 139 59 95 29
Mobile: (+33) 6 08 61 60 39
Fax: (+33) 134275446
catherine.bismuth1@ libertysurf.fr
ROSTER: Mécanique Celeste

UK TOM HOGAN
Tom Hogan Management
22 Norburn Road
Longsight
Manchester
M13 0QQ
Tel: (+44) (0)161 2255 392
tomhogan49@hotmail.com
ROSTER: Blue Gary (band)

NOR BJORN HOLBAEK-HANSSEN
Bahama Management
Midtaasen 55B
Oslo 1166
Tel: (+47) 22290840
Fax: (+47) 22290845
Mobile (+47) 90549044
hohansse@online.no
ROSTER: Paal Flaata

USA RANDI HOLDEN
RTC Entertainment
1743 O'Leary Court
Newbury Park, CA
91320
Tel: (+1) 805 498 4764
RTC_Entertainment@msn.com

ROB HOLDEN   **UK**
Mondo Management/IHT Records
Unit 2D
Clapham North Arts Centre
26-32 Voltaire Rd
London
SW4 6DH
Tel: (+44) (0)20 7720 7411
Fax: (+44) (0)20 7720 8095
rob@ihtrecords.com
www.davidgray.com
ROSTER: David Gray (artist,
IHT/East West/RCA), Orbital (band,
London WEA), Tennason (HTI),
Adam Snyder (HTI), Damien Rice
(DRM/HTI)

SIMON HOLLAND   **UK**
Ophidia Entertainment
12 Pleydell Avenue
London
SE19 2LP
Tel: (+44) (0)20 8653 1051
simon.holland@ophidia.co.uk
ROSTER: Junk TV (band), Zee
(artist/songwriter), Stone Foundation
(band)

TERRY HOLLINGSWORTH   **UK**
Ten Times Better Management
61-69 Osborne Road
Jesmond
Newcastle-upon-Tyne
NE2 2AN
Tel: (+44) (0)7931 867605
Fax: (+44) (0)191 221 1777
tphollingsworth@hotmail.com
ROSTER: Aka (band), Weave (band),
Yen (band)

JOHAN HOLLSTÉN   **FIN**
Welldone Productions Oy

349

Pikiaukio 2 as 1
FIN-20900 Turku
Tel: (+358) 2 2585085
Fax: (+358) 2 2585425
Mobile: (+358) 400 520215
johan.hollsten@welldone.fi
www.welldone.fi
ROSTER: The Crash

SWE GERT HOLMFRED
The Managemment
Walhallavägen 50
114 23 Stockholm
Tel: (+46) 8 673 24 70
Fax: (+46) 8 673 24 71
Mobile: (+46) 702 56 55 15
gert.holmfred@themanagement
    .nu
www.themanagement.nu
ROSTER: Fredrik Kempe, Dilba,
Lambretta, Maarja, Street Scene,
Javiero

SWE LINDA HOLMGREN
Talent Trust AB
Kungsgatan 9c
411 19 Gothenburg
Tel: (+46) 339 95 91
Mobile: (+46) 701 89 95 91
Linda.holmgren@talent-trust
    .se
www.talent-trust.se
ROSTER: Olle Ljungström

**AUS JUSTIN HOLSTEIN/
LUKE EARTHLING**
EE Entertainment
PO Box 591
Sumner Park
QLD 4074
Tel: (+61) (0)7 3376 0229
Fax: (+61) (0)7 3376 0229
Mobile: (+61) (0)410 557 148
Email: info@rhythmacerecords.com
Website: www.rhythmacerecords.com
ROSTER: Rollerball

SIMON HOLTOM UK
Twisted Records Ltd & Twisted
Music Ltd
Cooper House
2 Michael Road
London
SW6 2AD
Tel: (+44) (0)20 7736 3433
Fax: (+44) (0)20 7736 3643
simon@twisted.co.uk
www.twisted.co.uk
ROSTER: Simon Posford
(artist/songwriter), Benji Vaughan
(artist/songwriter), Ned And Maf
Scott (artist/songwriter)

MICHELLE HO UK
First Floor Flat
58 Anselm Road
London
SW6 1LJ
Tel: (+44) (0)20 7427 3431
Fax: (+44) (0)20 7385 2677
myc.ho@virgin.net

O'BRAIN HOOI UK
13B Ravenhill Road
London
E13 9BU
Tel: (+44) (0)20 8472 9748
Fax: (+44) (0)20 8548 1596
obrainhooi@btconnect.com
ROSTER: Sarah Anderson
(artist)

CHARLOTTE HORNSBY UK
Horny Music Management Ltd
PO Box 33855
London
N8 7XE
Tel: (+44) (0)20 8340 9142
Fax: (+44) (0)23 9247 7302
charlotte@hornymusic.co.uk

FRED HORSLEY CAN
TMA Music

125 Willingdon St
Fredericton
New Brunswick E3B 3A4
Tel: (+1) 506 454 6366
Fax: (+1) 506 454 6356
fhorsley@nbnet.nb.ca
ROSTER: Jon Fidler, Dionisus

UK DAVID HOWELLS
Darah Music Ltd
21c Heathmans Rd
Parsons Green
London
SW6 4TJ
Tel: (+44) (0)20 7731 9313
Fax: (+44) (0)20 7731 9314
admin@darah.co.uk
ROSTER: Steve Mac
(producer/composer), Nicky Chinn
(songwriter)

POL AIDAN HOYLE
Burning Candle
UL Podstaroscich 5
Warszawa
01-573
Poland
Tel: (+48) 22 839 0311
Fax: (+48) 22 839 0311
ROSTER: Wojtek Staroniewicz
(artist/songwriter, Allegro), Kamalbir
Nandra (artist/songwriter), Andrew
Fryer (producer, Real Music,
Warsaw), Raivo Tafenau (band),
Sergio Bastos (artist), Gilbert Gabriel
(songwriter), Steve Lambert
(songwriter)

UK JUSTIN HSU
On10 Music Entertainment
Ltd
16-17 Manson Place
Flat 10
London
SW7 5LP
Tel: (+44) (0)20 7581 2588

justin@on10music.com

DICK HUEY USA
Toolshed
137 Sixth Avenue
Nyack, NY
10960
Tel: (+1) 845 358 7411
dhuey@beggars.com
ROSTER: Danielle Howell

DAVID HUGHES AUS
David Hughes Management P/L
PO Box 253
Camberwell
VIC 3124
Tel: (+61) (0)3 9815 1988
Fax: (+61) (0)3 9815 1977
Mobile: (+61) (0)418 377 752
Email: hughesmgt@ozEmail.com.au
Website: www.bachelorgirl.com
ROSTER: Bachelor Girl

OD HUNTE UK
Treasure Hunte Productions &
Management
12 Eversham Rd
London
N11 2RP
Tel: (+44) (0)20 8372 0141
Fax: (+44) (0)20 8372 3875
odhunte@thp-online.com
www.thp-online.com
ROSTER: CC Martin (artist)

JO HUNT UK
CMW
2 Leckwith Place
Cardiff
CF11 6QA
Wales
Tel: (+44) (0)29 20 387620
Fax: (+44) (0)29 20233022
touring@communitymusicwales.org
.uk
www.communitymusicwales.org.uk

ROSTER: Jarcrew (band), Nadia
(artist), JT Mouse (artist/songwriter),
Untouchablez (band)

CAN ANNE HUTTER
Out West Management Inc
109, 7007 4A St SW
Calgary
Alberta T2V 1A1
Tel: (+1) 403 255 9721
Fax: (+1) 403 640 7310
annhutter@outwestman.com
www.outwestman.com
ROSTER: dallah bill

AUS MARK HUXLEY
Hoax
Tel: (+61) (0)3 9807 3685
Mobile: (+61) (0)408 995 749
Email: mark@x-posure.net
Web: www.x-posure.net
ROSTER: The Hired Hands

AUS LOREN IBBOTSON
Dark Horse Management
12 Cherrywood Grove
Menai
NSW 2234
Mobile: (+61) (0)408 510 081
Email: drkhorse@tpg.com.au
Web: www.midnightswim.com
ROSTER: Midnight Swim

UK JOHN INGHAM
Ballistic Management
64 Seymour Grove
Old Trafford
Manchester
M16 OLN
Tel: (+44) (0)161 682 7801
ROSTER: Paul Homes (artist), 4 Play
(band), Most Wanted (band)

USA PAUL INSINNA
New Horizons Management
286 Hall Ave

White Plains, NY
10604
Tel: (+1) 914 686 3414
Fax: (+1) 212 904 0703 NY
Paulinsinna@cs.com

CHARLES INSKIP   **UK**
INS-YNC
74 Harberton Rd
London
N19 3JP
Tel: (+44) (0)20 7263 5299
Fax: (+44) (0)20 7263 5299
charlie@ins-ync.co.uk
www.ins-ync.co.uk
ROSTER: The Afghan Whigs/Greg
Dulli (band)/(artist) (Birdman); The
Auteurs/Luke Haines (band)/(artist)
(Hut); Black Box Recorder (One Little
Indian); Kings Of Convenience/Erland
Oye (band)/(artist) (Source)

JOHN IRELAND   **UK**
Unique & Natural Talent
57 Elgin Crescent
London
W11 2JU
Tel: (+44) (0)20 7792 1666
johnny.ireland@virgin.net
ROSTER: A White Static (band)

JANINE IRONS   **UK**
Crosby Irons Associates Ltd
Unit 1
73 Canning Road
Harrow
Middlesex
HA3 7SP
Tel: (+44) (0)20 8424 2807
Fax: (+44) (0)20 8861 5371
jinfo@dunejazz.com
www.dunejazz.com
ROSTER: Gary Crosby (artist), Denys
Baptiste (artist), Guava (band), Nu
Troop (band), Jazz Jamaica (band),
Jazz Jamaica All Stars (band), Robert

Mitchell (artist), Tomorrow's Warriors (band), Juliet Roberts (artist), Soweto Kinch (artist)

UK KATIA ISAKOFF
Hairpin Management
Unit 12-13
14 Conlan Street
London
W10 5AR
Tel: (+44) (0)20 8960 7123
Fax: (+44) (0)20 8960 7123
Katia@hairpinmanagement.co.uk
hairpinmanagement.co.uk
ROSTER: Velasonic (band), Steve D'Agostino (artist/songwriter)

UZB OLEG ISHENKO
Guli-Bonu Producer Center
Bobur Str 20
Room 207
Tashkent
700100
Uzbekhistan
Tel: (+99 8712) 552 458
Fax: (+99 8712) 552 458
olgerdviz@mail.ru
www.karen.uz
Rostser: Karen (artist), Abbos (band), Nargiza (artist)

UK CLAUDE ISMAEL
Unique Corp Ltd
15 Shaftesbury Centre
85 Barlby Road
London
W10 6BN
Tel: (+44) (0)20 8964 9333
Fax: (+44) (0)20 8964 9888
nevermind7ent@aol.com
ROSTER: Tank (artist)

UK PETE JACKSON
Creation Management Ltd
2 Berkley Grove
Primrose Hill

London
NW1 8XY
Tel: (+44) (0)20 7483 2541
Fax: (+44) (0)20 7722 8412
creation.management@dial.pipex.com
ROSTER: Kathryn Williams (artist, EastWest), The D4 (band, Infectious/ Mushroom), Mew (band, Epic)

PATRICK JACOBS   **UK**
Patrick Jacobs International
Management
The Cottage
London Road
Wembley
HA9 7EU
Tel: (+44) (0)7092 126 199
Fax: (+44) (0)20 8900 2073
management@tashasworld.com
ROSTER: Tasha's World (artist)

SAFTA JAFFERY   **UK**
Taste Media Ltd
263 Putney Bridge Road
London
SW15 2PU
Tel: (+44) (0)20 8780 3311
Fax: (+44) (0)20 8785 9894
sjpdodgy@easynet.co.uk
www.sjpdodgy.co.uk
ROSTER: Dan Wise (producer), Sodi (producer), Ron Saint Germain (producer), Nick Griffiths (producer), Robin Millar (producer), Pat Moran (producer), Ian Caple (producer), Tony Mansfield (producer), John Cornfield (producer), Michael Brauer (Mixer), Muse (band), Vega4 (band), Serafin (band), Jim Warren (producer), John Leckie (producer)

JENNI JAMES   **AUS**
The Elements Music
GPO Box 1442
Melbourne
VIC 3001

Tel: (+61) (0)3 9818 1915
Mobile: (+61) (0)414 963 246
Email: jenni@theelements.com.au
Web: www.theelements.com.au
ROSTER: Glasshouse, The Elements

UK   TERRY JAMES
Alpha 9 Records
42 Courtfield Rd
Ashford
Middlesex
TW15 1JR
Tel: (+44) (0)7050 651364
Fax: (+44) (0)7050 662856
terry@alpha9.co.uk
www.alpha9.co.uk
ROSTER: Ollie Impossible (band),
Glow (band), Days Of Worth (band),
3rd Time Lucky (band),
Incline/Clarsay (DJ/producer), Maxine
Cook (songwriter)

UK   CHRISTIAN JEAN-FRANCOIS
Method Productions
Global House
92 De Beauvoir Road
London
N1 4EN
Tel: (+44) (0)20 7241 6880
Fax: (+44) (0)7092 380 952
christian@method-productions.com
www.method-productions.com
ROSTER: Sean Cummings (artist),
Andrew Bennett (artist), Nicole Perez
(artist)

FRA   MATHIAS JEANNIN
Dare Dare Music
83 rue de Reuilly
75012 Paris
Tel: (+33) 146392530
Mobile: (+33) 6 07 89 32 62
Fax: (+33) 1 58 05 20 61
daredare@noos.fr
ROSTER: Elsa, Washington Dead
Cats, Michel Crosio, Juju Messengers,

Patrice Lazareff

BARNEY JEAVONS   UK
Geronimo! Management
29 Gillian Avenue
Aldershot
Hants
GU12 4HS
Tel: (+44) (0)1252 408 040
barneyjeavons@supanet.com
ROSTER: Reuben (artist)

CHRIS JEFFERSON   USA
CDJ Mgmt/Production Group, Inc
7517 Kentucky Ave North
Brooklyn Park, MN
55428
Tel: (+1) 612 384 3488
cj1903@aol.com

PETER JENNER   UK
Sincere Management
Flat B
6 Bravington Road
London
W9 3AH
Tel: (+44) (0)20 8960 4438
Fax: (+44) (0)20 8968 8458
peter.jenner@sinman.co.uk
ROSTER: Billy Bragg (artist),
Jerry Burns (artist), Andy Kershaw
(broadcaster), Eddi Reader
(artist)

TOMAS JERNBERG   SWE
Talent Trust AB
Kungsgatan 9c
411 19 Gothenburg
Tel: (+46) 339 95 94
Mobile: (+46) 701 899 594
tomas.jernberg@talent-trust.se
www.talent-trust.se
ROSTER: Division of Laura Lee

JOAKIM JOHANSSON   SWE
Lucy Production &

Management
Sekundantvägen 18
462 60 Vänersborg
Tel: +46 521 611 80
Mobile: +46 739 15 66 10
joakim@lucy-production.com
www.lucy-production.com
ROSTER: Sparks of Seven

SWE MORGAN JOHANSSON

Moondog Entertainment AB
Box 4276
102 66 Stockholm
Telephone
+46 8 578 679 09
(Mobile)
+46 733 14 82 09
morgan@luger.se
ROSTER: The (International) Noise
Conspiracy, Helacopters, Refused,
Looptroop

USA CHEREANE JOHNSON

WEPRICC Management Ltd
PO Box 131
Germantown, MD
20875
Tel: (+1) 301 972 0066
   ext 9811
Fax: (+1) 202 777 2644
NELJSPOT@aol.com

AUS LEIGH JOHNSON

RPJ Promotions Pty Ltd
PO Box 541
Sth Melbourne
VIC 3205
Tel: (+61) (0)3 9690 8800
Mobile: (+61) (0)416 060 021
rpjpromotions35@bigpond.com
ROSTER: Carmen Hendricks

AUS KAT JOHNSTON

Greymalkin Music
Suite 6
222 Queens Pde

Nth Fitzroy 3068
Mobile: (+61) (0)413 55 66 02
Email: shahrecs@alphalink.com.au
Web: www.nightswimmer.com
ROSTER: Nightswimmer

ANDREW JONES   UK

14 Welford Place
London
SW19 5AJ
Tel: (+44) (0)20 8879 6360
r5akj@hotmail.com

BRYON JONES   UK

Brown Sugar Management
63 Charterhouse Street
London
EC1M 6HJ
Tel: (+44) (0)20 7253 9792
Fax: (+44) (0)20 7253 9053
Bryon@brownsugarmanagement
   .com
ROSTER: Melodi Brown (band), Ani
Popper (artist)

JILLAINE JONES   AUS

50 Green Street
Prahran
VIC 3181
Tel: (+61) (0)3 95102642
Mobile: (+61) (0)421 494 357
Email: jillaine@jillainejones.com
Web: www.jillainejones.com

KATY-HELEN JONES   UK

Maad 4 Music Company
PO Box 183
Tweedale
TF4 2WB
Tel: (+44) (0)1952 502 138
Fax: (+44) (0)1952 502 138

MARCUS JONES   AUS

MJM (Marcus Jones Management)
PO Box 242
Fitzroy

VIC 3065
Tel: (+61) (0)408 966 911
Email: marcus@emjay.com.au
ROSTER: Adam Lachlan,
Jimeoin (touring), Maya, Mike
Mcleish.

UK PAUL JONES
Ethix Management Ltd
100 Kinsgate Road
London
NW6 2JG
Tel: (+44) (0)20 7691 1960
Fax: (+44) (0)7005 963041
paul@ethixmamagement.com
ROSTER: Olie Childs (artist), Renton
(band), Lethal Peach (band)

FRA EMILIE JOSEPH-EDOUARD
Furax
85 rue du Fbg du Temple
75010 Paris
Tel: (+33) 153191246
Mobile: (+33) 616471902
emilie@furax.fr
ROSTER: Daara J, Toma Sidibe

UK TARA JOSEPH
Ruby Talent Ltd
Apartment 9
Goldcrest
1 Lexington Street
London
W1F 9TA
Tel: (+44) (0)20 7439 4554
Fax: (+44) (0)20 7439 1649
tara@ruby-talent.co.uk
ROSTER: Appleton (band)

USA C MIA JUHNG
200 East 24th Street, #810
New York, NY
10010
Tel: (+1) 212 995 8432
vanillasoy@aol.com

JON JULES　　　**UK**
Diamond Artist Management
Hatch Farm Studios
Hatch Farm
Chertsey Road
Addlestone
KT15 2EH
Tel: (+44) (0)1932 831677
Fax: (+44) (0)1932 831725
info@diamondartistmanagement.com
www.diamondartistmanagement.com
ROSTER: 3rd Edge (band)

NICK KANAAR　　　**UK**
Collyer-Bristow
4 Bedford Row
London
WC1R 4DF
Tel: (+44) (0)20 7242 7363
Fax: (+44) (0)20 7405 0555
www.collyerbristow.com

DESH KAPUR　　　**AUS**
Dk Music Management
Suite 6
147 Carr Street
West Perth
Western Australia 6005
Tel: (+61) (0)8 9227 0897
Mobile: (+61) (0)402 649 536
Email: styb@iinet.net.au
ROSTER: Cartman, The Avenues,
Daniel Bull

KARI KARJALAINEN (LAWYER) FIN
Blue Buddha Management Ltd
Tallberginkatu 1 / 40,
FIN-00180 Helsinki
Tel: (+358) 9 6859321
Fax: (+358) 9 68593224
Mobile: (+358) 40 5564110
info@bbmgmt.com
www.bbmgmt.com (agency
www.piikkikasvi.fi)
ROSTER: Quintessence, 22
Pistepirkko, Jo Hope

Robert Katavic
Robert Katavic Management
PO Box 26
South Melbourne
VIC 3205
Tel: (+61) (0)3 9352 7878
Fax: (+61) (0)3 8610 1039
Email: info@katavic.com
Web: www.katavic.com
ROSTER: Boomtime, Manic Opera, Merjah

UK **JOHN KAUFMAN**
Right Management
177 High Street
Harlesden
London
NW10 4TE
Tel: (+44) (0)20 8961 3889
Fax: (+44) (0)20 8961 4620
john.rightrecordings@btopenworld.com
ROSTER: The Paddies (band), Legs Larry Smith (artist/songwriter), Malcolm Roberts (artist/songwirtcr)

USA **COLLEEN KEANE**
Shut Up & Rock Management
8021 Lasaine Avenue
Northridge, CA
91325
Tel: (+1) 818 437 9355
colleen@shutupandrock.net

USA **JOEL KELLUM**
8100 Westlawn Avenue
Los Angeles, CA
90045
Tel: (+1) 310 670 7754
Mobile: (+1) 310 344 2053
Jbkellum@aol.com

UK **GARRY KEMP**
Top Banana Management Ltd
Sinclair House
The Avenue
W Ealing

London
W13 8NT
Tel: (+44) (0)20 8758 7508
Fax: (+44) (0)20 8758 7505
garry@topbananaman.co.uk
www.topbananaman.co.uk
ROSTER: Alchemy (band), Prodigal Sun (band)

STEPHEN KEMPNER **UK**
Sheridans
14 Red Lion Square
London
WC1R 4QL
Tel: (+44) (0)20 7774 9444
Fax: (+44) (0)20 7841 1391

JENNIFER KERSIS **UK**
Netjets Management Ltd
Level 2
60 Sloane Avenue
London
SW3 3DD
Tel: (+44) (0)20 7590 5110
Fax: (+44) (0)20 7590 5111
jkersis@netjets.com
www.netjets.com

GULNORA KHUDAYBERGANOVA **UZB**
Guli-Bonu Producer Center
Bobur Str 20
Room 207
Tashkent
700100
Uzbekhistan
Tel: (+99 8712) 552 458
Fax: (+99 8712) 552 458
gulnara@albatros.uz
www.karen.uz
ROSTER: Karen (artist), Abbos (band), Nargiza (artist)

ERROL KING **UK**
Capricorn Management Services
55 Granville Court
Balmes Rd

London
N1 5SP
Tel: (+44) (0)7957 423 271
eking2@edfman.com
ROSTER: Steven Lorenzo
(artist/songwriter), Shelomy
(artist/songwriter)

UK   STEPHEN KING
Creation Management Ltd
2 Berkley Grove
Primrose Hill
London
NW1 8XY
Tel: (+44) (0)20 7483 2541
Fax: (+44) (0)20 7722 8412
stephenking@dial.pipex.com
ROSTER: Kathryn Williams (artist,
EastWest), The D4 (band, Infectious/
Mushroom), Mew (band, Epic)

AUS   ANDI KIPPLING
Andi Kippling Management
PO Box 1373
Woden
ACT 2606
Mobile: (+61) (0)411 984 019
Email: andikippling@bigpond.com
Web: www.metheconqueror.com
ROSTER: Me The Conqueror

CAN   DOUG KIRBY
Wow! Artist Management
1451 White Oaks Blvd
Oakville
Ontario L6H 4R9
Tel: (+1) 905 844 2631
Fax: (+1) 905 844 9839
doug@livetourartists.com
www.livetourartists.com
ROSTER: Rita Chiarelli, Michael
Kaeshammer, Julian Sas

GER   WERNER KIRSAMER
Künstlermedia GmbH
Heinrich-Kahn-Str 27

89150 Laichingen
Tel: (+49) 07333 9670 0
Fax: (+49) 07333 9670 30
info@kuenstlermedia.de
www.kuenstlermedia.de
ROSTER: Gaby Albrecht, Die Schäfer,
Jantje Smit, Simone Christ, Michael
Thürnau, Geschwister Hofmann,
Marianne & Michael, Oswald Sattler,
Edelweiss Express, Joe Cocker
Double, Angela Wiedl, Patrick
Lindner, Claudio de Bartolo, Harlekin,
Marie Christin

MARCUS KNIGHT   AUS
Galaxy Management Australia
PO Box 349
Reservoir
VIC 3073
Tel: (+61) (0)3 9402 0943
Fax: (+61) (0)3 9402 1888
Mobile: (+61) (0)421 656 295
Email:
marcusknight@optusnet.com.au
Website: galaxygroup.com.au
ROSTER: Tash, Paul Cecchinelli,
Theo Marantis

HIIKMAH KOHLE   UK
218c Randolph Avenue
London
W9 1PF
Tel: (+44) (0)207 328 0891
hiikmahkohle@hotmail.com
ROSTER: Zaidah (artist), Rikky
Riviera (artist)

DANIEL KOHN   AUS
Seven Seventy/Grant Thomas
Management
PO Box 200
Potts Point
NSW 1335
Tel: (+61) (0)2 93577722
Fax: (+61) (0)2 93577733
Mobile: (+61) (0)416110774

Email: daniel@gtmgt.com.au
ROSTER: Waikiki

FIN JUHA KOIVISTO
Profest Oy
PB 180
FIN-60101 Seinajoki
Tel: (+358) 6 4212713
Fax: (+358) 6 4148622
Mobile: (+358) 400 803058
juha.koivisto@provinssirock.fi
www.profest.com

FIN TAPIO KORJUS
Rockadillo Production Oy
Ilmarinkatu 12 A 2
FIN-33500 Tampere
Tel: (+358) 3 2131260
Fax: (+358) 3 2131297
tapio@rockadillo.fi
www.rockadillo.fi
ROSTER: Trio Töykeät, RinneRadio,
Wimme, Pekka Pohjola, Piirpauke,
Sakari Kukko, U-Street All Stars

UK JULIA KOSKY
Brighton Boulevarde Productions
Suite 3
392 Oxford Street
Paddington
NSW 2021
Tel: (+61) (0)2 9380 4085
Fax: (+61) (0)2 9380 4775
Email: julia@thehive.com.au
ROSTER: Baggsmen, Deepchild,
Buchman, Andy B

DEN JEASPER KROLL
Clockwize Management
Vestergade 6 A, 3
Copenhagen K
DK-1456
Tel: (+45) 3391 6760
Fax: (+45) 3391 6761
mail@clockwize.dk

ROSTER: Kick The Kangaroo, Sascha
Dupont, Garbo, Yellowbellies, Vivid
Suspense

VINCENT KRUGER NLD
Euf Prods Musicmanagement
PO Box 11177
1001 GD Amsterdam
Tel: (+32) 20 427 99 12
Fax: (+32) 20 420 63 47
vincent@eufprods.com
www.eufprods.com
ROSTER: New Cool Collective, Floris,
Yinka, Raise the Roof, Sfeq-3000

NADJA KUENSTER
Danem Productions UK
9 Sunny Side
Liverpool
L8 3TD
Tel: (+44) (0)151 707 0025
nadja@danem.net
www.danem.net
ROSTER: Sweetmonk (band),
Natasha Gannt (artist/songwriter),
Sabina (artist/songwriter)

JOS KUIJSTERS NLD
Massif Music Management
PO Box 424
5000 AK Tilburg
jos.kuijsters@massifmusic.com
www.massifmusic.com
ROSTER: Danny Vera, IM, Krezip,
La Flor Azul

LIZA KUMJIAN-SMITH UK
Little Giant Music
Top Floor
21 Greek Street
London
W1V 5LG
Tel: (+44) (0)20 7287 7444
Fax: (+44) (0)20 7287 7444
liza@littlegiantmusic.com
www.littlegiantmusic.com

ROSTER: Nick Hayward (artist), Stephen Bliss (songwriter), Lydia (artist), Sugerfree (band)

UK DAVID LANDAU

Bonzorama Management
177 High Street
Harlesden
London
NW10 4TE
Tel: (+44) (0)20 8961 3889
Fax: (+44) (0)20 8961 4620
dlandau@talk21.com
ROSTER: TC Curtis
(artist/songwriter), Jim Fitzsimmons
(songwriter)

NLD JACCO VAN LANEN

MANA Music
Otterstraat 69
3513 CK Utrecht
Tel: (+32) 6 24 51 48 70
Fax: (+32) 30 223 28 82
jacco@manamusic.nl
www.manamusic.nl
ROSTER: Mill, Wealthy Beggar,
Stuurbaard Bakkebaard, Taxi To The
Ocean

CAN ROB LANNI

Coalition Entertainment Management
202-10271 Yonge St
Richmond Hill
Ontario L4C 3B5
Tel: (+1) 905 508 0025
Fax: (+1) 905 508 0403
rob@coalitionent.com
www.coalitionent.com
ROSTER: Our Lady Peace, Finger
Eleven, Joydrop, Simple Plan, Idle
Sons, Tom Barlow

CAN ALAIN LANTHIER

Alien Management
795 St-André
Montréal

Quebec H2L 5C2
Tel: (+1) 514 827 2566
Fax: (+1) 514 844 2248
info@impresario.ca,
impresario@videotron.ca
www.impresario.ca
www.myriamrobert.ca
www.mollia.ca
ROSTER: Myriam Robert, Mollia

ALINE LAPLACE   **FRA**

Pour Qu'elle Revienne
6 rue Gustave Rouanet
75018 Paris
Tel: (+33) 146061566
Mobile: (+33) 613457532
alinelaplace@yahoo.fr
ROSTER: Les Martine, Catch

DIDI LAROSE   **UK**

NCM Productions Ltd
10 St Albans Mansion
Kensington Court Place
London
W8 5QH
Tel: (+44) (0)20 7938 4000
Fax: (+44) (0)20 7938 3001
didi@ncmproductions.com
www.ncmproductions.com
ROSTER: ID (band)

JUHA LASSILA   **FIN**

Head of Finance
Blue Buddha Management Ltd
Tallberginkatu 1 / 40,
FIN-00180 Helsinki
Tel: (+358) 9-6859321
Fax: (+358) 9-68593224
info@bbmgmt.com
www.bbmgmt.com (agency
www.piikkikasvi.fi)
ROSTER: Quintessence, 22
Pistepirkko, Jo Hope

NATALIE LATHAM   **AUS**

Puddle Duck Stduio

714 Nicholson St
Nth Fitzroy
VIC 3068
Tel: (+61) (0)3 9482 4604
Fax: (+61) (0)3 9489 8605
Email: gnat@puddleduckstudios.com
Web: www.puddleduckstudios.com
ROSTER: Dirty Little Secret, Mr
Ladybug

CAN ERIC LAWRENCE
Coalition Entertainment Management
202-10271 Yonge St
Richmond Hill
Ontario L4C 3B5
Tel: (+1) 905 508 0025
Fax: (+1) 905 508 0403
eric@coalitionent.com
www.coalitionent.com
ROSTER: Our Lady Peace, Finger
Eleven, Joydrop, Simple Plan, Idle
Sons, Tom Barlow

UK PETER LAY
Red Boots Management
PO Box No 207
Gloucester
GL4 6YB
Tel: (+44) (0)1452 537731
Fax: (+44) (0)8700 940790
peter@redbootsman.com
www.redbootsman.com
ROSTER: Journey's End (band),
Potvin (band), Slyce (band), Giorgio
Pretti (artist), Zaira
(singer/songwriter), Alev Emine
(singer/songwriter), Iain Edwards
(songwriter)

UK CARMEN LAYTON-BENNETT
7 Eagle Court
69 High Street
Hornsey
London
N8 7QG
Tel: (+44) (0)20 7561 7910

Fax: (+44) (0)20 7561 7888
carmen@sibelius.com

RYAN LAZARUS   UK
First Provincial Credit
8 Shirehall Gardens
London
NW4 2QS
Tel: (+44) (0)20 8214 1414
Fax: (+44) (0)20 8214 1415
ryanlazarus@yahoo.com

PAUL LEDBURY   UK
Red Boots Management
PO Box No 207
Gloucester
GL4 6YB
Tel: (+44) (0)1452 537731
Fax: (+44) (0)8700 940790
peter@redbootsman.com
www.redbootsman.com
ROSTER: Journey's End (band,
Attack Records/Filmworks), Ripcage
(band, Attack Records/Filmworks,
Michael's Bones (band), Dennison
Brown (band)

JAMIE LEE   AUS
Shrunken Headz
3 Brodie Cres
Christies Beach 5165
Mobile: (+61) (0)417841931
Email: percussionqueen@bigpond
.com
Web: ww.mp3.com.au/shrunkenheadz
ROSTER: Shrunken Headz

ADRIAN LEIGH   UK
Ley-line Management
77 Tavistock Rd
London
W11 1AR
Tel: (+44) (0)20 7565 7114
Fax: (+44) (0)20 7373 8376
adrian@leylinepromotions.com
ROSTER: The Bed (band)

NOR RUNE LEM
Gunnar Eide Concerts
Sonja Henies plass 2
Oslo 0185
Tel: (+47) 23163260
Fax: (+47) 22174075
rune@gec.no
www.gec.no
ROSTER: Maria Mena

USA LEONIE MESSER
Magnolia Music Management, Inc
PO Box 151151
San Rafael, CA
94915
Tel: (+1) 415 888 3134
Fax: (+1) 415 840 0699
Mobile: 415 720 9544
leonie@magnoliamusicmanagement.com
www.magnoliamusicmanagement.com
ROSTER: Darren Hayes, Specificus,
Robert Conley (producer/engineer)

UK COLIN LESTER
Wildlife Entertainment Ltd
Unit F
21 Heathmans Road
London
SW6 4TJ
Tel: (+44) (0)20 7371 7008
Fax: (+44) (0)20 7371 7708
ROSTER: Travis (band), Craig David
(artist), Brand New Heavies (band),
Jake Bullit (artist), The Sofa Club
(band), Jody Wildgoose (artist),
Martyn Joseph (artist)

UK GAUTAM LEWIS
Creation Management Ltd
2 Berkley Grove
Primrose Hill
London
NW1 8XY
Tel: (+44) (0)20 7483 2541
Fax: (+44) (0)20 7722 8412
ricochet.mnat@dial.pipex.com

ROSTER: Mew (band, Sony), The D4
(band, Infectious), Kathryn Williams
(artist, EastWest), Kill City (band,
Poptones)

MARK LEWIS UK
Top Dollar Productions
117 Sunnybank Road
Unsworth
Bury
Lancashire
BL9 8LL
Tel: (+44) (0)20 7461 0005
Fax: (+44) (0)20 7461 0005
marktopdollar@yahoo.co.uk
www.cheekstheband.com
ROSTER: Cheeks (artist)

KISHIA M LINDSEY USA
DKVision Management, Inc
38-11 Ditmars Blvd, #673
Astoria, NY
11105
Tel: (+1) 718 392 1814
mdtobe05@yahoo.com

ROBERT LINNEY UK
MBL
1 Cowcross Street
London
EC1M 6DL
Tel: (+44) (0)20 7253 7755
Fax: (+44) (0)20 7251 8096
robert.linney@virginnet.co.uk
ROSTER: The Chemical Brothers,
The Avalanches, The Psychonauts

SUE LINSEN AUS
Bunza Entertainment
PO Box 4989
North Rocks
NSW 2151
Tel: (+61) (0)2 9630 0666
Fax: (+61) (0)2 8569 0371
Mobile: (+61) (0)421 329 401
Email: sue@bunza.com.au

ROSTER: Jonah's Road, Marz, Dr Cool, Quadraphonic

UK   JULIETTE LLOYD-PRICE
IE Music Ltd
111 Frithville Gardens
London
W12 7JG
Tel: (+44) (0)20 8600 3400
Fax: (+44) (0)20 8600 3401
jules@iemusic.co.uk
ROSTER: Robbie Williams, Sia, Archive, Craig Armstrong

UK   ADRIAN LLOYD
Tarrystone Flat
High Street
Cookham
Berks
SL6 9SQ
Tel: (+44) (0)7967 328152
adlloyd@slb.com

UK   PAUL LOASBY
One Fifteen
1 Prince Of Orange Lane
Greenwich
London
SE10 8JQ
Tel: (+44) (0)20 8293 0999
Fax: (+44) (0)20 8293 9525
info@onefifteen.com
ROSTER: Jools Holland (artist), Jools Holland and His Rhythm & Blues Orchestra (band, Warners), Cathedral (band, Dreamcatcher), Janice Long (DJ), Sam Brown (artist), Francesca Longrigg (artist), Shilpa Mehta (presenter), Laurie Latham (producer), Clive Arrowsmith (producer), Clearlake (artist, Domino, The Keys (artist, Too Pure), Sweettoof (artist), Edwina Hayes (artist), BBC Big Band

UK   SIMON LONG
Collins Long Solicitors

24 Pepper St
London
SE1 0EB
Tel: (+44) (0)20 7401 9800
Fax: (+44) (0)20 7401 9850
info@collinslong.com

BRIAN LORD   **AUS**
Brian Lord Entertainment
PO Box 987
Echuca
VIC 3564
Tel: (+61) (0)3 5480 2277
Fax: (+61) (0)3 5480 6654
Mobile: (+61) (0)4 0767 4400
Email: brian@brian-lord.com.au
Website: www.brianlord.com/
ROSTER: Brian Lord

RICK LOWE   **UK**
Rick Lowe Management
Suite 7
123-125 Gloucester Place
London
W1U 6JZ
Tel: (+44) (0)20 7486 6641
ROSTER: Michael Groth (songwriter, MCS), Nicky Rubin (songwriter, MCS)

GARY LUCK   **AUS**
Backtrack Music
GPO Box 1603
Canberra City
ACT 2601
Tel: (+61) (0)2 6291 2023
Fax: (+61) (0)2 6291 2023
Mobile: (+61) (0)411 100 786
Email: backtrack@webone.com.au
ROSTER: Esteban, Trysette, ArcticBand, Grayson Manor, Everyst, Deanna Bogart, Everything, Deluc, Lynda McLaughlin, Patrick Leonard, Ali Handal, Cindy Alexander

PETRI H LUNDÉN   **SWE**

Talent Trust AB
Kungsgatan 9c
411 19 Gothenburg
Tel (+46) 339 95 90
Mobile: (+46) 701 89 95 95
petri.lunden@talent-trust.se
www.talent-trust.se
ROSTER: The Cardigans, Weeping
Willows, Peter lemarc, Joey Tempest,
Parker

UK **JOHN LUXTON**
56 Drakefell Rd
London
SE14 5SJ
Tel: (+44) (0)20 7277 8622
john.luxton@dial.pipex.com
ROSTER: Storm In October
(band)

UK **RICHARD LYNCH**
Charabanc Management &
  Promotions
18 Sparkle Street
Manchester
M1 2NA
Tel: (+44) (0)161 273 5554
Fax: (+44) (0)161 273 5554
charabanc@btconnect.com
ROSTER: Fi-Lo Radio
TOM LYTH
41 Church St
Leigh
Lancs
WN7 1AY
Tel: (+44) (0)1942 679852
tomlyth@btinternet.com
ROSTER: Cava (band), Titus
Toiletseat (musical comedy act), Andy
Lyth (drummer/session musician)

UK **DIDIER M'PUNGE DIYAVOVA**
Euro-Event Corporation Ltd
135 Northwood Tower
Marlowe Road
London

E17 3HL
Tel: (+44) (0)20 8503 6424
mpdidier@aol.com
www.euroeventcorporation.com

JANIS MACILWAINE **UK**
First Move Management Ltd
137 Shooters Hill Road
Blackheath
SE3 8UQ
Tel: (+44) (0)1322 303039
Fax: (+44) (0)1322 303033
firstmoves@aol.com
www.firstmove.biz
ROSTER: Theo (artist), XLR 8 (artist/
songwriter), Hot Proper-T (band), LE
Ments (band), Harmony (band)

DEREK MACKILLOP **UK**
Twenty First Artists
1 Blythe Road
London
W14 0HG
Tel: (+44) (0)20 7348 4800
Fax: (+44) (0)20 7348 4801
ROSTER: Elton John (Mercury), Mis-
Teeq (Telstar), Luan Parle (Sony),
James Blunt (TBO), Phil Ramone
(producer)

AL MALIK **UK**
Iconoclast Media Ltd
26c Melrose Road
Wandsworth
London
SW18 1NE
Tel: (+44) (0)20 8425 0465
Fax: (+44) (0)7092 109723
al@iconoclastmedia.com
www.iconoclastmedia.com
ROSTER: DVD (band), Jindy Sandhu
(artist)

RENA MALKAH **CAN**
KA Talent Management
2A Edmund Cresc

Richmond Hill
Ontario L4B 2X9
Tel: (+1) 416 712 7611
Fax: (+1) 905 731-6860
rmalkah@primus.ca
www.untamed.ca
ROSTER: Untamed

UK **DAVID MANDERS**
Liquid Management
65 Shirland Rd
Maida Vale
London
W9 2EL
Tel: (+44) (0)20 7286 6463
Fax: (+44) (0)20 7286 2334
david@liquidmanagement.net
ROSTER: Zanderman (band),
Lightversusdark (band), Minibar
(band)

USA **DENTON MANDERSON**
DK Vision Management, Inc
38-11 Ditmars Blvd, #673
Astoria, NY
11105
Tel: (+1) 646 752 5303
Dkvision2003@yahoo.com
www.DKV-Management.com

USA **RICK MANDRIOTA**
Negative Evidence Mgmt
334 Main Street, #125
Matawan, NJ
07747
Tel: (+1) 908 216 5020
negativeevidence@yahoo.com
www.negativeevidence.com
ROSTER: 21 Against

UK **NATALIE MANGAN**
Z Management
The Palm House
PO Box 19734
London
SW15 2QL

Tel: (+44) (0)20 8874 3337
Fax: (+44) (0)20 8874 3599
john@zman.co.uk
www.zman.co.uk
ROSTER:
PRODUCERS: Chris Potter, Jony
Rockstar, Pete Craigie, Sly & Robbie,
Goetz, Simon Law & Lee Hamblin,
Dave Meegan, Stuart Crichton
PROGRAMMERS: Chris Brown, Tim
Wills, Ron Aslan, Mark Hayley, Jony
Rockstar, May Heyes
ENGINEERS: Chris Brown, Dave
Meegan-engineer, Tim Wills, Sie
Medway Smith, Chris Potter, Goetz,
Max Keyes
REMIXERS: Dave Meegan, Tim
Wills, Stuart Crichton, Chris Potter,
Goetz, Peter Craigie, Sly & Robbie
ARTISTS: Pave, The Flips, Narotic
Thrust, Una Mas

PHIL MANNING **AUS**
Teamwork Productions Pty Ltd
PO Box 302
Dulwich Hill
NSW 2203
Tel: (+61) (0)2 9558 4361
Fax: (+61) (0)2 9559 2669
Email: teamwork@magnet.com.au
ROSTER: John Paul Young, Graeme
Connors, Rosemary Rae

VICKI MANN **AUS**
TCB Music
PO Box 5131
Wheeler Heights
NSW 2097
Tel: (+61) (0)2 9971 5422
Fax: (+61) (0)2 9971 2410
Mobile: +61 (0)4122 23357
Email: tcbmusic@bigpond.com
Web: www.tcbmusic.com.au
ROSTER: ZAAB, Luxury, Medenea

JARI MÄNTTÄRI **FIN**

Petroleum Music Agency
Mäkelänkatu 25 B 6
FIN-00550 Helsinki
Tel: (+358) 50 5240745
Fax: (+358) 9 7532328
Mobile: (+358) 50 5240745
jari.manttari@petroleumagency.com
www.petroleumagency.com
ROSTER: Neverwood, Reagan, Shade

FRA JEAN-RAPHAËL MARANINCHI
Association Fouchtra
22 Ter rue Berthollet
94110 Arcueil
Mobile: (+33) 686550805
maraninchi@hotmail.com
Jean.MARANINCHI@warnerchappell
.com
ROSTER: Fouchtra

AUS ALFRED MARKARIAN
Alfred Markarian Management
1087 Victoria Road
West Ryde
NSW 2114
Tel: (+61) (0)2 9804 0600
Fax: (+61) (0)2 9804 0644
Mobile: (+61) (0)408 282 849
Email: arvest@idx.com.au
ROSTER: Whisper Under Water, Kev
Orkian, Arax, Karnig

AUS MARK
CC Artist Management
Email: info@close-call.net
Website: www.close-call.net
ROSTER: Close Call

UK ROSE MARLEY
Silk Studios
23 New Mount Street
Manchester
M4 4DE
Tel: (+44) (0)161 282 8380
Fax: (+44) (0)161 282 8381
rosemarley@silkstudios.co.uk

ROSTER: Un-Cut (artist/songwriter),
Lee Stanley (producer), Charlotte
Gordon (songwriter)

MARC MAROT   **UK**
Terra Firma Management
8 Glenthorne Mews
115a Glenthorne Road
Hammersmith
London
W6 0LJ
Tel: (+44) (0)20 8846 8528
Fax: (+44) (0)20 8741 4289
marc@terraartists.com
ROSTER: Paul Oakenfold (DJ,
Mushroom), Richard Ashcroft (artist,
Hut), Lemon Jelly (band, XL
Recordings)

DENISE MARTIN   **UK**
Z Management
The Palm House
105 Oakhill Road
London
SW15 2QL
Tel: (+44) (0)20 8874 3337
Fax: (+44) (0)20 8874 3599
denise@zman.co.uk
www.zman.co.uk
ROSTER:
PRODUCERS: Chris Potter, Jony
Rockstar, Pete Craigie, Sly & Robbie,
Goetz, Simon Law & Lee Hamblin,
Dave Meegan, Stuart Crichton
PROGRAMMERS: Chris Brown, Tim
Wills, Ron Aslan, Mark Hayley, Jony
Rockstar, May Heyes
ENGINEERS: Chris Brown, Dave
Meegan, Tim Wills, Sie Medway
Smith, Chris Potter, Goetz, Max
Keyes
REMIXERS: Dave Meegan, Tim
Wills, Stuart Crichton, Chris Potter,
Goetz, Peter Craigie, Sly & Robbie
ARTISTS: Pave, The Flips, Narotic
Thrust, Una Mas

FRA CAROLINE MARTINEZ
Avatar
109 rue Francis Lopez
34090 Montpellier
Mobile: (+33) 662181274
athenaismanager@aol.com
ROSTER: Athenaïs

UK KIM MARTIN
3RS Management
24 Clarence Street
Exeter
SA 5019
Tel: (+61) (0)411 730 385
Email: threeroundsshy@hotmail.com
Web: threeroundsshy@live.com.au
ROSTER: three rounds shy

UK LIONEL MARTIN
Blujay Management Ltd
55 Loudoun Rd
St Johns Wood
London
NW8 ODL
Tel: (+44) (0)20 7604 3633
Fax: (+44) (0)20 7604 3639
info@blujay.co.uk
ROSTER: Chris Sheehan, Delrosario,
Beulah

FRA BERNARD MARTINS
BM Management
Le Guerin Bat A1,
Av A Daudet
83130 La Garde
Tel: (+33) 494217421
Mobile: (+33) 661221545
Fax: (+33) 494935082
bmmartins@aol.com
ROSTER: Orelie

USA MIKE MARUCCI
Marucci Artist Management, Inc
1016 Pine Crest Road
Annapolis, MD
21403

Tel: (+1) 410 626 1475
Fax: (+1) 410 295 0535
mmarucci@erols.com

JIM MASYK   **CAN**
Twang Music Management
PO Box 90024
1488 Queen St W
Toronto
Ontario M6K 1L0
Tel: (+1) 416 666 6694
Fax: (+1) 416 535 4040
jim@linkhorn.com
www.twangmusic.com
www.linkhorn.com
ROSTER: John Borra

MICHAEL J MATTHEWS   **USA**
MJM Management Company LLC
PO Box 630372
Houston, TX
77263
Tel: (+1) 281 277 6626
mjmmgmt@webtv.net

TINA MATTHEWS   **UK**
Small World
18a Farm Lane
Trading Centre
101 Farm Lane
London
SW6 1QJ
Tel: (+44) (0)20 7385 3233
Fax: (+44) (0)20 7386 0473
smworld@dircon.co.uk
ROSTER: Ian Curnow
(producer/writer), Anders Kallmark
(programmer/writer/producer/remixer/
engineer), Peter Kearney (songwriter),
Blair MacKichan (songwriter/
producer/ artist/ musician), Glen
Skinner (producer/writer/engineer)

PRISCILLA J MATTISON, ESQ   **USA**
Two Bala Plaza, Suite 300
Bala Cynwyd, PA

19004
Tel: (+1) 610 660 7774
Fax: (+1) 610 668 0574
smattison@aol.com
ROSTER: Plastic Eaters, Christian
Josi (co-manager)

CAN NANCY MAYER

Silver Star Management
#232, 4936 Yonge St
Toronto
Ontario M4N 6S3
Tel: (+1) 416 410 9983
Fax: (+1) 416 686 0399
sstar@passport.ca,
nancy_mayer_mgmt@hotmail.com
www.carsoncole.com
ROSTER: David Deacon, Red Suede
Red, Carson Cole

UK RICHARD MAYES

Unique Corp Ltd
15 Shaftesbury Centre
85 Barlby Road
London
W10 6BN
Tel: (+44) (0)20 8964 9333
Fax: (+44) (0)20 8964 9888
rm@richardmayes.com
ROSTER: Ana Ann (artist)

UK MANTWA MAYIZA

Maies Gospel Promotions Ltd
Unit M7
Shakespeare Business Centre
245a Coldharbour Lane
London
SW9 8RR
Tel: (+44) (0)20 7207 1602
Fax: (+44) (0)20 7207 4619
enquiries@agape-music.com
www.agape-music.com
ROSTER: Fr Carlito Lassa
(artist/songwriter), Pstr Lifoko Du
Ciel (artist/songwriter), Ev Ntumba
David (artist/songwriter), Ev Sonny
Okunsun (artist/songwriter), Sr Mimi
Mavatiku (artist/songwriter), Fr Kool
Matope (artist/songwriter), Groupe
Gaiel (band), Groupe Agape (band)

PAUL MAYNARD UK

Impact Management
315 Eastwood Rd
Rayleigh
Essex
SS6 7LH
Tel: (+44) (0)1702 522457
paul@maniczone.com
ROSTER: The Rubber Gods (band),
Little Egypt (band), Tony Lovatt
(producer)

GARY McCLARNAN UK

Potential Development
18 Sparkle Street
Manchester
M1 2NA
Tel: (+44) (0)161 273 3435
Fax: (+44) (0)161 273 3695
mailbox@pd-uk.com
ROSTER: Mr Scruff (artist/producer),
Homelife (band), Toolshed (band),
Sam Duprez (producer/artist), Dan
Dwayre (producer), Black Lodge
(artist), Fingathing (band), Mayming
(band), Seaming To (artist)

DANNY McCLOSKEY USA

Next Step Music Management
419 N Larchmont Blvd, #5
Los Angeles, CA 90004
Tel: (+1) 323 665 8876
Fax: (+1) 323 785 2146
jdinsf@earthlink.net
ROSTER:
ARTIST MANAGEMENT: Sparrows
Point, Act Of Faith
SONG MANAGEMENT (film/TV
placement): Cleopatra Records
(catalogue), Slewfoot Records
(catalogue), Heyday Redcords

(catalogue), Spitshine Records (catalogue), Good Ink Records (catalogue), Kickin' Records (catalogue), Shabaz (Ark 21 Records), Rico Bell (of The Mekons, Bloodshot Records), Townes Van Zandt (Tomato Records)

UK MICHAEL McDONAGH

Michael McDonagh Music
Managment Ltd
The Studio
3c Wilson Street, Winchmore Hill
London
N21 1DP
Tel: (+44) (0)20 8447 8882
Tel: (+44) (0)20 8882 7679
caramusicltd@dial.pipex.com
ROSTER: James McNally (artist),
Sunbear (band), Steve Carroll (artist),
Cyan2 (band), The Popes (band),
Remix (band)

UK BEN McDONALD

D-No Entertainment
46 Cavendish Street
Mansfield
Nottinghamshire
NG18 2RU
Tel: (+44) (0)1623 428625
dnoentertainment@aol.com
ROSTER: BoDiesel (band)

UK ALAN McGEE

Creation Management Ltd
2 Berkley Grove
Primrose Hill
London
NW1 8XY
Tel: (+44) (0)20 7483 2541
Fax: (+44) (0)20 7722 8412
creation.management@dial.pipex.com
ROSTER: Kathryn Williams (artist,
EastWest), The D4 (band,
Infectious/Mushroom), Mew (band,
Epic)

CHRIS McGEEVER UK

Total Management
Flat 2, 7 Milnthorpe Rd
Meads, Eastbourne
East Sussex
BN20 7NS
Tel: (+44) (0)1323 645879
Fax: (+44) (0)1323 728 608
chrismcgeever@totalise.co.uk
www.catherinetran.com
ROSTER: Catherine Tran (artist)

ZITA McHUGH UK

Z Management
The Palm House
105 Oakhill Road
London
SW15 2QL
Tel: (+44) (0)20 8874 3337
Fax: (+44) (0)20 8874 3599
zita@zman.co.uk
www.zman.co.uk
ROSTER:
PRODUCERS: Chris Potter, Jony
Rockstar, Pete Craigie, Sly & Robbie,
Goetz, Simon Law & Lee Hamblin,
Dave Meegan, Stuart Crichton
PROGRAMMERS: Chris Brown, Tim
Wills, Ron Aslan, Mark Hayley, Jony
Rockstar, May Heyes
ENGINEERS: Chris Brown, Dave
Meegan, Tim Wills, Sie Medway
Smith, Chris Potter, Goetz, Max Keyes
REMIXERS: Dave Meegan, Tim
Wills, Stuart Crichton, Chris Potter,
Goetz, Peter Craigie, Sly & Robbie
ARTISTS: Pave, The Flips, Narotic
Thrust, Una Mas

GARY McINTYRE CAN

Gary McIntyre Management Inc
851 Hibernia St
Montréal
Quebec H3K 2T7
Tel: (+1) 514 931 6404
Fax: (+1) 514 931 8533

garymcintyre@sympatico.ca
ROSTER: Freeworm, Jean-François
Fortier, Patrick Prévost

UK MALCOLM McKENZIE
McKenzie Brothers Music
99a Regents Park Road
London
NW1 8UR
Tel: (+44) (0)20 7483 0491
malcolm@mckenziebrothers.com
ROSTER: Peter Shoulder
(artist/songwriter), ME Roberts
(artist/songwriter)

UK JOHN McLEAN
Die Hard Promotions Ltd
The Fishergate Centre
4 Fishergate
York
YO10 4FB
Tel: (+44) (0)1904 466720
Fax: (+44) (0)870 706 5095
john.mcclean@diehardproductions.co.uk
www.diehardproductions.co.uk
ROSTER: Sevenball (band), Beyond
All Reason (band)

USA ROBERT McLIN
Special People Management
10406-B Golden Meadow Drive
Austin, TX
78758-4919
Tel: (+1) 512 973 9150
rmclin@io.com

CAN HARRIET McLOUGHLIN
MCL Management
33 Queen St W
Main Floor
Brampton
Ontario L6Y 1L9
Tel: (+1) 905) 793 3044
Fax: (+1) 905 793 5011
harrietm@rogers.com
ROSTER: ic6, Mary Cherry

MAURICE McNABB UK
Cherry Moon Ltd
Site 28
15 The Beeches
Hightown Road
Glengormley
Co Antrim
N Ireland
BT36 7DL
Tel: (+44) (0)2890 842123
Fax: (+44) (0)2890 844299
cherrymoon@cherrymoon.net
www.cherrymoon.net
ROSTER: Trina Be (female vocalist)

RAYMOND MEADHAM UK
A'n'R Music Management Ltd
PO Box 388
Northampton
NN4 0ZA
Tel: (+44) (0)1604 763367
Fax: (+44) (0)1604 763367
anrmusic@aol.com
ROSTER: LJ (artist/songwriter), CCQ
(band)

DAVID MEINERT USA
Fuzed Music
351 W Olympic Place
Seattle, WA
98119
Tel: (+1) 206 352 5365
Fax: (+1) 206 374 2700
david@fuzedmusic.com
ROSTER: Maktub, The Master
Musicians Of Jajouka, Mountain
Con, The Catheters

ANNETTE MEISL GER
La Gala – International
Cultureprojects
PO Box 30 08 08
50778 Köln
Tel: (+49) (0)221 5504314
Fax: (+49) (0)221/9553508
info@lagala.de

www.lagala.de
ROSTER: Alma, Calypsocation,
Havana Open, Sonidotres, Fanfara
Din Cozmesti, Felix Dima Cuarteto,
Sultan Tunc

UK BEN MEKIE
18 A Edenvale Street
London
SW6 2SF
Tel: (+44) (0)7812 600 454
ben.mekie@btopenworld.com
ROSTER: Numb (band)

UK CAROLINE MELVILLE
K-La Music
3 Greenland Road
London
NW1 OAS
Tel: (+44) (0)20 7424 9501
kali@orange.net

NLD MAARTEN MENDELAAR
Swing Support
Postbus 47
4930 AA Geertruidenberg
Tel: (+32) 162 521 188
maarten@swingsupport.org
www.swingsupport.org
ROSTER: Carlo de Wijs, D'Wijs, Re-3
Project, Marjon van Iwaarden

UK JONATHAN MERRICKS
Kenwood Studios
23 Kewnwood Park Road
Sheffield
S7 1NE
Tel: (+44) (0)114 249 9222
Fax: (+44) (0)114 249 9333
jon@kenwoodstudios.co.uk
www.kenwoodstudios.co.uk

UK WARREN MIDDLETON
1st 4 UK Artists
4 Spencer Walk
Tilbury

Essex
RM18 8XJ
Tel: (+44) (0)1375 845212
Fax: (+44) (0)1375 845212
warren@1st4ukartists.co.uk
www.1st4ukartists.co.uk
ROSTER: Buster Bloodvessel (artist),
Bad Manners (band), The Beat (band)

SARAH MILLAR   UK
Sister Management
27 Lexington St
London
W1 3HQ
Tel: (+44) (0)20 7287 9601
Fax: (+44) (0)20 72879602
sister.mgmt@virgin.net
www.sister-pr.com
ROSTER: Rufus Stone
(artist/songwriter)

BOB MILLER   UK
Robert Miller Music Management
Suite 237
78 Marylebone High St
London
W1U 5AP
Tel: (+44) (0)7971 402973
millermusic@hotmail.com
ROSTER: Christine Collister
(artist/songwriter, Topic Records),
Corinne Bailey (artist/songwriter),
Helen (band), Frank
(artist/songwriter, Skott Records),
Spiteri (band, EMI Venezuela), Jorge
Spiteri (songwriter, Bug Music Ltd),
Stephen Alpert (songwriter, Bug
Music Ltd), House of Mishco (dance
production team), Steve Lima
(producer/writer, Tommy Boy
Records/Skott Records), Temple of
Light (dance production team),
Original Sinnaz (dance production
and remix team), Ollie Bagnell
(writer), Cargo Cult (band), Katie
Gough (artist)

UK PETER MILLS
Ghost Management
RHU Corner Pursers Lane
Peaslake
Surrey
GU5 9RG
Tel: (+44) (0)1306 731 536
Millspeterj@aol.com
ROSTER: Katie Lote
(singer/songwriter), Francesca Jackson
(singer/songwriter), Richie Sharp
(singer/songwriter)

FRA FREDERIC MIRAILLES
40 rue de Rochechouart
75009 Paris
Tel: (+33) 1 42 80 17 92
Mobile: (+33) 6 09 68 43 14
Fax: (+33) 1 42 80 17 92
frederic.mirailles@veda.com.fr
www.veda.com.fr
ROSTER: Manou, Abdell le Saint

USA JULI MIRANDA
T-Babie
2920 Kent, Apt 200
Bryan, TX
77802
Tel: (+1) 979 774 3191
jltmiranda@hotmail.com

FRA NANS MIRON
17 rue Marx Pormoy
75018 Paris
Tel: (+33) 142090784
Mobile: +33611513351
nans.miron@free.fr
ROSTER: Yann Matisse

UK MISTER CHRIS
Zenfoism
9 Chesshyre Avenue
Ancoats
Manchester
M4 7ET
Tel: (+44) (0)161 275 9326

Fax: (+44) (0)161 275 9326
misterchris@zenfo.co.uk
www.zenfo.co.uk
ROSTER: Zenfo (band), Gavstaar
(artist/ songwriter), SP (artist)

PRAVIN MISTRY   **UK**
Mistry Management
52 Broadmead Avenue
Northampton
NN3 2QY
Tel: (+44) (0)1604 714 203
pmistry@another.com

MATTHEW MOLINE   **AUS**
7th Dimension
PO Box 6187
Fairfield
QLD 4103
Tel: (+61) (0)7 3342 7507
Fax: (+61) (0)7 3342 7507
Mobile: (+61) (0)418 807 778
Email: matt@7thdimension.com.au
Website: www.7thdimension.com.au
ROSTER: Doch, Chad Morro,
Johnson Stompers

UNIE MOLLER   **UK**
Sexy Music
Yew Tree House
Dovecote Close
Haddenham
Buckinghamshire HP17 8BS
Tel: (+44) (0)778 995 7999/(0)774
8858 927
Fax: (+44) (0)1844 290 528
unie@sexyrecords.co.uk
ROSTER: Redd Angel
(artist/songwriter), Yolanda
(artist/songwriter), The Cronics (band)

JACK MOLYNEUX   **AUS**
JMM Jack Molyneux Management
PO Box 9112
Scoresby
VIC 3179

Tel: (+61) (0)3 9763 1146
Fax: (+61) (0)3 9763 1763
Mobile: (+61) (0)412 353 662
Email: jmm@bluep.com
Web: www.heavenscent.com.au
ROSTER: Heaven Scent

UK NICK MOORE
16 Ainger Rd
Primorse Hill
London
NW3 3AS
Tel: (+44) (0)20 78365256
nick.moore@zoom.co.uk
www.artistnetwork.com

UK JONATHAN MORLEY
Northern Lights Management
120 Ashurst Rd
London
N12 9AB
Tel: (+44) (0)20 8446 8103
Fax: (+44) (0)20 8342 8213
jonny.lights@virgin.net
ROSTER: Tina Dickow
(artist/songwriter), Core (band),
Richard Rainey (producer)

UK SEAMUS MORLEY
Fume Productions Ltd
109x Regents Park Rd
Primrose Hill
London
NW1 8UR
Tel: (+44) (0)20 7681 7982
Fax: (+44) (0)20 7916 3302
info@fume.co.uk
www.uglyrecords.co.uk
ROSTER: Adam Wren (producer),
Will Hensal (artist/songwriter)

UK FERDI MORRIS
VF Management International
Phoenix Sound
Engineers Way
Wembley

Middlesex
HA9 0ET
Tel: (+44) (0)20 8733 8185(6)
Fax: (+44) (0)20 8733 8199
shaz@vfmanagementinternational.com
ROSTER: Rube, Hands Off, Leslie
Loh, Tee Morris, Taofeeq Sanusi,
Oliver, Flirtations, Pearly Gates

CHRIS MORRISON UK
CMO Management (International)
 Ltd
Westbourne Studios
Studio 223
242 Acklam Road
London
W10 5JJ
Tel: (+44) (0)20 7524 7700
Fax: (+44) (0)20 7524 7701
susie@cmomanagement.co.uk
ROSTER: Blur (band, EMI), Elastica
(band), Midge Ure (artist, BMG),
Morcheeba (band, China/Warners),
Ooberman (band), Gorillaz (band,
EMI Records), Fionn Regan
(singer/songwriter), Turin Brakes
(band, Source Records), Siobhan
Donoghay (singer, London Records),
Jamie Hewlett (artist)

MELIKA MORRISON UK
Simones Internationale
12a Rosebank
Holyport Road
London
SW6 6LJ
Tel: (+44) (0)20 8861 3900
Fax: (+44) (0)20 7381 1571
ROSTER: Lounge Lizard (band),
Zeinab (vocalist/songwriter)

NIGEL MORTON UK
Moneypenny Management & Agency
The Stables
Westwood House
Main Street, North Dalton

Near Driffield
East Yokshire
YO25 9XA
Tel: (+44) (0)1377 217815
Fax: (+44) (0)1377 217754
nigel@adastey.demon.co.uk
www.adastra-
music.co.uk/moneypenny
ROSTER: Eliza Carthy
(artist/songwriter), Black Umfolosi

UK   HEATHER MOUL
East Side Management
260 Summerset Gardens
Creighton Road
London
N17 8JY
Tel: (+44) (0)20 8493 0294
Fax: (+44) (0)8712 105213
heather@eastside-records.co.uk
www.eastside-records.co.uk

CAN   ALLEN MOY
Divine Industries
Box 191
#101-1001 W Broadway
Vancouver
British Columbia
V6H 4E4
Tel: (+1) 604 737 0091
Fax: (+1) 604 737 3602
allenm@divineindustries.com
http://www.divineindustries.com
ROSTER: 54-40, Chin Injeti, Tom
Wilson, Copyright, The Special
Guests

GER   MSC PROMOTION GMBH
Elisenstr 32
63739 Aschaffenburg
Tel: (+49) 6021 38678 0
Fax: (+49) 6021 38678 24
kontakt@msc-promotion.de
www.msc-promotion.de
ROSTER: Management of television
presenter

JOHN MUHAMMAD   **UK**
44 Carlingford Road
London
N15 3EH
Tel: (+44) (0)7932 984441
Fax: (+44) (0)20 8888 5468
john_muhammad@hotmail.com
ROSTER: Mozaic (artist), Unit 5
(band)

RIIKKA MUINONEN   **FIN**
Manager
Blue Buddha Management Ltd
Tallberginkatu 1 / 40,
FIN-00180 Helsinki
Tel: (+358) 9 6859321
Fax: (+358) 9 68593224
info@bbmgmt.com
www.bbmgmt.com (agency
www.piikkikasvi.fi)
ROSTER: Quintessence, 22
Pistepirkko, Jo Hope

DENNIS MUIRHEAD   **UK**
Muirhead Management
Michelin House
81 Fulham Road
Chelsea
London
SW3 6RD
Tel: (+44) (0)20 7351 5167
Fax: (+44) (0)870 136 3878
dennis@muirheadmanagement.co.uk
www.muirheadmanagement.co.uk
ROSTER: Denis Woods
(producer/musician/writer), Richard
Bennett (artist/producer/writer), Billy
Swan (artist/songwriter/producer) RS
Field (producer/musician/songwriter),
Sun Studio – Memphis, Tennessee
(706 Records), James Lott
(producer/musician), Hugely Music
Publishing (Hugh Pagham), Acoustic
Design Group (John Flynn), IPA
(music publishing), music industry
consultant, mediator - ADR

Chambers, consultant lawyer

UK   RUPERT MUIR
Silvercube Management
Apartment 4
21 College Road
Newton Abbot
Devon
TQ12 1EG
Tel: (+44) (0)1626 324945
Fax: (+44) (0)1626 324945
silvercubemail@aol.com
www.silvercube.net
ROSTER: The Plumrecordings (band),
Hombres Imposible (band)

AUS   JOANNE MULCAHY
ME Music Management
Tel: (+61) (0)3 9704 6288
Fax: (+61) (0)3 9704 7729
Mobile: (+61) (0)4 14571137
Email: jom@bigpond.nct.au
Web: www.memusic.com.au
ROSTER: Leah Haywood, Daniel
James, Dreamlab Inc, Hal Okello

UK   PAULINE MUNRO-THOMSON
3 Meade Court
Walton Strret
Walton On The Hill
Surrey
KT20 7RN
Tel: (+44) (0)1737 814693
pauline_mt@hotmail.com

AUS   JOHN MURRAY-SMITH
Definite Records Ltd
PO Box 37614
London
NW7 2WX
Tel: (+44) (0)20 8959 0468
Fax: (+44) (0)20 8959 8392
john@jmsm.demon.co.uk
www.DefiniteRecords.Net
Ambelique (artist/songwriter,
Definite/Various), AJ Franklin
(artist/songwriter, Definite/Various),
Dave Barker (artist/songwriter,
Definite/Various), Brother Yahya
(artist/songwriter, Definite Records
Ltd), Winston Francis
(artist/songwriter, Definite/Various),
Dennis Alcapone (artist/songwriter,
Definite/Various), Chosen Few
(artist/songwriter, Definite/Various),
Ansel Collins (artist/songwriter,
Definite/Various)

MARK MURRAY   AUS
Pinnacle Artist Management
34 Cunningham St
Kiama Downs
NSW 2533
Tel: (+61) (0)2 42 378474
Mobile: (+61) (0)418 148 194
pinncleartistmanagement@hotmail
   .com
ROSTER: Trample & Ded Phoenix

MAX MYLVAGANAM   UK
9 Walton Close
Harrow
Middx
HA1 4UY
Tel: (+44) (0)20 8933 2511
Fax: (+44) (0)20 8933 2511
ROSTER: XX (band), Sandra Whelan
(artist)

LUC NATHALIE   FRA
Open Bar
97 Avenue Jean Jaures
75019 Paris
Mobile: (+33) 634305493
LNC2@wanadoo.fr
ROSTER: Wally

SHEILA NAUJOKS   UK
Kabuki
85 Camden Street
London
NW1 0HP

Tel: (+44) (0)20 7916 2142
Fax: (+44) (0)870 051 0158
sheila@kabuki.co.uk
www.kabuki.co.uk
ROSTER: Lahannya
(artist/songwriter)

UK **PHIL NELSON**
First Column Management
The Metway
55 Canning St
Brighton
Sussex
BN2 2EF
Tel: (+44) (0)1273 688 359
Fax: (+44) (0)1273 624 884
firstcolumn@btconnect.com
ROSTER: The Levellers (band, Eagle
Rock/Bug), The Milk And Honey
Band (band, Idea/BMG), Aqualung
(band, B Unique/Warner) (Warner
Chappell/ Steve Zapp), Charlie Myatt
(artist, Victoria) (Chrysalis -
publishing)

CAN **JOHN NEMETH**
Nemeth Professional Services
826 Church Dr
Lefroy
Ontario L0L 1W0
Tel: (+01) 705 456 6226
Fax: (+1) 416 762 3859
executivereligion@rogers.com
ROSTER: Clint Wilkinson, Jesse
Wilkinson, Trevor Devrn

UK **ELODIE NERVA**
Mint Management
69c Middle Lane
Crouch End
London
N8 8PE
Tel: (+44) (0)20 8340 1348
Fax: (+44) (0)20 8340 1348
elodienerva@hotmail.com
www.thegladstones.com

ROSTER: The Gladstones (band)

STUART NEWTON   **UK**
SANE
78 Barnards Hill
Marlow
Bucks
SL7 2NZ
Tel: (+44) (0)1628 473991
stuart@stutunes.co.uk

SYLVAIN NGUYEN LE   **FRA**
Le Periscope Sarl
51 Bld Gambetta
38000 Grenoble
Tel: (+33) 476432730
Mobile: (+33) 619341065
Fax: (+33) 476431386
sylvain@periscope-management.com
ROSTER: KUB

SHERRY NICHOLLS   **UK**
Leaves of Music Management
28 Sandford Avenue
London
N22 5EH
Tel: (+44) (0)20 8881 8865
leavesofmusic@aol.com
ROSTER: Jimmy Haynes Band
(artist), Xonnel Nicholls (artist)

JUSTINE NICHOLS   **UK**
Full Circle Music
PO Box 857
Darlinghurst 2021
Tel: (+61) (0)2 93601870
Mobile: (+61) (0)414 804 551
Email: jmnichols@bigpond.com
Website: www.fullcirclemusic.com.au
ROSTER: Full Circle

MICHAEL NICHOLSON   **UK**
Sven Gali Management
Flat 1
23 Wheler Street
London

E1 6NR
Tel: (+44) (0)20 7247 2050
mikenicholson78@hotmail.com
ROSTER: Blofeld (band)

UK CONSTANTINA NICOLAOU
Constantina Nicolaou Management
The Barn Studios
Burnt Farm Ride
Goffs Oak
Herts EN7 5JA
Tel: (+44) (0)1707 877707
Fax: (+44) (0)1707 877708
niclaw@tisclai.co.uk
ROSTER: Shena (artist/songwriter)

UK KEITH NORMAN
Uncle Buddha
12 Holmsfield
Keyworth
Notts
NG12 5RD
Tel: (+44) (0)115 914 8035
k.norman@ntlworld.com
ROSTER: Mybe (band)

UK CHRIS NORTON
Mondo Management/IHT Records
Unit 2D
Clapham North Arts Centre
26-32 Voltaire Rd
London
SW4 6DH
Tel: (+44) (0)20 7720 7411
Fax: (+44) (0)20 7720 8095
chris@ihtrecords.com
Rotser: David Gray (artist, IHT/East
West/RCA), Orbital (band, London
WEA), Tennason (HTI), Adam Snyder
(HTI), Damien Rice (DRM/HTI)

AUS DARREN NURICK
DPN Entertainment
25 Athena Avenue,
St Ives
NSW 2075

Fax: (+61) (0)2 9983 1847
Mobile: (+61) (0)410 500 828
Email: info@franktheband.com
Website: www.franktheband.com
ROSTER: Frank

JONE NUUTINEN   FIN
Eastborder Management Ltd.
Tallherginkatu 1 G /36
FIN-00180 Helsinki
Tel: (+358) 9 6813 9980
Fax: (+358) 9 6962 8080
mail@eastborder.com
www.eastborder.com,
www.urbanited.com
ROSTER: Velcra, SubUrban Tribe

CHRIS O'BRIEN   AUS
Solitaire Management
PO Box 631
Brentford Square
VIC 3131
Tel: (+61) (0)3 9873 3553
Fax: (+61) (0)3 9873 1175
chris@solitairemanagement.com.au
ROSTER: Bodyjar, For Amusement
Only

TERRY O'BRIEN   UK
Playpen Management
19 Churston Close
162-164 Tulse Hill
London
SW2 3BX
Tel: (+44) (0)20 8671 8014
terry@playpen.fsbusiness.co.uk
ROSTER: Jim Moray, Salsa Celtica

TOM O'CONNOR   UK
7 Princes Yard
London
W11 4PH
Tel: (+44) (0)20 7221 8242
tomoconnoruk@hotmail.com
ROSTER: Houston 500 (band), Wry
(band)

UK ELISA ODLE
Elisa
28 Cowgate Road
Greenford
Middlesex
UB6 8HQ
Tel: (+44) (0)20 8575 8975
Fax: (+44) (0)20 8575 8975
elisaodle@yahoo.co.uk
ROSTER: Jo Caleb Group (band)

UK RICHARD OGDEN
Richard Ogden Management Ltd
7 Russell Gardens
London
W14 8EZ
Tel: (+44) (0)207 751 1300
Fax: (+44) (0)207 348 0831
richard@richardogdenmanagement.com
ROSTER: Bomfunck MCs (band),
Nerina Pallot (artist), Tatiyana Rige
(artist)
Consultancy for: Ricky Martin
(artist), Sandy And Junior (artist),
World Cup 2002 (project)

UK THELMA OGDEN
Richard Ogden Management Ltd
7 Russell Garden
London
W14 8EZ
Tel: (+44) (0)207 751 1300
Fax: (+44) (0)207 348 0831
richard@richardogdenmanagement.com
ROSTER: Bomfunck MCs (band),
Nerina Pallot (artist), Tatiyana Rige
(artist)
Consultancy for: Ricky Martin
(artist), Sandy And Junior (artist),
World Cup 2002 (project)

UK YVONNE OLMAN
Big Blue Music
113a Churchill Road
London
NW2 5EH

Tel: (+44) (0)20 8452 7106
Fax: (+44) (0)20 8452 7106
yo@bigbluemusic.biz
www.bigbluemusic.biz
ROSTER: Phoebe (artist), Leighton
Jones (artist/songwriter, ABC
Records), Tom Ritchie
(artist/songwriter)

LORDA OMEISSAH   AUS
Lorda Omeissah Management
GPO Box 813
Greenacre
NSW 2190
Tel: (+61) (0)2 9642 0619
Fax: (+61) (0)2 9786 3348
Mobile: (+61) (0)413 044 332
Email: lorda@ozEmail.com.au
ROSTER: Nessa Morgan, Rick Price

STUART ONGLEY   UK
SGO Ltd
Po Box 34994
London
SW6 6WF
Tel: (+44) (0)20 7385 9377
Fax: (+44) (0)20 7385 0372
stuart@sgomusic.com
www.sgomusic.com
ROSTER: Chris Eaton, 3 Man Island,
Lunasa, Carly

UWE OTTE   GER
Otte Show-Productions
Am Berg 5
21244 Buchholz
Tel: (+49) (0)4181/28790
Tel: (+49) (0)4181/287920
Uweotte@aol.com
ROSTER: Jochen Brauer Band,
Bernd Hampel Showband,
Pasadena Roof Orchestra, Dirk Jecht
Band, Vicky Leandros, Johnny
Logan, Bonny M, George McCrae,
Abba Again, Erkan Aki, Jennifer
Rush

CAN KAREN PACE
Pacemaker Productions
#3, 748 Gerrard St E
Toronto
Ontario M4M 1Y6
Tel: (+1) 416 465 3993
Tel: (+1) 416 465 4433
kjp@ca.inter.net
ROSTER: renann

USA MARK PALERMO
246 Garfield Place
Brooklyn, NY
11215-2207
Tel: (+1) 917 482 1077
mhpalermo@aol.com

UK RENATO PAOLI
CNR Management
PO Box 894
Woking
Surrey
GU21 8ZJ
Tel: (+44) (0)1483 480694
Fax: (+44) (0)1483 473100
renatopaoliuk@yahoo.com
ROSTER: Draven (band)

AUS MARIO PAOLUCCI
blowmusic limited
PO Box 2192
Kew
VIC 3101
Tel: (+61) (0)3 9457 3209
Fax: (+61) (0)3 9347 8679
Mobile: (+61) (0)146 016 427
Email: mariopaolucci@bigpond
    .com
Web: www.blowmusic.com
ROSTER: Low Frequency
Occupation, Lorena Novoa, Gemma
Bishop, Ashley Evans, Anthony
Callea.

UK RUSSELL PAPER
Slum City Music

1 Woodroyd Terrace
Bradford
West Yorkshire
BD5 8PQ
Tel: (+44) (0)1274 738 537
Fax: (+44) (0)1274 738 537
ROSTER: Bradford Boyz (band)

**ROZ PAPPALARDO & AUS
CHANEL LUCAS**
women in docs
PO Box 3743
South Brisbane
QLD 4101
Tel: (+61) (0)408 730 551 or (+61)
(0)414 538 448
Fax: (+61) (0)7 3846 0603
management@womenindocs.com
Website: www.womenindocs.com
ROSTER: women in docs

GILLES PAQUIN CAN
Paquin Entertainment Group
395 Notre Dame Ave
Winnipeg
Manitoba R3B 1R2
(204) 988-1120
(204) 988-1135
gilles@paquinentertainment.com
www.paquinentertainment.com
ROSTER: Fred Penner, Norman
Foote, Amanda Stott, Ma Anne
Dionisio

SARAH PARHAM CAN
Coalition Entertainment Management
202-10271 Yonge St
Richmond Hill
Ontario L4C 3B5
(905)508-0025
(905) 508-0403
sarah@coalitionent.com
www.coalitionent.com
ROSTER: Finger Eleven, Idle Sons

NEIL PARKES UK

Collyer-Bristow
4 Bedford Row
London
WC1R 4DF
Tel: (+44) (0)20 7242 7363
Fax: (+44) (0)20 7405 0555
www.collyerbristow.com

UK TIM PARRY
Big Life Management Ltd
67-69 Charlton Street
London
NW1 1HY
Tel: (+44) (0)20 7554 2100
Fax: (+44) (0)20 7554 2154
biglife@biglife.co.uk
www.biglife.co.uk
ROSTER: Badly Drawn Boy (artist,
XL), Elizabeth Troy (artist, Talking
Loud), Youth (producers), Jazz
Coleman (producers), The
Beatmasters (producers), The Shining
(band, Zuma), Queen Adreena (band,
Rough Trade)

UK TONY PATOTO
Furious? Records
PO Box 40
Arundel
BN18 OUQ
Tel: (+44) (0)1243 558444
Fax: (+44) (0)1243 558455
tunatater@aol.com
www.delirious.co.uk
ROSTER: Delirious? (band, Furious?
Records)

UK JAMES PATRICK
Garden Cottage
Rectory Lane
Brasted
Kent
TN16 1JU
Tel: (+44) (0)1959 562 565
nakedtruthrecords@yahoo.co.uk
ROSTER: Canteen (band)

LARRY PATTERSON   UK
6 Parker Mews
Covent Garden
London
WC2B 5NT
Tel: (+44) (0)20 7916 9618
lpatterson13@aol.com
ROSTER: Adam Realtime (producer),
Pauline Henry (artist/songwriter)

JEROME PAUL-HAZARD   FRA
Nola Musique
9 Avenue Pasteur
93270 Sevran
Tel: (+33) 170022560
Mobile: (+33) 681857575
Fax: (+33) 170985007
nola@chello.fr
ROSTER: Lulendo

SARAH PAYNE   UK
RLPG
3 Glencoe Rd
Weybridge
Surrey
KT13 8JY
Tel: (+44) (0)1932 820059
Fax: (+44) (0)1932 820059
sarah.s.payne@virgin.net
ROSTER: Angels Vs Aliens (band)

COLIN PEEL   UK
Inductive Management
PO Box 20503
London
NW8 0WY
Tel: (+44) (0)20 7586 5427
Fax: (+44) (0)20 7483 2164
inductivemusic@ntlworld.com
ROSTER: The Butterfly Effect (band)

JEAN-MARC PEIGNARD   FRA
Univers N9uf
33 rue Bad Aussee
78370 Plaisir
Mobile: (+33) 684334020

jjmarc@netcourrier.com
ROSTER: L'homme Vers...

FRA VALERIE PELLERIN
Art Svp Selon Valerie Pellerin
55 rue Montmartre
75002 Paris
Tel: (+33) 153301895
Mobile: (+33) 611025288
valerie.pellerin@cerruti.com
ROSTER: Yann Weber, Chassagnac

UK STEPHEN PENNY
Royalty Records
20 Tarn Howes Close
Thatcham
Berkshire
RG19 3TS
Tel: (+44) (0)1635 863 787
royaltyrecords@pop-music.uk.com
www.pop.music.uk.com
ROSTER: The Sea Monkeys (band),
Terry Munday (artist), Anji (artist)

UK FELIX PEPLER
Flat 2
110 Becklow Road
Shepherds Bush
London
W12 9HJ
Tel: (+44) (0)20 8932 5450
felixpepler@ntlworld.com
ROSTER: Flow Motion (band)

UK ANDREA PETCH
Funkmeister Ltd
4 Albert Terrace Glasshouse
Harrogate
HG3 5QN
Tel: (+44) (0)1423 712503
Fax: (+44) (0)1423 712503
andrea@funkmeister.co.uk
ROSTER: Codex (band)

USA JEFF PETERS
TBA Artist Management
16501 Ventura Blvd, Penthouse 601
Encino, CA
91436
Tel: (+1) 818 728 2638
Fax: (+1) 818 728 2601
jpeters@tbaent.com

MICHELLE PETHERS UK
Crashed Management
41 Van Diemens Close
Chinnor
Oxfordshire
OX39 4QE
Tel: (+44) (0)1844 353 154
Fax: (+44) (0)1844 353 154
info@hedroom.co.uk
www.hedroom.co.uk
ROSTER: Hedroom (band), John
Pethers (songwriter)

SAMI PEURA FIN
Sam Agency Oy Ltd
Tallberginkatu 1 C / 102
FIN-00180 Helsinki
Tel: (+358) 9 68593232
Fax: (+358) 9 68593233
Mobile: (+358) 40 5900290
www.samagency.fi
ROSTER: Paleface

KIM PEZZANO AUS
KMP Consultants
PO Box 346
Gladesville
NSW 1675
Tel: (+61) (0)2 9809 0966
Fax: (+61) (0)2 9809 0966
Mobile: (+61) (0)415 494 922
Email: kimroc@zipworld.com.au
ROSTER: Rose Tattoo, Pete Wells
Band, Lucy Desoto Band, Pete, Angry
And The DFB (Damn Fine Band),
Bellhops

POLO PIATTI UK
PPM Artists Management

Ingersol House
9 Kingsway
Covent Garden
London
WC2B 6XF
Tel: (+44) (0)20 7240 3432
Fax: (+44) (0)20 8478 2101
music@ppmlondon.com
www.ppmlondon.com
ROSTER: Sweet Vendetta (band),
Dax O'Callaghan (artist), Zahara
(artist)

UK DONATELLA PICCINETTI
Silverbird Limited
Amersham Common House
133 White Lion Road
Amersham
Bucks
HP7 9JY
Tel: (+44) (0)1494 766 754
Fax: (+44) (0)1494 766 745
donatella@leosayer.com
ROSTER: Leo Sayer
(singer/songwriter)

CAN BRYAN PICKELL
Bryan Pickell & Associates
RR #1
Blyth
Ontario NOM 1H0
Tel: (+1) 519 525 1916
Fax: (+1) 519 524 1530
mgmt@silence-band.com
www.silence-band.com
ROSTER: Silence

FRA DANTES PIGEAUD
Sono Gt
19 rue Bridaine
75017 Paris
Mobile: (+33) 6 15 13 68 57
Fax: (+33) 1 44 54 53 49
dantes.sonogt@voila.fr
ROSTER: Tanger, Mike Rimbaud,
Ciao! Manhattan

STACEY PIGGOTT   AUS
Two Fish Out Of Water
PO Box 1041
Burleigh Heads
QLD 4220
Tel/fax: (+61) (0)7 5535 1225
Mobile: (+61) (0)414 313 222
Email: staceypiggott@optusnet.com.au
Web: www.dirtylucy.com.au
ROSTER: Dirty Lucy

MARTIN PIKE   UK
Stereophonic Management
PO Box 3787
London
SE22 9DZ
Tel: (+44) (0)20 8299 1650
Fax: (+44) (0)20 8693 5514
duophonic@btopenworld.com
ROSTER: Stereolab (band), Broadcast
(band), High Llamas (band)

SANDOR PIROTH   UK
52 North Holme Court
Thorplands
Northampton
NN3 8UX
Tel: (+44) (0)1604 245519
sanz1@btopenworld.com
ROSTER: Nataya (artist)

**PLATINUM MANAGEMENT PTY AUS
LTD**
Directors: Simon Lucas, Robert
Specogna
PO Box 145
Jamberoo
NSW 2533
Tel: (+61) 2 42360672
Fax: (+61) 2 42360671
Mobile: (+61) (0)416 080 505
Email: simon@platinummanagement
.com.au
Web: www.platinummanagement
.com.au
ROSTER: Mesh Radio, Scott Stone,

Tania Nichamin, Joe Macari, Adrian Sotomayor (aka Monious)

UK AMANDA PLETZER & RUPERT PLETZER
Muddy Music
PO Box 144
Northgate
QLD 4013
Tel: (+61) (0)7 3266 3027
MuddyMusic@bigpond.com
ROSTER: Deborah Conway, Tommy Ryan

NOR KNUT HARALD PLEYM
KHP Management
Brekka 47
Porgrunn 3917
Tel: (+47) 35567459
Fax: (+47) 93176789
Mobile: (+47) 90887204
knut@justentertainment.no
ROSTER: D Sound, Surferosa

USA FRED PORTER
Endangered Species Artists Mgmt
4 Berachah Avenue
South Nyack, NY
10960-4202
Tel: (+1) 845 353 4001
Fax: (+1) 845 353 4332
muzik@verizon.net
www.musicandamerica.com
ROSTER: Anna, Jason Wilson And Tabarruk, David Seering

CAN JAMES PORTER
RAMJAM Artist Management
218 Carlton St
Toronto
Ontario M5A 2L1
Tel: (+1) 416 966 9404
Fax: (+1) 416 966 9274
ramjamman@bellnet.ca
ROSTER: Stephan Moccio, The Immigrants, Kyp Harness

KARI POSSI FIN
Manager
Blue Buddha Management Ltd
Tallberginkatu 1 / 40,
FIN-00180 Helsinki
Tel: (+358) 9 6859321
Fax: (+358) 9 68593224
Possi: (+358) 50 5641950
Karjalainen: (+358) 40 5561110
info@bbmgmt.com
www.bbmgmt.com (agency
www.piikkikasvi.fi)
ROSTER: Quintessence, 22 Pistepirkko, Jo Hope

BILL POUGHER UK
Eversholt Music Ltd
46 Gillingham St
London SW1V 1HU
Tel: (+44) (0)20 7802 2114
Fax: (+44) (0)20 7802 2132
Mobile: (+44) (0)7799 842052
Email: bill@grosvenortm.co.uk
Web: www.brookedoherty.com
ROSTER: Brooke Doherty

MARK POWELL UK
Mark Powell Music Mangement
56 Alexandra Road
St Albans
Herts
AL1 3AZ
Tel. (+44) (0)1727 835306
Fax: (+44) (0)1727 759244
MandVPow@aol.com
ROSTER: Caravan (band, Intense Records), Nektar (band, Bellaphone), Sonja Kristina (artist)

PRESTON POWELL USA
Jazzateria Network (Rastafaria)
PO Box 720
Nyack, NY
10960
Tel: (+1) 845 353 8505
Fax: (+1) 845 353 8503

preston@jazzateria.com
www.jazzateria.com
ROSTER: dj-9, Midnite, Marc Cary,
Leo Gandelman, Indigenous People,
Jimmy McGriff, Reuben Wilson,
Masters Of Groove

AUS POWERFUNK RECORDS
PO Box 652
Darwin
NT 0801
Tel: (+61) (0)401 110 332
Fax: (+61) (0)8 89997493
Mobile: (+61) (0)401 110 332
Email: Paul@powerfunk.com
Website: www.powerfunk.com
ROSTER: NEO (www.theneo.com)

UK FRANK PRESLAND
Twenty First Artists
1 Blythe Road
London
W14 OHG
Tel: (+44) (0)20 7348 4800
Tel: (+44) (0)20 7348 4801
ROSTER: Elton John (Mercury), Mis-
teeq (Telstar), Luan Parle (Sony),
James Blunt (TBO), Phil Ramone
(producer)

FRA VALERIE PRIAM
Val'kyrie
9 rue Pierre de Coubertin
94510 La Queue en Brie
Mobile: (+33) 621354576
valkyrico@msn.com

GER CYRIL PRIEUR
Ste Itc
Seegartenstrasse 10
8008 Zurich
Tel: (+41) 4113848040
Mobile: (+41) 793125825
Fax: (+41) 1 384 80 49
cyrilprieur@bluewin.ch
ROSTER: Patricia Kaas, Stephan

Eicher, Mayane Delem

TIM PRIOR   UK
ARM (Artist & Rights Management)
The Old Lamp Works
Rodney Place
London
SW19 2LQ
Tel: (+44) (0)20 8542 4222
Fax: (+44) (0)20 8542 9934
tim@arm-eu.com
ROSTER: Nils Petter Molvaer, Ray
Wilson

DARREN PULLIN   UK
Sonrise Artists
Western House
31 Richardson Street
Swansea
SA1 3JF
Tel: (+44) (0)705 007 5959
darren@sonriseartists.co.uk
www.sonriseartists.co.uk

SARA QAZI   USA
ARM Management
1036 N Laurel Ave, Apt 3
West Hollywood, CA
90046
Tel: (+1) 323 848 6960
Fax: (+1) 323 848 6960
saraqazi@yahoo.com

KEVIN QUINLAN   UK
6 Kingsley Road
Wimbledon
London
SW19 8HF
Tel: (+44) (0)20 8542 0554
quinlanmusic@hotmail.com
www.quilanmusic.com
ROSTER: Quinlan (artist/producer),
Rush Hour (band), Stuart Headey
(artist)

ROLAND RADMANN   GER

Stars And More
Raiffeisenstr 8
66802 Überherrn
Tel: 06836/919445 /-6
Fax: 06836/919447
RadmannR@aol.com
www.starsandmore.info
ROSTER: Dance of the World, Stars of Paradise, Pierre Danoux, Peter Stern & die Mondharmoniker, Die Barmherzigen Plateausohlen, Jonicoel

GER ARMIN RAHN
Dreimühlenstr 7
80469 München
Tel: (+49) 089 775044
Fax: (+49) 089 7250660
info@arminrahn.com
www.arminrahn.com
ROSTER: Chris Norman, Saragossa Band, Weather Girls

CAN ROB RAPITI
BLR Entertainment
22 East 33rd St
Hamilton
Ontario L8V 3T1
Tel: (+1) 905 730 6874
Fax: (+1) 905 318 3898
blr@mountaincable.net
www.blrentertainment.com
ROSTER: Adam's Rib

AUS TERRY RASMUSSEN
i4Ni Management
7/8 Winnie Street
Cremorne
NSW 2090
Tel: (+61) (0)2 9953 1162
Mobile: (+61) (0)419 110 697
Email: tex_ras@yahoo.com.au
ROSTER: Stonewall, Different Breed, Pugjelly

UK DAVID RAVDEN

Blujay Management Ltd
55 Loudoun Rd
St Johns Wood
London
NW8 ODL
Tel: (+44) (0)20 7604 3633
Fax: (+44) (0)20 7604 3639
info@blujay.co.uk
ROSTER: Chris Sheehan, Delrosario, Beulah

JOHN RAVENHALL   UK
Scandalous Music Ltd
46 Chalk Hill
Watford
Herts
WD19 4BX
Tel: (+44) (0)1923 255 389
Fax: (+44) (0)1923 255 308
j.ravenhall@virgin.net

MARIE REBAUD   FRA
9 rue du Bucq 3
5000 Rennes
Tel: 33299323588
Mobile: (+33) 6 14 32 46 42
Fax: (+33) 299323588
marie.rebaud@free.fr
ROSTER: Paris Combo, Etiennes Grandjean

DAVID REECE   AUS
Savi Artist Management
26 Byron Street
Elwood
VIC 3184
Tel: (+61) (0)3 9696 2943
Fax: (+61) (0)3 9686 0545
Email: david_reece@optusnet.com
     .au
www.saviartistmanagement.com
ROSTER: NuBreed, Ivan Gough, Dirty Fours, Traveller, Titanium Breaks, Dark Alley, Deep Funk Project, Digital Mind Control, The Free Radicals.

NOR **REMO REHDER**
MBS
PO Box 337
Sandvika 1301
Tel: (+47) 67522860
Fax: (+47) 67522861
remo@farmenas.com
www.farmenas.com
ROSTER: Mo'Mac Trio

CAN **JANA REID**
AMI – Amsterdam Management
International
PO Box 370
Campbellford
Ontario K0L 1L0
Tel: (+1) 705 653 2700
Fax: (+1) 705 653 2709
jana@amihere.com
www.amihere.com
ROSTER: Steve Fox, Liona Boyd,
Leslie Nielson

FRA **MONYA REKIK**
Legalizik Project
14 rue Baudin
93100 Montreuil
Tel: (+33) 148701765
Mobile: (+33) 662835091
legalizik@aol.com
ROSTER: Legalizik, Oliv'et Ses Noyaux

GER **MATHIAS REMMEL**
Rema Concerts GmbH
Am Weinberg 2
63579 Freigericht
Tel: (+49) 06055 20276 + 2028
Fax: (+49) 06055/2029
info@rema24.de
www.rema24.de
ROSTER: Jens Jürgens, BMP
(Bayrische Music Power), King Creole,
MISS

UK **IAN RENDALL**
Grassroots Xchange

Studio 471
2 Old Brompton Road
London
SW7 3DQ
Tel: (+44) (0)20 7386 5763
ian@grassrootx.com
www.grassrootsx.com

BERNARD M RESNICK, ESQ **USA**
Two Bala Plaza, Suite 300
Bala Cynwyd, PA
19004
Tel: (+1) 610 660 7774
Fax: (+1) 610 668 0574
bmresnick@aol.com
www.bernardresnick.com
ROSTER: Plastic Eaters, Christian
Josi (co-manager)

PERRY RESNICK **USA**
RZO
421 Hudson St, Suite 523
New York, NY
10014-3651
Tel: (+1) 212 765 7550
Fax: (+1) 212 757 9821
presnick@rzo.com

JEF RICHAERTS **NLD**
Gerry van der Zwaard Management
& Agency
Postbus 90221
1006 BE Amsterdam
Tel: (+32) 20 689 99 99
Fax: (+32) 20 689 99 00
jef@vdzwaardmanagement.nl
www.vdzwaardmanagement.nl
ROSTER: Birgit

HOWARD RICKLOW **UK**
Collyer-Bristow
4 Bedford Row
London
WC1R 4DF
Tel: (+44) (0)20 7242 7363
Fax: (+44) (0)20 7405 0555

Howard.Ricklow@collyerbristow.com
www.collyerbristow.com

AUS LUKE RINALDI
Sweet Mate Promotions
PO Box 83
Northbridge
Western Australia 6865
Tel: (+61) (0)8 9228 0087
Fax: (+61) (0)8 9328 5180
Mobile: (+61) (0)417 967 136
Email: sweetmates@hotmail.com
Website: www.redjez.com
ROSTER: Capital City, Red Jezebel,
Team Jedi

FRA XAVIER RISSELIN
Artistik / Ceci-Dit
11 rue de la Hobette
08090 Warnecourt
Tel: (+33) 324353881
Mobile: (+33) 616966440
artistik@wanadoo.fr

AUS PETER RIX
Peter Rix Management
PO Box 957
Crows Nest
NSW 1585
Tel: (+61) (0)2 9966 5511
Fax. (+61) (0)2 9966 5444
Email: info@rixman.com.au
ROSTER: Marcia Hines

UK DAVID ROBERTS
DR Projects
PO Box 9956
Birmingham
B30 2XW
Tel: (+44) (0)121 242 5900
Fax: (+44) (0)121 242 5900
david@drprojects.co.uk
www.drprojects.co.uk
ROSTER: Jinrai (band)

UK RUSSELL ROBERTS

Sheridans
14 Red Lion Square
London
WC1R 4QL
Tel: (+44) (0)20 7774 9444
Fax: (+44) (0)20 7841 1391
rroberts@sheridans.co.uk

TOM ROBERTS **UK**
Upshot Communications
5th Floor
2-12 Pentonville Rd
Angel
London
N1 9PL
Tel: (+44) (0)20 7837 6597
Fax: (+44) (0)20 7293 5564
tomroberts@upshotcom.com
www.upshotcreek.com
ROSTER: James Jackman
(artist/songwriter, Sony Publishing),
Niall Flynn (artist/songwriter, Sony
Publishing), Arianne Schrieber
(artist/songwriter)

DEIRDRA ROBINSON **UK**
Z Records Ltd
The Factory
1 Coleridge Lane
Crouch End
London
N8 8EA
Tel: (+44) (0)20 8342 8948
Fax: (+44) (0)20 8347 5930
drobinson@zrecords.ltd.uk
ROSTER: Jakatta (artist,
MOS/Universal), Dave Lee (producer,
Universal)

MAGGIE RODFORD **UK**
AE Copyrights Ltd
18 Rodmarton Street
London
W1H 3FW
Tel: (+44) (0)20 7486 6466
Fax: (+44) (0)20 7224 0344

mrodford@air-edel.co.uk
ROSTER: Anne Dudley
(artist/songwriter), Hans Zimmer
(songwriter), Thomas Morse
(artist/songwriter), Sam Babenia
(songwriter), James Shearman
(songwriter), Paul Grabowsky
(artist/Composer/producer)

FRA CENDRYNE ROE
Nomades Kultur
La Ferme de Napollon
280 Av des Templiers
13400 Aubagne
Tel: (+33) 442037275
Mobile: (+33) 615441898
Fax: (+33) 442037282
cendyroe@juancarmona.com
ROSTER: Juan Carmona

UK VINCENT ROETHLING
Vega Management
26 Horseshoe Close
Camberley
Surrey
GU15 4DJ
Tel: (+44) (0)7967 638 430
vincent@vegamanagement.co.uk
www.vegamanagement.co.uk
ROSTER: Fume (band)

AUS DANNY ROGERS
Lunatic Entertainment Australia
PO Box 1047
Carlton
VIC 3053
Tel: (+61) (0)3 9923 6089
Fax: (+61) (0)3 9923 6089
Mobile: (+61) (0)421 695 669
Email: propella@aol.com
www.lunaticentertainment
.com
ROSTER: Gersey, The Anyones

USA JANELLE ROGERS
Green Light Go Entertainment

PO Box 20526
Ferndale, MI
48220
Tel: (+1) 248 761 9370
GreenLightGoEnt@aol.com

OYSTEIN RONANDER   NOR
Bureau Storm
Inkognitogt 8
Oslo 0258
Tel: (+47) 22121010
Fax: (+47) 22121019
oystein@bureaustorm.no
www.bureaustorm.no
ROSTER: Big Bang

ANNIE ROSENBLATT   FRA
Ah! Les Fourmis
11 Bis rue du Coq
Français 93260
Les Ilas
Tel: (+33) 143620723
Fax: (+33) 149720844
annierose@libertysurf.fr
ROSTER: Soapkills, Wab

ROBERT ROSE   UK
Manoueuvre Music Ltd
225 Bellingham Road
Catford
London
SE6 1EQ
Tel: (+44) (0)20 8697 3396
Fax: (+44) (0)20 8697 3396
robertdrose@hotmail.com
ROSTER: Da'VinChe (producer),
Mr D (producer), Knock Out
(producer), Roxy (Arist), Status
(artist)

JACK ROSS   CAN
The Agency Group
59 Berkeley St
Toronto
Ontario M5A 2W5
Tel: (+1) 416 368 5599

Fax: (+1) 416 368 4655
jross@theagencygroup.com
ROSTER: Moxy Fruvous

FRA JEAN-MARIE ROUILLON
Vacarme
89 Bd Picpus
75012 Paris
Tel: (+33) 143465687
Mobile: (+33) 686301231
jmrouillon@aol.com
ROSTER: Ibouka

UK KEITH ROWE
Slap Back Management
27 Sherbourne Drive
Cox Green
Maidenhead
Berkshire
SL6 3EP
Tel: (+44) (0)1628 675999
Fax: (+44) (0)1628 676985
slapback1@btinternet.co.uk

AUS MARCELLA ROYBAL
Pussycat Music Management
PO Box 243
Cherrybrook
NSW 2126
Tel: (+61) (0)2 9899-9944
Fax: (+61) (0)2 9899-2555
Mobile: (+61) (0)410-52-1990
Email: mgt@pussycatmusic.com
Website: www.butterfly9.com
ROSTER: Butterfly 9

UK HAZEL RYAN-BUCHER
Bob Wilson Bakandji Man
41 Auburn Road
Kingston
TAS 7050
Tel: (+61) (0)6339 3667
Mobile: (+61) (0)43 930 5445
Email: hazelryan@netspace.net.au
Website: www.bobwilson.com.au
ROSTER: Bob Wilson

BERNADETTE RYAN AUS
Bernadette Ryan Management
PO Box 374
Clifton Hill
VIC 3068
Tel: (+61) (0)3 9639 2524
Fax: (+61) (0)3 9639 2504
Email: b.m.r@bigpond.com
ROSTER: Architecture in Helsinki,
Dexter, James De La Cruz, New
Buffalo, Royce

SIMON RYDER UK
Shifty Management
Shifty Management
Ashbury Mews
82C Darby Road
Liverpool
L19 9AW
Tel: (+44) (0)151 236 0891
Fax: (+44) (0)151 236 0891
info@shiftymanagement.co.uk
www.shiftymanagement.co.uk
ROSTER: Lorimer, First Time Down,
Mike Crossey – producer

GEORGE SAID AUS
Bomb Records/Bomb Music Publishing
PO Box 139
Crows Nest
NSW 2065
Tel: (+61) (0)2 9436 0799
Fax: (+61) (0)2 9437 5980
Mobile: (+61) (0)418 279 959
Email: gsaid@bombmusic.net
ROSTER: Disco Montego, Jeremy
Gregory

BERNARD SAINT-PAUL FRA
Bernard Saint-Paul Organisation
44 rue de Miromesnil
75008 Paris
Tel: (+33) 153308350
Mobile: (+33) 623839000
b.saint-paul@wanadoo.fr
ROSTER: Veronique Sanson,

Christine Biais, Anissa, Christopher
Sanson

AUS MATTHEW SALLEO
Killcrushdestroy
PO Box 2043
Ellenbrook
WA 6069
Tel: (+61) (0)8 9296 7925
Mobile: (+61) (0)408 070 181
management@killcrushdestroy.com
www.killcrushdestroy.com/management/
ROSTER: Mr Sandman, Civilised,
Dyslexic Fish

AUS MARIO SALTALAMACCHIA
Montana Music Agency
186 Thompsons Road
Bulleen
VIC 3105
Tel: (+61) (0)3 9858 2806
Fax: (+61) (0)3 9858 2806
Mobile: (+61) (0)411467262
montana_music@optusnet.com
.au
ROSTER: Drivaside

USA AL SALZILLO
Nightside Entertainment, Inc.
10 Crabapple Lane
Greenville, RI
02828
Tel: (+1) 401 949 2004
Fax: (+1) 703 997 5995
al@nightsideentertainment.com
www.nightsideentertainment.com
ROSTER: The Becky Chace Band,
Chad Burdick, Dante Mazzetti, Bill
Petterson

FRA SAMUEL BENZAKIN
82 rue des Martyrs
75018 Paris
Tel: (+33) 142239896
Mobile: (+33) 6 82 85 08 82
s.benzakin@voila.fr

ROSTER: Cali, Ginger Ale

ALBERT SAMUEL UK
ASM Ltd
42 City Business Centre
Lower Road
Rotherhithe
London
SE16 2XB
Tel: (+44) (0)20 7740 1600
Fax: (+44) (0)20 7740 1700
asm@mission-control.co.uk
ROSTER: Oxide-Neutrino
(artist/producer, East West), So Solid
Crew (artist/producer, Relentless),
Blazin' Squad (artists, EastWest)

DAVID SAMUEL UK
ASM Ltd
32 St Olav's Court
Lower Rd
London
SE16 2XB
Tel: (+44) (0)20 7740 1600
Fax: (+44) (0)20 77401700
asm@mission-control.co.uk
ROSTER: Romeo (artist, Relentless
Records), Alexia (artist, Messy Records)

SUSAN SANDFORD SMITH UK
26 Grenville Road
London
N19 4EH
Tel: (+44) (0)20 7686 1953
Fax: (+44) (0)20 7686 1953
susie@sosumimusic.com
ROSTER: Sufferkiss (band)

GARY SANDS AUS
Gary Sands Promotions
1 Bond Avenue
Victor Harbour
SA 5211
Tel: (+61) (0)8 8552 5621
Fax: (+61) (0)8 8552 5621
Mobile: (+61) (0)419034428

Email: garyfm99@granite.net.au
Web: theboogiemen.info
ROSTER: The Boogiemen, Gary Sands, Katrina Carpenter Trio

FIN JUSSI SANTALAHTI

Partysan Concert Promotion Oy
Kauppakatu 11 C 2nd Floor
FIN-33200 Tampere
Tel: (+358) 3 2223181
Fax: (+358) 3 2223185
jussi.santalahti@partysan.com
www.partysan.com

CAN DANIEL SAUVÉ

Jairo Entertainment Corp
134 Chemin des Renards
Rigaud
Quebec J0P 1P0
Tel: (+1) 647 287 6223
daniel@danielsauvedesigns.com
www.sharonbrooksmusic.com
ROSTER: Sharon Brooks

UK ANDREW SAVILL

Swampmeister
1 Conway Close
Knutsford
WA16 9DH
Tel: (+44) (0)7887 767400
andrewsavill@hotmail.com
www.swampmeister.co.uk
ROSTER: Hilton (band), Gary Hilton (artist/songwriter)

USA STEVEN SCHARF

Steven Scharf Entertainment
126 East 38th Street
New York, NY
10016
Tel: (+1) 212 779 1994
Fax: (+1) 212 779 7920
sscharf@carlinamerica.com

GER STEFAN SCHEPNITZ

Absolute Entertainment

Forstweg 21b
04821 Waldsteinberg
Tel: (+49) (0)34292/86955
Fax: (+49) (0)34292/86956
absoluteentertainment@t-online.de
www.absolute-entertainment.de
ROSTER: Patty Miller (only for Germany), Vorsicht Weiber, Fathers Best, Rose @ Vorberg, Alfons Knackenbusch

DOUGLAS SCHINDLER AUS

Livefeed Management
PO Box 350
Newtown
NSW 2042
Tel: (+61) (0)438 951741
Mobile: (+61) (0)438 951741
Email: info@livefeed.com.au
Web: www.livefeed.com.au
ROSTER: Andy Clockwise

DYLAN SCHLOSBERG UK

Herotech Management
24-25 Nutford Place
London
W1H 5YN
Tel: (+44) (0)20 7725 7064
Fax: (+44) (0)20 7725 7066
info@herotech.net
www.herotech.co.uk
ROSTER: Mercury Tilt Switch (band), Junior (band)

JO SCHMIDT AUS

PO Box 321
Birdwood
South Australia 5234
Tel: (+61) (0)8 85 685 516
Mobile: (+61) (0)409 176 342
Email: jo@joschmidt.com
Website: www.joschmidt.com
ROSTER: Jo Schmidt

JUTTA SCHMIDT GER

Schmidt & Salden GmbH & Co Event

KG
Am Schulzehnten 7
63546 Hammersbach
Tel: (+49) (0)6185/8186 0
Fax: (+49) (0)6185/8186-30
info@glenn-miller.de
www.glenn-miller.de
ROSTER: The World Famous Glenn
Miller Orchestra directed by Will
Salden (Europe)

USA LISA SCHMIDT
Crisis Management, Inc
1288 West Laurelton
Teaneck, NJ
07666
Tel: (+1) 201 837 9440
Fax: (+1) 201 837 1775
crisismgt@aol.com

GER BERNHARD SCHUH
Veranstaltungsbüro Bernhard Schuh
Pfarrgasse 4
69121 Heidelberg
Tel: (+49) (0)6221/475186
Fax: (+49) (0)6221/472141
Bernhard.Schuh@rondo-classico.de
www.rondo-classico.de
ROSTER: Rondo Classico, Enrico Conte

USA GEOFFREY SCHUHKRAFT
On Music
1903 Midvale Avenue
Los Angeles
CA 90025
Tel: (+1) 310 231 0268
Fax: (+1) 310 478 3949
Email: geoffrey@schuhkraft.com
ROSTER: Antonio, Conscious Pilot,
CrashPalace, Diana ah Naid, Ronn
Moss, ZINC

CAN JACK SCHULLER
Mainstage Management Inc
1351 Grant St
Vancouver

British Columbia V5L 2X7
Tel: (+1) 604 253 2662
Fax: (+1) 604 253 2634
schuller@festival.bc.ca
ROSTER: James Keelaghan, David
Francey

PAUL SCOTT   **UK**
Royalty Records
Unit 30
Norris House
Hoxton
London
N1 5PU
Tel: (+44) (0)20 7729 3065
Fax: (+44) (0)20 7729 3065
royaltyrecords@pop-music.uk.com
www.pop-music.uk.com
ROSTER: The Sea Monkeys (band),
Terry Munday (artist), Anji (artist)

VERA SCOTT   **USA**
PO Box 1554
Clarkston, MI
48347
Tel: (+1) 248 625 5809
verascott@earthlink.net

ELAINE SEALY   **UK**
Symbyence Artist Management
1 Graham Road
Harrow Weald
Harrow
HA3 5RP
Tel: (+44) (0)20 8842 4199
jesealy@aol.com

GARY SEENEY   **UK**
Melting Ice Ltd
430 Stratford Road
Shirley
Solihull
West Midlands
B90 4AQ
Tel: (+44) (0)121 733 1763
Fax: (+44) (0)121 680 4392

gary.seeney@virgin.net
ROSTER: Natasha (artist)

UK DAMIEN SENN
5 Linden Mansions
Hornsey Lane
Highgate
London
N6 5LF
Tel: (+44) (0)20 8340 9953
damien@leigh-franklin.com
www.leigh-franklin.com
ROSTER: Franklin (band)

UK JONATHAN SHALIT
Shalit Entertainment & Management
7 Moor Street
Soho
London
W1D 5NB
Tel: (+44) (0)20 7851 9155
Fax: (+44) (0)20 7851 9156
jonathan@shalitglobal.com
ROSTER: Celestine (artist), Chris
Porter (producer/writer), Claire
Sweeney (actress/artist), Jamelia
(artist), Ruthie Henshall
(actress/singer), Big Brovaz (band),
Skillz (producer), Fingaz (producer),
James Alexander (artist), Adam Argyle
(artist), Future (band)

UK RAJEEV SHARMA
123 Repton Road
West Bridgford
Nottingham
NG2 7EN
Tel: (+44) (0)7967 695967
rajeev@ntlworld.com

UK JULIAN SHARPLES
Sharples & Co
13 The Towpath
Oxford
OX1 2TA
Tel: (+44) (0)1865 243 007

Fax: (+44) (0)1865 243 007
julian@sharplesandco.com
ROSTER: Ju Ju Men (band), Julian
Sharples (songwriter)

DARREN SHAW   **AUS**
Damn Shaw Management &
Productions
PO Box 324
Northcote
VIC 3071
Tel: (+61) (0)3 9350 5054
Mobile: (+61) (0)409 681814
damnshawmanagement@optusnet
.com.au
ROSTER: The Tenants, Mighty Boy,
Pidd, Marilyn Veil

JACK SHEEHAN   **UK**
9 Ferrycarrig Avenue
Coolock
Dublin 17
Tel: 3531 8672447
jack@rmgehart.ie
Kuba(band)

SHEEQ   **AUS**
Adelaide
South Australia 5000
Tel: (+61) (0)438 842644
Email: sheeq@sheeq.com
Website: www.sheeq.com
ROSTER: Sheeq

TOMMY SHOWS   **USA**
Sound Creative, Inc
11333 Orchard Lane
Reston, VA
20195
Tel: (+1) 703 867 6737
tommy@tomyshows.com

LIZ SHULMAN   **USA**
No Ordinary Artists
42 Calvin St, #3L
Somerville, MA

02143
Tel: (+1) 617 666 0773
liz@noordinary.org

USA BILL SIDDONS
Siddons & Associates
584 North Larchmont Blvd
Los Angeles, CA
90004
Tel: (+1) 323 462 6156
Fax: (+1) 323 462 2076
siddons@earthlink.net

DEN SARAH SILVERSTONE
Silverstone Management
Slotsgade 2
2nd floor
Copenhagen N
DK-2200
Tel: (+45) 35 37 62 00
Fax: (+45) 70 10 00 76
Mobile: +45 40 50 50 16
silverstone@hardworking.dk
www.silverstone-management.dk
ROSTER: SAYBIA, Kashmir, Kitty
Wu, Odessa

UK ELIZABETH SKEAVINGTON
Collins Long Solicitors
24 Pepper St
London
SE1 0EB
Tel: (+44) (0)20 7401 9800
Fax: (+44) (0)20 7401 9850
info@collinslong.com

UK SAMANTHA SLATTERY
Nettwerk Management
8730 Wilshire Blvd, Suite 304
Los Angeles, CA
90211
Tel: (+1) 310 855 0668
samantha@nettwerk.com

UK SAMANTHA SLATTERY
Nettwerk Management

Clearwater Yard,
35 Inverness Street
London
NW1 7HB
Tel: (+44) (0)20 7424 7500
Fax: (+44) (0)20 7424 7501
samantha@nettwerk.com
www.nettwerk.com

LAURA SLAVIN USA
Laura Slavin Productions
2260 W Holcombe Blvd, Box 302
Houston, TX
77030-2008
Tel: (+1) 713 665 6338
Fax: (+1) 713 665 4705
LVSlavin@aol.com
ROSTER: Doug Burtchaell

DAVE SMITH UK
Popmusicbusiness
3rd Floor
24 Lever St
Manchester
M1 1DX
Tel: (+44) (0)1282 870 727
Fax: (+44) (0)1282 870 727
dave@popmusicbusiness.com
popmusicbusiness.com
ROSTER: A-Funk (band), Elston
Majeska (artist), Jonny Berliner (band)

DAVID SMITH UK
Lateral Artist Management Ltd
PO Box 29391
London
W2 1GE
Tel: (+44) (0)20 8257 9470
Fax: (+44) (0)20 8257 9470
lateral@ntlworld.com
Dynamo Dresden (band)
www.dynamodresden.co.uk
www.joski.co.uk
ROSTER: Joski (band)

DENNIS SMITH UK

Taste Media Ltd
263 Putney Bridge Rd
London
SW15 2PU
Tel: (+44) (0)20 8780 3311
Fax: (+44) (0)20 8785 9892
dennis@sawmills.co.uk
www.tastemedia.com
ROSTER: Dan Wise (producer), Sodi (producer), Ron Saint Germain (producer), Nick Griffiths (producer), Robin Millar (producer), Pat Moran (producer), Ian Caple (producer), Tony Mansfield (producer), John Cornfield (producer), Michael Brauer (mixer), Muse (band), Vega4 (band), Serafin (band), Jim Warren (producer), John Leckie (producer)

AUS IAN SMITH
Ian Smith Management
4a/470 Sydney Rd
Balgowlah
NSW 2093
Tel: (+61) (0)2 9907 0076
Fax: (+61) (0)2 9948 6005
Mob: (+61) (0)414 324 355
Email: ian@ismith.com.au
Website: www.hepfidelity.com
ROSTER: Diesel/Mark Lizotte

UK JON SMITH
JS Management
PO Box 188
Barnstaple
North Devon
UB4 9LG
info@jondsmith.co.uk
www.jondsmith.co.uk
ROSTER: Aeroplane Blonde, Sour Mash

UK STEVE SMITH
Ear To The Ground
128-130 Curtain Road
1st Floor Suna House

Shoreditch
London
EC2A 3Ar
Tel: (+44) (0)20 7739 8183
Fax: (+44) (0)20 7498 420
stevesmith@eartotheground.org
ROSTER: Simian (band, Scurse [recording and publishing])

TOMMY JAY SMITH   **UK**
International Management
Starkey Lodge
Starkey Castle
Wouldham
Kent
ME1 3TR
Tel: (+44) (0)1634 869 448
Fax: (+44) (0)1634 868 452
tommyjaysmith@intman12.fsnet.co.uk

TONY SMITH   **UK**
Tony Smith Personal Management
25 Ives Street
London
SW3 2ND
Tel: (+44) (0)20 7590 2600
Fax: (+44) (0)20 7225 0299
ROSTER: Genesis (band), Phil Collins (artist), Mike And The Mechanics (band)

RICK SMOOT   **USA**
550 Poipu Drive
Honolulu, HI
96825
Tel: (+1) 808 497 3594
ricksmoot2000@yahoo.com

LARS SONCK   **FIN**
LAPS Productions
Abrahaminkatu 17 B 25
FIN-00180 Helsinki
Tel: (+358) 50 462 8897
Fax: (+358) 50 462 8897
sonck@welho.com
ROSTER: REdrama

FRA LAURENCE OUFKIR SOUKAÏNA
11 Quai de Metz / Bp17
75019 Paris
Tel: (+33) 142085242
Mobile: (+33) 615046431
sloufkir@hotmail.com
ROSTER: Kachaca, Nasat Mirini

FRA CHRISTOPHE SOULARD
Mexican Stand Off
109 Bd Deaumarchais
75 Paris
Tel: (+33) 142710444
Mobile: (+33) 686088848
mexican@wanadoo.fr
ROSTER: Erwann, Cyril Paulus,
Xavier Pace

UK DOUGIE SOUNESS
No Half Measures Ltd
Studio 19
St George's Studios
93-97 St George's Road
Glasgow
G3 6JA
Tel: (+44) (0)141 331 9888
Tel: (+44) (0)141 331 9889
info@nohalfmeasures.com
www.nohalfmeasures.com
ROSTER: Cosmic Rough Riders
(band), Tippi (artist), The Hazey Janes
(band), Daniel Wylie (singer/songwriter)

UK JANINE SPIKINGS
Spiked Management
Top Flat
12 Avington Grove
London
SE20 8RY
Tel: (+44) (0)7776 184075
spiked_j@yahoo.co.uk
ROSTER: Tempertwig (band)

CAN RON SPIRITO
Freeway Entertainment Group
240 Johnston Ave
Willowdale
Ontario M2N 1H6
Tel: (+1) 416 250 1039
r.spirito@sympatico.ca
ROSTER: Rubber Snake, The Mark
Inside

GRAHAM STAIRS   CAN
popguru sound & vision ltd
64 Tanbark Cresc
Toronto
Ontario M3B 1N6
Tel: (+1) 416 444 4859
Fax: (+1) 416 444 2814
popguru@idirect.com
www.popguru.com
ROSTER: Sister Someone, Hush
Hush, Goldfish Productions

STEVE STAVRINOU   UK
Art:X Management
25 Berkshire Gardens
London
N13 6AA
Tel: (+44) (0)20 8372 2698
stevestav@blueyonder.co.uk

SHIRIN STEINMANN   GER
Comedia GmbH
Raderberger Str 202
50968 Köln
(+49) (0)221/9231 326
Fax: (+49) (0)221/9231 849
info@comediagmbh.de
www.comediagmbh.de
ROSTER: Linus Show, Linus & The
Good Vibrators

PAUL STEPANEK   AUS
PSM – Paul Stepanek Management
PO Box 343
Willoughby
NSW 2068
Tel: (+61) (0)411 577336
Fax: (+61) (0)2 94154009
Email: stepane@attglobal.net

Website: www.sickpuppies.net,
www.thedeadabigails.com,
www.harpermead.com
ROSTER: Sick Puppies, The
Dead Abigails, Kyle Harper
Mead

CAN STEVEN HENDRY
Broken Shoe Productions
379 Strawberry Cresc
Waterloo
Ontario N2K 3J3
Tel: (+1) 519 585 9684
shendry@hotmail.com
ROSTER: Jeff Poolton

AUS ROSCO STEWART
Westlink Management
PO Box 233
Leederville
Western Australia 6902
Tel: (+61) (0)8 9228 2059
Fax: (+61) (0)8 9228 2059
rosco@westlinkmultimedia.com
ROSTER: Spencer Tracy

UK DAVID STOPPS
Friars Management Ltd
33 Alexander Road
Aylesbury
Buckinghamshire
HP20 2NR
Tel: (+44) (0)1296 434 731
Fax: (+44) (0)1296 422 530
DavidStopps@fmlmusic.com
www.fmlmusic.com
ROSTER: Howard Jones
(artist/producer), dba, Miriam
Stockley. The Dawn Parade, Shaz
Sparks, Mark Latimer, Martin
Grech

UK JAZZ SUMMERS
Big Life Management Ltd
67-69 Charlton St
London

NW1 1HY
Tel: (+44) (0)20 7554 2100
Fax: (+44) (0)20 7554 2154
sarah@biglife.co.uk
www.biglife.co.uk
ROSTER: Badly Drawn Boy (artist,
XL), Elizabeth Troy (artist, Talking
Loud), Youth (producers), Jazz
Coleman (producers), The
Beatmasters (producers), The Shining
(band, Zuma), Queen Adreena (band,
Rough Trade)

ARNE SVARE   NOR
Stageway
Skuteviksboder 11
Bergen 5035
Tel: (+47) 55559696
Fax: (+47) 55312046
arne.svare@stageway.no
www.stageway.no
ROSTER: Lene Marlin, Sissel,
Karoline Krüger

BARRY SWAYN   AUS
Bare Knuckle Publishing & Recording
156 Weeroona Street
Rye
VIC 3941
Tel: (+61) (0)3 59855991
Fax: (+61) (0)3 59855529
Email: bswayn@satlink.com.au
Web: www.thesitch.com.au
ROSTER: The Sitch, Ashdown Pound
& Swayn, Chantal Vitalis, Kris
Demeanor

KATHRINE SYNNES   NOR
BPop Management
Postbox 9329, Grönland
Oslo 0175
Tel: (+47) 22171508
Fax: (+47) 90691318
kathrine@bpop.no
www.bpop.no
ROSTER: Gluecifer, Cato Salsa

Experience, Number Seven Deli,
Uncle's Institution

UK CHRISTOPHER TANN
Orchard Road Studios
Orchard Road
Orchard Road Court
Finedon
Northants
NN9 5JG
Tel: (+44) (0)1933 398038
Fax: (+44) (0)1933 398038
c.tann@orchardroadstudios.com
www.orchardroadstudios.com
ROSTER: Hard Fought Years-Band
(Orchard Records)

UK STEVE TANNETT
Blujay Management Ltd
55 Loudoun Rd
St Johns Wood
London
NW8 0DL
Tel: (+44) (0)20 7604 3633
Fax: (+44) (0)20 7604 3639
info@blujay.co.uk
ROSTER: Chris Sheehan, Delrosario,
Beulah

FIN MARIA TARNANEN
Belides Oy
Tallberginkatu 1/36
FIN-00180 Helsinki
Tel: (+358) 9 6962 8030
Fax: (+358) 9 6962 8080
Mobile: (+358) 40 7072371
maria.tarnanen@belides.fi
www.belides.fi
ROSTER: Ismo Alanko

USA H RICHARD TASHJIAN, ESQ
Tashjian and Tashjian
500 N Central Ave
Glendale, CA
91203
Tel: (+1) 818 500 8810

rt@tashjianlaw.com

MICHELE TAYLER   **USA**
MTM
43 Chestnut Woods Road
Redding, CT
06896
Tel: (+1) 203 938 5544
mtayler@soniadada.com

HOWI TAYLOR   **UK**
18 Renton Avenue
Guiseley
LS20 8EE
Tel: (+44) (0)208 579 6900
Fax: (+44) (0)208 354 3836
howibass@hotmail.com

ROB TAYLOR   **UK**
Blue Hippo Management
188 Shenley Fields Road
Selly Oak
Birmingham
B29 5BP
Tel: (+44) (0)121 475 7452
Fax: (+44) (0)121 475 7452
bluehippo42@aol.com
ROSTER: Ben Okafor (artist), John
The Revelator (artist), Caleb Quaye
(artist), Kiddo (DJ), Ilene Barnes
(artist), Sarah Francis (artist)

ROBERT TAYLOR   **UK**
Burton Taylor Music
23 Belvedere Gardens
St Albans
Herts
AL2 3EN
Tel: (+44) (0)1727 768675
Fax: (+44) (0)870 133 4360
burton@music-it.demon.co.uk
ROSTER: Burton Taylor (artist/
songwriter), Richard Moffat (songwriter),
Stephanie Motta (songwriter)

JOHN TELFER   **BRA**

Basement Music
Av Paulista 2416
São Paulo, Brasil
01310-300
Tel: (+1) 011 5511 3259 7726
Mobile: 011 5511 9942 4266
john@johntelfer.net

CAN WILLIAM 'SKINNY' TENN

Pandyamonium/William Tenn
Management
164 Kingston Rd
Toronto
Ontario M4L 1S7
Tel: (+1) 416 690 6421
Fax: (+1) 416 778 5429
skinny@pmwtm.com
ROSTER: Hayden, Merlin, Hawksley
Workman, Cash Brothers, Flashlight,
Harlots

UK ANDREA TERRANO

Terrano Sounds
2b Plato Road
London
SW2 5UR
Tel: (+44) (0)20 7924 0496
Fax: (+44) (0)20 7924 0496
terrano@uk2.net
ROSTER: Tania Tee (artist, Mute
Publishing), Latin Soul (band, Just
Music), BB (artist/songwriter,
www.makestar.com), Big 4 Real
(artist), Tom Lindon (producer),
Iguana Productions (band)
(Ministry Of Sound), Tao Rose
(band)

UK ZAADI TESSIER

Richard Ogden Management Ltd
7 Russell Garden
London
W14 8EZ
Tel: (+44) (0)207 751 1300
Fax: (+44) (0)207 348 0831
richard@richardogdenmanagement.com

ROSTER: Bomfunck MCs (band),
Nerina Pallot (artist), Tatiyana Rige
(artist)
Consultancy for: Ricky Martin
(artist), Sandy And Junior (artist),
World Cup 2002 (project)

FRANCK TESTAERT   FRA

Papa's Production
115 rue Marechal Joffre
76600 Le Havre
Tel: (+33) 23519003
Mobile: (+33) 610092710
franck@papasprod.com
ROSTER: Mob's et Travaux, Folie
Ordinaire, Tokyo/Overtones,
Aminima, Lycanthrope

ALAIN THIBAULT   CAN

Alain Thibault Management
#6, 1027 Montée Masson
Laval
Quebec H7C 1S3
Tel: (+1) 450 661 8532
athibault@vidcotron.ca
ROSTER: Panache

MARY THIESSEN   USA

Measurement Arts
4041 Richmond
San Diego, CA
92103
Tel: (+1) 619 251 4376
mthiessenm@aol.com
ROSTER: Mindstain, Beverly
Killbillies, Rob Kwait

DENZIL THOMAS   UK

Eat Your Greens
57a Dulwich Road
Herne Hill
London
SE24 0NJ
denzil.thomas@ntlworld.com
ROSTER: Mikabomb (band), Apes
(band)

CAN LOUIS THOMAS
Quay Entertainment Services Ltd.
1674 Hollis St
Halifax
Nova Scotia B3J 1Y7
Tel: (+1) 902 491 1991
Tel: (+1) 902 491 1839
louis@atlanticmusicgroup.com
www.atlanticmusicgroup.com
ROSTER: Great Big Sea, Crush

UK STEVE THOMAS
Top Farm
The Lane
Wyboston
MK44 3AS
Tel: (+44) (0)1480 403 222
Fax: (+44) (0)1480 403 232
sthomas@mxcomms.com
ROSTER: Bowfinger (band)

UK ALAN THOMPSON
Funky Star Artist Management
The Apple Basement
4 Moray Place
Glasgow
G41 2AQ
Tel: (+44) (0)7977 224258
Fax: (+44) (0)141 423 0149
alan@funkystar.org.uk
www.funkystar.org.uk
ROSTER: Geoff Martyn
(artist/songwriter)

UK DEBRA THOMPSON
DNA Management
24B Alexandra Road
London
N8 OPP
Tel: (+44) (0)20 8520 4442
Fax: (+44) (0)20 8520 2514
debra.t@breathemail.net
ROSTER: Fuze (band), Hoodlum Priest
(artist/writer), The Rubbish (band)

CAN DONNA THOMPSON

Soulchild Management
100, 194 Pinewood Ave
Toronto
Ontario M6C 2V7
Canada
Tel: (+1) 416 879 7685
Fax: (+1) 416 879 4553
donna.t@attcanada.ca
ROSTER: Kalle Pace

DAN THORPE UK
27 Lime Road
Southfield
Bristol
BS3 1LS
Tel: (+44) (0)1179 022222
danny_thorpe@hotmail.com
ROSTER: Gavin Thorpe (artist), Wax
On Wax Off (band)

ROGER TICHBORNE UK
Texmain Ltd
29 Millway
London
NW7 3QS
Tel: (+44) (0)20 8959 3987
Fax: (+44) (0)20 8906 9991
roger.tichborne@btinternet.com
ROSTER: The Falsedots

INGO TIEDEMANN GER
Tiedemann 'Art Production' GmbH
Blankeneser Chaussee 30a
22869 Hamburg-Schenefeld
Tel: (+49) (0)40 256398
Fax: (+49) (0)40 256646
contact@tiedemann.de
www.tiedemann.de
ROSTER: Carlo von Tiedemann
(Moderation), Baccara, Goombay
Dance Band, Oliver Lopes, Pascal,
Gottlieb Wendehals, A 4U, Die ABBA
Revival Show

WILL TIPPER UK
WTM

21 Lowman Road
London
N7 6DD
Tel: (+44) (0)20 7686 9264
Fax: (+44) (0)20 7686 9264
wtipper@excite.com
www.herbaliser.com
ROSTER: The Herbaliser (band, Ninja Tune), Chris Bowden (artist/songwriter, Ninja Tune), Easy Access Orchestra (band, Irma), Dust (band, Bar De Lune)

USA VIVEK TIWARY
Starpolish
1 Irving Place, Suite P8C
New York, NY 10003
Tel: (+1) 212 477 6698
Fax: (+1) 212 477 5259
vivek@starpolish.com
www.starpolish.com
ROSTER: Junior

UK BOOMY TOKAN
Sledge Entertainment
48A Delafield Rd
London
SE7 7NP
Tel: (+44) (0)20 8387 8485
sledgeuk@hotmail.com
www.sledgeuk.com
ROSTER: Meresa Maye (gospel artist)

SWE MARCUS TÖRNKRANTZ
Törnkrantz Music
Råsundavägen 108
169 50 Solna
Tel: (+46) 8 446 67 34
Mobile: (+46) 702 18 75 33
marcus@infobahn.nu
ROSTER: Bob Hund, The Teenage Idons, Revlin, Bergman Rock

UK HOWARD TOSHMAN
Glowball Music Ltd

Unit 106, Belgravia Workshops
159/163 Marlborough Road
London N19 4NF
Tel: (+44) (0)20 8203 0073
Fax: (+44) (0)20 8202 7404
howard.t@virgin.net
ROSTER: Sweet Female Attitude (artist, Warners), Tracy Kilrow (songwriter), Summer Burkes (songwriter), Tom Palin (writer), Fubar (band), Lance Burman (writer)

LEE TREDREA UK
Manic Management
Flat 7
50 Avenue Rd
Highgate
London
N6 5DR
Tel: (+44) (0)20 8371 7033
l_tredrea@hotmail.com

SAM TROMANS UK
Me Me Me Management
105 Canalot Studios
222 Kensal Road
London
W10 5BN
Tel: (+44) (0)20 8960 8060
Fax: (+44) (0)20 8960 1344
sam@me-me-me.co.uk
www.me-me-me.co.uk
ROSTER: Patrick Duff (artist/songwriter), Karime Kendra (artist/songwriter), TNT (artist), Reagn (artist)

LINDON TROTMAN UK
Boss Records & Management
84 Holyrood Crescent
St Albans
Herts
AL1 2LP
Tel: (+44) (0)1727 857852
Fax: (+44) (0)1727 857852

bossrecs@aol.com
ROSTER: Richy Quarshie (band),
Lloyd Charles (band)

CAN PAUL TUCHSCHERER
Artist Management & Promotion
(AMP)
716 Durie St
Toronto
Ontario M6S 3H3
Tel: (+1) 416 763 7220
Fax: (+1) 416 763 6422
ampmanager@hotmail.com,
ampmusic@sympatico.ca
www.angelfire.com/on3/amp
www.hydrofoil.net
www.pleistoscene.com
www.derekj.net
ROSTER: hydrofoil, Derek J,
Pleistoscene

UK MARK TURNER
24/7 Management Ltd
48 Carden Crescent
Patcham
Brighton
Sussex
BN1 8TQ
Tel: (+44) (0)1273 553 833
Fax: (+44) (0)1273 562 272
24-7@mistral.co.uk
ROSTER: Daisy Hicks
(artist)

SWE HENRIK UHLMANN
Global Artist Management
PO Box 3166
Tel: (+46) 40 680 21 50
Mobile: (+46) 707 95 73 00
henrik@extensivemusic
　　.com
www.ga-management.com
ROSTER: Dr Bombay, SAM,
Sally Oldfield, Primadonna, Karma
Club, Diana Fox, Kathy Kelly,
Down Low

JEAN MARC VALAY　　　FRA
Koncert
12 rue Villebois
Mareuil
94300 Vincennes
Tel: (+33) 143286962
Mobile: (+33) 608731051
jmvalay@wanadoo.fr
ROSTER: La Souris Deglinguee

**SABINE VAN DE　　　　UK
WATTYNE**
OPL Management Ltd
4 The Limes
Northend Way
London
NW3 7HG
Tel: (+44) (0)20 8209 0025
oplmanagement@aol.com
ROSTER: Maneki-Neko (band)

JAN VAN MESDAG　　　UK
I Love Music Ltd.
31 Wardour Street
London
W1D 6PT
Tel: (+44) (0)20 7434 2256
Fax: (+44) (0)20 7734 7456
jan.vanmesdag@btconnect.com
ROSTER: Kevin Ferguson
(artist/songwriter)

DUTCH VAN SPALL　　　UK
Big Help Multimedia
Deppers Bridge Farm
Deppers Bridge
Southam
CV47 25Z
Tel: (+44) (0)1926 614640
dutch@dreamville.demon.co.uk
www.pride-rock.co.uk
ROSTER: Fat Rhino (band), Rosa
(singer/songwriter)

RUSSELL VAUGHT　　　UK
Luna Park Management

Studio J
52 Florida Street
London
E2 6AL
Tel: (+44) (0)7092 285786
Fax: (+44) (0)870 1345476
russellvaught@hotmail.com
ROSTER: Tommy B
(artist/producer/DJ)

NLD NATHALIE VAN VEENENDAAL
Siren Bemiddeling
Bolestein 184
1081 EA Amsterdam
Tel: (+32) 20 403 85 15
Fax: (+32) 20 403 85 85
nathalie@siren.nl
www.siren.nl
ROSTER: ZUCO 103, Izaline
Calister, Graham B, Tony Allen (NL),
Frederic Galliano (NL), Red Nose
District

FIN SEPPO VESTERINEN
Hinterland Oy
PO Box 194
FIN-00121 Helsinki
Tel: (+358) 400 850116
Fax: (+358) 9 671491
Mobile: (+358) 400-850116
seppo@heartagram.com
ROSTER: HIM, The Rasmus

FRA BEATRICE VIELLE
Musiques En Balade
3 Allee du Rhone
77150 Lesigny
Tel: (+33) 160021020
Mobile: (+33) 680425237
musibala@musique.net
www.musiquesenbalade.com
ROSTER: Fawzy Al-Aiedy, I Donni de
l'Esilieu, Tangora

NOR STEINAR VIKAN

Ramalama Management
Bispegata 12
Oslo 0152
Tel: (+47) 22170940
Fax: (+47) 22170933
ramalama@online.no
ROSTER: DumDum Boys

FRANCK VORGERS FRA
Pure Son'g
43 rue de la Rochefoucauld
75009 Paris
Tel: (+33) 1 53 21 06 97
Mobile: (+33) 6 62 43 06 97
Fax: (+33) 1 53 21 06 97
puresong@noos.fr
ROSTER: Maria Teresa, FARAKA,
Nancy Murillo, Erotokritos, La
Coccinelle, Le Diable à Quatre, Alex
Jacquemin Quartet

DOBS VYE UK
Adage Music Management
22 Gravesend Road
London
W12 0SZ
Tel: (+44) (0)20 8743 2065
dobs@adagemusic.co.uk
ROSTER: James Reynolds
(producer/programmer/mixer),
Dobster, Tabla Rasa, Mim

BJORN OLE WAAGE NOR
NAMA Management
Karl Johansgate 2
Oslo 0154
Tel: (+47) 22420000
Fax: (+47) 22417952
entertainment@nama.no
www.nama.no
ROSTER: Harald Heide Steen, Jonas
Fjeld, Jon Eikemo

CHRISTINE WADE UK
Moneypenny Management & Agency
The Stables

Westwood House
Main Street, North Dalton
Near Driffield
East Yokshire
YO25 9XA
Tel: (+44) (0)1377 217815
Fax: (+44) (0)1377 217754
chris@adastey.demon.co.uk
www.adastra-
music.co.uk/moneypenny
ROSTER: Eliza Carthy (artist/
songwriter, Warner Bros US), Slo-Mo
(artist/songwriter), Al Scott (producer)

UK MARC WADSWORTH
Marc Wadsworth Management
195 Hollydale Road
London
SE15 2TG
Tel: (+44) (0)20 7771 2835
Fax: (+44) (0)20 7635 0825
marc.wads@mcr1.poptel.org.uk
ROSTER: Donna Williams
(singer/songwriter)

UK DIANE WAGG
Deluxxe Management
40 Loveday Rd
London
W13 9JS
Tel: (+44) (0)20 8579 6900
Fax: (+44) (0)20 8354 3836
diane@deluxxe.co.uk
ROSTER: A Girl Called Eddy (artist),
Eliza Newman And Skandinavia
(artist), Theory Of Everything (band)

UK PAUL WALDEN
The Flying Music Company Ltd
110 Clarendon Road
London
W11 2HR
Tel: (+44) (0)20 7221 7799
Fax: (+44) (0)20 7221 5016
info@flyingmusic.co.uk
www.flyingmusic.com

ROSTER: 4 The Boyz (pop group)

GUNTHER WALKER   **UK**
Solar Management Ltd
42-48 Charlbert Street
London
NW8 7BU
Tel: (+44) (0)20 7722 4175
Fax: (+44) (0)20 7722 4072
info@solarmanagement.co.uk
www.solarmanagement.co.uk
ROSTER: Zero 7 (band), Jimmy
Sommerville (artist), Nigel Godrich
(producer), Dave Eringa (producer),
Stephen Hague (producer), Sally
Herbert (songwriter), Yo Yo
(songwriter), Graeme Stewart
(producer)

JENNIE WALKER   **YSA**
The Jennie Walker Company
435 West 57th St, #15-S
New York, NY 10019
Tel: (+1) 212 541 7456
jennie@jenniewalker.com

PHILIP WALKER   **UK**
LG Connections Ltd
The Hollies
Chimes Court
Huddersfield
HD5 0DU
Tel: (+44) (0)1484 512474
Fax: (+44) (0)1484 454430
philip.walker@lgconnections.co.uk
www.lgconnections.co.uk
ROSTER: Stricken (band), Tetsuo
(band), Divide (band)

JOHN WALLER   **UK**
John Waller Management &
   Marketing
The Old Truman Brewery
91 Brick Lane
London
E1 6QL

Tel: (+44) (0)20 7247 1057
Fax: (+44) (0)20 7337 0732
john.waller@dial.pipex.com
ROSTER: Mark Nevin (artist/writer),
Isabel Fructuoso (artist/writer), Eva
Luna (artist), David Saw
(artist/writer), Cast Of Thousands
(band)

AUS GARY WALTON
vaguemusic
PO Box 2265
Prahran
VIC 3181
Tel: (+61) (0)414 509 119
Email: vaguemusic@iprimus.com.au
Website: www.lauren.com.au
ROSTER: Lauren

UK DAVID WANLESS
Swansong Enterprises Ltd
186 Kings Road
Harrogate
North Yorkshire
HG1 5JG
Tel: (+44) (0)1423 545179
swansongent@aol.com
ROSTER: Chris Lawrence
(artist/songwriter)

UK NICK WARBURTON
RNA Artist Management
3 Giles Close
Oxford
OX4 4NU
Tel: (+44) (0)1865 717217
nickwarburton@tiscali.co.uk
ROSTER: Ben McIntosh (producer),
Jamie Hollings (producer), Rythmical
Noise Authority (band)

UK JAMES WARE
Aware Management Services Limited
144 Camden High Street
London
NW1 ONE

Tel: (+44) (0)20 7468 2637
Fax: (+44) (0)20 7287 5731
jware@davenportlyons.com
ROSTER: Penguin Cafe Orchestra
(band)

PETER WARK   USA
Worldwide Entertainment Group
411 Lafayette Street, 3rd floor
New York, NY
10003
Tel: (+1) 212 420 0893
Fax: (+1) 212 420 0752
pwark@wweg.com
www.wweg.com
ROSTER: Courtney Love, Duncan
Sheik, Carlos Alomar, Robert Earl
Keen, Marah w/Paul Dickman

CHRIS WARREN   UK
Split Music
13 Sandys Road
Worcester
WR1 3HE
Tel: (+44) (0)1905 29809
Fax: (+44) (0)1905 613023
split.music@virgin.net
www.splitmusic.com
ROSTER: The Next Room
(producers), Dead Next Door (band)

VEGARD WASKE   NOR
Bureau Storm
Inkognitogt 8
Oslo 0258
Tel: (+47) 22121010
Fax: (+47) 22121019
vegard@bureaustorm.no
www.bureaustorm.no
ROSTER: Jaga Jazzist

KAREN WATERS   AUS
Karen Waters (Artist Management)
PO Box 565
Bourke
NSW 2840

Tel: (+61) (0)418 614 359
Email: kazwaters@bigpond.com
ROSTER: Nick Buck, Fiona
Kernaghan, Paul Costa

CAN MARK WATSON

Watson Entertainment Productions &
   Services
268-1326 Huron St
London
Ontario N5V 2E2
Tel: (+1) 519 679 2283 or 416 873
   6609
Fax: (+1) 416 873 6602
mwatson@sympatico.ca
www.essentialsmusic.com
www.blendmusic.com
www.dannioniell.com
ROSTER: The Essentials, BLEND,
Danni O'Neill

AUS PENNY WEBER

Jam Packed Entertainment
PO Box 1260
St Kilda
South Australia 3182
Tel: (+61) (0)3 9534 2446
Fax: (+61) (0)3 9534 2446
Mobile: (+61) (0)412285422
Email: jampacked@iprimus.com.au
ROSTER: Offcutts, Virtue, Lindsay
Gravine

AUS ANNA WEBSTER

Pure Music
196 Barridale Dve
Kingsley
Perth
WA 6026
Tel: (+61) (0)407 380 629
annawebster2000@hotmail.com
Website: www.equadoronline
   .com
ROSTER: Equador

FRA JEAN PIERRE WEILLER

73 Bld Kellerman
75013 Paris
Tel: (+33) 1 45 88 47 74
Mobile: (+33) 6 85 12 20 87
Fax: (+33) 1 53 62 97 23
JPWeiller@aol.com
ROSTER: I Muvrini, No Jazz

DAVID WEISZ AUS

Weisz Management
3/392 Oxford St
Paddington
NSW 2021
Tel: (+61) (0)2 93804264
Mobile: (+61) (0)407185542
Email: davidweisz@optusnet.com.au
Website: www.gelbison.com.au
ROSTER: Gelbison

LEA WESTERN UK

Hartwood
Youngswood Way
Alverstone Garden Village
Isle Of Wight
PO36 0HE
Tel: (+44) (0)1983 408052
Fax: (+44) (0)1983 408052
lea@skybunker.com
www.skybunker.com

DEAN WESTON UK

Bubkiss
The Oast House, Eden Lodge, Liss
Hampshire
GU33 6JQ
Tel: (+44) (0)1730 892611
bubkiss72@hotmail.com
www.bubkiss.net
ROSTER: Bubkiss (artist/songwriter)

JOHN WESTON UK

JW Management
380 Longbanks
Harlow
Essex
CM18 7PG

Tel: (+44) (0)1279 304526
jpweston@ntlworld.com
ROSTER: Silverwish (band)

AUS WHAT MANAGEMENT

Alistair Cranney
PO Box 10131
Adelaide Business Centre
Adelaide
SA 5000
Tel: (+61) (0)8 83583594
Fax: (+61) (0)8 83583594
Aus Mobile: (+61) (0)419956699
UK Mobile: (+44) (0)7813487930
answers@whatmanagement.com
Web: www.whatmanagement
    .com
ROSTER: Merri-May, Things Of
Stone And Wood

UK DEREK WHITE

Axis Productions
46 Brook Street
Aston Clinton
Aylesbury
Bucks
HP22 5ES
Tel: (+44) (0)1296 631 898
Fax: (+44) (0)1296 630 321
dw@hopkinson-white.demon.co.uk
ROSTER: The Kynd (band)

UK JON WHITE

Jon White Agency Limited
81 Haliburton Road
St Margaret's
Twickenham
TW1 1PD
Tel: (+44) (0)20 8400 7540
Fax: (+44) (0)20 8400 7540
jon@white-limited.com
www.white-limited.com
ROSTER: Girlinky (band), Series-7
(band), King Mantis (band), I Love
UFO(band), Cult Of Celebrity (band),
People In Jars (band)

KEVIN WHITE UK

Multiplay Music Ltd
19 Eagle Way
Harrold
Bedford
MK43 7DA
Tel: (+44) (0)1234 720785
Fax: (+44) (0)1234 720664
kevin@multiplaymusic.com
www.multiplaymusic.com
ROSTER: Dominoo (band), Pelle
Nylen (writer/producer), Lutious
(writer/producer), Ken Rose
(writer/producer)

NIALL WHITE UK

TLT Management
71 Townsend Street
Cheltenham
Glos
GL1 9HA
Tel: (+44) (0)1242 573195
Fax: (+44) (0)1242 573195
thelasttaxi@talk21.com
www.lasttaxi.co.uk
ROSTER: The Last Taxi (band)

SOPHIE WHITE AUS

Tel: (+61) (0)414531008
Email: sophiewhite@hotmail.com
Website: www.sophiewhite.com

DAVE WHITNEY UK

Dreamscape Music Limited
3 Squirrels Farm
Oak Farm Lane
Sevenoaks
Kent
TN15 7JU
Tel: (+44) (0)1732 822424
Fax: (+44) (0)1732 822243
davewhitney@dreamscapestudios
    .com
ROSTER: Nicky Cook (songwriter),
Martin Bushell (songwriter), Tony
Momrelle (songwriter)

SWE JEPPE WIK
The Managemment
Walhallavägen 50
114 23 Stockholm
Tel: (+46) 8 673 24 70
Fax: (+46) 8 673 24 71
Mobile: (+46) 707 92 32 50
jeppe.wik@themanagement.nu
www.themanagement.nu
ROSTER: Fredrik Kempe, Javier,
Maarja, Dilba, Lambretta

UK CLIFF WILKINSON
23 Sheringham Avenue
Twickenham
Middlesex
TW2 6AW
Tel: (+44) (0)20 8755 4745
ROSTER: Serese (band)

UK DAVID WILLIAMS
Jungle Management
High Veld
Newlands Drive
Maidenhead
Berkshire
SL6 4LL
Tel: (+44) (0)1628 785481
Fax: (+44) (0)1628 781684
will@junglemanagement.com
ROSTER: Blofeld (band), Street
Regal (band), Fat Man Kicks Cat
(band)

CAN TRACY ELIZABETH WILLIAMS
ATH Entertainment
246 Scott St
Fort Frances
Ontario P9A 1G7
Tel: (+1) 807 274 0660
Fax: (+1) 807 274 0661
athent@jam21.net
ROSTER: Daughter Judy

USA TAMARA WILSON

Tamara Wilson, Inc
401 69th Street, #9D
Miami Beach, FL
33141
Tel: (+1) 305 815 1489
tamara123@earthlink.net

SUE WINCOTT **UK**
Crucible Management
7 Elder Avenue
London
N8 9TA
Tel: (+44) (0)20 8292 4299
Fax: (+44) (0)20 8292 4299
info@crucible-management.co.uk
ROSTER: The Mediaeval Baebes
(band), Jamie Lawson (artist),
Supervia (band)

MARK WINDERS **AUS**
Brandon Promotions & Management
PO Box 69
Prospect
Adelaide
SA 5082
Tel: (+61) (0)8 8344 5802
Fax: (+61) (0)8 8344 5802
Mobile: (+61) (0)408 022 748
Email: brandonp@chariot.net.au
ROSTER: Tidal, Diatribe, Skintilla.

COEN TER WOLBEEK **NLD**
Mojo Management
Postbus 2686
1000 MR Amsterdam
Tel: (+32) 20 521 00 10
Fax: (+32) 20 521 00 19
C.ter.Wolbeek@mojo.nl
www.mojo.nl
Daniël Lohues, Brainpower, Sita,
Wipneus & Pim, SKIK, Edsilia
ROSTER: Rombley, Twarres, Kirsten,
Dyzack

ALAN WOLMARK **USA**
CEC Management

1123 Broadway
Suite #317
New York, NY 10010
Tel: (+1) 212 206 6765
Fax: (+1) 212 807 9288
CECUS@aol.com
ROSTER: Ben Folds, Crashland, Darren Jessee, Natasha Atlas, The Eighties Matchbox B-Line Disaster, John Alagia (producer)

UK   DAVID WOOD
One Way Management T/A Outburst
    Music Ltd
71 High Street East
Wallsend
Tyne & Wear
N28 7RJ
Tel: (+44) (0)191 262 4999
Fax: (+44) (0)191 263 7082
mdwood33@aol.com
www.geordiestuff.co.uk
ROSTER: Alan B Evans (artist), Debbie (artist), DJ Rob, DJ Spike

USA   BLAIR WOODS
Big WalkUp Artist Mgmt
362 Rhode Island Street
Buffalo, NY
14213
Tel: (+1) 716 882 1923
BlairW@aol.com

UK   MARK WOOD
Modern Wood Management
50a Waldron Road
London
SW18 3TD
Tel: (+44) (0)20 8947 2224
Fax: (+44) (0)20 8946 6545
mark.modernwood@virgin.net
ROSTER: Imogen Heap (artist), Nik Kershaw (artist), Jethro East (programmer), Frou Frou (band), Clarkesville (band), Sonara, Audiogene

DONNA WOODWARD   UK
Valley Music Ltd
11 Cedar Court
Fairmile
Henley on Thames
Oxon
RG9 2JR
Tel: (+44) (0)1491 845840
Fax: (+44) (0)1491 413667
donna@valleymusicuk.com
www.valleymusicuk.com
ROSTER: Tom Jones (artist, V2)

MARK WOODWARD   UK
Valley Music Ltd
11 Cedar Court
Farmile
Henley On Thames
Oxon
RG9 2JR
Tel: (+44) (0)1491 845 840
Fax: (+44) (0)1491 413 667
mark@valleymusicuk.com
www.valleymusicuk.com
ROSTER: Tom Jones (artist, V2)

DAVID WOOLFSON   UK
Parliament Management
PO Box 6328
London
N2 0UN
Tel: (+44) (0)20 8444 9841
Fax: (+44) (0)20 8442 1973
info@parliament-management.com
ROSTER: Letrix (band), Rob Reed (Writer), Tina Booth (Writer)

FAY WOOLVEN   UK
In Phase Management
PO Box 756 A
Surbiton
Surrey
KT6 6YZ
Tel: (+44) (0)20 8390 4583
Fax: (+44) (0)20 8288 1597
mail@inphasemanagement.com

ROSTER: Cradle Of Filth (band), Reef (band, Sony), Reactor (band)

UK **CORAL WORMAN**
Strongroom Management (SRM)
120-124 Curtain Rd
London
EC2A 3SQ
Tel: (+44) (0)20 7426 5132
Fax: (+44) (0)20 7426 5102
coral@strongroom.com
www.strongroom.com/management
ROSTER: Mike Nielsen (producer/mix and recording engineer/programmer), Luke Gifford (mix and recording engineer/programmer), Dave Pemberton (producer/mix and recording engineer/ programmer), Gaetan Schurrer (programmer/writer), Aidan Love (programmer/writer/ remixer), OTT (mix and recording engineer/ programmer/writer/producer), Alex Valentine (singer/songwriter), Mark McGuire (producer/engineer/ Pro Tools)

UK **AMANDA WRIGHT**
Bright Spark Management Ltd
59 High Street
Chipstead
Sevenoaks
Kent
TN13 2RW
Tel: (+44) (0)7973 988069
amanda@bspromotions.com
www.bspromotions.com
ROSTER: HERBiE (band)

UK **DAVID WRIGHT**
14 Inham Fields Close
Gunthorpe
Notts
NG14 7FH
Tel: (+44) (0)115 9663584
davewright11@hotmail.com
www.bornlaid.co.uk
ROSTER: Born Laid (band)

KLAUS WÜNSCH **GER**
Veranstaltungsbüro Wünsch
Schumannstr 5
55595 Hargesheim
Tel: (+49) (0)671 45001
Fax: (+49) (0)671 31126
wuenschdirwas@va-wuensch.de
www.va-wuensch.de
ROSTER: Michael Klostermann & seine Musikanten, Zauber der Operette, Johann Strauß Gala, Dancing Queen, The Black Gospel Singers, Antonia feat Sandra S, Broadway Classics, Dancing Feet

STEFAN ZAGORSKI **AUS**
Architecture Label Pty Ltd
PO Box 207
Camperdown
NSW 2085
Fax: (+61) (0)2 9451 9440
Email: arc-info@architecturelabel.com
Web: www.architecturelabel.com
ROSTER: SPOD, Death Cab For Cutie, Disco Doom, Further, Knievel, The Dismemberment Plan, The Head, Thinktank

SEBASTIEN ZAMORA **FRA**
Zamora Productions
10 rue Erard
75012 Paris
Mobile: (+33) 6 60 38 48 35
Fax: (+33) 1 43 72 42 00
sebastien@zamoraprod.com
ROSTER: Aston Villa, Les Wampas, Les Yeux Noirs

AREND VAN DER ZEE **NLD**
Birdsong Artist Management
Postbus 2025
3440 DA Woerden
Tel: (+32) 348 419 234
birdsongcentral@cs.com
www.racoon.nl
ROSTER: Racoon

Appendix 3
Directory Of MMF Offices

**MMF AUSTRALIA AND
NEW ZEALAND**
Selena Quintrell
PO Box 590
Surrey Hills
NSW 2010
Australia
Tel: (+61) 2 9310 4268
Fax: (+61) 2 9698 6247
selenaq@immf.net

MMF CANADA
Karen Pace
#3, 748 Gerrard St East
Toronto
Ontario M4M 1Y6
Canada
Tel: (+1) 416 465 3993
Fax: (+1) 416 465 4433
KJP@ca.inter.net
www.mmfcanada.com

MMF DENMARK
Jeasper Kroll
Vestergade 6 A, 3
Copenhagen K
DK-1456
Denmark
Tel: (+45) 3391 6760
Fax: (+45) 3391 6761
mail@clockwize.dk

MMF FRANCE
Didier Zerath
16 Rue Escudier
Boulogne
92100
France
Tel: (+33) 1 41 31 02 28
Fax: (+33) 1 41 31 02 28
dze@noos.fr
www.mmffrance.com

MMF NORWAY
Eivind Bryoy
Karl Johansgate 2
Oslo
0154
Norway
Tel: (+47) 24145500
Fax: (+47) 24145501
eivind@nextto.no

MMF FINLAND
Kari Possi
Blue Buddha Management
Tallberginkatu
1 Box 40
Helsinki
00180
Finland
Tel: (+35) 89 68 59 32 21
Fax: (+35) 89 68 59 32 24
possi@bbmgmt.com

MMF HOLLAND

Wim Reijnen
PO Box 58363
HJ Amsterdam
1040
Netherlands
Tel: (+31) 20 777 4271
Fax: (+31) 20 524 1602
wim@immf.net

IDKV (GERMANY)

Michael Bisping
Rahlstedter Str 92 A
Hamburg
Hansestadt Hamburg
22149
Germany
Tel: (+49) 40 675699 0
Fax: (+49) 40 675699 30
info@ass-concerts.de

MMF USA

Steve Garvan
7919 Fairfax Court
Niwot

Colorado
8053
USA
Tel: (+1) 303 652 3489
Fax: (+1) 303 652 3610
steve@garvanmanagement.com

MMF UK

James Sellar (General Secretary)
1 York St
London W1U 6PA
Tel: (+44) (0)870 8507 800
Fax: (+44) (0)870 8507 801
Email: info@ukmmf.net
Web: www.ukmmf.net

MMF SWEDEN

Carl Blom
Gotabergsgatan 2
34 Goteborg
SE-411
Sweden
Tel: (+46) 31 701 75 20
Fax: (+46) 31 701 75 30
carl.blom@flagstone.se

MMF
Music Managers Forum
7 Russell Gardens
London W148EZ
Tel: 020 7751 1894   Fax: 020 7603 4411
info@ukmmf.net   www.ukmmf.net

MEMBERSHIP APPLICATION FORM

PLEASE COMPLETE THIS FORM IN BLOCK CAPITALS

NAME OF MEMBER/S: ....

COMPANY NAME: ....

ADDRESS: ....

....

.... Post Code: ....

Tel:.................................... Fax.................................. Mobile...................................... .

Email.. Website....................................
(VERY IMPORTANT, eg TO RECEIVE BULLETINS)

Please inform us of which acts you are currently managing.   (Please use other side if necessary)

NAME	TYPE (ie BAND/ARTIST/PRODUCER)	RECORD CO. IF SIGNED
....	....	....
....	....	....
....	....	....

I/We would like a one year membership with the MMF as:

A Company member (for up to three named members) ☐

Full Individual Membership ☐

Associate Individual Membership (non-voting) – See Notes ☐

Overseas Individual Membership (non-voting) – See Notes ☐

Please make cheques payable to 'The Managers Forum Ltd'.

....

OFFICE USE ONLY   Passed by council:...

FEE ENCLOSED   £..................... ....   INV # ....   MEM NO ....

MEMBERSHIP TYPE   ....   DATE REC ....   EXPIRY DATE ....

CARD ☐   INV ST ☐   DIR ☐

CURRENT MEMBERSHIP RATES

At present there are three levels of membership. All prospective applications are reviewed by the Council.

COMPANY

For up to three named full members. This is representative of a saving on 3 individual full members.

£350 excluding VAT
£411.25 inclusive

FULL INDIVIDUAL MEMBERSHIP

£200 excluding VAT
£235 inclusive

ASSOCIATE MEMBERSHIP

This is a subsidised membership level for those managers that are new to the music industry and have no income stream from their artists.

£68.08 excluding VAT
£80 inclusive

This is on the proviso that you upgrade to a full membership rate as soon as an income stream from your artist/roster has been established. The Associate level membership does not entitle you to vote on any MMF related decisions at AGMs/EGMs etc.

OVERSEAS MEMBERSHIP

If you are from overseas and there is no regional MMF you may join as an Overseas Member for a flat fee of £100.
VERY IMPORTANT:
- You must pay up front. The Direct Debit scheme is not available.
- All payments must be by bankers draft, or bank transfer / CHAPS, with bank charges payable at your end.

LENGTH OF MEMBERSHIP

All membership rates listed above apply for a year.

| 1st January | 1st April | 1st July | 1st October |

Applications for membership can be received at any time throughout the year but please note your application will be deemed to start from the closest previous date listed above. EG, if you submit an application on the 4th May your membership will be deemed to be renewable on the 1st April the following year.

ONLINE LATE 2003

www.mmf-training.com

STOP

Music Industry
Training Ahead

MMF

Training Office
+44 (0)161 228 3993

Who knows where they could take you.....